THE CUBAN MISSILE CRISIS REVISITED

Also by James A. Nathan

Foreign Policy Making and the American Political System
(with James K. Oliver)

The United States Foreign Policy and World Order
(with James K. Oliver)

The Future of United States Naval Power
(with James K. Oliver)

THE CUBAN MISSILE CRISIS REVISITED

edited by
James A. Nathan

9/96

St. Martin's Press
New York

"Before 'The Missiles of October': Did Kennedy Plan a Military Strike Against Cuba?" by James Hershberg was first published in different form in *Diplomatic History* 14 (Spring 1990): 163-98 and is reprinted by permission.

"The Traditional and Revisionist Interpretations Reevaluated: Why Was Cuba a Crisis?" by Richard Ned Lebow was first published in a different form as "Domestic Politics and the Cuban Missile Crisis: The Traditional and Revisionist Interpretations Reevaluated," in *Diplomatic History* 14 (Fall 1990): 471-92 and is reprinted by permission.

"The Kennedy-Khrushchev Letters: An Overview" by Philip Brenner and the full text of all the correspondence between President Kennedy and Chairman Khrushchev on the Cuban Missile Crisis first appeared in a special issue of *Problems of Communism*, Spring 1992.

Chapter 3 © Barton J. Bernstein 1992
Chapter 6 © Philip Brenner 1992

First published in the United States of America in 1992

Printed in the United States of America

ISBN 0-312-06069-6 (cloth)
ISBN 0-312-09725-5 (paper)

Library of Congress Cataloging-in-Publication Data
The Cuban missile crisis revisited / edited by James A. Nathan.
    p. cm.
  Includes index.
  ISBN 0-312-06069-6
  1. Cuban Missile Crisis, 1962. I. Nathan, James A.
E841.C85 1992
973.922—dc20   91-47951
                                               CIP

For Lisa, Alex, and Michael Lincoln

TABLE OF CONTENTS

Preface ix

Notes on Contributors xi

1. The Heyday of the New Strategy: The Cuban Missile Crisis
   and the Confirmation of Coercive Diplomacy
   James A. Nathan 1

2. The Cuban Missile Crisis: An Overview
   Raymond L. Garthoff 41

3. Reconsidering the Missile Crisis: Dealing with the Problems
   of the American Jupiters in Turkey
   Barton J. Bernstein 55

4. The View from Washington and the View from Nowhere:
   Cuban Missile Crisis Historiography and the Epistemology
   of Decision Making
   Laurence Chang 131

5. The Traditional and Revisionist Interpretations Reevaluated:
   Why Was Cuba a Crisis?
   Richard Ned Lebow 161

6. Thirteen Months: Cuba's Perspective on the Missile Crisis
   Philip Brenner 187

7. President Kennedy's Decision to Impose a Blockade in the Cuban Missile Crisis: Building Consensus in the ExComm After the Decision
Elizabeth Cohn 219

8. Before "The Missiles of October": Did Kennedy Plan a Military Strike Against Cuba?
James G. Hershberg 237

9. The Kennedy-Khrushchev Letters: An Overview
Philip Brenner 281

Index 297

PREFACE

Several years ago, the director of the National Security Archive, Scott Armstrong, asked me to help chair a panel of historians, policy analysts, and participants in the Cuban missile crisis at a meeting of the Society of American Historians convening in Williamsburg, Virginia in 1988. At that time the National Security Archive was gathering materials on the Cuban missile crisis and wanted to make the community of historians of American foreign policy aware of the Archive's existence.

Though I knew Scott Armstrong as a much-celebrated journalist, I knew nothing of the National Security Archive. I soon discovered that Scott had helped to found an institution that intended to become a major independent resource for scholars and journalists. The mission that the National Security Archive set for itself was bold indeed: to establish openness and transparency in the foreign policy and defense processes.

This book marks one of the many successes of the early efforts of the Archive. This book also commemorates the thirty years that have passed since the world stood at the edge of a dangerous precipice, the shaky foundations of which have only recently been uncovered. This collection also represents a distillation of the new wisdom gathered by researchers using the resources of the National Security Archive and the records recently opened by the American, former Soviet, and Cuban governments.

Pittsburgh's Richard Ned Lebow has interviewed many of the surviving Soviet policymakers from the Khrushchev years. Philip Brenner of The American University was instrumental in gathering heretofore unknown documents from the Cuban and American governments, as well as the long-withheld correspondence, some of which is excerpted here, between President Kennedy and Chairman Khrushchev. Ambassador Raymond Garthoff, a former senior intelligence analyst now at the Brookings Institute, has long followed unfolding intelligence revelations pertaining to the crisis. Laurence Chang, now at Stanford, and Jim Hershberg, coordinator of the Cold War International History Project of the Woodrow Wilson Center, have had long associations with the National Security Archive. Mr. Chang was one of the most sensitive researchers who first dedicated himself to the task of assembling material relevant to the Cuban missile crisis. Dr. Hershberg used Archive material to develop startling information on the U.S. preparations for war in the months leading up to the events of October 1962. Stanford University professor Bart Bernstein's early insight about the centrality of the American missiles stationed in Turkey and Italy has been vindicated by events. Documents assembled by Professor Bernstein were at the core of the Archive's original collection on the Cuban missile crisis. Professor Bernstein's characteristically careful reexamination of the crisis is original to this volume and is as welcome as it is important. As for myself, I had not thought much about the crisis for years until Scott remembered me and reawakened my interest in the affair.

I truly enjoyed the opportunity to think the matter anew, and my own contribution draws liberally from the insights and documents assembled by the other authors in this collection. The support attendant to my new position as Khalid bin Sultan Eminent Scholar at Auburn University at Montgomery allowed me to complete the work of writing, editing, and harassing my fellow authors, so that we were able to accommodate a demanding schedule.

My association with the authors in this study and with my editor at St. Martin's Press, Simon Winder, has been a source of immense satisfaction. They all have my thanks.

James A. Nathan

NOTES ON CONTRIBUTORS

JAMES A. NATHAN is a former U.S. Foreign Service officer. He has taught at the University of Delaware, Johns Hopkins (School of Advanced International Studies), the Naval War College, and the Army War College. He is presently Khalid bin Sultan Eminent Scholar, Auburn University at Montgomery.

RAYMOND L. GARTHOFF is a senior U.S. Foreign Service officer and Senior Fellow at the Brookings Institution. He was Ambassador to Bulgaria in 1977-79, and a Senior Foreign Service Inspector General from 1974 to 1977. Prior to that, Mr. Garthoff was deputy director of Political Military Affairs. In 1962, Mr. Garthoff was a special assistant for Soviet Bloc Affairs and was active in the Cuban missile crisis decision-making process.

BARTON J. BERNSTEIN is Professor of History and Mellon Professor Interdisciplinary Studies at Stanford University, where he specializes in foreign policy and science. Dr. Bernstein is co-director of the International Relations Program and the International Policy Studies Program. He has been writing on the Cuban missile crisis since 1962.

LAURENCE CHANG is a doctoral student in political science at Stanford University. Mr. Chang wrote this article while he was an information analyst at the National Security Archive in Washington, D.C., where he was project editor of *The Cuban Missile Crisis, 1962*, a comprehensive declassified U.S. government document (National Security Archive, Chadwyck-Healey, Inc., 1990).

RICHARD NED LEBOW is a professor at the University of Pittsburgh's Graduate School of Public and International Affairs. Professor Lebow is a former professor at Cornell, the National War College, and scholar-in-residence at the CIA.

PHILIP BRENNER is chairman of the department of International Politics and Foreign Policy, American University, Washington, D.C., and the author of *From Confrontation to Negotiation: U.S. Relations with Cuba* (Westview, 1988). Mr. Brenner has been at the forefront of a largely successful movement to declassify documents from the Soviet Union, Cuba, and the United States that bear on the Cuban missile crisis.

ELIZABETH COHN is a doctoral student at American University and former director of the Central American Historical Institute, Washington, D.C.

JAMES G. HERSHBERG holds a Ph.D. from Tufts University. He is the coordinator of the Cold War International History Project at the Woodrow Wilson International Center for Scholars in Washington, D.C. and the author of *Harvard to Hiroshima,* a study of James B. Conant, to be published in 1993 by Alfred A. Knopf.

1

The Heyday of the New Strategy: The Cuban Missile Crisis and the Confirmation of Coercive Diplomacy

James A. Nathan

CLIO AND THE CUBAN CRISIS

The Cuban missile crisis has been of special interest to those growing numbers of civilians who have a professional interest in the use and management of military power. The successful and determinedly civilian orchestration of the great panoply of persuasion that was brought to bear on the Soviets in the Caribbean seemed to herald an era wherein vastly expanded power, blessedly, had become a relevant, useful, and rational instrument of American policy. The triumphant and apparently lopsided position of the United States in the aftermath of the Cuban crisis reinforced the venerable American hope that a stable international order could be sustained if it were underwritten by America's readiness to employ effective force. What was novel in contemporary "crisis management," political science Robert Tucker observed a few years later, was "the intensity of the aspiration to exercise a far greater measure of control. . . . A growing confidence in the ability . . . to manage crises [was] accompanied by a growing confidence that force [might] be employed in a regulated manner."[1]

"There is no such thing as strategy," an exultant Robert McNamara claimed in Cuba's aftermath, "only crisis management."[2] The belief that force could be managed for discrete diplomatic ends was exhilarating, for it resolved a dilemma that had been building for nearly 200 years: On the one hand, force had seemed to have expanded beyond any meaningful purpose; on the other, diplomacy had withered as a meaningful exercise in moderating the conduct of states. But in the early 1960s, a new nexus between force and order seemed, to the crisis managers, clear. Force could be married to diplomacy, they asserted. And the union promised no less than the achievement of a stable, liberal international regime predicated on ample reserves of American power directed by a confident, savvy national security elite. There was no need for deterrence to come to any kind of unlimited test since limited coercion could form an unmistakable and undeniable politico-military grammar. Force, it seemed, could be proportionate and effective. If force could be made a discrete instrument of bargaining, the inner dynamic of Soviet expansionism could be tamed and defeated without incommensurate dangers. The Cuban missile crisis seemed to offer the promise that the sterile and fruitless Kabuki of diplomacy, replete with archaic conference halls and interminable discussion, could be replaced by the management center, the telex, and rapid-fire "signals" divined by those savvy minds who were alert to war's horrors, yet not inured to them.

The Clausewitzian Heritage

From the mid-seventeenth to the onset of the twentieth century, war and peace were ambiguous concepts, defined as much by legal artifacts as by the empirical reality of the battlefield. Wars began by declarations and ultimatums, and they ended with treaties and conferences. Short of war, there were an abundance of military maneuvers and demonstrations of intent that were undertaken in the absence of much public concern. European publics were largely unaware, ill-informed, and disengaged from war. The worst of most wars were fought at sea or in outposts distant from the capital. Battles might be intense, but the costs were largely limited to professional armies and navies. The stakes of conflicts were relatively small. From the Treaty of Westphalia to the onset of the Napoleonic Wars, capitals and courts were rarely at risk. The consequences of defeat, in contradistinction to earlier practices, were neither slavery, slaughter, nor forcible conversion. Rather, a kind of custom of redistributive recompense evolved. Gains or losses were summed up and parsed out in the form of military alliances, dynastic marriages, or overseas colonies. Before the Napoleonic Wars, as Carl von Clausewitz noted, an unlimited struggle was only a theorist's abstraction and not the reality of the battlefield.[3]

By the middle of the eighteenth century, there had emerged a kind of "international society" of resonant interests. As Clausewitz put it, "Political relations . . . [had] become so sensitive a nexus that no cannon could be fired . . . without every government feeling its interests affected."[4] In this "classic" international "system," the familiar palliatives of diplomatic adjustment were well tolerated.[5] War was an adjunct of diplomacy. In the end, diplomats settled up at the bargaining table what soldiers had determined on the battlefield. When, for instance, France ceded Canada after the Seven Years War, Voltaire sniffed that it was not worth worrying about a few "miserable acres of snow."[6]

To Clausewitz, the warrior and the diplomat had a kind of regulatory synergy, sharing an end not of victory, but of a stable peace. War, to Clausewitz, was but a "stronger form of diplomacy."[7] And the battlefield was merely an extension of the conference chamber: "Suppose one merely wants a small concession from the enemy. One will only fight until some modest quid pro quo has been acquired, and a moderate effort should suffice for that. The enemy's reasoning will be much the same. . . . [W]e must be willing to wage such minimal wars which consist in merely threatening the enemy with negotiations held in reserve."[8]

The Ascendancy of Force

Clausewitz's specter was "pure war," which, of "its own independent will . . . usurp[s] the place of policy the moment it [is] brought into being." Clausewitz's great fear was that war would become "pointless and devoid of sense,"—a "thing unto itself."[9] Once war compelled animosities too intense, it lost its integration with the broader world of statecraft.[10] If war were left to the generals or left to its own inner expansive logic, then war's political nature would be suffused. Then the ensuing havoc would not end with any settlement. The carnage would cease only with the annihilation of the enemy.

By the end of the nineteenth century, war could consume not just professional armies, but great sections of whole societies as well. At the same time war began to lose its utility as a means of establishing "normal change," war's "legitimacy" as an instrument of statecraft eroded. Once war began to approach its terrible and absolute form, the only remaining rationale for its employment was to defeat the cause of war itself. As Raymond Aron put it, wars "might not have started out to bring about a change of a particular view of life, but as operations mounted . . . it was essential to inflate the purposes of victory. . . . [P]eace would be durable only if dictated unconditionally after crushing the enemy. The demand for total victory was not so much the expression of political philosophy as a reflex action to total war."[11]

Apocalyptic Power

By the mid-1950s, the Eisenhower administration had given atomic weapons a central place. Yet nuclear weapons were challenged as excessive even by those who depended on them. As Eisenhower, who was assailed by suggestions that he develop nuclear weapons that were more "useful," explained:

> No matter . . . how certain that within 24 hours we could destroy Kuibyshev and Moscow and Leningrad and Baku and all the other places . . . I want you to carry this question home with you. Gain such a victory, and what do you do with it? Here would be a great area from the Elbe to Vladivostok and down through South East Asia torn up and destroyed and without government. . . . I ask you what would the civilized world do about it? I repeat, there is no victory in any war except . . . through our dedication . . . to avoid it.[12]

Not many elements of any given Soviet challenge could be depicted as worth the conjury of atomic victory. Atomic weapons were disproportionate to any normal valuation as a policy objective. Atomic victory neither implied the bending of an enemy to one's will or even defeating his army. Nor did it capture what Clausewitz had in mind when he wrote of war "in the extreme." Rather, victory implied the elimination of an enemy's society altogether. It was not "politics by other means," but what the Nuremberg lawyers spoke of when they wrote the laws of genocide.

Once the Soviets achieved a kind of nominal strategic nuclear parity, war, defined in terms of nuclear weapons, was a coin too fearful in consequence to be redeemed. Yet, while nuclear weapons might paralyze one side, there was, in the emerging American community of defense intellectuals, a fear that these same weapons would embolden the Soviets. As Henry Kissinger explained: "It can be argued that fear of all-out war is bound to be mutual... but . . . [i]f the Soviet block can present its challenges in less than all out form, it may gain a crucial advantage. Every move on its part will then pose the appalling dilemma of whether we are willing to commit suicide to prevent encroachments, no one of which seems to threaten our existence directly, but which may be a step on the road to our ultimate destruction."[13]

THE DEPRECIATION OF DIPLOMACY
AND THE NEW STRATEGISTS

The dreary history of the interwar period seemed to reveal that Western negotiation with totalitarian regimes had reaped only more demands. Finally, when the West said "no—no more," Hitler found the final "no"—coming from Munich's "worms"—just as unconvincing as all the others.[14] The incandescent image of Chamberlain and his folded umbrella burned with idectic certainty in the collective memory of American policymakers.[15]

To William Bundy, in the early 1970s, Munich was the "basic datum" of American foreign policy: "The rejection of armed action contribute[d] to the most ghastly human phenomena. To Kennedy, Johnson, Rusk, my brother... McNamara . . . [war] could prevent vast evil and open the way to progress. War was viewed . . . not as *Catch-22* or *M*A*S*H* or even *Patton* . . . but as the only way to deal with world order."[16]

As a result of the interwar experience, negotiations with "revolutionary" totalitarian powers—powers that would not recognize the legitimacy of the extant international order—were discredited in the West. But whatever the sad spectacle of Munich might have meant, it could have been overcome, one supposes, had not Roosevelt's wartime diplomacy been discredited as well.[17] After the war, Yalta became an oath in American domestic politics.[18] The Republican party's platform of 1952, drafted by John Foster Dulles, denounced the Yalta accords as "secret understandings" that "aided communist enslavements."[19] The negotiators of Yalta had, it was charged, put the capstone on "twenty years of treason."[20]

If it was the business of diplomats to make it unnecessary to fight, they had failed with the onset of the Second World War.[21] If it was their business to lay the foundation for a firm peace, then there too was failure. After the war, diplomats (who had been in Asia when Chiang Kai-shek was forced to flee from Mao's troops or who had been with Roosevelt at Yalta) were accused, at a minimum, of having known the enemy too well—and, at a maximum, of deserting American interests for those of our adversaries. Dean Acheson, George C. Marshall, and the State Department were pilloried. To Indiana Republican Senator William Jenner, for instance, General Marshall was a "front man for traitors . . . a living lie . . . an errand boy . . . a stooge, or a co-conspirator for this administration's crazy assortment of collectivists, cut-throats and Communist fellow traveling appeasers."[22]

In the classic diplomatic tradition, diplomacy and negotiation were nearly synonymous. The diplomat's function was to bring "intelligence and tact to the conduct of official relations" in order to "harmonize" divergent national interests.[23] A concrete manifestation of a diplomat's undertaking was a treaty. The sum of treaties derived by negotiation formed a tissue of "positive" international law. International law, and the relationships it implied, made international society more predictable and hence more orderly. But international law and diplomacy hardly seemed relevant to Soviet power, which was characterized by George Kennan as "[i]mpervious to logic . . .

and committed to the belief that with the U.S. there can be no permanent modus vivendi."[24]

In "legitimate" international systems, negotiations serve to bridge differences.[25] But the postwar world, as Harry Truman told Congress in 1947, was a struggle between two ways of life: "One . . . based upon the will of the majority, and . . . distinguished by free institutions . . . free speech . . . and freedom from oppression. . . . The second . . . based upon the will of a minority . . rel[ying] upon terror and oppression."[26] In a struggle between good and evil, negotiations that led to compromise would not only not work, but if Truman's analysis obtained, they would be wrong.

By the late 1940s, diplomacy had become not so much a method of ameliorating the clash of interest as a self-defeating vestige of an ancient and irrelevant civility. Conferences were still staged. Diplomats met. Communiqués were issued. But meetings were believed to be little more than venues for mean-spirited propaganda, or complex traps to lure good-willed Western innocents.[27] At a conference in 1954, Secretary of State John Foster Dulles asked one of his aides whether he might not be satisfied if the Soviet foreign secretary would accept free elections and the reunification of Germany. "Why yes," his aide responded. "Well, that's where you and I part company," Dulles retorted. "[B]ecause I wouldn't. There'd be a catch in it."[28] To Henry Kissinger, it was clear that the Soviets saw "no value in making concessions. Either they are unnecessary on the basis of the relationship of forces; or else they reflect the relationship of forces and are not concessions, strictly speaking."[29] Similarly, Clark Clifford advised Harry Truman in 1946: "The language of military power is the only language the disciples of power understand. . . . Compromise and concessions are considered, by the Soviets, to be evidence of weakness and they're encouraged by our 'retreats' to make new and greater demands."[30]

As the diplomat and his craft fell into disrepute, all that remained was force pressed to a ferocity beyond the scale of comprehension. Of course, there was a belief that one could get agreements of a sort with the Soviets, yet these could hardly be more than truces. The dilemma of the Cold War—of total stakes and total weapons—called to mind Cicero's lament: "What," he asked, "can be done against force, without force?"[31]

At all conference tables, there had been the shadow of the Warrior. But once the shadow took form, the Diplomat had all but been defeated. Success achieved by force, François de Calliers wrote, "rests on an insecure foundation. . . . [for m]enaces always do harm to negotiations, since they often push a party to extremes to which they would not have resorted but for the provocation."[32]

For most of history, force was diplomacy's nemesis: the sum and symbol of diplomacy's failure. As Henry Kissinger wrote, "In any negotiation, it is understood that force is the ultimate recourse. It is the art of diplomacy to keep the threat potential, to keep its extent indeterminate and to commit it only as a last resort. For once power has been made actual, negotiations in the proper sense cease. A threat to use force which proves unavailing does not return the negotiation to the point before the threat was made. It destroys the bargaining position altogether for it is a confession not of finite power, but of impotence."[33]

To the "new strategists,"[34] the great given was that while classic diplomacy had no real utility, a kind of functional diplomacy[35] had developed wherein adversaries would bargain with each other through the mechanism of graduated increments of military force in order to achieve a "negotiated" accord.[36] This odd, "vicious" "diplomacy of violence" gave a kind of perverse and pernicious twist to the ancient practices of official "gentlemen" who directed their energies toward the search for settlements.[37] As former State Department official and Harvard economist Thomas Schelling explained, "[t]he power to hurt is bargaining power. . . . [its] only purpose, unless sport or revenue, must be to influence somebody's behavior[,] to coerce his decisions or choice; to be coercive, violence has to be anticipated. And it has to be avoidable by accommodation. . . . To exploit it is diplomacy—vicious diplomacy, but diplomacy."[38]

As soon as the Soviets acquired deliverable strategic weapons, in the mid-1950s, Eisenhower began to indicate that he was willing, for his part, to move toward a settlement. As he told the Soviets at Geneva in 1955, "[Once] it was that wars began where diplomacy fails, [now] diplomacy must begin because war has failed."[39] But diplomacy was not the Eisenhower administration's long suit. Dulles had cooperated with Senator Joseph McCarthy in "cleaning out" the State Department. Dulles was, as Eisenhower had noted, "a sort of international prosecuting attorney" more than he was a classic statesman.[40] And although Dulles may have ruminated in private about various initiatives with the Soviets, there is little evidence that he pursued any of them with as much energy as he expended in doggedly opposing summit meetings and the independent diplomatic undertakings of allies.[41]

Kennedy and the State Department

The Kennedy team, perhaps with the exception of the president himself, also had a low regard for the diplomatic enterprise as well as its nominal embodiment, Secretary of State Dean Rusk.[42] Rusk felt he had the ear of the president, and bore in silence the scorn of those "gossips" who later committed their opinions of him to paper—a practice Rusk, in turn, felt, along with his great tutor, General George Marshall, abused a public trust for one's private purse.[43] To the Kennedy courtiers, Rusk could not win for losing. The "gentle, gracious Rusk," as Ted Sorensen put it, was "almost *too* amiable" when asked to respond to White House initiatives; he was "*too* eager to disprove charges of State Department softness by accepting Defense Department toughness." And Rusk bore with "*too* much composure . . . criticism . . . aimed at the frequent sterility of the State Department bureaucracy."[44]

Rusk garnered general disdain from Kennedy's entourage and was the object of water cooler jokes. Once, recalled Sorensen, "I solemnly handed him . . . a [bogus] clipping from a Costa Rican newspaper which contained a faked photograph of . . . Kennedy 'on his way' to Palm Beach . . . promis[ing] an outsized . . . aid grant. Rusk looked at the . . . clipping and nodded gravely that any commitment made would have to be kept."[45]

Rusk was criticized as "irrevocably conventional," a man who "rejoiced . . . in tedium and unembarrassed banality."[46] He was said to be "inscrutable," "compulsively colorless" and "Buddha like," though even his detractors said he was "splendid" in negotiations. But, carped Arthur Schlesinger, "inscrutability [was] inadequate as a principle of life."[47]

To the bright, assertive, and self-consciously masculine Kennedy team, State seemed as if it had been denatured. The professional foreign service was criticized as an insipid swamp of diplomatic gobbledygook. The foreign service personnel system was said to engender only bromides instead of action-filled recommendations that the Kennedy team was looking for. Kennedy complained to *Time* magazine's Hugh Sidey that State had "all those people over there. . . . [T]hey are constantly smiling. I think we need to smile less and be tougher."[48]

Kennedy took matters into his own hands, creating ad hoc alternatives to the professionals, using advisers to distill whatever wisdom there was from deep within the "opaque" interior of the national machinery.[49] He organized foreign policy at the top. The president appointed and received ambassadors at his own initiative and encouraged American ambassadors to report directly to him.[50] Kennedy was his own secretary of state; and some speculated that that was the reason he kept Rusk on long after painful burlesques about him rode the cocktail circuit.

To Kennedy, foreign policy was hardly the array of minute and delicately crafted agreements that might take the hard edge off the more abrading aspects of international society or that make international relations more predictable, and hence, "orderly." Rather, diplomacy was an action tool of the Cold War, partly defensive and partly apiece with his effort "to get the country moving." Just because a country had "gone communist, didn't mean it couldn't be gotten back," he once said. But due care had to be taken. "Domestic policy," he cautioned, can "only defeat us[;] foreign policy could kill us."[51]

The Kennedy Administration's View of War and Politics

The lethal element of international relations was the Kennedy team's preoccupation. Kennedy, and especially McNamara, grappled with the problem of central deterrence at a time when it was clear that the use of strategic weapons could be suicidal, yet much of American defense planning focused on somehow actually using nuclear weapons. When Kennedy, urged on by Eisenhower, focused on the Laotian problem in 1961, the new president was startled to discover that the Joint Chiefs of Staff seemed obsessed with nuclear weapons. Robert Kennedy recalled the 1961 meetings on Laos, when the military unanimously recommended sending in at least 60,000 (and perhaps 160,000) U.S. troops,[52] armed with tactical nuclear weapons: "They were to be brought in through two airports. Someone questioned what we would do if only a limited number landed and then the Communist Pathet Lao knocked out the airports and then attacked our troops, limited in numbers, and not completely equipped. The [military] representative said we would then have to destroy Hanoi and possibly use weapons."[53]

The Kennedy methodology in Laos could be seen as an augury. The president had sought to make it appear as if an armed solution might be necessary at the same time he strove to engineer, through diplomacy, a well-veiled exit from an unsupportable position, and to mask that retreat as a kind of personal victory.[54] A Geneva Conference on Laos was initiated in May of 1961. In June of 1962, the conferees agreed to a neutral government. All sides covertly and liberally violated the agreement, but the Laotian issue nearly disappeared from the headlines.[55] Kennedy had finessed the matter by pure dint of the distance of Laos from the concerns of most Americans, and with the help of court scribes. As Arthur Schlesinger later rhapsodized, "This . . . first experiment in Kennedy diplomacy under pressure . . . [was] marked by restraint of manner, toughness of intention, and care to leave his adversary a way of escape without loss of face."[56]

But the Bay of Pigs disaster, the continuing Cuban irritant, the eroding position of a client South Vietnamese government, the apparent inability of

Kennedy to get Khrushchev to refrain from changing the status of Berlin at Vienna, the sheer bellicosity of the Soviets, the disturbing Soviet initiatives in Africa, and the venomously reckless rhetoric of the Soviets' would-be associates, the Chinese, all seemed to require vigilance, and precluded an appearance of yielding to changes that would seem to embolden the tide of Soviet power. If retreats were to happen elsewhere the next time, they would have to be even more befogged than they had been by Harriman's discussions in Geneva on the Laotian question. It would be best of all, of course, if events were said to have unfolded as a result of an American determination at arms.

From the onset, the Kennedy administration was preoccupied by the issue of proportioning appropriate responses to military tests. During the transition, the Kennedy team had given some thought to mounting a conventional defense to conventional threats in Europe, but were given a choice by military planners—the legacy of the Eisenhower years—between "humiliation and all-out nuclear action."[57] Kennedy's remedy, as he told NATO's military committee, was to search "for a sensitive and flexible control of all arms and especially over nuclear weapons . . . and to [exercise] control from the highest authorities all the way downward . . . after any initiation of hostilities . . . and at any level of escalation."[58]

Kennedy, his brother tells us, read historian Barbara Tuchman's tales of folly, miscalculation, and military plans that compelled actions far beyond the bounds of proportion defined in terms of interest.[59] Tuchman's twofold lesson drawn from the onset of World War I was that military planners should not be allowed to remain autonomous from the world of the statesmen; and that war should not occur as an act of civilian capitulation to "military necessity."[60] The Kennedy administration was not prepared to be grabbed at the forelock by military machines; and the Kennedy team was certainly unwilling to be a prisoner of military professionals whom they were starting to see, well before the Cuban missile crisis, as trigger-happy.

CUBA'S EUROPEAN CONTEXT

Even though Cuba and other geographic "threats" consumed inordinate amounts of time, they were "side issues," peripheral to the real center of American concerns.[61] Europe was at the heart of American postwar foreign policy. The key to Europe was Germany. Without German manpower, the only defense of Europe could be the thinning reed of nuclear deterrence. Without a dense German defense in depth—even though that defense risked the potential loss of about 80 percent of the German "substance"—the defense of the rest of Europe was almost inconceivable. Nuclear weapons might deter a Soviet invasion; but the Soviets could only be stopped from a determined thrust running to the English Channel with a barrier of German manpower.

The emotional pivot to the German question rested in the exposed occupied enclave of Berlin. After Dulles died, Eisenhower determined to seek a peaceful solution to the recrudescent Berlin crisis, spurred, to be sure, by Khrushchev's periodic deadlines and threats. In the early part of 1960, the prospect of meaningful talks over the Berlin question materialized and then evanesced when an American U-2 reconnaissance plane was curiously downed over Sverdlovsk on May 1, 1960.[62] Substantive negotiations stalled thereafter until mid-May 1961, when Khrushchev invited Kennedy to meet with him in Vienna the next month. The Vienna meeting went badly, as a startled young president encountered a bullying Khrushchev. Khrushchev reaffirmed his December deadline for an accommodation over Berlin. If Kennedy insisted on the right of the Western powers after a December peace treaty was signed, and if the West crossed the East German manned frontier, then that crossing would be repelled by force. "I want peace," said Khrushchev, "but if you want war, that is your problem." Kennedy retorted: "It is you, not I, who wants to force a change." It was, thought Dean Rusk, a "brutal" exchange.[63]

The older man may have confused Kennedy's courtesy for vacillation. "It was not a good meeting," recalled a one-time special assistant to Foreign Minister Andrei Gromyko. "[T]he impression in the Foreign Ministry was that it went badly. Kennedy failed to deal with Nikita. . . . To find that an American President can be bullied and won't react. . . . It really surprise[d] me."[64]

As tension mounted in anticipation of the December deadline set by Khrushchev, an increasing number of refugees fled the East. Thirty thousand departed in July alone. Just after midnight Sunday morning, August 13, 1961, East German troops began to tear up the streets at the western edge of the divide that separated the Soviet Zone of Berlin from the occupying Western allies. Road blocks and barricades appeared. Four days later, a bleak concrete wall sealed the city in twain. By October 26, 1961, American tanks faced Soviet tanks on the Friedrichstrasse, nearly muzzle to muzzle. A senior Soviet official in Berlin at the time said that if the American tanks "followed the orders given to them—and those orders were to destroy the Berlin wall—our tanks would then open fire."[65] In those "strange and moody days," as Arthur Schlesinger recalled them, Kennedy himself estimated the chances of nuclear war at 20 percent.[66]

American draft calls tripled. The reserves were reactivated, and the Strategic Air Command (SAC) was put on ground alert. Three and one-half billion dollars were allocated to civilian defense, including household radiation detectors and a national air raid siren system.[67] George Kennan, who had been called back from retirement to serve as ambassador to Belgrade, declared that the White House had reacted with a "terrifying presumption" to a "transient situation," and he was not about to stand idly by and let a group of rash novices "blow up the world" without speaking out.

The first step in ending the crisis came with an apparent Soviet tactical retreat. "They've gotten themselves in a difficult situation, and they don't know how to get themselves out of it. They're looking for a way out, I'm sure. So let's give them one," Khrushchev said, as he turned his guns around.[68] Khrushchev then announced that he would not seek a peace treaty with his East German subordinates because the Western powers had shown "understanding," and, he might have added, East Germany seemed to have been securely imprisoned. The crisis faded. But the lesson that Kennedy inferred from the whole interaction with Khrushchev, from the spring to the winter of 1961, was, in Kennedy's own words, "that son of a bitch doesn't pay attention to words, he has to see you move."[69] The contest had transmuted to a question of national guts, and it had become personal.

Cuba and the Credibility of the Nuclear Threat

Less than a month after Georgy Bolshakov, a special KGB liaison from the Soviet embassy, told Robert Kennedy that Khrushchev had given personal assurances that there would be no Soviet defensive missiles in Cuba, missiles were discovered.[70] "He can't do that to me," John F. Kennedy is said to have complained to National Security Adviser McGeorge Bundy on hearing the startling news on October 15. President Kennedy was disturbed by the audacity of the move much more than he was bothered by the arithmetic of mutual atomic damage. He was also affronted.[71]

> I don't know if they're aware . . . I can't understand their viewpoint . . . if they are aware of what we said at the press conferences [where the administration warned in September against placing missiles in Cuba] I say . . . I don't think there is any record of the Soviets ever making this direct a challenge, really.[72]

To Kennedy, Khrushchev seemed as if he was both "rubbing his nose in the dirt" and being reckless.[73] The sum of the Soviet action constituted both a national and personal test. As he told the American people, this "secret, swift, and extraordinary" decision to base strategic missiles for the first time outside of Soviet soil "is a deliberately provocative and unjustified change in the status quo which cannot be accepted by this country if our courage and our commitments are ever to be trusted again by friend or foe."[74]

As Henry Kissinger once said, "The whole problem with the nuclear age [was that] until power is used, it is . . . what people think."[75] Clearly, the appearance of a radical revision in the strategic equation was serious. Since deterrence rests as much on a psychological relationship as it does the balance of forces, a shift form the well-advertised "missile gap in reverse" of the year before to a position where, as Kennedy fretted, "they look like they're coequal with us," was bound to be unsettling, especially if the most well-advertised component of containment had, it seemed, been reversed by a strategic shortcut. If, as Kennedy summed up the experience in public a few months later, the Soviets had succeeded in keeping their missiles in Cuba, "it would have politically changed the balance of power. It would have appeared to, and appearances contribute to reality."[76]

McNamara had, well before the crisis, abandoned "static" measures of nuclear advantage reckoned in terms of raw megatonnage delivered to an ever more expansive list of targets.[77] Undoubtedly this "bean counting" was somewhat surreal and its impact was largely "psychological," as one of the participants in the Executive Committee of the President (ExComm) deliberations put it.[78] But according to U.S. analysts at the time, the 24 medium-range ballistic missiles (MRBMs) and some 12 to 16 intermediate-range ballistic missiles (IRBMs) discovered in Cuba had raised the number of targets the Soviets could lethally cover in the United States by 40 percent.[79] On the merits of what was known, the missiles severely eroded the possibility of an unanswered U.S. first strike against the Soviets.[80] This had been something central to U.S. Air Force planners, but was not critical in the mind of the secretary of defense who believed, before the crisis, that a disarming first strike was a chimera.[81] Clearly, however, in their own terms, the missiles seemed to give the Soviets some of the leverage they had lost when the missile gap had been revealed as a myth the year before.

In September, Kennedy said to his advisers, "I should have said . . . that we don't care. But when we said we're not going to [tolerate them] and then they go ahead and do it, and then we do nothing, then . . . our risks increase. They've got enough to blow us up now anyway. I just think it's just a question of . . . a political struggle as much as [a] military" issue.[82] McNamara joined the conversation with his own underscore: "[T]his is a domestic political problem."[83]

It was not just that Kennedy or his closest advisers felt the press of domestic politics (they probably did, although later they claimed they did not), but that the domestic credibility of the administration could not, in their minds, be disaggregated from national credibility when the real issue was the diabolic antinomies of the day: nuclear war or global totalitarianism.[84] As journalist Jonathan Schell observed in the context of Vietnam, a few years later: "A blow to the image of toughness was not just a blow to the pride of the men of government or a political setback for them . . . it was a blow to the heart of the national defense."[85]

THE FEARFUL OPTIONS AND NUCLEAR CREDIBILITY

McNamara proposed at first a warning that the United States was about to "take out" the offending missiles. If there was a Soviet response, then the Soviet Union would be struck as well, presumable with a disarming atomic first strike. "Now if this alternative doesn't seem to be a very acceptable one . . . wait until you work out the others," he said darkly.[86] Later, McNamara would claim that U.S. plans that detailed strategic nuclear exchanges were "unreal."[87] But clearly the military was under the impression that "it might be necessary to make a compensatory attack against the USSR" as a follow-on to an invasion of Cuba.[88] Although there were doubters in the ExComm, even among the "doves," most seemed to feel that if Cuba was invaded, then the Soviets would be forced to move in an area where the Russians had an equivalent geostrategic advantage, and where the United States had an equivalent exposure.[89]

An invasion was expected, at least as Robert Kennedy's memoirs have it, "by Monday or Tuesday," October 29 or 30.[90] It is possible that an invasion could have been mounted; the Soviets, even though they suffered high casualties, and a significant strategic and political loss, might not really have done much, as some analysts and some of the participants in the crisis now maintain.[91] But an equivalent riposte was expected. Dean Acheson argued convincingly that the missiles based in Turkey would be lost and proposed a follow-on nuclear strike within the Soviet Union after the Soviets had struck Turkey.[92]

Some, therefore, in the ExComm were willing to "write off" an attack on Turkey if a Soviet attack was confined to the Jupiter sites. "We were going to let him [Khrushchev] have his strike in Turkey, as I understood it last week," said Bundy. "Yeah, that's right," replied McNamara. But if allied forces in Berlin were squeezed, it raised prospects so frightening that McNamara said he was not "prepared to address" them.[93]

By October 27, the ExComm had become convinced that whatever the missiles' ultimate strategic meaning, their symbolic meaning was both unmistakable and no longer tolerable. The longer missiles stayed on in Cuba, the more irretrievable the situation would become. The longer operational missiles were in place, the more certain it was that they changed the Soviet bargaining position vis-à-vis the United States, and diminished the standing of the United States in the world.[94] Further, if the crisis persisted, the majority in the ExComm feared that the extant high-voltage stasis could not be sustained. Shooting could start anywhere, and then the United States would have put in jeopardy not just its control of events, but control of the rhythm of combat as well. With all the dangers, the Joint Chiefs of Staff and its chairman Maxwell Taylor were clear with their recommendation in favor of a strike no later than Monday, if for no other reason than that after then the military would start to lose its edge—as planes and men wore down under the strain of peak readiness, and because with each surveillance flight, more planes and pilots were exposed to hazards.[95]

The consensus that the crisis had to be resolved within 48 hours was further crystalized by the receipt of two quite different messages. The first was a rambling private letter from Khrushchev offering to exchange the missiles for a promise that the United States would not invade Cuba. The second, more formal message was also broadcast on radio. It mentioned the obsolete, but nonetheless recently operational, U.S. missiles in Turkey, near the Soviet border.

Soon after the second message was in hand, an Air Force U-2 surveillance flight was shot down over Cuba with the loss of a pilot. U.S. intelligence overflights were essential to see if the Soviets were either readying a preemptive strike, or if they were "standing down."[96] General Taylor, the one military man who commanded real respect in the Kennedy camp, argued: "[W]e must not fail on surveillance. We can't give up twenty-four hours at this stage." McNamara seconded Taylor's insistent observation. He "fully agreed" and President Kennedy added his assent.[97] Reconnaissance planes would scour the island at two-hour intervals.[98]

It was expected that U.S. planes would be attacked. The president was hardly compelled by the logic of targeting a few of the offending Soviet-manned antiaircraft batteries.[99] The momentum of events, it was clear in the ExComm discussions, pointed to striking Soviet surface-to-air missiles (SAMs). But a small-scale strike at just one offending air-defense battery would kill Soviets, and perhaps in the melee, a medium-range ground-to-ground nuclear-tipped missile would be fired on the United States. The Joint Chiefs wanted an all-out coordinated air strike launched at Cuba "right away," but agreed to a limited single strike first, with the understanding that if another attack on U.S. aircraft occurred, there would be a thoroughgoing extirpation of the offending SAM site.[100] An initial attack of 2,000 sorties would cover an estimated 16,000 Soviet troops, but, in fact, there were over 40,000 Soviet personnel and their equipment on the island. An invasion would follow some days later.[101] McNamara conceded part of the argument to the military. Invasion, he affirmed, was now "inevitable" once military hostilities began.[102]

The throbbing press of events wore on the deliberants. Secretary Rusk, on contemplating the reaction of the "hawks" to the news of the downed U-2, found his eyes brimming with tears. Acheson brought him up sharply: "Pull yourself together, Dean, you're the only Secretary of State we have."[103] Robert Kennedy wrote about the time left in terms of hours: "The President was not optimistic nor was I. He ordered twenty-four troop carrier squadrons of the Air Force Reserve to active duty. They would be necessary for invasion. The expectation was that there would be a military confrontation by Tuesday, possibly tomorrow."[104]

Strategic Plans

A kind of hollowness to the much-vaunted U.S. "damage limiting" plans by which McNamara had hoped to confine nuclear destruction to military targets appeared at the onset of the crisis, when U.S. strategic aircraft were shifted by Kennedy to civilian airfields.[105] This made a "token" Soviet counterforce, "damage limiting" strike against military targets, if they were going to bother, seem somewhat far-fetched. Indeed, the early strategic nuclear targeting plans of the McNamara years, according to the Joint Chiefs, were "designed to be executed as a whole."[106] Moreover, the Joint Chiefs told the president, "limiting attack to military targets has little practical meaning as a humanitarian measure . . . [because of] fallout."[107] Although "strikes could be withheld against targets," the Joint Chiefs cautioned about "excessive . . . options . . . which could contribute to confusion and lower our assurance of success." "It must be clear," they warned, "that any decision to execute only a portion of the entire plan would involve acceptance of grave risks."[108]

To the Soviets, the sheer number of American strategic weapons aloft or on alert pointed to the inexorable conclusion that if there was an American nuclear assault on the Soviet Union, the limits would not be meaningful to the Soviet recipients.[109] Whether or not the Soviets understood or knew U.S. targeting plans, there was pressure on Khrushchev to act. Soviet military doctrine, notes Raymond Garthoff, called for preemption if there was "positive indication that the United States was preparing imminently and irrevocably for a first strike."[110] The obvious danger was that Khrushchev was coming to feel that argument for war would develop its own logic and prepare for it.[111] Perhaps, as the editor of Khrushchev's memoirs noted, had Khrushchev been more "normal," that is, had he believed along with Soviet and American "deterrence theorists" that nuclear weapons could not just be an instrument of bluff, he would have acted to use them, for he would have assumed that American thinking would be tracking an equivalent line of thought.[112]

Later, McNamara and Bundy would claim that not only was there little likelihood that the Strategic Integrated Operations Plan (SIOP) would ever become relevant, but that any use of nuclear weapons was remote and even farfetched.[113]

If nuclear weapons were not a realistic option, one wonders why, on more than a few occasions, McNamara recalled wondering if October 27 would be the last Saturday he ever saw: "I remember the sunset. We left about the time the sun was setting in October, and I, at least, was so uncertain as to whether the Soviets would accept replying to the first instead of the second . . . that I wondered if I'd ever see another Saturday sunset like that."[114]

Near Misses

For his part, President Kennedy put the odds for war at between one in three and even.[115] Clearly, most of the participants in those events found them harrowing. Robert Kennedy reported that he felt, on October 25, that "we were on the edge of a precipice with no way off. . . . President Kennedy had initiated the course of events, but he no longer had control over them."[116] The sense of dread was soon superseded by the elation that accompanied success. But years later, researchers Raymond Garthoff and Scott Sagan assembled a lengthy list of worrisome—but, at the time, unapprehended—near misses and communication and control failures that could have triggered an inadvertent chain of events that could have brought the United States and the Soviets over the edge of war and into the abyss.

  • American intelligence had learned that their premier informant, Colonel Oleg Penkovsky, had been arrested on October 22. Penkovsky's arrest had dangerous implications. The Soviets, as Raymond Garthoff suggests, might have inferred that the information that Penkovsky relayed to U.S. Intelligence verified that the United States did, indeed, have sufficient nuclear punch to exercise the Joint Chiefs' preferred first SIOP option, a devastating coordinated first strike. In addition, Penkovsky had been given some coded signals, including, according to Garthoff, "one to be used in the ultimate contingency: imminent war. When he was arrested, he . . . chose to use the signal for imminent Soviet attack! . . . [A]bout to go down, he evidently decided to play Samson and bring the temple down on everybody else as well."[117] Penkovsky's provocative signal was suppressed within the CIA, and neither the CIA director nor the ExComm were told of his dire last call.

• Orders to cease the U-2 flights near the Soviet borders were either not received or ignored.[118] In one "Strangelove" incident, an authorized U-2 entered Soviet airspace.[119] Soviet MiGs scrambled to shoot the spy plane down. The U-2's SOS alerted Galena Air Force Base in Alaska, and a group of American fighter aircraft rose to escort the errant plane back to base. Not known at the time in the White House was the fact that the American fighter group scrambling to rescue the U-2 some 100 miles into Soviet air space had been armed with nuclear weapons that could be fired on each pilot's own authority.[120]

• The commander in chief of the U.S. Strategic Air Command, in an uncoded signal, alerted all his units to the highest peacetime alert, "DefCon 2." Most of the actions relevant to this alert would have been picked up in due course, but the Soviets must have been puzzled by the bravura with which these moves were broadcast.[121] This unprecedented intensification of peacetime readiness for war was taken openly so that the Soviets could pick the message up and be suitably daunted.[122] "[T]his remarkable display of American power," writes Garthoff, "was unauthorized and unknown to the President, the Secretary of Defense, the Chairman of the Joint Chiefs, and the Excomm as they so carefully calibrated and controlled action in the intensifying confrontation."[123]

• In those same heated hours, the FBI informed the White House that the Soviet mission in New York had prepared to burn its archives. Some analysts took this as preparation for war, notwithstanding the fact that none of the Soviet strategic forces within the Soviet Union had been put on alert.[124]

• An Atlas intercontinental ballistic missile (ICBM) was test launched from Vandenberg Air Force Base in California on the afternoon of October 26, 1962. The missile that was tested sat side by side with others that were fully loaded, already on alert. At the least, the test flight might well have appeared as a nuclear "stray" had the Soviets been able to observe it.[125] At the most, it could have been seen like the wandering U-2, as a precursor to an all-out attack.

• At the height of the crisis, at least one CIA covert action team was roaming Cuba. The activities of Operation Mongoose were suspended, apparently only as an afterthought, on October 30, 1962, by Robert Kennedy.[126] Nonetheless, the CIA-sponsored unit decided, on its own authority, to blow up a factory on November 8.[127] One might speculate what might have happened if any of the clandestine units operating in Cuba had decided to fire on Soviet missiles, vulnerable as they were reported to have been to rifle fire, or if they had attempted to kill Castro or his close associates, or if they had killed any of the high Soviet officials on the island at the time.

• The main instrument of control of the tempo of pressure was the blockade run by the Navy. McNamara sensed that the Navy might not be responsive to what the president had in mind and went to the "Flag-Plot," or Naval Operations Center, where he could talk to ship commanders directly.

McNamara's colloquy with the Chief of Naval Operations, Admiral George Anderson, has been often told:

McNamara: *"When that ship reaches the line, how are we going to stop it?"*

Anderson: *"We'll hail it."*

McNamara: *"In what language—English or Russian?"*

Anderson: *"How the hell should I know?"*

McNamara: *"What will you do if they don't understand?"*

Anderson: *"I suppose we'll use flags."*

McNamara: *"Well, what if they don't stop?"*

Anderson: *"We'll send a shot across the bow."*

McNamara: *"Then what if that doesn't work?"*

Anderson: *"Then we'll fire into the rudder."*

McNamara: *"What kind of ship is it?"*

Anderson: *"A tanker, Mr. Secretary."*

McNamara: *"You are not going to fire a single shot at anything without my express permission, is that clear? Do you understand that?"*

Anderson: *"The Navy has been running blockades since the days of John Paul Jones and if you and your deputy will go to your offices, the Navy will run the blockade."*

McNamara wheeled to return to his office.

Anderson: *"Don't worry, Mr. Secretary, we know what we are doing here."*[128]

In fact, all six Soviet submarines near the quarantine were shadowed. One sub was "surfaced," unknown to the ExComm, by a low-level depth charge and disabled.[129] In any case, the Soviets were not informed of where the quarantine was supposed to have been until October 27, 1962—"Black

Saturday"—when George Ball suggested to the president that they be notified.[130]

The quarantine had a flexible definition in practice. A Soviet freighter loaded with nuclear weapons, the *Poltava*, was designated the Navy's "first target" and pursued ahead of the official quarantine line by a U.S. destroyer at maximum speed, notwithstanding an order to recall another pursuing destroyer that had caught the notice of the defense secretary.[131] The Navy had established the quarantine at a distance of 500 miles from Havana and Cape Maysi[132] when the president ordered the Navy to draw the line closer in to shore in order to give the ships steaming toward Cuba more room and time to turn away instead of submitting to the American interdiction. But the Navy kept the quarantine where it was until Monday, October 29, the day after Khrushchev's last open communication to Kennedy signaled the end of the crisis.[133]

Years later, McNamara pontificated, "Some things you can't foresee, and you can't process all the relevant information at once."[134]

Virtue and Necessity: The Jupiters

In the wake of the crisis's successful resolution, the innate self-confidence suffused the profound relief of the moment. The national security group ExComm, who had handled the Cuba material, code-named, meaningfully, "Elite," felt that they had mastered the merger of politics and force. The ability to oversee force became the coin of an exclusive realm. National security managers occupied a narrow circle with few apprentices and still fewer fully accredited practitioners.[135] As Roger Hilsman put it, crisis management in foreign affairs had become "like blue cheese . . . [an] acquired taste."[136]

Despite Kennedy's determination not to "gloat" after the crisis, some of the Kennedy decisionmakers found celebration irresistible. To Arthur Schlesinger, the Cuban missile crisis displayed "the ripening of an American leadership unsurpassed in the responsible management of power . . . [a] combination of toughness . . . nerve and wisdom, so brilliantly controlled, so matchlessly calibrated that [it] dazzled the world."[137]

The common characterization of the ExComm was that it was a paragon of organizational effectiveness. As one student of decision making, Thomas Halper, wrote, "The Executive Committee was important in helping plumb the reality of the situation. . . . The men chosen were calm, rational, and frank. . . . [T]he Committee was the scene of intellectual conflict . . . and not emotional quarreling arising from interpersonal friction. . . . [The ExComm] permitted . . . the freedom essential for effective discussion . . . and made the best use of available time. . . . [T]he information and skills brought to bear to the task were additive. Both in scope and depth, the President and his advisors had a decisive edge over the President alone."[138]

But the ExComm conversations, as now disclosed in declassified transcripts, hardly show a cool delineation of alternatives or a deliberate dissection of well-gamed actions. The voices are halting. The sentences are incomplete. Thoughts ramble. Memories slip and options ooze into the ether. At several points, McNamara's distraction was abundantly clear. One deputy remembers him nearly hysterical: "He turned absolutely white [when he got the news of the stray U-2] and yelled hysterically, 'This means war with the Soviet Union.'"[139] The meetings were long, inconclusive, and terrifying. Robert Kennedy recalled, "The strain and hours without sleep were beginning to take their toll. . . . That kind of pressure does strange things to human beings, even to brilliant, self-confident, mature, experienced men."[140] There were reports that one assistant secretary was so disconcerted and fatigued that he drove into a tree at 4 A.M.[141] The initial judgment on the meetings of the acid-tongued former secretary of state, Dean Acheson, seemed, as usual, on the mark: They were "repetitive" and "leaderless" and he stopped attending them since they were "a waste of time."[142]

The Excomm transcripts do make clear that President Kennedy tended to favor a trade of the Jupiters, as the second public message of Khrushchev suggested. Although a trade might have looked reasonable at home and overseas, it could also have constituted something of an embarrassment within NATO and provided an opening to right-wing critics. But if a trade were not made, and there had been war, even if it was "limited," then Kennedy was also aware that there would be bitter recriminations.[143] How could the carnage of battle be justified when the price of avoiding it was the small change of obsolete, vulnerable missiles that the administration was hoping to stand-down soon in any case? As Kennedy ruminated, "We can't very well invade Cuba with all its toil, when we could have gotten them out by making a deal on the missiles in Turkey. If that's part of the record, I don't see how we'll have a very good war."[144]

By the afternoon of October 27, the president's conviction was, he told his advisers, that "we will get the Soviet strategic missiles out of Cuba by invading or trading."[145] The president had earlier sent his brother to explore with Anatoly A. Dobrynin an offer of a pull-out of the Jupiter missiles in Turkey in exchange for a withdrawal of Soviet missiles in Cuba, on the evening of October 27. But, meanwhile, the president indicated to the ExComm that he was moving closer to a military solution: If "our reconnaissance planes are fired on tomorrow . . . then we should take out the SAM sites in Cuba by air action."[146]

Kennedy, it seems, was negotiating both with his advisers and the Soviets. To his largest group of advisers he wanted to appear as resolute as possible. Hence, only at the eleventh hour, and then only to a small circle of intimates, was Kennedy willing to show some of the flexibility that he had apparently come up with on his own.

Between the afternoon and evening meetings of October 27, "Black Saturday," Kennedy convened a group of advisers: Rusk, McNamara, Robert Kennedy, George Ball, Roswell Gilpatric, Llewellyn Thompson, Sorensen, and Bundy. Their collective decision was to authorize Robert Kennedy to tell Dobrynin that the missiles in Turkey would come out after the crisis had been resolved.[147] Not known to this "mini" ExComm, however, was the approach that Robert Kennedy made to Ambassador Dobrynin regarding a swap of the Jupiters for the missiles in Cuba. Then, very late that night, Rusk and President Kennedy took further measures to end the crisis via a quid pro quo. Secretary Rusk was given authority to authorize, on a signal, the UN secretary-general to announce in public the offer of an exchange of the U.S. missiles in Turkey for the missiles in Cuba.[148]

It was a complex game. Informally, the president had authorized his brother to see if Ambassador Dobrynin would accept a "private understanding" (already broached in discussions with Dobrynin some days earlier) with Khrushchev to quietly exchange the Jupiters for the missiles and to offer publicly to guarantee that the Cubans would be free from American invasion. Formally, there was to be a "no invasion" pledge for removal of the missiles. Informally, there was to be a trade: the United States would pull its missiles out of Turkey and Italy, if the Soviets would withdraw their missiles first from Cuba. If the arrangement Robert Kennedy was offering the Soviets were made public, the attorney general stated, it "would damage the relationship."[149] But if Khrushchev rejected the offer, the president was prepared to go forward with the offer of a public trade.

Mid-morning the next day, Khrushchev responded via Moscow radio, accepting Robert Kennedy's offer without mentioning, as Kennedy insisted, the imminent withdrawal of the Jupiters.[150] John F. Kennedy was thus salvaged for 25 years from the ignominy of having to make his eagerness to initiate a public swap known to most of his advisers for 25 years. Kennedy had stood firm. He was tough. And he had prevailed.

The implications of the Kennedy-Dobrynin meeting were, in the words of Arthur Schlesinger, "muted."[151] As rendered by Sorensen, the legend was that the Kennedys were only offering Khrushchev a face-saving method that would, in fact, "strengthen our stand."[152] There would be no public compromise. The crisis was portrayed as a "test of will" that highlighted the Soviet transgression of the political-nuclear status quo. As Kennedy's Boswell put it, the president wanted to "concentrate on a single issue—the enormity of the introduction of the missiles and the absolute necessity of their removal."[153]

Before the Senate Foreign Relations Committee, Rusk was asked by Senator Bourke Hickenlooper to affirm that a "deal" or "trade" had in "no way, shape or form, directly or indirectly been connected with the settlement . . . or had been agreed to?" Rusk replied, "That is correct, sir."[154]

In 1963, McNamara told the House Appropriations Committee "without any qualifications whatsoever there was absolutely no deal . . . between the Soviet Union and the United States regarding the removal of the Jupiter weapons from either Italy or Turkey."[155]

McGeorge Bundy writes of the forthright swap: "As far as I know, none of the nine of us told anyone else what had happened. We denied in every forum that there was any deal."[156] As a result, the lesson to all but a select group of Kennedy intimates was that Kennedy had determined events by dictating a virtual ultimatum. The chroniclers of the 1960s claimed the Soviets merely capitulated. This was the expurgated sum of Robert Kennedy's ultimatum to Dobrynin: "We had to have a commitment by tomorrow. . . . [I]t was a statement of fact. . . . [I]f they did not remove those bases, we would remove them."[157] Roger Hilsman, the senior State Department intelligence officer in the crisis, reached the only conclusion he could have from the "facts" as they were portrayed at the time: Khrushchev simply "backed down."[158] Dean Rusk's phrase, recalling a childhood game, "we were eyeball to eyeball, and the other fellow blinked," was said to have told it all.

One result of the misleading way the crisis legend was retold was that the new national security managers who proliferated after Cuba routed those who had most favored negotiations. In an article in the *Saturday Evening Post*, one of the last "moderates," Adlai Stevenson, was widely attacked for "advocating a Munich." The source of the story, it was rumored, was the president himself.[159] In front of each other, the ExComm members were afraid of being sullied by the taint of "Munich"—to sound anything less than bold. As McGeorge Bundy explained, only the "cautious" and "hawkish" Rusk, who had a reputation as not "insensitive to the interests of allies, and [un]eager to make unwise concessions to the Soviets" could make it "easier on us" to propose the swap (that Kennedy seems to have had already told his brother to take to the Soviets informally days before).[160] Later, Abram

Chayes, Kennedy's State Department legal counselor, noted at an ExComm reunion: "Max Taylor said that there were three options—talk the missiles out of Cuba, shoot 'em out, and squeeze 'em out. There was a fourth, buy 'em out. This one gets talked about less than the others because of the power of the Munich stigma and because it sounds a lot less courageous. But, in fact, we did, in part, buy 'em out, and the President seems to have been willing to go a lot farther."[161]

The apparent rewards of toughness and the gains that were the seeming fruits of a determined position of strength edged out those alternatives not framed in terms of coercion. A "moderate" in these terms was limited to suggesting limited violence. As Undersecretary of State George Ball explained his "devil's advocacy" about Vietnam (a "modest" troop ceiling of around 70,000 men and a series of bombing halts): "[I]f I had said let's pull out overnight or do something of this kind, I obviously wouldn't have been persuasive at all. They'd have said, 'That man's mad.'"[162]

While peaceful options to resolve potentially lethal conflicts were at a discount, military options suggested by military men were also depreciated as a result of the way in which the Cuban crisis was celebrated in print.[163] Robert Kennedy's amanuensis (Arthur Schlesinger) has him remembering the "many times . . . I had heard the military take positions which, if wrong, had the advantage that no one would be around at the end to know."[164] "The military are mad," the president was reported as concluding.[165] The military's enthusiasm for preemptive attacks on the Soviet Union, and Air Force Chief of Staff General Curtis LeMay's wish to attack Cuba even the day after the Soviets announced the missiles were to be withdrawn, drew great walls of well-advertised scorn from the Kennedy national security *consigliere*.[166]

Later, for instance, a story circulated in Georgetown's tonier salons that reflected the civilian wisdom of the day. Chairman of the Joint Chiefs Lyman Lemnitzer briefed Kennedy on Vietnam, but he had pointed not to the Mekong Delta, but rather the Yangtze Valley.[167] In sum, the military were not just dangerous, they were fools and to the degree there were "failures" in the Cuban crisis, those failures were adjudged the result of an incomplete control exercised over a rather loutish military. The conclusion was clear: The professional military either posed most of the risks, or exacerbated them. Robert Kennedy said: "[T]his experience pointed out for all of us the importance of civilian direction and control."[168] The president occurred: "The first advice I'm going to give my successor is to watch the generals and to avoid the feeling that just because they are military men their opinion on military matters is worth a damn."[169]

Years later, Peter Rosen, a defense analyst, reflected on the consequence of the Kennedy team's distrust in Vietnam: "It must be said that the generals were and are often wrong. Their advice was often bad. The military, however, was fighting the war and had the data and personal experience that was crucial. Bad relations meant the civilians and the soldiers were less likely to work together to develop good strategy. Instead, the civilians were inclined to turn to limited war theory. It enabled them to make strategy of a sort without help from the generals. It gave them power over the generals."[170]

The new security managers believed they had discovered a modern alchemy of melding force to diplomacy. Sub-nuclear, and indeed sub-conventional, violence could, in the right admixture, be instrumental overseas and supportable at home.[171] Later, these confident assumptions were placed on a vast testing ground in Southeast Asia. In a rare, self-revelatory rumination, McNamara said, years later:

> At least people like Helmut Schmidt and Dennis Healey . . . have a chance to rise through government positions . . . with some experience and expertise in defense under their belts. But Americans are always putting people in positions of high authority . . . who have almost nothing in the way of prior qualifications, and that carries risks. . . . It's *very* dangerous to bring the President of Ford Motor Company—or even worse, General Motors [laughter]—to be Secretary of Defense. . . . I really think it is vitally important to have people in top administration positions who have some prior expertise in national security matters."[172]

But the new national security managers were not overseeing an alien institution. Many of them had had great success in military organizations, serving with heroism and distinction. Bundy had worked on the planning for D-Day with Admiral Kirk and General Bradley. When things were winding down in Europe, he transferred to the infantry in order to be in on the invasion of Japan. McNamara was an Air Force planner in the war working with Robert Lovett in bringing the latest, life-saving business management techniques to supply and support the Air Force. Hilsman, a West Point graduate, was a guerilla fighter with Mosby in the Burma theater.

The Kennedy national security clique's evident disdain for the military did not stem from a "know nothing" ignorance of armed force, but from their affection for the appealing theory that they had mastered a great secret of avoiding the Hobson's choices presented by nuclear war. Alas, as Rosen points out, all those theories—abstracted from the "pauses," "squeezes," "signals," and "messages" that were adduced from the blockade, the nuclear alerts, the mobilizations, and the dispersal of the bombers in SAC[173]—about the transmittal of "political meaning" through coercion (to any extent that they may have succeeded in Cuba) manifestly failed in Vietnam.

It is unclear, moreover, how "clear" those signals were in execution—and most importantly, how accurately they were interpreted in Moscow or in Cuba. The once ebullient quintessential crisis manager, Robert McNamara, told his old associates in a kind of coda of the crisis managing craft that there ought to be a "law" that states "It is impossible to predict with a high degree of confidence what the effects of the use of military force will be because of accident, miscalculation, misperception, and inadvertence. You can't manage crises; it's a dangerous metaphor, because it's misleading."[174]

CUBA AND THE AMERICAN CENTURY

The Cuban missile crisis revived the sense of an American mission. Time-Life publisher Henry R. Luce once rhapsodized in a widely circulated editorial that Americans must "accept wholeheartedly our duty and opportunity as the most powerful and vital nation in the world and in consequence to exert upon the world the full impact of our influence for such purposes as we see fit, and by such means as we see fit."[175]

After the crisis, Arthur Schlesinger, Jr., could lyrically resurrect this tradition: "But the ultimate impact of the missile crisis was wider than Cuba, wider than even the Western hemisphere. . . . Before the missile crisis people might have feared that we would use our power extravagantly or not use it at all. But the thirteen days gave the world—even the Soviet Union—a sense of American determination and responsibility in the use of power which, if sustained, might indeed become a turning point in the history of the relations between East and West."[176]

The crisis seemed to reaffirm the utility of nuclear weapons and maintaining "positions of strength and resolve."[177] Roger Hilsman was but one of the Kennedy-era advisers who were convinced that "the best judgement" of the meaning of the confrontation was that "the Soviets backed down in the face of a threat that combined conventional and strategic power."[178] The "immense" benefits of the shadow of U.S. nuclear preponderance continued to drive perceptions and policy.[179] As one Kennedy adviser, Paul Nitze, was to insist his entire professional life, "[T]he decisive factor" in October 1962, was "our undoubted nuclear superiority."[180] Henry Kissinger echoed Nitze's confidence in the utility of the American nuclear advantage: "The crisis could not have ended so quickly and decisively but for the fact that the United States can win a general war if it strikes first and can inflict intolerable damage . . . even if it is the victim of a surprise attack."[181]

But after the Cuban crisis, the option of "low-level violence" became more plausible and even more necessary. After all, the symbolic or "psychological capital" of deterrence rested on the notion of resolve. And one way to demonstrate political will was through the assertion of conventional force. A successful use of armed force could demonstrate "resolve" without the threat of organizing a nuclear holocaust. The latter threat was bound to deteriorate with the advent of a viable Soviet retaliatory capability in any case, and the knowledge that the Soviets had collapsed once under a nuclear threat and might not be willing to be quite so passive again upped the ante and the risks of "nuclear gamesmanship." So, after Cuba, a success in limited war became even more of an imperative.

As Daniel Ellsberg recalled: "McNamara's tireless and shrewd efforts in the early sixties, largely hidden . . . to this day . . . [were to] control the forces within the military bureaucracy that pressed the threat and use of nuclear weapons. . . . [I]n this hidden debate, there was strong incentive . . . for the civilian leaders to demonstrate that success was possible in Indochina without the need either to compromise the Cold War objectives or to threaten to use nuclear weapons."[182]

Of course, the underlying assumptions of the planners of limited war—as they emerged victorious from the Cuban crisis—were as old as the Cold War. They dated from Truman's Manichean presentation of a bitter bipolar global confrontation where a gain to one party necessarily would be a loss to the other. Later, a world of diverse centers of power, with elements of superpower cooperation, where gains and losses would be less easily demonstrable, would not be so congenial to a military remedy. A multipolar world would be less hospitable to the belief that the only options available to policymakers were either military force or retreat. Maneuver and negotiation would reappear. But such a development was to come about only after a militarized vision of diplomacy had been tested in Vietnam and found wanting.

As the Cold War has faded, it is unclear if the old twin of force, the diplomat, can be rehabilitated. But in a world made more traditional by the collapse of the leading revolutionary faith, nuclear crisis would not have its old salience, nor would nuclear weapons compel us in the same directions. The long-neglected temporizing repertoire of the statesmen—the conference chamber and the treaty—may once again restore a balance to the unnatural 50-year union of the warrior to the diplomat. After the Cold War, force could well return to its proper role: a last recourse that serves as a latent adjunct to order, and not its surrogate.

NOTES

The author wishes to thank Ray Garthoff and Bart Bernstein for their very careful reading and comments on an earlier draft. The remaining mistakes and interpretations are, however, my own.

1. Robert E. Osgood and Robert W. Tucker, *Force, Order, and Justice* (Baltimore: Johns Hopkins University Press, 1967), p. 343.
2. Cited by Coral Bell in *The Conventions of Crisis: A Study in Diplomatic Management* (London: Oxford University Press, 1984), p. 2.
3. Carl von Clausewitz, *On War,* ed. and trans. Michael Howard and Peter Paret (Princeton, NJ: Princeton University Press, 1984), I, p. 647.
4. Carl von Clausewitz, *Von Krieg,* 19th ed., ed. Werner Hahlweg (Bonn, 1980), p. 590. Cited and translated by Hugh Smith, "The Womb of War: Clausewitz and International Politics," *Review of International Studies* 16, no. 1 (January 1990), p. 49.
5. Clausewitz, however, disputed the restraint of law and morality on war as "self-imposed," "imperceptible limitations." Clausewitz, *Von Kreig,* p. 75; Smith, "The Womb of War," p. 46.
6. Ludwig Dahio, *The Precarious Balance* (New York: Vintage Books, 1962), p. 115. On the issue of whether, in fact, this system was indeed "moderate," see James A. Nathan, "The Heyday of the Balance of Power: Frederick the Great and the Decline of the Old Regime," *Naval War College Review* (July-August 1980), pp. 53-67.
7. Clausewitz, *On War,* pp. 69, 488, 501.
8. Ibid., p. 604.
9. Ibid, p. 644.
10. Ibid, p. 706.
11. Raymond Aron, *The Century of Total War* (Boston: Beacon Press, 1954) p. 28.
12. In a 1954 conversation with military officers, cited in James C. Hagerty, *The Diary of James C. Hagerty,* ed. Robert H. Ferrell (Bloomington, IN: Indiana University Press, 1983), p. 69.
13. Henry Kissinger, *Nuclear Weapons and Foreign Policy* (New York: W. W. Norton, 1969), p. 11.
14. Leonard Mosely, *On Borrowed Time: How World War II Began* (New York: Random House, 1969), p. 383.
15. See Richard Neustadt and Ernest May, *Thinking in Time: The Uses of History in Decision Making* (New York: Free Press, 1988), p. 89.
16. Transcript of remarks made by William P. Bundy, University of Delaware, October 16, 1973.
17. Robert J. Beck, "Munich's Lessons Reconsidered," *International Security* 14, no. 2 (Fall 1989), pp. 161-91. By 1947, Harry Truman had concluded

that the Soviets had not kept a "single agreement," and that the only American recourse was to "resort to other methods." *Public Papers of the Presidents of the United States: Harry S Truman* (Washington, DC: U.S. Government Printing Office, 1947), p. 239

18. Athan G. Theoharis, *The Yalta Myths: An Issue in US Politics, 1945-1955* (Columbia, MO: University of Missouri Press, 1970), p. 23-86ff.

19. Theodore Draper, "Neoconservative History," New York Review of Books 32 (January 16, 1986) p. 5. Stephen Ambrose, *Eisenhower*, vol. I (New York: Simon and Schuster, 1983), p. 543.

20. Any authority will do. My choices are Charles Webster, *The Art of Diplomatic Practice* (New York: Barnes and Noble, 1962), p. 42; and Ernest Satow, *A Guide to Diplomatic Practice*, vol. 1 (London: Longman, 1922), pp. 1-4.

21. Michael Howard, *War and the Liberal Conscience* (New Brunswick, NJ: Rutgers University Press, 1978), p. 132.

22. *Congressional Record*, 81st Cong., 2d sess., 96, 1414-7.

23. See Satow, *A Guide to Diplomatic Practice*, pp. 1-3. François de Callier's definition is from his *De la manière de negocier avec les souverains*, published in 1716. De Callier's book was the basic Western handbook on the subject well into the twentieth century. See Harold Nicholson, *The Evolution of Diplomacy* (New York: Collier Books, 1966) p. 85.

24. George F. Kennan, "Excerpts from the Telegraphic Message from Moscow of February 22, 1946," in *Memoirs, 1925-1950* (Boston: Little, Brown, and Company, 1967), pp. 557-8. Kennan's views in private were always more complex than his most oft-quoted analysis. See David Mayers, "Containment and the Primacy of Diplomacy: George Kennan's Views, 1947-8," *International Security* 11, no. 1 (Summer 1986), pp. 124-62.

25. These distinctions have been at the heart of Henry Kissinger's academic corpus. See Henry Kissinger, *A World Restored* (Boston: Houghton Mifflin, 1957), pp. 1-8, 138-9, 143, 172; and Henry Kissinger, "Classical Diplomacy: The Congress of Vienna," in John Stoessinger and Alan F. Westin, eds., *Power and Order: Six Cases in World Politics* (New York: Harcourt Brace and World, 1964), pp. 1, 29-30.

26. Harry S Truman, "The Truman Doctrine: Special Message to the Congress on Greece and Turkey," 180th Congress, 1st sess., March 24, 1947, p. 19.

27. As Dulles, who was then the Republican observer at the Moscow conference in September 1947, reported to the Senate Foreign Relations Committee: "Soviet foreign policy . . . depends little on getting results by diplomatic negotiations. It depends on getting results by penetrating the political parties and organizations from other countries." Daniel Yergin, *Shattered Peace: The Origins of the Cold War and the National Security State* (Boston: Houghton Mifflin, 1977), p. 301. The argument pervaded the academy. As Zbigniew Brzezinski put it: "Totalitarians completely reject the traditional patterns of diplomatic behavior. . . . Diplomatic protocol serves to limit... conflict . . . [but] the diplomatic notes of totalitarian regimes are . . . tools which are aimed either at forging domestic opinion or shattering the morale

of an opponent." Carl J. Friedrich and Zbigniew K. Brzezinski, *Totalitarian Dictatorship and Autocracy* (New York: Frederick Prager, 1962), p. 58.

28. Richard Goold-Adams, John Foster Dulles: A Reappraisal (Westport, CT: Greenwood Publishing Group, 1962), p. 293.
29. Kissinger, *Nuclear Weapons and Foreign Policy*, p. 57.
30. Clark M. Clifford and George Elsey, "American Relations with the Soviet Union," a report submitted to Harry S Truman on September 24, 1946. Reprinted in *Arthur Krock, Memoirs: Sixty Years on the Firing Line* (New York: Funk and Wagnalls, 1968), pp. 431.
31. Cited by Kenneth Waltz in *Man, the State and War* (New York: Columbia University Press, 1959), p. 159.
32. Nicholson, *The Evolution of Democracy*, p. 88. De Calliers, Louis XIV's secretary and a diplomat of long experience, wrote this in 1716. See ibid., p. 85-6.
33. Henry Kissinger, "The Congress of Vienna," *World Politics* 8 (July 1956), p. 277.
34. The phrase is James King's, who circulated several influential manuscripts on the subject. King's work greatly impacted Robert Endicott Osgood's *Limited War* (Chicago: University of Chicago Press, 1957), esp. p. 282ff., and Osgood's *Limited War Revisited* (Boulder, CO: Westview Press, 1979). Both books were heavily indebted to King. Indeed, Osgood had read King's manuscripts, but failed to credit them, to King's own dismay.
35. As Dean Rusk proudly explained about Korea: "[W]e . . . tried to use the right amount of force that [was] required, without letting our objectives escalate." "The Revisionist Historians," transcript of PBS television broadcast of "Firing Line," January 27, 1974 (Columbia, SC: Educational Communications Association, 1974), pp. 7-8.
36. Osgood, *Limited War Revisited*, p. 11.
37. Nicholson, *The Evolution of Diplomacy*, pp. 86-88.
38. Thomas C. Schelling, *Arms and Influence* (New Haven, CT: Yale University Press, 1966) p. 2.
39. Blanche Wiesen Cook, *The Declassified Eisenhower* (Garden City, NY: Doubleday, 1981) p. 154.
40. Entry for May 14, 1953 in Robert H. Ferrell, *The Eisenhower Diaries* (New York: W. W. Norton, 1981), p. 237.
41. Richard H. Immerman, "Conclusion," in Richard H. Immerman, ed., *John Foster Dulles and the Cold War* (Princeton, NJ: Princeton University Press, 1990), p. 274.
42. Rusk was an unknown to Kennedy. They had met only once, briefly, and perhaps Kennedy felt early on that Rusk ill-served him, as Rusk himself once confided, when Rusk did not question more strongly plans for the Bay of Pigs. Arthur M. Schlesinger, Jr., *Robert Kennedy and His Times* (New York: Ballantine Books, 1978), p. 466. Schlesinger dates Rusk's isolation from the Kennedy inner circle at this time. However, Schlesinger's bias in the matter of Rusk is evident. For example, he claims Rusk may have had a "nervous breakdown" during the Cuban crisis, when we now know that

Rusk played a serious and potentially critical role in the resolution of the crisis. Nonetheless, at Hawks Cay, at least, he refused to recant. David Welch, ed., *Transcript of the Proceedings of the Hawks Cay Conference, Marathon, Florida, 5-8 March 1987*, final version (Center for Science and International Affairs, Harvard University, April 1988), mimeograph 22, p. 61.

43. Thomas J. Schaenbaum, *Waging Peace and War* (New York: Simon and Schuster, 1988), p. 276ff., 286; conversations with Dean Rusk conducted by the author, January 1970 in Washington, D.C., and October 1975 in Newark, Delaware.

44. Theodore Sorensen, *Kennedy* (New York: Bantam Books, 1969), p. 303; Schlesinger, *Robert Kennedy and His Times*, p. 559.

45. Sorensen, *Kennedy*, p. 303.

46. Arthur Schlesinger, Jr., *A Thousand Days* (Boston, Houghton Mifflin, 1965), p. 402.

47. Ibid., p. 403, 404.

48. Ibid., p. 376.

49. Ibid., p. 392.

50. Ibid., p. 394.

51. Ibid., p. 395.

52. Ibid., p. 315. There was the impression that the preferred goal was 160,000 troops to be equipped with tactical nuclear weapons. See ibid., p. 316.

53. Robert F. Kennedy, *Thirteen Days* (New York: New American Library, 1969), pp. 117-18.

54. Lawrence J. Bassett and Stephan E. Pelz, "The Failed Search for Victory: Vietnam and the Politics of War," in Thomas G. Paterson, ed., *Kennedy's Quest for Victory: American Foreign Policy, 1961-1963* (New York: Oxford University Press, 1989), p. 231.

55. John Prados, *The President's Secret Wars* (New York: William Morrow, 1985), p. 271-74.

56. Schlesinger, *A Thousand Days*, p. 317.

57. Marc Trachtenberg has found a couple of memos from the Eisenhower years that give the impression that Dulles was aware that, as the secretary put it privately, "massive nuclear destruction was running its course," and that the United States "must fight defensive wars that do not involve the total defeat of the enemy." Marc Trachtenberg, "Making Sense of the Nuclear Age," in Marc Trachtenberg, *History and Strategy* (Princeton, NJ: Princeton University Press, 1990), p. 267, fn 7. But notwithstanding Eisenhower's "hidden" distrust of massive retaliation, his record seems to be as much as a "brinksman" as Dulles on more than a few occasions. Hence, about the Berlin issue, Eisenhower was reported to have told a congressional delegation in March 1959, "[H]is basic philosophy was . . . 'to push [the] whole stack of chips into the pot.' . . . He expressed the conviction that the actual decision to go to all-out war will not come, but if it comes, we must have the crust to follow through." Memo of a conference

held March 6, 1959; cited by Trachtenberg, "Making Sense of the Nuclear Age," p. 265, fn 3. Catherine Kelleher, *Germany and the Politics of Nuclear Weapons* (New York: Columbia University Press, 1975), pp. 159, 164.

58. *The New York Times,* April 11, 1961, cited by Kelleher, *Germany and the Politics of Nuclear Weapons,* p. 161.

59. Kennedy, *Thirteen Days,* p. 105.

60. General staffs, in the words of Barbara Tuchman, "goaded by time-tables, were pounding the table . . . to move lest their opponents gain an hour's head start." Barbara Tuchman, *Guns of August* (New York: Macmillan, 1962), p. 72; and Marc Trachtenberg, "The Meaning of Mobilization in 1914," *International Security* 15, no. 3 (Winter 1990/91), p. 123.

61. Schlesinger, *A Thousand Days,* p. 362.

62. See some of the still unanswered questions on this incident that are raised in James A. Nathan, "A Fragile Detente," *Military Affairs* 39, no. 3 (October 1975), p. 97-104, and a discussion of the U-2.

63. Schaenbaum, *Waging Peace and War,* pp. 335-6.

64. Arkady Shevchenko interview with John Newhouse, cited in John Newhouse, *War and Peace in the Nuclear Age* (New York: Alfred A. Knopf, 1989), p. 151.

65. Newhouse, *War and Peace in the Nuclear Age,* p. 160.

66. Schlesinger, *A Thousand Days,* p. 363.

67. "Radio and Television Report to the American People on the Berlin Crisis," July 25, 1961, *Public Papers of the President* (Washington, DC: United States Government Printing Office, 1961), p. 534-36.

68. Nikita Khrushchev, *Khrushchev Remembers: The Last Testament* (Boston: Little, Brown, and Company, 1990), p. 507.

69. Schlesinger, *A Thousand Days,* pp. 369-370.

70. It is still unclear whether Kennedy himself felt the missiles were much more than symbolic threat and an indication of such a wanton disregard of American interests (as well as his own political interests). The Chiefs of Staff and their chairman, Maxwell Taylor, took the military threat quite seriously. "These missiles," he said, "can become a very, a rather important adjunct and reinforcement to . . . the strike capability of the Soviet Union. The Secretary of Defense, Robert McNamara, disagreed, saying, "I myself don't believe it's primarily a military problem. It's primarily a domestic political problem." Transcript of ExComm meeting, 6:30-7:55 P.M., October 16, 1962, pp. 45-48.

71. "Off the Record Meeting on Cuba," October 16, 1962, 6:30-7:45 P.M., JFK Library, p. 75.

72. Ibid., p. 78.

73. Schlesinger, *A Thousand Days,* p. 363.

74. Roger Hilsman, *To Move a Nation* (Garden City, NY: Doubleday, 1967), pp. 210-11.

75. Cited by Jonathan Schell in *The Time of Illusion* (New York: Alfred A. Knopf, 1967) p. 354.

76. Speech of Deputy Secretary of Defense Roswell Gilpatric on October 21, 1961. Cited by Hilsman, *To Move a Nation,* pp. 163-64; "Off the Record Meeting on Cuba," October 16, 1962, pp. 57-8; McGeorge Bundy, *Danger and Survival* (New York: Vintage, 1988), p. 452.

77. Welch, ed., *Transcripts of the Proceedings of the Hawks Cay Conference,* p. 142.

78. The Executive Committee of the President was an ad hoc group most of whose members had high-level responsibilities. They included George W. Ball, undersecretary of state; McGeorge Bundy, special adviser to the president on national security affairs; C. Douglas Dillon, secretary of the treasury; Roswell L. Gilpatric, deputy secretary of defense; U. Alexis Johnson, deputy undersecretary of defense for political affairs; Robert F. Kennedy, attorney general; Edward M. Martin, assistant secretary of state for inter-American affairs; John H. McCone, director of the CIA; Robert S. McNamara, secretary of defense; Paul Nitze, assistant secretary of defense for national security affairs; Dean Rusk, secretary of state; Theodore C. Sorensen, special counsel to the president; General Maxwell D. Taylor, chairman of the Joint Chiefs of Staff; Lieutenant General Joseph F. Carroll, director of the Defense Intelligence Agency; Lyndon B. Johnson, vice president of the United States; Adlai E. Stevenson, ambassador to the United Nations; Llewellyn E. Thompson, ambassador-at-large and former ambassador to the Soviet Union; Donald Wilson, deputy director of the United States Information Agency; and for a while, Dean Acheson, former secretary of state. Two days after the missiles were first reported, Sorensen submitted a memorandum to the president: "These missiles, even when fully operational, do not significantly alter the balance of power—i.e., they do not significantly increase the potential megatonnage capable of being unleashed on American soil, even after a surprise American nuclear strike." See Theodore Sorensen, "Memorandum for the President," October 17, 1962, Sorensen Papers, John F. Kennedy Library, Boston, Massachusetts, box 48, "Cuba" folder; "Off the Record Meeting on Cuba," October 16, 1962, 6:30-7:55 p.m., p. 58, John F. Kennedy Library, Boston, Massachusetts (henceforth Off the Record transcript).

79. Raymond Garthoff, "Memo on the Military Significance of the Soviet Missiles Bases in Cuba," October 27, 1962, Department of State declassified document, reprinted in Garthoff, "The Meaning of the Missiles," Washington Quarterly 5, no. 4 (Autumn 1982) pp. 78. In fact, the Soviet deployment augmented the Soviet strike capability by about 100 percent if they had been armed.

   Medium-range ballistic missiles (MRBM) have a range from 300 to 1,000 miles. Intermediate-range ballistic missiles (IRBM) have a range from 1,000 to 3,500 miles.

80. David Welch, ed., *Transcript of the Proceedings of the Hawks Cay Conference,* p. 31, 53.

81. Cited by Scott Sagan in *Moving Targets: Nuclear Strategy and National Security* (Princeton, NJ: Princeton University Press, 1989), p. 29.

82. "Off the Record Meeting on Cuba," October 16, 1962, p. 58.

83. Ibid., p. 89.

84. Douglas Dillon remembered: "I agree with Mac Bundy totally. I *never* heard in the Excomm any comment about public opinion or how our choices would fly politically or anything else like that." Welch, ed., *Transcript of the Proceedings of the Hawks Cay Conference*, p. 116.

85. Schell, *The Time of Illusion*, p. 369.

86. "Off the Record Meeting on Cuba," October 16, 1962, pp. 46-47.

87. Welch, ed., *Transcript of the Proceedings of the Hawks Cay Conference*, p. 31.

88. Frank Sieverts, "The Cuban Crisis," National Security Files 1962, box 49, pp. 75-76.

89. Transcript of ExComm meetings on the Cuban missile crisis, October 27, 1962, Presidential Recordings, JFK Library, p. 46.

90. Kennedy, *Thirteen Days*, p. 109.

91. Welch, ed., *Transcript of the Proceedings of the Hawks Cay Conference*, p. 141ff.

92. Sorensen, *Kennedy*, p. 773.

93. Ibid., p. 51.

94. Welch, ed., *Transcript of the Proceedings of the Hawks Cay Conference*, p. 71. The point is Raymond Garthoff's.

95. Transcript of ExComm meetings on the Cuban missile crisis, October 27, 1962, pp. 26, 45; Welch, ed., *Transcript of the Proceedings of the Hawks Cay Conference*, p. 110.

96. Transcript of ExComm meetings on the Cuban missile crisis, October 27, 1962, p. 36.

97. Ibid., p. 46.

98. Frank Sieverts, special assistant to the assistant secretary of state for public information, "The Cuban Crisis," 1962. Prepared for the ExComm on McNamara's request, declassified November 14, 1984, JFK Library, National Security files, box 49, p. 186.

99. Transcript of ExComm meetings on the Cuban missile crisis, October 27, 1962, p. 42.

100. This is McGeorge Bundy's recollection in Welch, ed., *Transcript of the Proceedings of the Hawks Cay Conference*, p. 95.

101. Transcript of ExComm meetings on the Cuban missile crisis, October 27, 1962, p. 39. Troop estimates are in Raymond Garthoff, *Reflections on the Cuban Missile Crisis* (Washington, DC: Brookings, 1989) p. 34.

102. Transcript of ExComm meetings on the Cuban missile crisis, October 27, 1962, p. 42.

103. Schoenbaum, *Waging Peace*, p. 321.

104. Kennedy, *Thirteen Days*, p. 109.

105. Marc Trachtenberg has found a revealing transcript of an interview with Air Force General Bruce K. Holloway, who says of the SIOP: "This is the one play I can certainly say something nice about Mr. McNamara. He never

reversed us to my knowledge while I was . . . on the SIOP." "The influence of McNamara's declaratory policy on the SIOP," says Trachtenberg, "was slighter than many people assume." Trachtenberg, *The Cuban Missile Crisis: History and Strategy* (Princeton, NJ: Princeton University Press, 1990), p. 249, fn 37.

106. Scott Sagan, ed., "SIOP-62: The Nuclear War Plan Briefing to President Kennedy," *International Security* 12, no. 1 (1987), p. 49.

107. Ibid., p. 50-51. SIOP-63, a year later, does not appear to be that much different. See Desmond Ball, "The Development of the SIOP, 1960-1983," in Desmond Ball and Jeffrey Richelson, eds., *Strategic Nuclear Targeting* (Ithaca, NY: Cornell University Press, 1986), pp. 57-67

108. Sagan, ed., "SIOP-62," p. 49.

109. Lawrence Freedman, The Evolution of Nuclear Weapons (London: Macmillan, 1981), p. 244. To be sure, American strategic planning had evolved from manufacturing "a smoking radiating ruin" at the end of two hours to attempts to "withhold cities" and perhaps other targets as well. See Ball, "The Development of the SIOP, 1960-1983," p.

110. Garthoff, *Reflections on the Cuban Missile Crisis,* p. 156.

111. Robert P. Berman and John C. Baker, *Soviet Strategic Forces: Requirements and Responses* (Washington, DC: Brookings, 1988), p. 88. To the Soviets, the sheer number of American strategic weapons aloft or on alert pointed to the inexorable conclusion that if there was an American nuclear assault on the Soviet Union, the limits would not be meaningful to the Soviet recipients.

112. Bill Taubman in Welch, ed., *Transcript of the Proceedings at the Hawks Cay Conference,* p. 179.

113. McNamara in Welch, ed., *Transcript of the Proceedings at the Hawks Cay Conference,* pp. 68, 100, 108, 109. As Frank Sievert's report ("The Cuban Crisis, 1962," JFK Library, National Security File, box 49, pp. 75-76) indicated, "it might be necessary to make a compensatory strike against the USSR" if surviving Soviet missiles struck the United States from Cuba. Bundy, *Danger and Survival,* pp. 455-58. Bundy believes that Kennedy would not have ordered an air strike or an invasion, even if Khrushchev had rejected all the proposals on the table. Rather, the president would have simply tightened the blockade. Rusk and Sorensen, arguably the two who knew the president's mind the best on this matter, hold a different view. For Rusk's views, see Schoenbaum, *Waging Peace,* p. 320-23.

114. Welch, ed., *Transcript of the Proceedings of the Hawks Cay Conference,* p. 140; and "A Transcript of a Discussion about the Cuban Missile Crisis," (Sloan Foundation, 1983), pp. 54-55. Courtesy of Arthur Singer.

115. Sorensen, *Kennedy,* p. 705.

116. Kennedy, *Thirteen Days,* pp. 70-71. Recently, there has been yet another purported revelation that would indicate that the crisis was even closer than anybody had suspected. At the fifth, and perhaps the last, in a series of conferences on the Cuban missile crisis, held in Havana in January 1992, General Anatoly I. Gribkov asserted that Soviet field commanders had

authority, on their own, to launch up to six nuclear armed short-range nuclear missiles on invading U.S. forces, had the U.S. tried to take the island. Gribkov's information was, however, not just startling, but in contradiction to the recollection of other, and seemingly better informed, (ex-Soviet) participants. See John Newhouse, "A Reporter At Large: Socialism or Death," The New Yorker, April 27, 1992, page 70ff.

117. Garthoff, *Reflections on the Cuban Missile Crisis*, pp. 64-65.

118. Graham Allison, *The Essence of Decision* (Boston: Little, Brown, and Company, 1971), p. 141.

119. Hilsman, *To Move a Nation*, p. 221.

120. Sagan, *Moving Targets*, p. 147.

121. Garthoff, *Reflections on the Cuban Missile Crisis*, p. 62; Scott Sagan, "Nuclear Alerts and Crisis Management," *International Security* 9, no. 4 (Spring 1988), p. 109. To be sure, the Soviets seemed to have made no preparations for nuclear conflict at all; see Sorensen, *Kennedy*, p. 713.

122. Raymond Garthoff in Welch, ed. *Transcript of the Proceedings of the Hawks Cay Conference*, p. 118.

123. Garthoff, *Reflections on the Cuban Missile Crisis*, p. 62.

124. Newhouse, *War and Peace in the Nuclear Age*, p. 178.

125. Scott D. Sagan, *Organizations, Accidents and Nuclear War* (forthcoming). Intercontinental ballistic missiles (ICBM) usually have a range of over 500 miles.

126. Sagan, "Nuclear Alerts and Crisis Management," p. 122, fn 64. Operation Mongoose was a CIA operation designed to bedevil and destabilize Fidel Castro's regime and, if possible, assassinate the Cuban leader.

127. Garthoff in Welch, ed., *Transcript of the Proceedings of the Hawks Cay Conference*, p. 149

128. On this famous conversation, see McNamara's comments in Welch, ed., *Transcript of the Proceedings of the Hawks Cay Conference*, pp. 93-94; Elie Abel, *The Missile Crisis* (Philadelphia: J. B. Lippincott, 1969), pp. 285-86; William A. Hamilton, "The Decline and Fall of the Joint Chiefs of Staff," *Naval War College Review* 24 (April 1972), p. 47; Jack Raymond, *Power at the Pentagon* (New York: Harper and Row, 1964), pp. 285, 286. Anderson, it is important to note, has maintained that there is substantial fiction in this account.

129. According to Scott Sagan, there is some ambiguity if U.S. actions disabled the Soviet sub that was observed being towed back from the area or if the sub simply broke down. See Scott Sagan, "Rules of Engagement," *Security Studies* 1, no. 1 (Autumn 1991), pp. 93, fn 63.

130. J. Anthony Lukas, "Class Reunion: Kennedy's Men Relive the Cuban Missile Crisis," *New York Times Magazine*, August 30, 1987, p. 51; Sagan, "Nuclear Alerts and Crisis Management," pp. 112-18; Bromley Smith, secretary to the National Security Council, "Summary," summary record of the NSC Executive Meeting No. 7, October 27, 1962, 10:00 A.M., p. 114.

131. Garthoff, *Reflections on the Cuban Missile Crisis*, p. 68.

132. Sieverts, "The Cuban Crisis," p. 188.

133. Garthoff, *Reflections on the Cuban Missile Crisis*, p. 68, fn 110; Sagan "Nuclear Alerts and Crisis Management," p. 110, fn 26.

134. Welch, ed., *Transcript of the Proceedings of the Hawks Cay Conference*, p. 92.

135. Abel, *The Cuban Missile Crisis*, p. 46.

136. Cited by John McDermitt in "Crisis Manager," *New York Review of Books* 1 (September 14, 1967), p. 8.

137. Schlesinger, *A Thousand Days*, p. 840-41.

138. Thomas Halper, *Foreign Policy Crisis* (Columbus: Charles E. Merrill, 1971), pp. 189-193. Halper's book is a gold mine of first-rate analysis and eclectic learning even though, perforce, much of the information on which he predicates his analysis has been superseded by the release of documents in the 1980s and early 1990s.

139. David Detzer, *The Brink* (New York: Thomas Y. Crowell, 1979), p. 281.

140. Kennedy, *Thirteen Days*, p. 22.

141. Robert Kennedy was reported to have believed that Dean Rusk "had a virtual complete breakdown mentally and physically." Schlesinger, *Robert Kennedy and His Times*, pp. 546-47.

142. Dean Acheson, "Dean Acheson's Version of Robert Kennedy's Version of the Cuban Missile Crisis," *Esquire* (February 1969), p. 77.

143. Smith, "Summary," p. 117.

144. John F. Kennedy's transcripts of Cuban missile crisis meeting, October 27, 1962, pp. 32-38; and Bundy, *Danger and Survival*, p. 430.

145. Smith, "Summary," p. 112.

146. See Richard Ned Lebow and Janice Gross Stein, *We All Lost the Cold War* (forthcoming) for details of this meeting; Smith, "Summary," p. 124.

147. Bundy, *Danger and Survival*, p. 432-33.

148. The letter was revealed for the first time at the Hawks Cay Conference; Rusk to Blight, February 25, 1987, in Welch, ed., *Transcript of the Proceedings of the Hawks Cay Conference*, p. 131.

149. Schlesinger, *Robert Kennedy and His Times*, p. 564.

150. Exactly the nature of this offer and its timing is still uncertain. Ambassador Dobrynin has contended, according to one secondhand report, that the initial overture was made by Robert Kennedy on Wednesday the 24th. Recent notes discovered in the Kennedy Library indicate the range of desiderata asked by Robert Kennedy included Soviet restraint of Cuba in the Western Hemisphere.

151. Schlesinger, *Robert Kennedy and His Times*, p. 563.

152. Sorensen, Kennedy, p. 699.

153. Schlesinger, *A Thousand Days*, p. 810.

154. "Briefing on Cuban Developments," January 25, 1963, *Executive Sessions of the Senate Foreign Relations Committee* (Historical Series), vol. 15, pp. 105-06, 111.

155. U.S. House Appropriations Committee, Department of Defense Appropriations for 1964, 88th Cong., 1st sess., 1963, part I, p. 57. This was also McNamara's position in 1968 when he wrote in an introduction to Robert Kennedy's memoir: "Perhaps his [JFK's] most difficult decision was the refusal, against the advice of his weaker brethren . . . to bargain the security of the Western world by yielding to the specious Russian offers of a face-saving accommodation at the expense of America's allies." Kennedy, *Thirteen Days*, p. 18.

156. Bundy, *Danger and Survival*, p. 434.

157. Kennedy, *Thirteen Days*, p. 108.

158. Hilsman, *To Move a Nation*, pp. 226, 215.

159. Richard J. Walton, *The Cold War and Counter Revolution* (Baltimore, MD: Penguin Books, 1972), p. 119. The article, "In a Time of Crisis," appeared on December 8, 1962, and was written by Stewart Alsop and Charles Bartlett. It could well have been Robert Kennedy, instead of his brother John, who spoke despairingly of Stevenson; see Schlesinger, *Robert Kennedy and His Times*, p. 556.

160. Bundy, *Danger and Survival*, p. 433.

161. Abram Chayes in Welch, ed., *Transcript of the Proceedings of the Hawks Cay Conference*, p. 170.

162. Leslie Gelb and Morton Halperin, "The Ten Commandments of the Foreign Affairs Bureaucracy," *Harpers* 244 (June 1972), p. 36.

163. Schlesinger, *A Thousand Days*, p. 831.

164. Kennedy, *Thirteen Days*, p. 26.

165. Ibid., pp. 44-45.

166. Ibid., p 119.

167. Hilsman, *To Move a Nation*, p. 512-13; and David Halberstam, *The Best and Brightest* (New York: Random House, 1972), p. 255.

168. Kennedy, *Thirteen Days*, p. 119

169. John Keegan, "The Human Face of Deterrence," *International Security* 6, no. 1 (Summer 1981), p. 147.

170. Stephen Peter Rose, "Vietnam and the American Theory of Limited War, *International Security* 7, no. 2 (Fall 1982), p. 99.

171. As McNamara put it later: "If you read Toynbee, you realize the importance of a democracy learning to cope with limited war. The greatest contribution Vietnam is making—right or wrong [is] beside the point—is that it is developing in the United States an ability to fight a limited war without developing public ire." Douglas Kiker, "The Education of Robert McNamara," *Atlantic Monthly* 219, no. 3 (March 1967), p. 53.

172. McNamara in Welch, ed. *Transcript of the Proceedings of the Hawks Cay Conference*, p. 163. The seriousness about this is apparent when one notes

that McNamara made this point twice in four days—once at the opening of the retrospective and once at the closing. See ibid., p. 13.

173. Brock Bower, "McNamara Seen Now Full Length," *Life* (May 10, 1978), p. 78. McNamara claimed then and later that the blockade was a "line of communication from President Kennedy to Khrushchev" that was useful to "send political message[s]."

174. Welch, ed., *Transcript of the Proceedings of the Hawks Cay Conference,* p. 162.

175. Henry Luce, *The American Century* (New York: Farrar and Rinhart, 1941), p. 23; and Henry Luce, *Life* (February 17, 1941), p. 63.

176. Schlesinger, *A Thousand Days,* pp. 840-41.

177. "If we have learned anything from this experience, it is that weakness, even only apparent weakness, invites Soviet transgression. At the same time, firmness in the last analysis will force the Soviets to back away." "Significance of the Soviet Backdown for Future US Policy," Document F, October 29, 1962, in Garthoff, *Reflections on the Cuban Missile Crisis,* p. 216.

178. Hilsman, *To Move a Nation,* p. 227.

179. The term is from Raymond Garthoff's 1962 evaluation. See Garthoff, "Significance of the Soviet Backdown for Future US Policy," p. 215.

180. In James Blight and David Welch, *On the Brink: Americans and Soviets Reexamine the Cuban Missile Crisis* (New York: Hill and Wange, 1989), pp. 147-148.

181. Henry A. Kissinger, "Reflections on Cuba," *Reporter* (November 22, 1962), pp. 21-24.

182. Daniel Ellsberg, *Papers on the War* (New York: Simon and Schuster, 1972), pp. 292-93.

2

The Cuban Missile Crisis: An Overview

Raymond L. Garthoff

THE SOVIET DECISION

On a spring day in 1962, Soviet Party leader Nikita Khrushchev, vacationing at a dacha in the Crimea, was visited by Defense Minister Rodion Malinovsky. As they were conversing, the marshal gestured toward the horizon to the south and remarked on the fact that medium-range nuclear missiles the United States was installing across the Black Sea in Turkey were just becoming operational. So far as we know, that is all the marshal said, and the next step was Khrushchev's reaction: Why, he mused, should the Americans have the right to put missiles on our doorstep, and we not have a comparable right? A few weeks later, while in Bulgaria, he carried the point one fateful step further: Why not station Soviet medium-range missiles in Cuba?

Khrushchev had long rankled at what he regarded as American flaunting of its political and military superiority, and successful cultivation of a double standard. Why shouldn't the Soviet Union be able to assert the prerogatives of a global power? One reason, of course, was that the United States *did* have superiority in global political, economic, and military power. Moreover, while the Soviet Union had enjoyed some spectacular successes—in particular, its primacy in space with the first earth satellite and first test of an intercontinental ballistic missile (ICBM) in the four years or so since that time, there had been reverses. In particular, after riding an inflated world impression of Soviet missile strength during American self-flagellation over a "missile gap," improved intelligence had now persuaded the American leaders—and the world—that the *real* missile gap, and a growing one, favored the United States.

Since Khrushchev personally had overplayed the Soviet hand on missiles, he had particular reason to want to offset the new, and to him, adverse gap. Indeed, if he wanted to carry forward his still-unsuccessful campaign on West Berlin, or even to prevent American exploitation of missile superiority in other political contests, some way had to be found to overcome the growing American superiority. Available Soviet ICBMs were not satisfactory; he needed several years to await the next generation. But the Soviet Union did have plenty of medium-range missiles (a category in Soviet usage that embraced both the Western categories of "medium-range" and "intermediate range" ballistic missiles, MRBMs and IRBMs). It would certainly help deal with the problem of Soviet strategic missile weakness if the Soviet Union could create ersatz ICBMs by deploying MRBMs and IRBMs near the United States, comparable to what the United States was doing in Turkey.

The second ingredient in concocting the decision to put Soviet missiles in Cuba was the interaction of Soviet and American relations with Castro's Cuba. By the spring of 1962, Cuba had become highly dependent on the Soviet Union, economically and politically. In turn, it was a declared socialist state and Castro was in the process of merging the old-line Cuban Communist party and his own 26th of July Movement, the former providing organizing ability and a structured ideology, the latter the leaders and the popular following.

Meanwhile, Cuban-American relations were precarious. The United States, frustrated by the defeat at the Bay of Pigs of the Cuban émigré invasion it had sponsored, had by no means lessened its hostility or given up its efforts to unseat Castro's regime. By the fall of 1961, the president had authorized a broad covert action program, Operation Mongoose, aimed at harassing, undermining, and optimally overthrowing the Castro regime. This effort included repeated and continuing attempts to assassinate Castro himself. While the Cuban and Soviet leaders did not (so far as it has been possible to ascertain) then know about high-level deliberations in Washington and planning papers on Operation Mongoose, they did know in considerable detail about the CIA operations in Miami sending reconnaissance and later sabotage teams into Cuba, and they knew about at least some of the assassination attempts.

Also, the United States, by February 1962, had extended its economic sanctions to a complete embargo against trade with Cuba, and had engaged in diplomatic efforts to get other countries to curtail trade. In January 1962, at Punta del Este, the United States had succeeded in getting the majority necessary to suspend Cuban participation in the Organization of American States (OAS). By the spring of 1962 the United States had also persuaded fifteen Latin American states to follow its lead and break diplomatic relations with Havana. In short, the United States was conducting a concerted political, economic, propaganda, and covert campaign against Cuba.

On the military side as well, the president had in October 1961 secretly instructed the Defense Department to prepare contingency plans for war with Cuba, with air attack and invasion alternatives. While secret, elements of these plans were tested in subsequent military exercises, and elements of the military forces needed to implement them were built up. Between April 9 and 24, when Khrushchev was brooding in the Crimea, a U.S. Marine air-ground task force carried out a major amphibious exercise, with an assault on the island of Vieques near Puerto Rico. Another exercise conducted from April 19 to May 11 on the southeastern coast of the United States involved more than 40,000 troops, 79 ships, and over 300 aircraft. While the exercise was publicly announced, the fact that it was designed to test an actual Commander in Chief, Atlantic (CINCLANT) contingency plan against Cuba was of course not disclosed. But the Cubans and Soviets assumed, correctly, that it was.

Under the circumstances, it was not surprising that Cuban and Soviet leaders feared an American attack on Cuba. There had been no decision in Washington to attack. But there were programs underway directed toward overthrowing the Cuban regime, and military contingency planning and preparation if the president decided to attack. The United States had the capabilities to attack, and its overall intentions were clearly hostile; any prudent political or military planner would have had to consider at least the threat of attack.

The Cubans sought Soviet commitments and assistance to ward off or meet an American attack. The Soviet leaders had given general, but not ironclad, public assurances of support. They were not, however, prepared to extend their own commitment so far as to take Cuba into the Warsaw Pact.

Khrushchev first raised the idea of deploying Soviet missiles in Cuba with a few close colleagues in May. Khrushchev's plan was to deploy in Cuba a small force of medium-range missiles capable of striking the United States, both to bolster the sagging Soviet side of the strategic military balance, and to serve as a deterrent to American attack on Cuba. The missiles would be shipped to Cuba and installed there rapidly in secrecy. Then, the Soviet Union would suddenly confront the United States with a fait accompli and a new, more favorable status quo. The impact of the move, and perforce

American acceptance of it, would bolster the Soviet stance (probably in particular in a new round of negotiation on the status of Berlin, although no concrete information is available on that point).

Anastas Mikoyan, a veteran Politburo member and close friend, expressed strong reservations on at least two points: Castro's receptivity to the idea, and the practicality of surreptitiously installing the missiles without American detection. Khrushchev readily agreed to drop the idea if Castro objected, but his sense of Castro's reaction was better than Mikoyan's. On the question of practicality, it was decided to send a small expert team headed by Marshal Sergei Biryuzov, the new commander in chief of the Strategic Missile Forces, incognito (as "Engineer Petrov"), to check out the terrain and conditions and advise on the practicality of secret deployment. The military, represented by Malinovsky and Biryuzov, favored the scheme because of what it would do to help redress Soviet strategic inferiority.

Khrushchev apparently brought the full Party Presidium (as the Politburo was then known), or rather its members available in Moscow at the time, into the decision-making process only in late May when the mission was about to depart for Havana to ascertain Castro's response and evaluate feasibility.

The military had necessarily been involved, and had been supportive, but not as decisionmakers. Andrei Gromyko, foreign minister but not then yet a member of the Party leadership, had also been consulted privately, and was present (though remaining silent) at the few deliberative meetings. Only recently have we learned that his private advice had been to caution Khrushchev on what he believed would be the strongly adverse American reaction, but not to oppose the whole idea directly. Similarly, the new Soviet ambassador to Havana, selected because he had the best personal rapport with Fidel Castro, Aleksandr Alekseev, initially doubted Castro's readiness to agree. But he supported anything that would strengthen Soviet-Cuban relations.

Castro readily agreed to the Soviet offer of missiles, believing that he was serving the broader interests of the socialist camp as well as enhancing Cuban security. Biryuzov, who evidently saw his task as fulfilling an assigned mission rather than providing input to evaluation of a proposal, reported that they could secretly install the missile system.

Formal orders were given to the Ministry of Defense on June 10, 1962 to proceed with the deployment, even though many details remained to be decided. In early July 1962, Cuban Defense Minister Raúl Castro visited Moscow, and he and Marshal Malinovsky drafted a five-year renewable agreement to cover the missile deployment. But despite the absence of any issue of disagreement, the draft agreement (always hand-carried, with oral instructions, as were all communications between Moscow and Havana on the matter—even encrypted messages were not trusted) went back and forth twice, and was never actually signed by Khrushchev and Castro. Khrushchev evidently held back because he feared Castro, who had wanted to make it public, would leak it once it had been signed.

THE AMERICAN FOCUS: SOVIET MISSILES IN CUBA

I

The "Cuban missile crisis" derives its name (in the United States; in the Soviet Union, with the accent on American hostility toward Cuba, it is called "the Caribbean Crisis") from the central role played by the Soviet missiles. As President Kennedy had warned on September 4, 1962, shortly before the first missiles actually arrived in Cuba, if such Soviet offensive missiles were introduced "the gravest issues would arise," and nine days later, he stressed that in that case "this country will do whatever must be done to protect its own security and that of its allies." It was, of course, too late to affect Soviet decisions long made and then reaching final implementation.

President Kennedy's declaration included another element, rarely recalled, to which he applied the same warning of "gravest" consequences: if, apart from missiles, the Soviet Union sent to Cuba "any organized combat force." If it had been apprehended that instead of missiles, Khrushchev had dispatched an expeditionary force of Soviet ground, air, and naval combat forces to deter an American invasion, would a crisis have emerged of similar dimensions to the one that emerged over the missiles? That question, posed as an alternative to installing missiles, is historically hypothetical. But what has not been appreciated until now is that the Soviets in fact *did* send such a combat force *in addition to* the missiles.

The Ministry of Defense in Moscow on June 10 received orders not only on the dispatch of a mixed division of Strategic Missile Force troops, comprising three regiments of R-12 (SS-4) and two regiments of R-14 (SS-5) medium-range missiles; but also a Soviet combat contingent including an integrated air defense component with a radar system, 24 surface-to-air missile battalions with 144 launchers, a regiment of 42 MiG-21 interceptors; a coastal defense component comprising 8 cruise missile launchers with 32 missiles, 12 Komar missile patrol boats, and a separate squadron as well as a regiment totalling 42 IL-28 jet light bombers for attacking any invasion force. In addition, a ground force of division size comprised four reinforced motorized rifle regiments, each with over 3,000 men, and 35 tanks. In addition, 6 short-range tactical rocket launchers, and 18 army cruise missile launchers were part of the contingent. This force was seen as a "plate glass" deterrent to U.S. invasion, and reassurance to Castro as an alternative to Cuban membership in the Warsaw Pact.

While most of the weaponry was discovered by American aerial reconnaissance during the crisis, even afterward the number of Soviet military personnel was underestimated by nearly half—22,000 instead of 42,000. The United States failed to discover that a major Soviet expeditionary contingent, under the overall command of a four-star general, General of the Army Issa Pliyev, was in Cuba in October-November 1962.

Recently, former Soviet General of the Army Anatoly Gribkov, who was responsible for planning the Soviet dispatch of forces to Cuba in 1962, has declared that 9 tactical nuclear weapons were sent for the ground force tactical rocket launchers, and with authorization for their use delegated to General Pliyev in case of an American land invasion. If true, this was one of the most dangerous aspects of the entire deployment, and this was not known in Washington.

The medium-range missiles capable of striking the United States, in contrast, were placed under strict control by Moscow: General Pliyev was not authorized to fire them under any circumstances, even an American attack, without explicit authorization by Khrushchev.

II

Ambassador Anatoly Dobrynin arrived at the State Department at 6:00 P.M. on October 22, 1962, at the request of Secretary of State Dean Rusk. His demeanor was relaxed and cheerful; a short time later, he was observed leaving "ashen-faced" and "visibly shaken." A few hours earlier, Foreign Minister Gromyko had departed from New York for Moscow at the end of his visit in the United States, making routine departure remarks to the press and evidently with no premonition of what the president would be saying while he was airborne. Incredibly, the Soviet leadership was caught by surprise by the American disclosure that the missiles had been discovered a week earlier and by the American "first step" action of imposing a quarantine, coupled with a demand that the missiles be removed.

Khrushchev has been reported to have initially in anger wanted to challenge the quarantine-blockade, but whether that is correct the actual Soviet response was cautious. The blockade was not challenged, and no counter-pressures were mounted elsewhere, such as Berlin (as had been feared in Washington). Even the Soviet response to the unparalleled American alert of its strategic forces and most forces worldwide was an announced, but actually hollow, Soviet and Warsaw Pact alert.

Khrushchev continued for a few days to believe that the United States might accept at least the partial Soviet missile deployment already in Cuba. But by October 26, it had become clear that the United States was determined. Moreover, the United States had rapidly prepared a substantial air attack and land invasion force. The tactical air combat force of 579 aircraft was ready, with the plan calling for 1,190 strike sorties on the first day. More than 100,000 Army and 40,000 Marine troops were ready to strike. An airborne paratroop force as large as that used on Normandy in 1944 was included in the preparation for an assault on the island. American military casualties were estimated at 18,500 in ten days of combat.

Soviet intelligence indicated on October 26 that a U.S. air attack and invasion of Cuba were expected at any time. Khrushchev then hurriedly offered a deal: An American pledge not to invade Cuba would obviate the need for Soviet missiles in Cuba and, by implication, they could be withdrawn. A truncated Soviet Presidium group (a Moscow "ExComm") had been meeting since October 23. We still know almost nothing about its deliberations, but it is clear that Khrushchev was fully in control.

Later on October 26, a new intelligence assessment in Moscow indicated that while U.S. invasion preparations continued, it was now less clear that an attack was imminent. Thus there might be some time for bargaining on terms for a settlement.

Meanwhile, Ambassador Dobrynin reported that Robert Kennedy had informed him that the United States was planning to phase out its missiles in Turkey and Italy; there might be opportunity to include that in a settlement. Moreover, the Soviet Embassy in Washington had reported that in a discussion between the KGB station chief, Aleksandr Fomin, and an American television correspondent with good State Department contacts, John Scali, the American—after checking with Secretary Rusk—had indicated that an American assurance against attacking Cuba in exchange for withdrawal of the Soviet missiles in Cuba could provide the basis for a deal, but that time was short.

A new message from Khrushchev to Kennedy was sent that night, October 26, proposing a reciprocal withdrawal of missiles from Cuba and Turkey, as well as the American assurances against invasion of Cuba. But on October 27, later called "Black Saturday" in Washington, an ominous chain of events, including the stiffened Soviet terms, intensified concern. In Moscow, Soviet intelligence again reported signs of American preparations for possible attack on Cuba on October 29 or 30. A very alarmed message was also received from Fidel Castro expressing—for the first time—Castro's belief that an attack was imminent (within 24 to 72 hours), and urging Khrushchev, in case of an invasion, to preemptively attack the United States. The effect of this call was to reinforce a decision by Khrushchev that Castro did not expect or want: prompt conclusion of a deal to remove the missiles in exchange for an American verbal assurance against attacking Cuba.

Other developments also contributed to moving Khrushchev, by October 28, to act on the basis he had first outlined on October 26. One was Castro's action on October 27 in ordering Cuban antiaircraft artillery to open fire on low-flying American reconnaissance aircraft. None were shot down, but the action clearly raised the risk of hostilities. Far more dangerous was the completely unexpected action of local *Soviet* air defense commanders in actually shooting down a U-2 with a Soviet surface-to-air missile. Khrushchev at first assumed that Cubans had shot the plane down, but at some point learned that even his own troops were not under full control. Although the much more restrictive instructions and other constraints still seemed to rule out any unauthorized firing (or even preparation for firing) of the medium-range missiles, the situation was getting out of control.

Kennedy's proposal on the evening of October 27 to exchange American assurances against invasion of Cuba for Soviet withdrawal of its missiles, coupled with a virtual ultimatum, was thus promptly accepted. Khrushchev did not risk taking the time to clarify a number of unclear issues, including what the Americans considered to be "offensive weapons." He accepted the president's terms and sent his reply openly over Radio Moscow, as well as via diplomatic communication.

III

Many additional aspects of the unfolding of the crisis and its settlement will not be reviewed here. This brief recounting of principal developments in Soviet decision making has several features to which we should direct our attention.

First of all, until recently we (the Western world, public, academic, and official) knew scarcely *any* of the facts recounted above. They have become known, piecemeal and from various Soviet sources, over the last few years. Some of this new information was disclosed or confirmed at a special symposium on the crisis, convened in Moscow in January 1989 with Politburo sanction, which brought together American, Soviet, and Cuban veterans of the crisis and scholars of it, and at the two follow-up conferences at

Antigua in January 1991 and Havana in January 1992, the latter with Fidel Castro's active participation.

Second, almost none of this information has been provided in official documentation. A purist awaiting access to the Soviet archives would still have nothing. While the Soviet authorities have permitted a number of Soviet officials (even including retired intelligence operatives) to say what they know (or, more precisely, what they recall or believe that they know and recall), there has been no parallel declassification of documentation.

For example, shortly before the Moscow conference, I asked former Ambassador Anatoly Dobrynin whether he could get declassified some of his dispatches to Moscow during the crisis. He countered by saying he would speak on that information, as he did. But his recollection was hazy and unclear on some points, and while his contribution was welcome, it was certainly no substitute for the actual records. Former Foreign Minister Andrei Gromyko, then one of the key surviving Soviet participants, at the Moscow conference, as in his recent two-volume memoir, told almost nothing of what he knew. The one exception was a detailed account of his meeting of October 18 with President Kennedy, on which he wanted to counter the American charge of evasion and deception. (Gromyko died some six months later.) The Soviet ambassador to Cuba at the time of the crisis, Aleksandr Alekseev, at the Moscow conference and in published articles, has provided some useful information, but he has not had access to the archives and there are identifiable errors in his account as well as uncertainty as to some other assertions. Sergo Mikoyan, son of the Soviet leader, has published and discussed in conferences and interviews some aspects of the crisis based on his father's unpublished memoir material (as well as his own observations). Fyodor Burlatsky, as a consultant at the Central Committee and sometime speech writer for Khrushchev, had access to a key letter from Khrushchev to Castro describing origins of the idea to place missiles in Cuba. Colonel General Dimitri Volkogonov, not a participant in the crisis but in 1989 chief of the Institute of Military History, had access to the Ministry of Defense archives and disclosed some important information from materials there at the Moscow conference (and in a later interview). General of the Army Gribkov provided additional, but also some contradictory, evidence on the military deployments at the Havana conference. Finally, senior Cuban officials at the Moscow and Havana conferences also provided some useful non-documentary information.

What is one to make of this new information from such sources? In some cases, the new "information" is contradictory and inconsistent. In some cases, it is clearly wrong. By the nature of the compartmentalization of access to information in the Soviet system in 1962 (and today), assertions honestly made are sometimes based on incomplete or incorrect information, in addition to being filtered through selective memory, sometimes also tainted by access to American accounts of the crisis. Yet in many cases the new data is from knowledgeable sources who were in a position to know certain facts, and in some of these cases there is persuasive confirmation from other sources. In short, it would be foolish to reject or ignore all such information, but also not prudent to accept it all. Each assertion needs to be judged on grounds of plausibility as well as confirming or unconfirming information from other sources. Would the source have had direct access to and knowledge of the reported information? How can its validity be tested?

Khrushchev's conversation with Malinovsky in the Crimea in April 1962 is reported by only one source: Burlatsky read (and helped to edit and write) the draft of a letter sent by Khrushchev to Castro in January 1963 in which Khrushchev recounted this initial priming conversation. Khrushchev did not mention it in his memoir. Indeed, his published recollections say the idea first occurred to him when he was in Bulgaria (May 14-20). Recently we acquired the actual January 1963 letter from the Cubans—and the reference to a conversation between Khrushchev and Malinovsky in the Crimea is not in it. Moreover, Gromyko said Khrushchev first raised the idea with him on the way home from Bulgaria. Yet it seems clear from several sources that the matter was discussed in late April and early May, and certain verifiable actions tend to confirm this earlier timing (e.g., the recall of Alekseev from Havana). Among those confirming the April-May meetings are Gromyko, Sergo Mikoyan, and Alekseev.

But even if we accept without reservation Burlatsky's recollection of the Khrushchev-Malinovsky conversation in April, we must reserve judgment on the accuracy of the conversation's retelling. For example, Burlatsky recalls Khrushchev as stating that Malinovsky complained about the American missiles being installed just over the horizon in Turkey, but *not* that Malinovsky came up with the idea of installing Soviet missiles in Cuba. It seems unlikely that Malinovsky would have made that suggestion, and there is no indication that he did. But if he did, unless he made some note of it or told someone at the time (who would now be an uncertain source), we shall never know. Malinovsky favored the idea in early May meetings in Moscow, but that tells us nothing about the genesis of the idea. It was probably Khrushchev's own idea, and all sources, information, and working assumptions about Soviet decision making are consistent with that conclusion. But we will probably never know for certain.

Until 1987, we did not even know whether Gromyko was *aware* of the decision to place the missiles in Cuba before the crisis broke. Now, from all accounts—Gromyko himself, Sergo Mikoyan, and Alekseev—it is clear that he directly participated in the deliberations. Yet even at the end of the Moscow conference in January 1989, we knew nothing about what, if any, advice Gromyko had given Khrushchev. Only in later interviews and articles in 1989 did Gromyko and Alekseev disclose that Khrushchev asked Gromyko's view privately and that Khrushchev was warned that it would provoke a strong American reaction. Gromyko, then not yet a member of the Presidium (Politburo), apparently said nothing in the meetings. (Alekseev confirms that at the time Gromyko had privately told him of the warning he had given Khrushchev.)

We have the late Anastas Mikoyan's account of his early discussions of the idea alone with Khrushchev and in the early meetings, as given to his son Sergo and now published by him in this volume. We have Alekseev's comments on the one meeting he attended. Several senior Soviet officials have expressed strong doubt that there are any records of these meetings in the Soviet archives, and one says a search was made and none found. That may well be the case, but we do not know.

Let me cite one other case. On the night of October 26-27, Fidel Castro wrote an alarmed message to Khrushchev. He wrote it, according to Alekseev, from a bunker at the Soviet Embassy in Havana, and with Alekseev's participation. We knew nothing about such a message before Alekseev described it in a memoir article published in November 1988 (except that Khrushchev had, publicly, in December 1962, referred to a Cuban warning of an imminent U.S. attack). At the Moscow conference, in informal conversations, Sergei Khrushchev said that Castro had urged the Soviet Union to fire its missiles against the United States in case of a U.S. invasion of Cuba.

When Castro's reported remarks leaked to the Western press in Moscow, it was denied at the conference, but the fact of the letter and its warning of imminent American attack was confirmed by both Cuban and Soviet officials. With the release late in 1990 of the messages exchanged between Castro and Khrushchev, we now know that Castro did indeed urge that if the United States launched an invasion of Cuba, not merely an air attack, the Soviet Union should not wait for the United States to make a nuclear strike on the Soviet Union, but should itself launch a preemptive strike.

To take but one last example: From the events of October 26-28, new light has been thrown on the addition of a call for removal of the U.S. missiles from Turkey in the second Soviet proposal for resolving the crisis (received in Washington the morning of October 27). As earlier noted, an informed senior Soviet participant in the crisis has told me that changing Soviet intelligence estimates on the threat of imminent American attack on Cuba importantly affected the timing of the urgent first message of October 26, the belief hours later that there was still time for bargaining leading to the second message, and the decision on October 28 to settle without delay. Confirmation or modification of this report from Soviet archives may someday be possible if Soviet reluctance to disclose data of that kind is surmounted.

The fact that President Kennedy, through his brother, conveyed to Dobrynin on October 27 his intention to withdraw the Jupiter missiles from Turkey was not publicly known at the time, and indeed was not then known to most members of the ExComm. It has, however, been known for 20 years. In recent years it has become known from American sources (and privately confirmed by Soviet sources) that the Soviets subsequently tried unsuccessfully to get the declared American intention conveyed in writing and converted into a commitment. But only now have Soviet sources suggested that Robert Kennedy had first indicated this intention to Dobrynin earlier, and that this early tipping of the American hand underlay the additional demand in the second message received on October 27. Again, there is no documentation to date, although Dobrynin's messages to Moscow would spell out at least his version of the exchanges. The available American records include no reference to meetings between Robert Kennedy and Dobrynin during that week other than on October 23 and 27, but there may have been no written record. Dobrynin states that they met "several times" during the week, almost daily, alternating between the Soviet embassy and the attorney general's office, including on October 24 and 25, as well as October 23 and 27.

There are a number of other aspects of the missile crisis on which Soviet sources have now provided first-hand or second-hand oral or published memoir accounts. One is whether Soviet nuclear missile warheads were actually in Cuba (it now appears that they were, but not arming the missiles). In only a few cases have Soviet archives been available to Soviet writers (Gromyko, General Volkogonov), and until 1990, in no case had original documentation been declassified and made available. Now, however, this is beginning to change. Opening up memoir sources and across-the-table exchanges at least marked a beginning. In 1990-1991, the Soviet and Cuban authorities have begun to release such valuable documentary sources as the crisis exchanges between Khrushchev and Castro, and additional messages from Khrushchev to Kennedy. Most of Ambassadors Dobrynin and Alekseev's crisis messages from Washington and Havana to

Moscow are also promised soon. One hopes there will be more such documentation, and not only with respect to the Cuban missile crisis of 1962.

NOTE

Source documentation and further discussion is provided in the revised edition of the author's book on the crisis. See Raymond L. Garthoff, *Reflections on the Cuban Missile Crisis,* rev. ed. (Washington, D.C.: Brookings Institution, 1989).

3

Reconsidering the Missile Crisis: Dealing with the Problems of the American Jupiters in Turkey

Barton J. Bernstein

I am particularly concerned that we may fail to understand the Soviet reaction to our own defense programs. A double standard which allows us to react angrily at the slightest rumor of a Soviet missile base in Cuba, while we introduce . . . missile set ups in Turkey . . . is dangerously self-defeating.

Chester Bowles to John F. Kennedy, April 22, 1961[1]

It's just as if we suddenly began to put a major number of MRBMs in Turkey. Now, that'd be goddam dangerous, I would think.

John F. Kennedy at the ExComm, October 16, 1962[2]

The Soviet Union had secretly established missile bases in Cuba while at the same time proclaiming . . . this would never be done. We had to have a commitment by tomorrow [Sunday, October 28] that those bases would be removed [or] we would remove them. [Soviet ambassador Anatoly Dobrynin] raised the question of our removing the missiles from Turkey. I said that there could be no quid pro quo . . . this was a decision that would have to be made by NATO. However, President Kennedy . . . had ordered their removal some time ago, and it was our judgment that, within a short time after this crisis was over, those missiles [Jupiters] would be gone.

Robert Kennedy, *Thirteen Days* (1969)[3]

President John F. Kennedy has been variously praised and blamed for his handling of the Cuban missile crisis in October 1962. For many, it was his great triumph: Seven days of wide-ranging deliberations and careful planning, and six days of the shrewd use of cautious threats, limited force, and wise diplomacy to achieve victory.[4] For critics, however, it was an unnecessary crisis or dangerously mishandled, or both: Kennedy should either have acceded to the Soviet missiles in Cuba, or at least tried private diplomacy before moving to the quarantine. Removal of the missiles was not worth the risk of nuclear war.[5]

In recent years, partly under the spur of new evidence, some critics and admirers, though not abandoning their basic assessments, have come to agree upon a chilling conclusion: Nuclear crises cannot be safely managed. Things go wrong. Communications within the bureaucracy or between adversaries may be misunderstood; fatigue and even paranoia may warp judgment; underlings and various agencies may do the unexpected; and "standard operating procedures" may not be adequately modified and monitored for the very different situation of crisis. Looking back upon the Cuban missile crisis 25 years later, former Secretary of Defense Robert McNamara asserted that "misinformation, miscalculation, misjudgment and human fallibility" may dominate.[6] "You *can't* manage crises," he concluded.[7] Such counsel, even if widely accepted, has not meant agreement on other aspects of the crisis.

Some assessments focus on Kennedy's response to the Soviet demand of Saturday, October 27, that America withdraw its missiles from Turkey. Publicly, Kennedy seemed to reject this Soviet proposal.[8] But did he? Until recently, there was considerable dispute on this subject. Some defenders claimed—on the basis of hints in Robert Kennedy's memoirs[9]—that the president actually struck a private bargain and, hence, indirectly acceded to the Soviet terms.[10] Critics, on the other hand, either denied that there was such an agreement[11] or stressed that it was dangerously loose.[12] When the Soviets were looking for a way out of the crisis, why, the critics ask, did Kennedy refuse to accept the Turkey-Cuba trade publicly and thus leave Khrushchev a choice between possible holocaust or humiliation? Wasn't Kennedy guilty of brinkmanship? What would Kennedy have done if Khrushchev had not retreated and accepted public humiliation?

New claims made by three former officials—Soviet ambassador Anatoly Dobrynin, presidential counsel Theodore Sorensen, and Secretary of State

Dean Rusk—have partly addressed these questions. Dobrynin recently asserted that the president, operating through Robert Kennedy on October 27, agreed privately to remove the Jupiters in Turkey as a part of an *explicit* deal. When Dobrynin revealed this private deal, Sorensen promptly concurred, admitting that *Thirteen Days* had intentionally misrepresented this arrangement.[13] And Rusk has stated that President Kennedy allowed him on the 27th to prepare a secret UN conduit for a possible public deal on the Jupiters. All this new information, as well as recently declassified ExComm transcripts, indicates that the president was considerably more flexible on the 27th than much of the earlier evidence and many of the early memoirists suggested.

The availability of much of this newer evidence has roughly paralleled changes in the Cold War and efforts by Kennedy's admirers to refurbish his image. Whereas in the mid-1960s, after his death, ExComm members tended to represent Kennedy as strong, resolute, and not given to substantial compromise when dealing with the Soviets, there has been a desire in more recent years to make him far less of a cold warrior and to establish his suppleness and willingness to compromise. None of this is to invalidate the recent claims about events in the missile crisis, but it is to point out that these revelations, coming after roughly a quarter century, are consonant with broader movements in foreign policy and with related desires to recast the image of John Fitzgerald Kennedy.

None of the new information *establishes* what Kennedy would have done if Khrushchev had insisted upon a public American *pledge* to remove the Jupiters. This chapter concludes that the president would quite probably have responded by first increasing pressure on the Soviets. But if that had failed, would Kennedy have yielded, issued such a public pledge, and thus risked weakening his credibility? Or might the president have invaded Cuba, and risked the consequences? This chapter's necessarily speculative interpretation of "what if," heavily informed by recent revelations, suggests that President Kennedy would have made a public deal to remove the Jupiters in order to settle the crisis.

This chapter, building on earlier work, also reexamines other issues involving the Turkey-Cuba missile trade and its background. New evidence strengthens earlier conclusions, first published in 1980, that Kennedy and not Eisenhower had deployed the Jupiters in Turkey, that these missiles were deployed in late 1961 and did not become operational until 1962, and that Kennedy never actually gave an order to remove these weapons until the end of the missile crisis. New evidence also reveals that some Kennedy advisers, before this 1961 deployment, had worried about a "double standard" and likened the Jupiters to Soviet missiles in Cuba. At about the same time,

Khrushchev independently engaged in a similar analysis, and thus Kennedy's emplacement of the Jupiters helped trigger the Soviet leaders' 1962 decision to put missiles in Cuba.

This chapter also analyzes administration responses to that Soviet emplacement, emphasizes that Kennedy actually forgot that his administration had recently put the Jupiters in Turkey, and argues that the administration contemplated a Turkey-Cuba missile trade during the crisis *before* Khrushchev publicly proposed it on October 27. After Khrushchev's offer, the president was probably the most willing of all the ExComm members to engage in some form of such a trade. Fortunately, Kennedy and his advisers did not know about the Kremlin's difficulties with Fidel Castro: Events in Cuba were hurtling dangerously out of Soviet control, and Castro's actions seemed likely to provoke an American military attack. The Soviets' inability to control Castro probably propelled Khrushchev to settle speedily for a private deal and not the public one on the Jupiters he desired.

HOW THOSE MISSILES GOT TO TURKEY: THE EISENHOWER BACKGROUND

The Eisenhower administration decided in 1957 to arrange to send missiles to Europe, largely to strengthen NATO, both militarily and psychologically. Even before Sputnik, partly to repair the "special relationship" torn by the Suez debacle, the administration promised Britain 60 Thors, "soft" intermediate-range ballistic missiles (IRBMs).[14] And shortly after Sputnik, when administration members feared a confidence or deterrence gap, the administration gained NATO's unanimous approval for the deployment of missiles on the continent. Most NATO allies, however, fearful of antagonizing the Soviet Union and in many cases of inflaming domestic opposition, refused the weapons. Ultimately, only Italy and Turkey would accept them.[15]

But in summer 1959, when Greece also seemed a likely recipient for the Jupiters, President Eisenhower privately expressed his worries about placing these IRBMs so near the Soviet Union. "If Mexico or Cuba had been penetrated by the communists," he said in the paraphrased words of the minutes, "and then began getting arms and missiles from [the Soviets], we would be bound to look on such developments with the gravest concern and in fact . . . it would be imperative for us [even] to take . . . offensive military action." Such thinking, however, did not block his administration's movement toward an agreement with Turkey to take some Jupiters.[16]

That summer, Premier Khrushchev complained to Vice President Richard Nixon about the developing American plan to place these weapons in

Turkey. Khrushchev threatened to retaliate for such American bases in Italy, Greece, and Turkey with Soviet missiles in Albania and Bulgaria. Toward the end of this conversation, Soviet First Deputy Premier Anastas Mikoyan charged that the Jupiter bases in Turkey were designed for "political domination." Shifting the analysis, Khrushchev told Nixon, "If you intend to make war on us, I understand; if not, why [do this]?"[17]

The American agreement with Turkey, completed in October 1959, provided for 15 Jupiters. The arrangements of ownership and custody were cumbersome: The missiles would be owned by Turkey; the nuclear warheads would be owned by the United States and held by its forces; the weapons could be launched only on the order of the Supreme Allied Commander-Europe (an American) on the approval of both the American and Turkish governments; and the sites would be manned by soldiers of both nations. It was, in principle, a single-veto system.[18]

The legal provisions raised serious questions about actual practices during a crisis. What would happen if only one nation decided to launch the missiles? How would the complex legal and custodial arrangements—with their checks and balances—actually operate? Could American troops stop the Turkish government, or even panicky Turkish troops, from acting unilaterally? What would happen if the Turks seized control of the weapons and warheads during a local crisis with the Soviets and launched the nuclear missiles, despite American objections? Such questions undoubtedly added to the fears of the Soviet Union, because the missiles would be close to the border. Could the Soviets trust the Turks? Should the United States?

The Jupiters were "soft," liquid-fuel IRBMs, taking hours to fire, quite inaccurate, very vulnerable, and hence only useful militarily for a first strike, and thus provocative. The Jupiter's skin was so thin that a sniper's bullet could puncture it and render it inoperable. "In the event of hostilities," one secret report warned, "the USSR with its ballistic missile capability logically could be expected to take out these bases on the first attack, which undoubtedly would be a surprise attack."[19] Put bluntly, the Jupiters would draw, not deter, an attack.

Yet various Turkish governments, both before and after the coup of 1960, wanted these weapons. They added prestige, emphasized Turkey's key role in NATO, and exaggerated the warmth of relations with a great power, the United States. To these Turkish governments, the missiles were political assets abroad, and possibly at home. Probably these men did not understand the strategic liabilities; perhaps they believed that the missiles, because of their first-strike capacity and the lurking ambiguities of actual control, were sufficiently frightening to deter the Soviets from pressuring Turkey.[20]

A week before Eisenhower departed from office in January 1961, he had a meeting on the troubling subject of the Jupiters. Atomic Energy Commission Chairman John McCone, having just returned from Europe, stressed that a high-powered rifle could knock out these weapons. Secretary of Defense Thomas Gates said, in the words of the minutes, the "deployments are actually more symbolic than useful." But he was wary of reversing agreements.[21] In the end, the Eisenhower administration, perhaps by intentional dawdling,[22] never delivered missiles to Turkey. Thus, when Kennedy became president, he inherited the agreement, with the Turks still expecting fulfillment, for America's sending the Jupiters. He made the decisions to deploy the missiles in Turkey.

KENNEDY PUTS THE JUPITERS IN TURKEY

Later, a fiction would emerge—promoted by Robert Kennedy's *Thirteen Days,* by some other administration stalwarts, and by trusting journalists and scholars—that Eisenhower's administration had actually installed the weapons in Turkey, that Kennedy had inherited this situation, and that the new president had sought to remove them and even *ordered* their removal well before the Cuban missile crisis but that he had been thwarted by subordinates. Bureaucratic politics and organizational loyalties had triumphed over presidential wishes and will, this interpretation stressed. In that fictional version, the president was shocked, dismayed, and angered to learn during the Cuban missile crisis that the Jupiters were still in Turkey.[23]

Such claims and recollections are misleading. During the crisis, Kennedy did manage briefly to forget that there were American missiles in Turkey, and he never seemed to recognize that his own government had actually installed them. But others reminded him of the Jupiters, and at least a few advisers undoubtedly recalled, during the October 1962 crisis, important parts of the administration's earlier decision to deploy these weapons. Key documents reveal that the actual deployment of the Jupiters did not occur until after Kennedy had been in the White House for at least half a year, and probably not until autumn 1961, and that the missiles did not become operational until March or April 1962.[24] These documents also reveal that there was considerable doubt within the government, prior to deployment, about the wisdom of putting these weapons in Turkey.

The first document, a partly declassified report by the Joint Congressional Committee on Atomic Energy, makes clear that the construction for the Jupiters had not even started when Kennedy entered the White House. On February 11, 1961, the committee stated, "construction . . . should not be permitted to *begin* on the . . . Jupiter sites [that are necessary for] placing 15 obsolete Jupiters in Turkey." Instead, according to the committee, the government should deploy to the area a Polaris submarine, with its 16 missiles, operated and controlled entirely by American personnel. That submarine, the committee emphasized, could be sent before 1962, when the Jupiters would become operational, and the Polaris would be "a much better retaliatory force."[25] It would be mobile, concealed, and thus virtually immune from a Soviet attack. As a result, unlike the Jupiters, the Polaris would add to deterrence and better protect America, NATO, and Turkey.

In late March 1961, Undersecretary of State Chester Bowles discussed these issues with the president and then sent him a brief report on the problem of missile bases in Britain and Italy, which had already been established, and in Turkey. A recent study by former Secretary of State Dean Acheson, Bowles noted, "stressed the vulnerability of these bases, their provocative 'first strike' nature as the Soviets see them, and their diminishing military importance in view of the greatly expanded Polaris and Minuteman programs." Bowles mentioned that both the Atomic Energy Commission and the Joint Committee on Atomic Energy were "concerned about" the installation of missiles in these countries.[26]

Kennedy directed that a special committee, drawn from the Departments of State and Defense and from the Central Intelligence Agency, "should review the question of deployment of IRBMs to Turkey and make recommendations to [him]." This three-agency committee was to be chaired by a representative from State,[27] which, unlike Defense, was probably not deeply troubled (aside from Undersecretary Bowles) by the provocative nature of the Jupiters and was likely therefore to serve as a partisan for Turkish interests and resist cancellation of the weapons. Had Kennedy wished to avoid sending the Jupiters to Turkey, he might well have sought a different bureaucratic interest to chair this committee. Had he been committed *not* to deploy the weapons, he could have *ordered* that arrangements be worked out accordingly.

In mid-April 1961, the question of whether or not to deploy the Jupiters still seemed open. Fearful that Kennedy might get unnecessarily tough in foreign policy, especially after the Bay of Pigs debacle, Undersecretary Bowles wrote out virtually a lecture of "do's and don'ts" for the chief executive. "I am particularly concerned that we fail to understand the Soviet reaction to our defense program," Bowles warned. "A double standard which allows us to react angrily at the slightest rumor of a Soviet missile base in Cuba, while we introduce . . . missile setups in Turkey . . . is dangerously self-defeating." Already in Kennedy's bad graces after the recent Bay of Pigs venture, which the undersecretary had let the press know he opposed, Bowles decided not to send his lengthy lecture.[28]

In May, according to Paul Nitze, he and Secretary of State Dean Rusk, acting on Kennedy's instructions, *tried* to persuade Turkey's foreign minister, Rauf Sarper, "that the Jupiters were already obsolete and should not be deployed in his country." Sarper was outraged.[29] That rebuff was probably predictable. But by the early summer of 1961, the Jupiters were still not in Turkey. On June 22, George C. McGhee, of State, reported to McGeorge Bundy, the president's special assistant for national security, "that action should not be taken to cancel *projected* deployment of IRBM's *to* Turkey." This conclusion was "based primarily," McGhee explained, "on the view that, in the aftermath of Khrushchev's hard posture at Vienna, cancellation . . . might seem a weakness." American credibility and the president's prestige required doing what the Defense Department regarded as militarily dangerous. And General Lauris Norstad, commander of NATO, according to McGhee, "underlined the military importance of sending IRBM's to Turkey. This makes it unlikely that any attempt [would succeed] to persuade the Turkish military that they should abandon this project."[30]

General Norstad's arguments remain unavailable. But it is clear that Norstad's reasoning helped undercut the analysis of Secretary McNamara and his "whiz kids," who hoped to make deterrence more reasonable and thus chafed at the resistance of allies, the American brass, and the State Department. Why did Kennedy accede to deploying the missiles? The documents are still classified. The most likely explanation is that McGhee's report summarized Kennedy's own thinking that summer. The president did not want to seem weak after the debacle at the Vienna summit, where he felt Khrushchev had bullied him. Nor did Kennedy wish to weaken the NATO alliance politically and deeply offend a key American ally, Turkey, by reneging on Eisenhower's commitment. Perhaps, as McNamara later hinted, the administration might have been tempted to promise a Polaris for the future, when it would be available, instead of deploying Jupiters *then*, in mid-1961. But there were no extra Polaris subs then, in the summer of 1961. As McNamara later explained, "[T]here would have been a psychological loss to the West of simply cancelling the program and failing to replace them—the missiles—simultaneously with some other more modern system."[31] Presumably, after the pain of Vienna faded, when credibility was reaffirmed and more Polaris subs became available, the administration could try a Jupiter-for-Polaris swap with the Turks. But in 1961, there was no felt need for haste, since the Jupiters were deemed a minor problem in a nuclear edifice that, for the new administration, required major overhauling and great expansion.

KENNEDY NEVER *ORDERED* REMOVAL
OF THE JUPITERS

According to some memoirists, President Kennedy raised with the State Department in early 1962 the issue of withdrawing the Jupiters. At the NATO meeting in May 1962 Secretary of State Dean Rusk found that the Turks still objected, primarily on political grounds, according to Roger Hilsman.[32] There is no evidence that the administration offered a Polaris as a substitute that spring, and probably the Turks would have found the submarine less attractive. The Turks did not seem to share the Defense Department's concern about an invulnerable deterrent, and the Jupiters offered two notable advantages the Polaris lacked: The missiles, because they were visible, added more tangible prestige; and they were subject, in principle, to some Turkish control.

By the summer of 1962, Hilsman claims, Kennedy again raised the matter of removing the Jupiters, this time with Undersecretary of State George Ball, and rejected the State Department's "case for further delay."[33] And in late August 1962, Kennedy raised this subject yet again, this time, surprisingly and dramatically, in the context of Cuba. While he did *not* order a withdrawal of the Jupiters, a *study* was ordered in an August 23, 1962 directive and the responsibility for the problem was shifted to the Department of Defense, which, unlike State, was more concerned about nuclear strategy than about maintaining warm relations with a dependent ally. National Security Action Memorandum No. 181, dated August 23, 1962, expresses Kennedy's thoughts and new fears—of missiles in Cuba and Soviet efforts to equate them with the Jupiters. Here is a segment of that memorandum:

> The President has directed that the following actions and studies be undertaken in the light of new Soviet bloc activity in Cuba.
>
> > What action can be taken to get Jupiter missiles out of Turkey? (Action: Department of Defense). . . .
> >
> > A study should be made of the advantages and disadvantages of making a statement that the U.S. would not tolerate the establishment of military forces (missile or air, or both?) which might launch a nuclear attack from Cuba against the U.S. . . .

> A study should be made of the various military alternatives which might
> be adopted in executing a decision to eliminate any installations in Cuba
> capable of launching nuclear attack on the U.S. What would be the pros
> and cons, for example, of pinpoint attack, general counterforce attack,
> and outright invasion? (action: Department of Defense)[34]

So far as the available records and recollections indicate, however, Defense
accomplished nothing in the next seven weeks to phase out the Jupiters.[35]
Probably Defense was again flirting with the possibility of substituting
deployment of a Polaris (there were nine) near Turkey for the Jupiters.

Did Kennedy really believe that this directive of August 23 would soon
remove the Jupiters? Given that his government had installed them, and they
had just recently become operational, he could not have been so foolishly
optimistic. Nor did the memorandum *order* the Department of Defense to
act. It asked "What action can be taken . . . ?" and stated that there would be
a meeting with the president in about nine days "to review progress on these
items." Thus it is too simple to conclude, as have some analysts, that Kennedy
ordered removal of the missiles and that the bureaucracy thwarted his
instructions.[36] Put simply, Kennedy had never ordered withdrawal of the
Jupiters. He *hoped* for such an action.

Why did Kennedy in August link the missiles in Turkey to the problem
of Cuba? Did he foresee that the Soviets would install surface-to-surface
missiles 90 miles from the United States? The memoirists tell us that neither
Kennedy nor his advisers, with the exception of CIA director John McCone,
deemed such Soviet action as likely.[37] Probably then, their concern was more
general: that the Soviets might justify a buildup of troops and even bombers
in Cuba by pointing to the Jupiters, which had recently become operational.[38]

The August 23 National Security Action memorandum had suggested the
danger of the Soviets equating "offensive" missiles in Turkey with those in
Cuba. So, even *before* a U-2 photographed the Soviet "offensive" missile
sites on October 14, a National Security Council staff member prepared a
strained, self-righteous document, characteristic of the administration's public pronouncements during the future crisis, stressing the political differences
between America's Jupiters in Turkey and Soviet missiles in Cuba: The
Soviet weapons were designed for aggression and secretly deployed; the
American weapons were defensive and openly deployed. Put simply, the
Soviet action was dangerous and dishonorable, the American peaceful and
honorable.[39]

KHRUSHCHEV'S DECISION:
RESPONDING TO THE AMERICAN JUPITERS

To Khrushchev, however, the world looked very different. Unlike Kennedy, the Soviet leader had not sponsored armed invasions of the rival camp's allies. And Khrushchev's earlier protests against the emplacement of missiles in Turkey had been virtually ignored. By early 1962, he knew that he was at a great disadvantage in deliverable strategic weapons. The addition of 15 Jupiters would simply worsen an already terrible situation for the Soviets. The balance of strategic weaponry was probably about 9 to 1 in America's favor. The United States already had over 100 intercontinental ballistic missiles (ICBMs) and the Soviets probably about a dozen. The strategic balance was scheduled to become predictably worse for the Soviets by October 1962, when the Soviets would have about 20 ICBMs and the United States over 170.[40]

By spring 1962, an astute Soviet analyst, looking at likely American nuclear capabilities as well as administration pronouncements about nuclear strategy, could have concluded that the United States was seeking to develop an effective counterforce capability: the ability in a first strike to destroy most of the Soviet strategic weapons and retain the ability to block Soviet retaliation (with the few Soviet weapons not destroyed) by threatening an American attack on Soviet cities and noncombatant populations.[41]

There is no evidence that Khrushchev engaged in this analysis, but there is considerable evidence that he was feeling beleaguered by the general American strategic buildup, underscored by the deployment of Jupiters in Turkey. According to one Soviet source, Premier Khrushchev, brooding about the Jupiters, decided in April 1962 to consider sending missiles to Cuba. That month, Marshal Rodion Malinovsky, the Soviet defense minister, had explained to Khrushchev that the Jupiters in Turkey could reach their Soviet targets in 10 minutes whereas Soviet ICBMs would require 25 minutes to reach their American targets. Apparently, Malinovsky had not been proposing a Soviet deployment of nuclear missiles in Cuba. That was undoubtedly Khrushchev's idea. In his view, such a deployment could somewhat offset the growing American strategic superiority, specifically counter the Jupiter deployment, and also help to protect Cuba from a feared Kennedy administration military assault on that Soviet ally.[42]

The protection of Cuba was an important problem. Probably it was not Khrushchev's primary motive for wanting to install missiles in Cuba, but those weapons, he undoubtedly believed, could both defend Cuba and expand the Soviet strategic arsenal. Cuba was an important issue, as both symbol and substance, for Khrushchev and the Kremlin. A successful United States attack there would be "a terrible blow," he later explained, because it would have "gravely diminish[ed] our stature throughout the world, but especially in Latin America. If Cuba fell, other Latin American countries would reject us." To halt the first of the "dominoes" from falling he would place missiles in this beleaguered Caribbean island.[43]

In late April and in May, Khrushchev discussed his plans with associates. At first, Deputy Premier Anastas Mikoyan was opposed, fearing, among other objections, that the missiles would be provocative to the United States. Marshal Malinovsky greeted the deployment as a useful "deterrent measure," and Mikoyan soon relaxed his objections after Castro agreed to the plan and the Soviet military indicated that the deployment could be conducted without American knowledge.[44]

In May 1962, soon after the Jupiters had become operational, Khrushchev publicly complained about their deployment. Speaking on Bulgaria's Black Sea coast, he said, "Would it not be better if the shores on which are located NATO's military bases and the launching sites for nuclear-armed rockets were converted into areas of peaceful labor and prosperity?" He blamed America (called "the imperialists") and the ruling circles in Turkey for this dangerous deployment.[45]

In another speech in Bulgaria that month, he accused Kennedy of threatening that the United States, under certain circumstances, might strike the first nuclear blow. "Is it wise to threaten someone who is at least your equal in strength?" Khrushchev rhetorically asked.[46]

Unlike the American agreements on the deployment of IRBMs to Turkey, Khrushchev aimed to keep the agreement with Cuba (and the actual emplacement of missiles) secret at least until the weapons were combat ready. Soviet Ambassador Dobrynin, who did not know about the deployment, assured both Robert Kennedy and Theodore Sorensen in early September that the Soviet military equipment being shipped to Cuba was purely defensive.[47]

On September 11, after President Kennedy had publicly denied that there were "offensive ground-to-ground missiles in Cuba" and warned that "the gravest issues would arise . . . were it to be otherwise," *Tass* asserted that the military equipment sent to Cuba is "designed exclusively for defensive purpose . . . there is no need for the Soviet Union to shift its weapons for the repulsion of aggression, for a retaliatory blow, to any other country, for instance Cuba . . . there is no need to search for sites for [our nuclear weapons beyond the boundaries of the Soviet Union."[48] That statement was deceptive and undoubtedly so intended; it was not clearly a lie.

In that public statement, *Tass* also complained about America's military bases, sometimes with nuclear weapons encircling the Soviet Union: American leaders "install rockets [missiles] in Turkey, Italy. . . ." In contrast, *Tass* argued, the United States refused to allow the Soviets "to strengthen the defenses" of allies who felt threatened. "What conceit! The U.S. apparently believes that in present conditions [it] can proceed to aggression with impunity." An attack on Cuba, *Tass* warned, "will be the unleashing of war."[49]

To Castro, during the year and a half after the Bay of Pigs attack, when American covert operations ("Mongoose") were hoping to overthrow him, the prospect of Soviet missiles should have seemed attractive. They could help defend Cuba and thus—if their presence was made known—deter a United States attack. Castro's acceptance of the missiles could also strengthen his relationship with the Soviet Union, contribute to its defense, and possibly help protect other Communist revolutions. Undoubtedly, Castro did not realize that the Soviet missiles could well threaten his regime by drawing, not deterring, a United States attack. In a warning in early October 1962, Cuban president Osvaldo Dorticós publicly told the United States, "aggression against Cuba can become transformed. . . into the start of a new world war."[50]

Contrary to Cuban wishes, Khrushchev tried to keep the missile deployment secret for a period, probably until after the early November 1962 American elections. That strategy failed because the Soviet military did not use the necessary camouflage in Cuba. As a result, the shocked president, relying upon U-2 surveillance, learned on October 16 what he had previously deemed very unlikely: The Soviets had placed missiles in Cuba. Ironically, that same day in Moscow, Khrushchev complained to American ambassador Foy Kohler that the United States had earlier placed missiles in Italy and Turkey.[51]

THE EXCOMM'S FIRST DAY

Upon learning on Monday evening, October 15, of the missiles in Cuba, national security adviser McGeorge Bundy had decided not to awaken the president. Let him get his sleep, Bundy thought, for the next days would be difficult and nothing could be decided immediately.[52] Tuesday morning, upon receiving the bad news, Kennedy decided to establish and then convene a special group of advisers, the Executive Committee (later dubbed "Ex-Comm") of the National Security Council, to help diagnose the problem and to devise ways of getting the missiles out of Cuba. The president was determined, according to memoirists, that doing nothing was unacceptable. He wanted to get missiles out of Cuba—quickly.

At the first ExComm meeting, held later that Tuesday morning, the group considered various options—air strike, invasion, diplomatic approaches, blockade, and different combinations. Many speakers dwelled on the military options—including the tactics and details, the time for preparations and the danger of reprisal. That first morning, as throughout the day, the possibility of a military solution frequently dominated.

In the discussions that morning, the assembled men briefly puzzled over why the Soviets had put missiles in Cuba. Perhaps a Berlin-for-Cuba trade was envisaged by Khrushchev, a few thought. There were also analogies to the American missiles in Turkey, as Secretary of State Rusk noted. Elaborating in part on CIA director John McCone's thinking, Rusk explained, Khrushchev knew that the United States had substantial nuclear superiority and "that we don't really live under fear of his nuclear weapons to the extent, uh, he has to live under fear of ours. Also we have nuclear weapons nearby, in Turkey and places like that."[53]

For the ExComm members, their knowledge about the Jupiters—a very minor matter for them in the preceding 21 months—was vague. The president, upon hearing Rusk's words about American missiles in Turkey, seemed surprised. He asked how many were there. "About fifteen, I believe," replied Secretary of Defense McNamara. Bundy added, "I think that's right. I think that's right."[54]

Significantly, not until the second ExComm meeting, held that Tuesday evening, did anyone during the sessions focus sharply on the military significance of the Soviet medium-range ballistic missiles (MRBMs). At the time, the Soviet emplacement was estimated as increasing the Soviet strategic missile arsenal by about 50 percent. (It may have actually tripled, or at least doubled, the Soviet arsenal of missiles capable of hitting the United States.) The Joint Chiefs of Staff believed that the additional weapons imperiled the United States. McNamara forcefully dissented. The added missiles did not change the strategic balance—"not at all," he asserted. In the ExComm, his assessment went unchallenged at the time.[55]

Accepting McNamara's conclusions, President Kennedy stated, "Last month, I should have said . . . that we don't care [about the Soviets putting missiles in Cuba]. But when we said we're not going to [accept it] and then they go ahead and do it, and then we do nothing. . . ."[56]

For President Kennedy, the problem was not essentially military. Rather, the Soviets had challenged America's and his own credibility and will. The Soviets had crossed a line he had drawn, largely for domestic purposes, and now he wanted to get the missiles out promptly. He felt he could not allow them to remain in Cuba.[57]

Military solutions, as McNamara stressed, posed profound dangers. Even American bombings would miss some of the MRBMs, which could then be unleashed against the United States. An American attack could mean a Soviet-American nuclear war, he warned. "I, I don't know quite what kind of a world we live in," he said, "after we've struck Cuba, and we, we've started it."[58]

Attorney General Robert Kennedy, contrary to the later claims in *Thirteen Days,* endorsed a military attack on Cuba—even if it meant war with the Soviets. Better now than later, he said. The attorney general even suggested creating a pretext for attacking Cuba; "sink the *Maine* again or something," he said.[59]

The president puzzled aloud about Soviet motives, noting that Khrushchev had even been cautious on Berlin. "[W]hat is the advantage" for Khrushchev putting the missiles in Cuba? the president asked. "It's just as if we suddenly began to put a major number of MRBMs in Turkey. Now that's be goddam dangerous, I would think."[60]

"Well, we *did,*" replied an ExComm member (possibly Bundy). The president, forgetting his own 1961 decision to deploy the Jupiters, said, "Yeah, but that was five years ago," under Eisenhower. Strangely, no one immediately corrected Kennedy to point out that *he* had made the crucial decisions.[61]

A few ExComm members, stressing that the Soviets were far behind in the ICBM race, suggested that Khrushchev might be acting to narrow the gap. One adviser (probably Bundy) said, "I'm sure his generals have been telling him for a year and a half that he had . . . golden opportunity to add to his strategic capability." Another thought Khrushchev might also be setting up a trade—probably involving Berlin.[62]

President Kennedy continued to be puzzled by the Soviet actions. "I don't know whether . . . they're aware of what we said at the press conference about Soviet missiles," he said. "I don't think there's any record of the Soviets making this direct a challenge, ever, really . . . since the Berlin blockade [of 1948]." Bundy pointed out, "We have to be clear . . . that they made this decision, in all probability, *before* you made your statements."[63]

Bundy acknowledged that the Soviets had not reversed their decisions *after* Kennedy's warnings of late August and September. The president and the others knew that these warnings, designed to refute domestic charges about Soviet missiles in Cuba, had not really been directed at the Soviets[64] and therefore had not been carefully phrased. The ExComm members may not have realized how vague those public statements had been. No one at the ExComm meetings that day pointed out this problem.

Whatever open course of action the president ultimately chose in order to deal with the MRBMs, advisers knew that there would have to be a public explanation. A few ExComm members stressed that Kennedy's hand would be strengthened if he could state that the Soviets had lied to him either publicly or privately. Bundy thought that Ambassador Dobrynin had not actually known about the missile plan when he had given his private assurances. Maybe, suggested one member, the president could get Soviet Foreign Minister Andrei Gromyko, in his forthcoming meeting with Kennedy, to lie about the missiles so that a record would be established. In the meantime, the best example of Soviet deceit anyone could cite was the Soviet public statement of September 11, "that there is no need for the Soviet Union to shift its weapons for the repulsion of aggression for a retaliatory blow to any other country, for instance Cuba."[65] The Soviet emplacement did not render that statement a lie, only a deception.

Kennedy was not interested in pinning down the matter of lying. Building on Bundy's earlier analysis that the Soviets had committed themselves to the missile venture before August, the president said, "Now, maybe our mistake was in not saying some time *before* this summer that if they do this we're [word unintelligible] to act."[66]

According to reports summarized at the meeting, American experts were divided whether, in Soviet calculations, this was a Soviet high-risk or low-risk venture. State Department intelligence analysts thought low-risk; Llewellyn Thompson, a Soviet expert and former ambassador to the Kremlin, thought high-risk. Would high-risk mean that the Soviets were desperate, or likely to retreat? Surprisingly, none made clear how the estimates of risk should shape American tactics.[67]

Toward the end of this evening session, Secretary McNamara, again offering his own judgment of the MRBM problem, emphasized, "I don't think there *is* a military problem here [in Cuba] this is a domestic, political problem . . . It's primarily a . . . domestic political problem."[68]

At the evening session, none directly challenged that analysis. It did not seem to alter their thinking about the problem or their commitment to secure the speedy removal of the missiles. There was general agreement, promoted partly by McNamara, that various groups would analyze possible courses, including a blockade and military action against Cuba and the missiles. McNamara also suggested that the president might issue a statement to Khrushchev warning, "if there is ever *any indication* that they're [the missiles in Cuba] to be launched against this country, we will respond not only against Cuba, but we will respond directly against the Soviet Union with, with a full nuclear strike." McNamara acknowledged that this alternative "doesn't seem to be a very acceptable one, but wait until you work on the others." His vague implication was that the threat of an American preemptive strike, in response to a Soviet indication, might start to look attractive.[69]

In this meeting, there had been men who shaded toward the "dove" or "hawk" side, and some had also ambled, in mulling aloud about ideas and questioning others' proposals, from one side to the other. But none had steadfastly proposed doing nothing, and none had persistently recommended attacking Cuba. Their conception of a solution could not include acceding to the missiles. Their conception might ultimately embrace military action.

Any analyst, with just these ExComm minutes, would find it very difficult, if not impossible, to predict what the administration would choose to do—blockade (quarantine), bombing, an invasion, or some combination. And an analyst's efforts to correlate or explain positions advocated on October 16 or later in terms of bureaucratic interest ("where you stand depends on where you sit")[70] would undoubtedly fail. Random guessing would probably work about as well.

OCTOBER 17-22:
AMERICA MIGHT HAVE TO TRADE THE JUPITERS

On October 16, the Jupiters in Turkey had not been central to the discussion. During the next six days, from the 17th through the 22nd, when the ExComm and other advisers deliberated on how the administration should respond, the prospect of trading the Jupiters received some support. United Nations Ambassador Adlai Stevenson, Secretary McNamara, and some others occasionally suggested trading missiles (Jupiters for those in Cuba) to settle the crisis. Apparently, the president flirted with this notion.

On Wednesday, the 17th, Stevenson warned Kennedy that world opinion would equate America's missile bases in Turkey with the Soviet bases in Cuba. Stevenson's memorandum was fuzzy, perhaps because he feared giving unwelcome counsel; he both warned that "we can't negotiate with a gun at our head" and suggested trading the bases in Turkey for those in Cuba. "*I feel you should make it clear that the existence of nuclear missile bases anywhere is negotiable before we start anything,*" he underlined.[71]

In fairness to Stevenson, when he offered this counsel on Wednesday, the ExComm was leaning toward an attack on Cuba to eliminate the missiles; in that context, he was probably more concerned to head off disaster than to phrase an exact plan for negotiations. His memo was unclear on key matters; and the problems of when, how, and under what conditions to offer a trade—whether explicit or informal—would bedevil thinking on this matter throughout the crisis.

The day after Stevenson's suggestion, Theodore Sorensen drafted a possible message to be handed to Khrushchev. It compelled him to remove the missiles from Cuba or face an immediate American attack on the island. Possibly to reduce the impact of this ultimatum, the draft also had President Kennedy offering "to discuss other problems on our agenda, including, if you wish, the NATO bases in Turkey and Italy to which you referred in your conversation with Ambassador Kohler." Lest such an offer seem to accept the virtual equivalence of the American bases with the Soviet missiles in Cuba, the draft stressed, they "are in no way comparable in the eyes of either . . . international law or world opinion."[72]

On Friday, the 19th, according to the ExComm minutes, "more than once during the afternoon Secretary McNamara voiced the opinion that the US . . . would at least have to give up our missile bases in Italy and Turkey and would probably have to pay more besides . . . to get the Soviet missiles out of Cuba."[73] On Saturday, McNamara again offered the same analysis: "We would have to be prepared to accept the withdrawal of US strategic missiles from Turkey and Italy and possibly agreement to [withdraw in the future from] Guantanamo." He added, "We could obtain the removal of the missiles . . . only if we were prepared to offer something in return."[74]

On Saturday, after the ExComm had finally seemed to agree on the quarantine, Stevenson attended the meeting and once more recommended a trade, this time to be announced along with the quarantine. His proposed settlement would have included withdrawal of Jupiters from Turkey and abandonment of Guantanamo. According to Arthur Schlesinger, Jr., who has seen the still-classified minutes, "everyone jumped on Stevenson." Why? Schlesinger claims that most feared that this proposed tactic, by *starting* with concessions, would "legitimize Khrushchev's action and give him an easy triumph." Robert Kennedy later added that the timing and the Guantanamo offer, not the Turkish bases, provoked the anger.[75] Probably, in addition, Stevenson himself provoked ire. He was an outsider, not respected by either Kennedy brother, and Stevenson's counsel, even when similar to that of the trusted McNamara, easily rankled the then-tired members of the ExComm.

President Kennedy "sharply rejected the thought of surrendering [Guantanamo]," according to the ExComm minutes. "He felt that such action would convey to the world that he had been frightened into abandoning our position."[76] He "emphatically disagreed," reports Schlesinger, "that the initial presentation to the UN should include our notion of an eventual political settlement." According to the minutes, "he agreed that at an appropriate time we would have to acknowledge that we were willing to take strategic missiles out of Turkey and Italy if this issue was raised by the Russians . . . But he was firm in saying that we should only make such a proposal in the future." The quoted minutes leave unclear whether the president was willing to countenance an explicit public trade of the Jupiters, or whether he was suggesting something private, hedged, even evasive.[77]

At that same Saturday meeting, though President Kennedy was thinking about a future trade involving the Jupiters, he did not bar the likelihood of an air strike on the missiles on Cuba a few days after announcing the quarantine. In preparation for such an attack, he "suggested," in the words of the minutes, "that we inform the Turks and the Italians that they should not fire the strategic missiles they have even if attacked." Apparently, he did not know about the veto system controlling the use of the nuclear warheads, and thus he believed that the Turks or Italians could attack on their own initiative.[78]

After the discussion at this Saturday meeting of a possible American air strike and its repercussions, "the President made clear [to the Saturday group] that in the UN we should emphasize the subterranean nature of the buildup . . . Only if we were asked would we respond that we were prepared to talk about the withdrawal of missiles from Italy and Turkey." Stevenson, wanting more, argued that the administration "must be more forthcoming about our giving up our missile bases in Turkey and Italy." Paul Nitze, while opposing Stevenson's proposal that the United States should make an offer, "said he would not object to discussing this question in the event that negotiations developed from our installation of the blockade."[79]

That weekend, one of the president's aides, probably Sorensen, drafted a message suggesting the possibility of an ultimate trade. Presumably intended for the president's public address announcing the presence of Soviet missiles in Cuba, that draft statement included a crucial sentence, "the United States stands ready to discuss with the Soviet Union the elimination of all strategic bases on foreign soil in the context of the disarmament treaties now under consideration, including the NATO bases in Turkey and Italy." That proposal disappeared before the final version of Kennedy's Monday night speech was put together.[80]

On Sunday morning, high-level State Department officials flirted with the Cuba-Turkey missile trade. At an evening meeting, convened by Robert Kennedy, a number of senior government officials agreed, in the words of Abram Chayes, the State Department legal adviser, "that the Turkish missiles would have to be given up in the end, as the price of settlement." Why not have the United States introduce this offer at the UN right after the announcement of the quarantine? Offered at the beginning, such a concession would have various liabilities and seem, according to Chayes's summary of attitudes, "rather weak and defensive . . . inconsistent with the sense of resolution and determination that was judged essential to the success of the quarantine."[81]

Suggesting a trade, W. Averell Harriman, Assistant Secretary of State for Far Eastern Affairs, counseled President Kennedy on likely Soviet purposes: "There has undoubtedly been great pressure on Khrushchev for a considerable time to do something about our ring of bases, aggravated by our placing Jupiter missiles in Turkey." Harriman hinted that such a trade might rescue Khrushchev, who, he thought, had been pushed to take such bold action by a tough group in the Kremlin.[82]

On Monday morning, the day the president announced the quarantine, Attorney General Robert Kennedy sketched the administration's public line, at least for the next few days. Fearful that Stevenson might be too soft in dealing with the Soviets at the UN, Robert Kennedy reportedly pulled aside Schlesinger, then serving as Stevenson's aide at the UN, to outline the administration's thinking: "We will have to make a deal at the end, but we must stand absolutely firm now. Concessions must come at the end of negotiation, not at the beginning."[83] Robert Kennedy's implication: The quarantine, if successful, would frighten the Soviets but not compel them to yield unless America also offered some quid pro quo. Did the attorney general have the Jupiters in mind? The deliberations of the past week, especially the Sunday-evening meeting, certainly suggested them as part of an exchange.

Why didn't the president order the dismantling of the Jupiters before they might become a public bargaining card in the crisis? Probably the time was too short and probably he was also tempted by the prospect of a future trade and unwilling to discard this extra card. Stevenson, among others, had warned of a potential liability: that the Jupiters would also make it harder to persuade the world why the Soviet missiles constituted a new kind of threat. But probably Kennedy was willing to take that risk in order to keep open future options, to protect himself from international embarrassment (wouldn't sudden dismantling suggest a Turkey-Cuba equivalence?), and to avoid domestic charges of weakness and a sellout.

Perhaps, however, in the rush of events, the president never focused sharply on dismantling the weapons. Presumably, he as well as most of the ExComm members still knew very little about them. Undoubtedly, Kennedy and his associates would have been shocked to learn that the *Air Force had turned over to the Turks control of the first Jupiters at some point in the 72 hours before President Kennedy's speech declaring the presence of Soviet missiles in Cuba.* "This was the first Jupiter launch position to be assigned [to] the Turks," an official Air Force history later noted laconically.[84]

In a background briefing to the press right after Kennedy's October 22 evening address, Secretary McNamara was asked to respond to the claim that the Soviets, by placing missiles in Cuba, were doing what the United States had done by putting missiles close to the Soviet Union. "There is no similarity," McNamara assured the press. The Turks and others were threatened by the Soviets, he explained, but Cuba "was not under the threat of nuclear attack or attack from this country."[85] Throughout the crisis, that would be the administration's *public* line of argument.

PLANS TO TRADE THE JUPITERS:
TUESDAY, OCTOBER 23, TO FRIDAY, OCTOBER 26

After the president's Monday evening speech announcing the quarantine, some American officials vigorously canvassed the possibility of trading the Jupiters in Turkey as part of the ultimate settlement of the crisis. There were basic questions, as they knew: Whether and, if so, how to exchange the Jupiters, ideally without appearing to do so? Would other weapons meet the military and political needs of NATO and Turkey? If so, could the United States withdraw the Jupiter missiles without offending most NATO nations, and Turkey in particular? "The danger in Turkey can be especially acute," one official warned. "If the Alliance or the US seems to be pulling away from [Turkey] it could lead to the fall of the present government."[86] An uneasy new coalition, shored up by its military and by American economic aid, the Turkish government could not afford to antagonize its powerful generals nor risk a crisis.[87]

Working within these constraints, Undersecretary of State George Ball, W. Averell Harriman, Harlan Cleveland, assistant secretary of state for international organization, Walt Whitman Rostow, director of the Policy Planning Council, and Stevenson, among others, scratched around for some solution involving the Jupiters. At times, this line seemed to capture the fancy of President Kennedy, but hard questions always lingered for him.[88]

Early in the week, President Kennedy apparently directed the State Department to consider withdrawing the missiles, which spurred Ball to consult key ambassadors. On Wednesday, the 24th, Ball notified Ambassador Raymond Hare in Ankara that a trade was being considered, and requested an assessment of the political situation in Turkey so "that [we will] not harm our relations with this important ally." Would Turkey accede to withdrawal of the Jupiters, Ball asked, if there was some military replacement, possibly deployment of an American-controlled Polaris, or establishment of a seaborne, multilateral nuclear force (MLF) within NATO?[89] Both notions had been knocking about Washington for more than a year, and the Kennedy administration, like Eisenhower's, had been flirting with the creation of a Multilateral Nuclear Force, under NATO, in order to restrain the desire of some Europeans nations, and especially France, for an independent deterrent.

Removal of the Jupiters as part of an explicit trade would injure NATO and American relations with Turkey, Hare replied. The Turks would greatly resent "that their interests were being traded off in order to appease an enemy." They were proud that, unlike the Cubans, they were not the "stooge" of a great power. Both Turkey's political prestige and military power were at stake, he claimed, and the Jupiters fulfilled both needs.[90]

Could these missiles be used to settle the Soviet-American conflict? Hare was not optimistic, but dutifully discussed some programs. He reluctantly suggested a secret agreement (without Turkey's knowledge) and then the prompt dismantling of the missiles. That course would prove attractive in Washington.[91]

On receiving Ball's secret cable, NATO Ambassador Thomas Finletter also replied that the Turks would bitterly resent a trade. He lectured the State Department on the dangers of a "horse trade." It could set a "pattern for handling Russian incursions" elsewhere and thus frighten other members of NATO, who "may wonder whether they will be asked to give up some military capability" the next time. Finletter, however, admitted that some NATO members—the "Norwegians, Danes and maybe even [the British] might be willing [to] accept Cuba-Turk deal 'to avoid nuclear war'. . . ."[92]

By Thursday, the 25th, while one special NSC committee was sketching the scenario for an air strike, another was outlining a "political path"—a summit meeting while the quarantine continued—to settle the crisis. "It would probably involve discussion over Berlin or, as a minimum, our missile bases in Turkey," the committee warned.[93] A linked proposal, probably from the same committee, suggested an offer "to withdraw our missiles from Turkey in return for Soviet withdrawal of . . . missiles from Cuba." To avoid a crisis in NATO and to assuage Turkey, such an offer "might be expressed in generalized form, such as withdrawal of missiles from territory [near] the other [great power]."[94]

On Friday, the 26th, Harriman was also urging negotiations to get the missiles out of Turkey. He endorsed the "defanging resolution" of Assistant Secretary Harlan Cleveland: Only nuclear powers should possess nuclear weapons and missiles, and thus American and Russia would not place these systems in the territory of non-nuclear powers. Such terms, Harriman explained, would compel the United States to pull missiles out of Turkey and Italy, but not Britain, which was a nuclear power, and Russia would have to withdraw its missiles from Cuba. By raising the terms to a level of generality, Harriman hoped to conceal what some could regard as a naked trade—missiles in Turkey and Italy for missiles in Cuba. *"Agreement should be put forward not as a trade over Cuba,"* he underlined, but *"as a first and important step towards disarmament."*[95] And he believed, sincerely, that the result would be both a way out of the crisis and a course toward more effective arms control. Harriman was seizing on the crisis to address more basic problems and also offering Khrushchev a way of avoiding humiliation.

At first glance, Harriman's plan seemed appealingly simple: The negotiations *might* be speedy, and the Soviets would recognize that they could take credit for forcing a trade and for promoting disarmament. But what would happen if the negotiations were not speedy? Wouldn't obtaining the endorsement of NATO and Turkey take too much time?

Even though virtually all the medium-range ballistic missile (MRBM) sites *had been operational* since the first day of the quarantine, and therefore the Soviets could have launched a first salvo of about half their 42 MRBMs, Kennedy and members of the ExComm continued to worry about the continued work on missile sites in Cuba. They seemed to fear that the Soviets would reduce the time required for launching an MRBM, and that they also were advancing quickly on 12 or 16 launchers for IRBMs (12 to 32 missiles), likely to be ready in about five weeks. The CIA was not sure whether nuclear warheads were in Cuba, but the administration assumed the worst.[96]

The ExComm minutes are scattered with demands that work on the missiles must soon stop. And Kennedy seemed to have a self-imposed deadline of roughly between Sunday, the 28th, to about Tuesday, the 30th.[97] As a result, plans involving a trade of the Jupiters had to meet his informal timetable. Those plans that seemed to involve lengthy negotiations would be found unacceptable, unless they stipulated a way of getting the Soviets promptly to halt work on the sites.

While Harriman's plan *may* have had this liability, two others—one from a special NSC committee, and the other from Rostow—certainly did. On Friday, the special committee offered a proposal, forwarded by Rusk without comment to Kennedy, for a "face-saving cover, if [the Soviets] wish, for a withdrawal of their offensive weapons from Cuba."[98] It was an elaborate, guardedly optimistic scheme suggesting a summit conference, to be preceded by the agreement of NATO and Turkey to accept an MLF and to remove missiles from Turkey and Italy.

Walt W. Rostow, sketching a similar plan, believed that he had devised a way out of the crisis while maintaining all of the "Free World assets" and actually strengthening the NATO alliance. His solution: Secure NATO's speedy approval for MLF, presumably with an agreement to dismantle the Jupiters. The Soviets, he acknowledged, "could read it [dismantling] as a way of helping them off the hook"; but it would "nail down the missile portion of the Alliance and [thus thwart Soviet efforts] to disrupt the confidence of the Alliance in the U.S." An additional attraction, for Rostow, was that it achieved goals he had long sought—a stronger NATO, establishment of MLF, and removal of dangerous weapons.[99] But how could these negotiations with NATO nations be completed in a few days?

Ideally, the analyst would like to know which ExComm members saw which proposals, and what kind of informal dialogue ensued. But, for the most part, that kind of evidence is not available. The special NSC committee's proposal went to Kennedy, as did Rostow's, and probably all the reports reached Bundy's desk.[100] By Friday, judging from the contents of the various memoranda, there had been substantial informal dialogue. Many advisers were looking for a road to a settlement, and the Jupiters constituted a possible one.

On Friday morning, the ExComm considered whether Kennedy should seek UN-arranged negotiations with the Soviets while they halted construction on the missile sites and, as Stevenson suggested, America suspended its quarantine. Could the crisis be settled this way? Stevenson, who seemed optimistic, "predicted that the Russians would ask for a new guarantee of the territorial integrity of Cuba and the dismantlement of U.S. strategic missiles in Turkey" in return for withdrawal of missiles from Cuba. Stevenson still regarded these terms as reasonable. But John McCone, the CIA director, was outraged. He resented linking the missiles of the two nations. McCone said, according to the minutes, "the Soviet weapons in Cuba were pointed at our heart and put us under great handicap to carry out our commitments to the free world."[101]

Kennedy did not bar the trade that Stevenson had outlined. According to the minutes' paraphrase, the president said, "we will get the . . . missiles out of Cuba only by invading or trading. He doubted that the quarantine alone would produce a withdrawal of the weapons." After Kennedy spoke, the dialogue quickly shifted from the Jupiters to Stevenson's proposal that the quarantine should be suspended during negotiations. Most strongly opposed that concession. The pressure must be maintained, they concluded, to help force a settlement. Curiously, they did not return to the issue of the Jupiters at that meeting.[102]

Later that Friday, the Soviets loosely indicated terms for settling the crisis: withdrawal of their missiles from Cuba and on-site inspection, in return for America's terminating the quarantine and pledging not to invade Cuba. There was not even a hint that America must dismantle its Jupiters; the Soviets were asking for less than many American officials had anticipated and than some had proposed to grant.[103]

That Friday night, the ExComm could find reason for satisfaction. The dangerous crisis would end with one American concession—a no-invasion pledge.[104] Only a few advisers, including McCone[105] and at least some of the Joint Chiefs,[106] were deeply unhappy that Castro would be safe from a United States attack. For the rest, the pledge was a small price to pay. According to Secretary Rusk, it was simply a reaffirmation of existing obligations: "We are committed not to invade Cuba [because we] signed the UN Charter and the Rio treaty."[107] Neither he nor the others mentioned the administration's efforts and hopes up to at least mid-October 1962 of overthrowing Castro.

But on Saturday morning, the ExComm's optimism speedily collapsed. A Soviet ship was approaching the quarantine line, and the FBI reported that the Soviet delegation was burning papers in likely preparation for war. Worst of all, a new Soviet message arrived, raising the terms of settlement to require a public deal removing the Jupiters from Turkey.[108] Soon, the ExComm would learn that American surveillance aircraft had been fired on over Cuba and that a SAM (surface-to-air missile) had shot down a U-2.

WOULD WESTERN ALLIES HAVE ACCEPTED A TRADE?

How would America's NATO allies, other than Turkey, have responded if the administration had met the Soviet terms and agreed publicly to withdraw the Jupiters? Could Kennedy have negotiated a private trade before the Soviets made their public demand? The leaders of most of the NATO allies understood the military liabilities of the Jupiters, so the issues were not primarily strategic (the loss of weapons) but psychological and international-political: the significance of an American concession on weaponry in Europe in order to deal with problems in the Caribbean.[109] Would Kennedy be viewed as a leader who sold out allies for America's interest? Or would he be seen as a leader who sought peace and would pay some reasonable price to avoid plunging NATO and America into war?

There is considerable evidence on the attitudes of the German, French, British, Italian, and Canadian governments, and scattered evidence for Belgium, the Netherlands, Greece, Denmark, and Norway. A formal trade, especially a public one, would have unnerved some governments, particularly the German, possibly the British, and probably the Dutch; it would have confirmed the analysis of President Charles de Gaulle of France, delighted Canada, and probably pleased the Italian, Greek, Danish, and Norwegian governments.

Konrad Adenauer, the firm chancellor of Germany, who always feared that American concessions anywhere might betoken abandonment of Berlin, would undoubtedly have opposed even a private trade.[110] But he had no real leverage and could not threaten to leave NATO or even acknowledge its weaknesses. Unwilling to move toward rapprochement with the Soviet Union, he and his party depended on the United States and NATO, both for military protection and political prestige. Any trade would have eroded his trust in Kennedy, but it would not have altered Adenauer's policies on the larger issues—Berlin, East Germany, the Warsaw Pact, and the Soviet Union. True, at home, he would have been compelled to defend himself and his party from charges that America would also sell out Berlin and thus from demands that an approach to the East was essential. But he would have succeeded, partly for his own reasons. Like Kennedy, Adenauer could have distinguished between Berlin and the Jupiters, which could have been defined as marginal and symbolic.

Charles de Gaulle's position was different. Already moving toward French withdrawal from NATO on the grounds that the alliance meant American domination and blocked France from an independent foreign policy, de Gaulle could use the missile crisis—whatever the outcome—to support his analysis. The United States had acted independently, without consultation with allies, he noted. The implication, which he would later exploit, was familiar: "annihilation without representation." In turn, had Kennedy publicly traded the missiles in Turkey, that act also would have confirmed de Gaulle's analysis: American would act on its own interests and abandon allies whenever convenient. Probably no likely action by Kennedy in the missile crisis—whether he traded or not—could have blocked de Gaulle's ambitions for an independent force.

That conception, so intimately related to his quest for national and personal grandeur, would not be punctured by decisions during the missile crisis.[111] While he officially supported the president in the crisis, the aged French leader hinted that immaturity had led Kennedy and the United States to overreact. De Gaulle's chiding words, as summarized by the American ambassador, were these: "The French for centuries had lived with threats and menaces, first from the Germans and from the Russians, but he understood the US had not had a comparable experience."[112]

Britain's Prime Minister Harold Macmillan had publicly supported the quarantine and privately worried, especially in the early days, that Khrushchev would wring concessions that would weaken the alliance. He feared that Khrushchev might have installed the missiles "to trade Cuba for Berlin." Fretting that the quarantine might be inadequate, Macmillan wrote in his diary, Kennedy may "'miss the bus'—he may *never* get rid of Cuban rockets except by trading them for Turkish, Italian, or other bases. Thus Khrushchev will have won his point." But by Friday, the 26th, when the Soviets seemed to be seeking a way out of the crisis, Macmillan was conciliatory. "If we want to help the Russians save face," he asked Kennedy, "would it be worthwhile our [immobilizing the Thors] in England during the . . . conference [proposed by the Soviets]?" Kennedy found the suggestion attractive, wanted to mull it over, but apparently told Macmillan that it might provoke the Soviets to insist on dismantlings in Turkey and Italy.[113]

Though Macmillan had proposed a temporary demobilization of his Thors, he later claimed that, despite the obsolescence of the Jupiters, he would not have agreed to the Soviet proposal on the 27th for their removal. Was this bravado created after the settlement? Perhaps.[114] But even if Macmillan might have privately questioned a public trade, as the dependent ally in the "special relationship" with the United States, he and his party would have probably defended such a trade publicly. Loyalty to America would have shaped the Conservative government's public statements.

During that week in late October, American analysts concluded that Britain, along with Norway and Denmark, would welcome a trade of the Jupiters to end the crisis.[115] They were undoubtedly correct about the two Scandinavian allies, which had steadfastly resisted the placing of any nuclear weapons on their soil. When the Soviets made their public demand for including the Jupiters in a settlement, Norwegian government officials endorsed removal of the weapons.[116]

Italy's center-left coalition government reluctantly supported the quarantine, tried to improve relations with the Soviets during the crisis, and anxiously urged Kennedy to negotiate with Khrushchev. On the 27th, when an American attack on Cuba seemed imminent, Premier Amintore Fanfani of the Christian Democrats wanted Kennedy to extend his deadline and probably favored the trade of Turkey's Jupiters. The Italian Socialist party, upon which the uneasy government coalition depended, had condemned the quarantine and probably welcomed the trade to end the crisis.[117]

In Canada, Prime Minister John Diefenbaker, long unhappy about America's dominance, was publicly tactful but privately critical of the president's actions. So troubled was Diefenbaker by Kennedy's unilateral decisions on the crisis and so fearful that Canada might be dragged into war that he wanted to bar Strategic Air Command (SAC) bombers from the use of Canadian airfields during the crisis.[118] His devout hope was that war could be avoided, and he did not seem to fear that concessions—and certainly not on the Jupiter—would seriously weaken the NATO alliance.

On Thursday, October 25, Andrew de Staercke, the Belgian ambassador to NATO, privately proposed the deal that the Soviets demanded two days later. He thought, wrote journalist Cyrus Sulzberger, "we should take the initiative in making such an offer." The bases were obsolete, the ambassador argued, and he did not see how the Soviets would withdraw their weapons unless the United States did something equal.[119] He apparently was not worried about the loss of prestige to the United States or the impact on NATO and seemed to believe that these matters were less important than a settlement. Unlike de Staercke, and presumably his government, Dutch officials privately opposed a trade on the grounds that it would undermine NATO's morale.[120] But Greek officials, while publicly discreet, seemed to lean toward de Staercke's analysis. When the Soviets demanded removal of the Jupiters, Greek officials privately indicated that this was an acceptable solution. "Compromise can be the only way out," one government member explained.[121]

In some important Latin American nations, despite their public statements supporting Kennedy, there was probably strong sentiment for a compromise involving the Jupiters, in either a public or private deal. The United States government had won unanimous support for the quarantine from the Organization of American States, but that unanimity had been secured, in at least a few cases, by some deft coercion. The main item on the OAS agenda had been United States economic aid, and Washington had first moved for a vote of support for the quarantine. The American message was clear: Aid could depend upon an affirmative vote.[122] Even then, some governments—including Brazil, Mexico, Bolivia, Argentina, and Uruguay—had feared providing full support for Kennedy's actions, as the State Department knew at the time.[123] Hostile to United States military intervention in Latin America, many governments there also worried about the backlash in their own countries from radical groups if the United States attacked Cuba. A trade, even a public one, for the Jupiters was attractive if an invasion was the alternative.

America's complex alliance system did rest partly upon faith in its credibility, but many governments also feared that efforts to affirm credibility could be rash and dangerous. They did not usually expect the United States to maintain blind allegiance, and, as the history of recent American foreign relations demonstrated, discretion, tempered force, and the willingness to compromise were also essential to operating the far-flung alliances.

THE SATURDAY CRISIS: EXCOMM DELIBERATIONS

Saturday was the most painful day of the crisis. For the president and the ExComm there were no easy answers: Should American promptly bomb the SAM sites, as the ExComm had previously agreed, in reprisal for the shootdown of the U-2? How should the administration respond to the Soviets' additional demand of publicly trading the Jupiters in Turkey to settle the crisis? The minutes reveal that the ExComm speedily disposed of the first question upon learning in the afternoon of the U-2 shootdown, but later in the day the president decided on military action if a plane was fired upon on Sunday. Throughout Saturday's three sessions, the ExComm and the president wrestled with the second question. That meant, for them, seeking to devise tactics for very different parties—the Soviet Union, Turkey, NATO, and the world public, as well as domestic America.

The transcript of the three sessions discloses sometimes desultory discussions, where speakers were oblique, rambling, and even confusing—both to later analysts and even to other ExComm members. Much of the problem was that these men were fatigued and frightened, carrying for 11 days the burden of perilous crisis, as they struggled to formulate advice with peace or war in the balance. Their use of convoluted phrasings, elaborate scenarios, and complicated hypotheticals and conditionals, replete with various contingencies and assumptions, could leave unclear—even to others at the session—whether a speaker was recommending a course of action, suggesting it as a possibility, simply analyzing pros and cons, or exploring it to emphasize its liabilities.

In the sessions, the president, Attorney General Robert Kennedy, Secretary of Defense Robert McNamara, national security adviser McGeorge Bundy, Secretary of State Dean Rusk, and special adviser for Soviet affairs Llewellyn Thompson were the most active participants. Surprisingly, the discussions, despite the president's frequent statement of inclinations, seem rather free and open. And contrary to many later reports, there was little evidence of rancor or acrimony among the men.

No one at the sessions spoke of his own fatigue, the future of his family if war came, or the destruction of America. Nor did they ever introduce moral or ethical standards to win a point or rebut an argument. They operated as tacticians and concealed whatever personal fears they felt. They knew—without any need for repeated reminders—that the decisions the president made could be truly momentous.

A few advisers wanted a prompt trade made publicly, as the Soviets demanded. Others hoped to arrange a way of pulling out the Jupiters, ideally without a clear trade. A public trade would injure Turkey, NATO, and America, according to their analysis. Was there some way of inducing Turkey to suggest withdrawal of these weapons? Or of placing their withdrawal in some broader context of disarmament? At various points, President Kennedy indicated that he did not want to yield to Soviet pressure, but that he would favor some sort of cosmetic arrangement to get rid of the Jupiters in order to settle the crisis. At a few junctures, he seemed desperate and prepared to countenance a more open trade. He also periodically emphasized that work on the Soviet missile sites must soon stop, and his lingering implication was that an attack might otherwise become necessary in the next few days. That was never the course he desired.

At times in the Saturday meetings, a few ExComm members, as well as the Joint Chiefs of Staff, suggested an attack—possibly first on the SAM sites and then on the missile sites, to be followed by an invasion. Such a proposal raised profound questions at the meetings: Would the Soviet Union then retaliate against Berlin or elsewhere? Wouldn't NATO and especially Turkey become a target? Could all-out war be avoided? An anxious group of weary men, hardly more than a dozen, assessed actions that could lead to war or peace. All recognized that the president, listening to their counsel and trying out his own notions in the group, had the constitutional and actual power of decision. The greatest burden and the final responsibility were his. He would have to choose what to do.

At the morning session, as through most of the day, the problem of how to respond to Khrushchev's Turkey deal was central. Assistant Secretary of Defense Paul Nitze, an ardent cold warrior since the Truman years, opposed the Soviet proposal at the beginning of the meeting: "It would be anathema to the Turks to pull the missiles out . . . the next Soviet step would be denuclearization of the entire NATO area."[124] His unstated implications were familiar: Concessions would only beget Soviet demands for more concessions. Where would America draw the line? Why should allies trust America's promises? Those concerns heavily influenced the discussion that day.

In the morning session, President Kennedy occasionally indicated that a trade might be necessary. Still not realizing that his own government had recently installed the Jupiters in Turkey, he said, "We last year tried to get the missiles out of there because they're not militarily useful." The Soviet offer, he acknowledged, would look to the UN "or any other rational men... like a fair trade." How, he wondered aloud, could his government justify military action against Cuba if the alternative was this trade?[125]

Facing what he admitted would look like a fair trade, the president felt that he had been politically cornered. Khrushchev had shrewdly played a clever card, and the president's associates had not protected him and the American government from this strategy. During the week, no arrangement had been worked out to get the Jupiters out of Turkey. "Now we've known this was coming for a week," he complained. The transcript reveals his dismay and testiness when he learned that the Turks had not even been approached about giving up the Jupiters:

JFK: How much negotiation have we had with the Turks?

Rusk: We haven't talked with the Turks. The Turks have talked with—the Turks have talked with us in—uh—NATO.

JFK: Well, have we gone to the Turkish government before this came out this week? I've talked about it now for a week. Have we had any conversation in Turkey, with the Turks?

Rusk: We've asked [ambassadors] Finletter and Hare to give us their judgments on it. We've not actually talked to the Turks?

Ball: We did it on a basis where if we talked to the Turks, I mean this would be an extremely unsettling business.

JFK: . . . [T]his is unsettling *now* George, because he's got us in a pretty good spot here, because most people will regard this as not an unreasonable proposal, I'll just tell you that.[126]

While scolding Ball, the president did not contend that he had actually ordered action on the Jupiters. Most likely, he had actually thought that discussions were being conducted; he had not ordered either discussions or withdrawal of the Jupiters. In this crisis, feeling that Khrushchev had cornered him, the president undoubtedly found it tempting to recall, in a self-serving way, that his earlier inclinations were clear and that subordinates should have acted upon his notions. In his mind, he may have converted those inclinations into desires. But he seemed to recognize that he had never given an order. His disappointment was sincere—about the situation and about the lack of initiative among key subordinates. But he was not about to take—and possibly not even to recognize—his own responsibility for the situation: the Jupiters being in Turkey. Yet, as he knew, presidential *desires* are most likely to be acted on when they are expressed as *orders*.

Bundy, picking up on Nitze's themes, warned that the Turks would conclude "that we are trying to sell [out] our allies for our interest. That would be the view in all of NATO. It's irrational, and it's crazy, but it's a *terribly* powerful fact."[127]

Only rather briefly, in the morning session, did the ExComm puzzle over the second letter—why the Soviets raised the ante, what it meant, and whether Khrushchev had been overruled? Surprisingly, the discussion never focused sharply on this important set of questions. Llewellyn Thompson, a former ambassador to the Soviet Union and the recognized Soviet expert in the ExComm, thought that Khrushchev was still in control and that he had gotten the idea for the Jupiter trade from Austrian Foreign Minister Bruno Kreisky's public suggestion. Bundy speculated that Khrushchev had been overruled in the Kremlin, thus forcing the Jupiter demand.[128] In the Ex-Comm, no one discussed what it might mean if Bundy was correct and hardliners in the Kremlin had come to the fore: Would that require more American flexibility? Might additional challenges emerge from the Kremlin? Most ExComm members simply assumed—as later proved correct—that Khrushchev was still in charge.

In the morning, when they discussed Kennedy's possible reply to the Soviet terms, C. Douglas Dillon, the secretary of the treasury and a Republican, proposed that the president send a message that placed the Jupiters in a broad European context. The president could tell the Soviets "that the Turkey proposal opens the way for a major discussion of a lot of tensions in Europe, including Berlin." That approach was quickly opposed by Rusk, among others, on the grounds that it would frighten the Germans.[129]

Kennedy "regretted that the Soviets had made the Turkish proposal in the most difficult possible way." Khrushchev had "put this out in a way that's caused the maximum tension and embarrassment," the president complained. Because the Soviet demand was public, "we have no chance to talk privately to the Turks about the missiles. . . ." At times that morning, the president favored removing the Jupiters, but he did not want to appear to be yielding to a Soviet demand, lest he lose prestige and credibility, injure Turkey and NATO, and give the Soviets a public victory.[130]

The Soviets have "a very good card" in the Jupiter offer, the president stressed. "This one is going to be very tough, I think, for us. It's going to be tough in England, I'm sure—as well as other places on the continent. . . .

Most . . . people think if you're allowed an even trade you ought to take *advantage* of it. Therefore it makes it more difficult to move with world support [if we reject it and then have to take military action]."[131]

The Soviets' suggested trade of their 42 MRBMs (then believed by American experts to constitute about a third of the Soviet strategic missile arsenal)[132] for 15 obsolete Jupiters was attractive on military grounds, Kennedy acknowledged. He thought that there might be a way of achieving a settlement without risking American prestige or injuring NATO. "We cannot propose to withdraw the missiles," he explained, "but the Turks could offer to do so. [T]hey must be informed of the great danger . . . and we have to face up to the possibility of some kind of a trade over the missiles."[133] In that morning session, Kennedy was the chief "dove"—but unwilling to make a prompt trade.

The minutes for the morning, like those for later that day, reveal a sense of desperation, that events were taking control, that action was restricted to unpalatable alternatives. The 42 MRBMs, even with the addition of 12, 16, or 32 IRBMs, did not alter the strategic balance[134] nor make a Soviet nuclear attack on the United States more likely. But no ExComm member challenged the dominating assumption: The United States could not delay for more than a few days. Yet, if the work on the sites ceased (even though nearly all the MRBMs were reported operational), "we could talk to the Russians," Kennedy said.[135]

The two-hour morning meeting ended with agreement on a brief public reply to Khrushchev's demand. That White House statement, widely interpreted in the press as outright rejection, was actually more subtle and elusive.[136] It left the door slightly ajar for some future agreement on the Jupiters, but never explicitly mentioned them. It sidestepped the Soviet demand, asserted that negotiations were impossible until work stopped (called a "standstill" in the ExComm) on the missile sites and they were rendered inoperable, declared that Cuba and European security could not be linked, but mentioned the possibility of post-settlement discussions on arms limitations in Europe and thus hinted (it seems, in retrospect) at a willingness to consider removal of the Jupiters after the resolution of the crisis.[137]

Neither the morning deliberations nor that public statement had resolved the basic problem of how to respond to the Soviet offer. At the beginning of the afternoon meeting, the president said that he did not expect Khrushchev to accept a standstill arrangement but believed that a Soviet rejection would somewhat shift world opinion and help the United States. Kennedy still hoped to prepare the way for a trade of the Jupiters and wanted support from the NATO Council, possibly even their recommendation for such action. But some advisers warned that NATO might instead disapprove and, in Ball's words, tie "our hands." Kennedy, in contrast, believed that if the stark alternative—an American invasion of Cuba and Soviet reprisal in Europe—was spelled out, the allies might well agree to a trade. Dillon warned, however, that there might be a different response: "Don't trade" and "Don't do anything in Cuba."[138] Adding to the negative counsel, Thompson pointed out that the Soviet terms would still allow Soviet planes and technicians in Cuba and "that would surely be unacceptable and put you in a worse position."[139]

To Kennedy, however, not accepting the Soviet offer looked far worse. As he said, "I'm just thinking about—what we are going to have to do in a day or so, which is [censored] sorties and [censored] days, and possibly an invasion, all because we wouldn't take missiles out of Turkey, and we all know how quickly everybody's courage goes when the blood starts to flow, and that's what's going to happen in NATO, when they—we start these things, and they grab Berlin, and everybody's going to say, 'Well that was a pretty good proposition.' . . . Today it sounds great to reject it, but it's not going to, after we do something."[140]

TROLLOPE PLOY ASCENDANT?

Some Excomm members were more inclined than the president to gamble at least briefly and not move toward the Turkey trade. Starting with Bundy in the morning, a few, including Sorensen, proposed disregarding the Soviets' Saturday letter and responding instead to their offer of Friday. (This tactic of actually accepting the earlier offer and of making no explicit reference to the later one would be dubbed the "Trollope ploy" after the plot in Anthony Trollope's novels where a young woman interprets a flirtation, an offer not made, as a marriage proposal.)[141] Kennedy feared that this tactic would simply delay matters while work on the missiles in Cuba continued and that Khrushchev would reply, "What about my second letter?" And then, Kennedy told the ExComm, "we're going to be screwing around for *another* forty-eight hours."[142]

Initially rejecting this Trollope ploy, Kennedy argued that the Soviets would not remove their missiles without a trade. Disagreeing, Thompson, the Soviet expert, advised, "There's still a chance we can get this line [working out a deal on the basis of the first letter] going." Thompson maintained that Kennedy's acceptance of the Friday offer, which required an American no-invasion pledge, would give Khrushchev a victory. He could "say 'I saved Cuba, I stopped an invasion' and he can get *away* with this..."

But Kennedy was still dubious. Because Khrushchev had made his Saturday letter public, the president said, "how can he take his missiles out of Cuba... if we just do nothing about Turkey?"[143] Nevertheless, the president was willing to be persuaded and soon decided to endorse the Trollope ploy.

The implications of guaranteeing not to attack Cuba raised no discussion in the ExComm. No one mentioned the various CIA attempts (some recently endorsed by Attorney General Kennedy) to overthrow Castro and the American-supported émigré attacks on Cuba in recent months.[144] There was brief consideration of asking Eisenhower to endorse the pledge, and thus presumably to defang GOP criticism, but no one pushed this political strategy.[145]

The president was under strong pressure to move away from trying negotiations and instead endorsing military action. In the middle of the afternoon session, General Maxwell Taylor, chairman of the Joint Chiefs of Staff, told the ExComm that the JCS recommended that the "big strike" on Cuba be executed no later than Monday morning unless there was firm evidence that the offensive weapons in Cuba were being dismantled, and that an invasion should soon follow.[146]

"That was a surprise," Robert Kennedy snidely remarked about the bellicose JCS counsel.[147] The President brushed aside this dangerous JCS advice and returned to the problems posed by the Turkey offer. President Kennedy kept saying that he wanted the Turks to propose, or at least calmly accept, withdrawal of the Jupiters. He knew, as others had pointed out, that a Polaris submarine could be substituted for the 15 Jupiters. He stressed, as he had earlier, that the crisis could soon get worse and that NATO members would bitterly regret getting dragged into a war if it could have been avoided by a settlement on the Jupiters.[148]

These considerations were briefly halted by the painful news in the afternoon that an American U-2 had been shot down over Cuba. "This is much of an escalation by them, isn't it?" asked the president. "Yes, exactly," replied McNamara, who opposed immediate escalation by the United States, saying that an attack on Cuba could still be delayed for a few days, until Wednesday or Thursday, if surveillance and the quarantine were maintained.[149]

Kennedy feared that the Soviets' Jupiter demand and then this shootdown constituted a Soviet decision to get much tougher. The Soviets "feel they must respond now," stated General Taylor. "The whole world knows we're flying [over Cuba]." Taylor wanted speedy retaliation against the SAM sites. The president, McNamara, and others seemed briefly to agree, but slowly they backed away. Such action, they understood, would kill thousands of

Soviet soldiers in Cuba and could start a risky chain of escalation—Berlin, Turkey, . . . [150]

The ExComm returned to the nagging problem of the Soviet demand on the Jupiters. McNamara proposed that the Turks and also NATO could be forced to accept an American trade with the promise of a Polaris as a replacement. Withdrawal of the Jupiters, he explained, could be justified to them "as relieving the Alliance" of a target. To dramatize the dangers to NATO and Turkey, a message could be sent to these European allies warning them that an American invasion of Cuba was likely and that the Jupiters were likely targets for Soviet retaliation. He acknowledged that an invasion might soon be necessary. At least one ExComm member concluded that McNamara was actually proposing defusing the Jupiters, informing the Soviets, and then attacking Cuba.[151]

Toward the end of this three-hour afternoon meeting, Vice President Lyndon Johnson, who seldom spoke, George Ball, and CIA director John McCone all pushed for a speedy trade of the Jupiters. Johnson reminded them that last week they had feared that Khrushchev would demand a trade involving Berlin. "We were afraid . . . he'd never offer this." Take it, said the vice president. "I'd say, sure, we'll accept your offer," advised Ball. Don't worry about NATO, he told a questioning Bundy, "if NATO isn't any better than that, it isn't that good to us." McCone, a conservative Republican, declared, "I'd trade those Turkish things out right now. I wouldn't even talk to anybody about it."[152]

This counsel evoked some comments about the ExComm's thinking during the past 11 days. "I said [last week] I thought it was the realistic solution to the problem," stated McNamara. Bundy recalled, "We were going to let him [Khrushchev] have his strike in Turkey, as I understood it last week . . . at least that was the way we talked about it." "Yeah, that's right," said McNamara. "That was one alternative."[153]

Unfortunately, these recorded recollections do not allow analysts to reconstruct with any assurance the details or the depth of the commitment to the earlier alternative of letting the Soviets strike Turkey that Bundy mentioned. He implied that it had been more than a theoretical option, that some ExComm members had seriously proposed it. Bundy's phrasing of "*let* him" suggests that they had not intended to retaliate—at least not against the Soviets. Perhaps a Soviet attack on the Jupiters had been viewed the preceding week as the necessary price for an American attack on the Soviet missiles in Cuba.

But on Saturday afternoon, Llewellyn Thompson, the acknowledged Soviet expert, found the advice from Johnson, Ball, and McCone unpalatable. Taking a tough position, Thompson stated: "These boys [the Soviets] are beginning to give way. Let's push harder. I think they'll change their minds when we take continued forceful action, stopping their ship [a tanker headed toward the quarantine line] or taking out a SAM-site." Don't send an ultimatum, he advised, just bomb a SAM site. He said that Khrushchev had either been overruled in the Kremlin or deceived by recent articles (Foreign Minister Kreisky's publicized suggestion and a similar column by Walter Lippmann recommending a trade of the Jupiters), and thus the Soviets had chosen to try the Turkey proposal.[154] No one asked Thompson why he was unworried if, as he speculated, Khrushchev might have been overruled in the Kremlin. Perhaps Thompson was implying that resisting the demand of the hardliners, if they were in power, would strengthen those who endorsed a softer line.

Johnson, hearing Thompson's advice, called him a "warhawk."[155] But the Soviet expert's counsel triumphed in the ExComm in a limited way. They agreed not to make a Turkey trade. There would be time for the Trollope ploy first. That message could be dispatched, and others for NATO and Turkey would be drafted warning of imminent crisis.

The president was not optimistic that the Trollope letter would succeed. But he did not seem uneasy about trying it—even if it meant losing a day, as he had lamented earlier. If it failed, as he thought likely, he would have to take the next step. Revealing his own inclinations, he said in the last recorded minutes of the afternoon meeting, "We can't very well invade Cuba . . . when we could have gotten them out by making a deal on the same missiles in Turkey."[156]

After this three-hour session, the president's "Trollope ploy" letter was delivered to the Soviets. It included a sharp warning: "The continuation of this threat, or a prolonging of this discussion concerning Cuba by linking these problems to the broader questions of European and world security, would surely lead to an intensification of the Cuban crisis and a grave risk to the peace of the world."[157] At the same time, aides were drafting a possible letter to Sunday's meeting of the NATO Council: "The United States is willing, if the other members of the NATO alliance so desire, to render the Jupiter missiles in Turkey inoperative by removal of their warheads and to notify the Soviet Government to such an effect prior to moving against the Soviet missiles in Cuba."[158]

SATURDAY NIGHT EXCOMM MEETING: HOPES AND FEARS

When the ExComm reconvened that evening at nine, the group discussed continuing aerial surveillance of Cuba, adding pressure on the Soviets, handling Sunday's special NATO meeting, responding on the Turkey-Cuba missile trade, and possibly invading Cuba.

The session opened with renewed concern about surveillance. Amid fears that another American plane might be shot down, McNamara urged low-level flights; if the plane was fired upon, there should be a prompt "attack on the attackers." The president wanted to delay retaliation while hoping for a favorable reply to his Trollope letter. But if an American plane was fired at on Sunday, he explained, then there would be retaliation on Monday after the issuance of a warning. Destroy "all those SAM-sites," he said.[159]

To add pressure on the Soviets, the president agreed on a publicized call-up of 24 Air Force reserve squadrons involving about 14,000 men. He also indicated that he would soon tighten the quarantine to block all petroleum, oil, and lubricants. But he decided to delay a decision on whether or not to stop a Soviet tanker that would soon reach the quarantine line.[160]

The president decided not to ask the NATO Council for advice nor to seek their support on Sunday for a possible trade. On his brother's recommendation, the president agreed that the message should tell NATO representatives that the United States had disregarded the Jupiter trade and accepted the Friday offer, that a U-2 had been shot down and the crisis was becoming more dangerous, and that the United States would soon call another meeting (probably on Monday) if the Trollope letter did not succeed.[161]

If the Soviets insisted upon the removal of the Jupiters, Robert Kennedy explained, the president could still make suggestions to the NATO Council. The attorney general left unclear whether such advice should be for yielding or standing firm. He ended by stating that if the NATO representatives "say, 'We want to hold fast,' then on Tuesday we go in [invade Cuba]." His implication was that war was very near.[162]

Such a frightening implication was soon softened by the president himself. He sketched to the ExComm what he thought he should tell America's ambassador to Turkey:

> Let's give him an explanation of what we're trying to do. We're trying to get it back on the original proposition of last night . . . because we don't want to get into this [Jupiters] trade. If it's unsuccessful, then we—it's *possible* that we may have to get back on the Jupiter thing. If we do, then we would of course want it

to come from the Turks themselves and NATO, rather than just the United States. We're hopeful, however, that that won't come. If it does, his judgment on how it should be handled . . . we're prepared to do the Polaris and others, does he think this thing can be made? We'll be in touch with him in twenty-four hours when we find out if we're successful in putting the Russians back on the original track.[163]

Technically, John F. Kennedy's sketch only outlined the *possibility* of a deal, if necessary. But at no point had the president chosen to stress the likelihood that he would select war instead. His words then, especially when read in the context of his many earlier statements that day, made clear that he was inclined, if necessary, to work out some kind of Jupiter trade. It was an inclination, not a commitment. There was no expressed decision.

At the end of that Saturday session, when McNamara asked Robert Kennedy whether he had any doubts about the decisions made, the attorney general replied, "I think we're doing the only thing we can . . ." McNamara seemed less confident and certainly more troubled. He told the ExComm that they should "have two things ready, a government for Cuba, because we're going to need one and secondly, plans for how to respond to the Soviet Union in Europe because sure as hell they're going to do something there." One ExComm member (unidentified in the transcript) offered his own ghoulish humor to end this chilling session, "Suppose we make Bobby mayor of Havana."[164]

About two hours after that comment, special messages went out to Finletter for Sunday's NATO meeting and for American ambassadors to deliver to Charles de Gaulle and Konrad Adenauer. Among the themes emphasized to Finletter was that he should not "hint of any [American] readiness to meet Soviet Jupiter exchange proposal" and that he "should strongly press the point that U.S. action in Cuba—if it becomes essential—will be directed at a potential threat to the total strategic balance endangering other NATO countries at least as much as the United States."[165] That last theme, reaching well beyond McNamara's earlier counsel that the Soviet missiles were not a military threat, was probably framed to prepare NATO allies to support such military action, if America chose to embark on such a course. Yet, this message could also be interpreted, after the passage of years, in a less frightening way: It was communicating to NATO allies America's steadfast commitment to the alliance and to the maintenance of credibility, and there was hope that the Soviets would learn of such American resoluteness and try to settle speedily.

The special messages from Kennedy to Adenauer and de Gaulle seem more alarming: "The situation is clearly growing more tense and if satisfactory responses are not received from the other side in forty-eight hours, the situation is likely to enter a progressively military phase." The implication could be interpreted as—invasion by Tuesday.[166]

Capturing some of the fear suggested by these messages, Secretary McNamara much later recalled his own anxieties earlier that Saturday evening when Kennedy's Trollope reply had been dispatched to the Soviets. "I remember the sunset. We left about the time the sun was setting in October, and I, at least, was so uncertain as to whether the Soviets would accept replying to the first instead of the second . . . that I wondered if I'd ever see another Saturday sunset like that."[167]

SATURDAY'S RFK – DOBRYNIN MEETING: CHANGING DISCLOSURES ABOUT A SECRET DEAL

So far, this discussion has omitted an important set of events that Saturday evening: Robert Kennedy's secret meeting with Soviet Ambassador Anatoly Dobrynin, at 7:45, before the evening session of the ExComm. Acting on the instructions of the president and Secretary Rusk, the attorney general invited Dobrynin to a private meeting at the Justice Department. According to Robert Kennedy's memoir, *Thirteen Days* (1969), the attorney general delivered both a virtual ultimatum and a loose promise. The ultimatum was: "If the [Soviets] did not remove these [missiles], we would remove them."[168] And in response to Dobrynin's question about America's withdrawing the Jupiters from Turkey, according to Robert Kennedy's secret memorandum, confirmed by his memoir, there was also a loose promise: "There could be no quid pro quo—no deal of this kind could be made [on removal of the Jupiters]. It was up to NATO to make the decision. I said it was completely impossible for NATO to take such a step under the present threatening position . . . If some time elapsed—and per . . . instructions—I said I was sure that these matters could be resolved satisfactorily."[169]

This 1969 revelation of a "carrot and stick" approach, coming as it did from a memoir by the president's brother, changed the interpretation of the missile crisis for some analysts.[170] They concluded that the president on October 27 had been privately more flexible and willing to carve out a reasonable settlement than his public statements of the day and some early memoirists had made him seem. Yet, crucial questions lingered: What would have happened if Khrushchev had rejected this private, hedged offer (dependent on Turkey and NATO) when he had demanded a firm public deal?

Would Kennedy have moved further toward a settlement, increased pressure on the Soviets, or risked war by taking military action in Cuba?

In the past few years, ExComm members have revealed new evidence—or at least made different claims from those in *Thirteen Days*—about Robert Kennedy's Saturday evening meeting with Dobrynin. This release of information, controlled by a few ExComm members, has encouraged further reinterpretation, with the "carrot" being described as more juicy. The accuracy of these revelations cannot really be checked, because the key documents—especially Robert Kennedy's own diary—remain unavailable to independent scholars. Under the impact of these revelations, Robert Kennedy's seemingly hedged, private offer has been redefined: first, as a firm, unhedged promise but not part of a deal; and now, more recently, as a private *deal* actually trading the Jupiters.

This set of revelations merits brief summary, for it can be instructive about the power of former government officials to control scholars', and plain citizens', knowledge and understanding of crucial events after some 30 years.

In 1983, a few ExComm members, including Bundy and McNamara, implied that Robert Kennedy had actually offered a firm, unilateral promise—not a deal, and not hedged by requiring Turkey's and NATO's approval—to remove the Jupiters.[171] More recently, Bundy, though claiming to deny that there had been any firm, private deal on the missiles and stating that Robert Kennedy had only made a "unilateral private assurance"—provided substantial evidence that there may well have been such a deal trading the Jupiters.[172]

Bundy and a few other ExComm members also provided valuable information about a secret meeting, held after the second Saturday session of the ExComm, leading to the attorney general's conference with Dobrynin that evening. Right after the second ExComm session, according to these new revelations, a small group met briefly with the president and Robert Kennedy: Rusk, McNamara, Bundy, Sorensen, Ball, Thompson, and Undersecretary of Defense Roswell Gilpatric. At that session, Rusk proposed that the attorney general should make a private arrangement on the Jupiters with the Soviet ambassador.[173]

According to Bundy's 1988 book, "the proposal was quickly supported by the rest of us and approved by the president. It was also agreed that knowledge of this . . . would be held among those present and no one else. Concerned as we were by the cost of a public bargain struck under pressure at the apparent expense of the Turks . . . we agreed without hesitation that no one not in the room was to be informed of this additional message."[174]

Shortly after Bundy's book appeared, Dobrynin complained in 1989 that American representatives were still refusing to acknowledge that the Jupiters were part of an *explicit* Soviet-American *deal* to settle the missile crisis.[175] Listening to Dobrynin, Sorensen promptly agreed with him. Sorensen confessed that he had long deceived virtually all Americans about this. Sorensen stated that the Jupiters were part of an explicit deal, that Robert Kennedy's own manuscript diary makes this clear, and that Sorensen had "edited out" this information before *Thirteen Days* was posthumously published. Here is Sorensen's own 1989 statement:

> Ambassador Dobrynin felt that Robert Kennedy's book did not adequately express that the "deal" on the Turkish missiles was part of the resolution of the crisis. And here I have a confession to make to my colleagues on the American side, as well as to others who are present. I was the editor of Robert Kennedy's book. It was, in fact, a diary of those thirteen days. And his diary was very explicit that this was part of the deal; but at that time it was still a secret even on the American side, except for the six of us who had been present at that meeting. So I took it upon myself to edit that out of his diaries, and that is why the Ambassador is somewhat justified in saying that the diaries are not as explicit as his conversation.[176]

According to Sorensen's newest version (1989), the president had also recognized the value to Khrushchev, in dealing with his colleagues in the Presidium, of being able to say privately, "we have been assured that the missiles will be coming out of Turkey."[177]

KHRUSHCHEV AND THE DANGERS
PROPELLING A SPEEDY SETTLEMENT

On Sunday, October 28, 1962, Khrushchev publicly yielded on the missiles in Cuba. He had accepted a *private* arrangement even though it did not meet his demand for a public deal. Why?

Khrushchev may have been largely pushed to accept because he had good reason to fear the imminence of war. Events were getting out of control. He was having great difficulties with Castro. The Cuban leader had agreed in the early summer to accept the Soviet missiles as a way of defending Cuba, maintaining solidarity with the Soviet Union, and possibly even protecting Communist revolutions elsewhere. Undoubtedly, Castro had not foreseen that the Soviet missiles, somewhat like the Jupiters in Turkey, might be more provocative than military useful. Certainly, he had not anticipated that they would provoke a crisis and seem to increase the likelihood of war.[178]

But by Friday, October 26, Castro secretly told Khrushchev that an American attack—against the missile sites, and possibly also an invasion—seemed very likely in the next three days. Castro promised, in a combination of bravado and desperation, that "we will firmly and resolutely resist attack, whatever it may be."[179]

In this secret message, Castro stated that the Soviets should launch a preemptive nuclear strike against the United States *if* it actually invaded Cuba and aimed to occupy it. For the Soviets, Castro argued, such an act "would be . . . clear legitimate defense." It was not vengeance that Castro claimed to be seeking, though that may well have been his motive. Rather, he explained, the dangerous alternative was for the Soviet Union to be the victim of a likely American preemptive strike against the Soviet heartland.[180]

Castro's frightening counsel arrived in Moscow shortly before Saturday's unsettling reports. On Saturday, Khrushchev concluded that the Cubans shot down a U-2, Robert Kennedy warned Dobrynin that another attack on an American surveillance plane would mean that the United States "would shoot back,"[181] and to make matters worse, Castro's October 26 message suggested that the Cubans would continue to attack American planes over the island.[182] Added to all of this, apparently, was Robert Kennedy's Saturday evening threat, delivered to Dobrynin: America would soon attack the missiles in Cuba if the Soviets did not speedily agree to remove them.[183]

For Khrushchev, even without Robert Kennedy's Saturday evening ultimatum of imminent American action to destroy the missiles in Cuba, the dangers had come to seem both powerful and escalating. What would happen, the Soviet leader had to worry, if the Cubans, as seemed likely, did shoot at American planes, and President Kennedy retaliated by bombing Cuban antiaircraft sites, or both Cuban and Soviet sites, and possibly the missiles themselves? How many of the 43,000 Soviets, and millions of Cubans, would have been killed? What then? If an invasion followed, would Soviet troops have used their *tactical nuclear* weapons? And then?

Under such pressures, with an ally the Soviets could not control, Khrushchev had to try to arrange a settlement speedily. Had he not been offered a private deal on the Jupiters, he might have still felt forced, by the likely events that Castro could unleash, to work out an even less satisfactory agreement along the lines of Friday's suggested terms—simply gaining a no-invasion pledge. Events were closing in, as Khrushchev (better than Kennedy and the ExComm) knew.

Khrushchev certainly could not take the risk of holding out for a public deal involving the Jupiters. By accepting the private deal, rather than the public one he had sought on Saturday, he could not save face internationally.

That would be a considerable price to pay—a lost opportunity partly smashed by Castro. Publicly, despite the announced likelihood of an American announced no-invasion pledge, Khrushchev would appear to all the world to have yielded to an American demand: Back down and risk public humiliation; or, delay, and have Cuba attacked and many of the 43,000 Soviets there killed; and, then back down or escalate.

KENNEDY'S FULFILLMENT OF THE SECRET DEAL: REMOVING THE JUPITERS

Americans and others, despite some dissents, long celebrated the handling of the missile crisis as Kennedy's "finest hour." Top American officials long concealed and even denied the Turkey-Cuba missile deal. On October 29, Rusk cabled Ambassadors Hare and Finletter that "no 'deal' of any kind was made involving Turkey."[184] In 1963, McNamara told the House Appropriations Committee, "without any qualifications whatsoever there was absolutely no deal . . . between the Soviet Union and the United States regarding the removal of the Jupiter weapons from either Italy or Turkey."[185] Such assurances were certainly less than candid. A small group of American officials, including McNamara and Rusk, generally agreed to lie in order to protect the NATO alliance, affirm national credibility, and help the administration and the president at home.

Acting soon after the crisis to fulfill the secret deal, President Kennedy authorized the removal of the Jupiters. McNamara personally promised that he would take responsibility for handling this matter, and he promptly delegated the task to John McNaughton, who was a trusted aide and the department's legal counsel. "And I said to John," McNamara later stated, "I'm going to tell you something. I don't want you to ask any questions about it. I don't want you to say to anybody else why it's being done, 'cause I'm not going to tell you, I just want you to do it, and I want every single missile removed out of Turkey."[186] Undoubtedly, McNaughton, a shrewd man, understood what he had not been explicitly told: that some kind of deal had been made, and that it had to be kept secret.

But the process of speedy removal was not easy. On November 9, Rusk advised President Kennedy that the 15 Jupiters in Turkey and 30 in Italy should not be withdrawn in "the near future." There were powerful political and military reasons, Rusk argued, against their prompt removal.[187]

The Jupiters could be useful in an American first strike, Rusk noted, because they were targeted against 45 of the 129 Soviet MRBM-IRBM sites. The Jupiters were also useful sponges in the event of a Soviet first strike, because the 45 missiles would be targets for Soviet weapons that would otherwise be aimed elsewhere, at Western Europe. Beyond such military arguments, according to Rusk, there were also strong political considerations. If the Jupiters were soon removed, American credibility would be found wanting, and allies besides Turkey and Italy might no longer trust the United States. But "as more modern and effective weapons systems come into being . . . and as the Cuban missile crisis recedes, the phasing out of the [Jupiters] would at a later time be entirely feasible."[188]

Rusk's political argument, though vague on how soon the crisis would recede, could certainly fit within the rough confines of Robert Kennedy's secret promise to Dobrynin that the missiles would come out in about five months. Rusk's military argument, despite the possible attractions of the Jupiters serving as a sponge, was quite weak. They might even be a menace on technological grounds. Treasury Secretary Douglas Dillon had recently told Kennedy that the weapons "were flops and this would have been proved if they had [used them during the recent crisis]."[189]

Within the government, other advisers who did not know about the deal strongly advised against withdrawing the missiles from Turkey. "[T]his could create one hell of a mess," concluded Robert Komer, a Bundy aide, in early November. "Early removal of JUPITERS would revive all [our allies'] latent fears [even though] our Cuban performance has greatly bucked [them] up," Komer told Bundy.[190] In early January 1963, Komer, still ignorant of the deal, tried to persuade the president not to remove the weapons. "Turkish political outlook is quite uncertain and we see trouble ahead," Komer reported.[191]

Komer's advice undoubtedly had no effect. Rusk's counsel may have slightly delayed the actual removal of the weapons, but the delay was not lengthy. Kennedy's order to McNamara would be implemented. In such cases, a presidential directive to a high-level adviser, when each man agrees on the importance of the command, is very likely to be efficiently enacted. Presidential will expressed as an *order* was not thwarted. Whatever the problems in removing the Jupiters, they were overcome. On April 25, 1963, six months after the Cuban missile crisis, McNamara informed President Kennedy, "the last Jupiter came down [in Turkey] yesterday," and it would be flown out at the end of the week.[192] A Polaris submarine with 16 missiles was deployed to the area to replace the Jupiters. That exchange of weaponry received little publicity, and American officials would long choose to deny that a secret deal had been made and fulfilled.[193] As a result, the missile crisis seemed to prove, for many years, that Kennedy's resolute toughness had produced a great triumph for him and for America.

WHAT WOULD JFK HAVE DONE IF KHRUSHCHEV HADN'T RETREATED ON SUNDAY?

But what if Khrushchev had not retreated by Sunday morning, October 28, and not agreed to remove the missiles from Cuba? What would the president have done? A few of the memoirists,[194] Robert Kennedy included, asserted that America would *soon* have attacked Cuba. That is dubious. Actually, there were some tentative plans, far short of invasion, to add more pressure first: tightening the quarantine to block all petroleum, oil, and lubricants.[195] Such action would have further injured Cuba's beleaguered economy and also added to the appearance of American resolve. Yet, how long might the president have stayed with this tightened quarantine and not further escalated, or settled, in the next few days—especially with forthcoming elections in the United States?

Some evidence has recently become available that helps address this question. In 1987, in a statement that even surprised former ExComm members, Dean Rusk said that the president, on that fateful Saturday evening, October 27, had directed him to open a secret conduit to the UN as an *option* for a public deal. According to Rusk, Kennedy "instructed me to telephone . . . Andrew Cordier, then at Columbia University, and dictate to him a statement which would be made by U Thant, the Secretary General of the United Nations, proposing the removal of both the Jupiters and the missiles in Cuba. Mr. Cordier was to put that statement in the hands of U Thant only after a further signal from us."[196] (In 1990, Rusk altered the implication of his recollection by explaining that *he* had actually proposed this Cordier route and that Kennedy had then approved setting up this option.)[197] Rusk himself seemed to believe that the president, if matters had become dangerously stalemated, would have used such a route: "It was clear to me that President Kennedy would not let the Jupiters in Turkey become an obstacle."[198]

Rusk's claims about setting up this Cordier route as an option seem truthful when read in the context of other recent revelations and claims.[199] Rusk's disclosure underscores Kennedy's flexibility and his resourcefulness. John F. Kennedy was devising a way, if necessary, of making a public deal but of having it appear as a UN proposal and thus blunting some criticism of himself for softness.

Would the president have seized upon this route or some similar arrangement to have struck such a public deal? Probably. He could have punctured some criticisms by also announcing that a Polaris submarine, stationed near Turkey, would actually offset the Jupiters and add, less provocatively, to both Turkey's and America's security. Yet, the president would still have appeared weak to many American citizens, an especially dangerous situation with congressional elections coming up, and weak to some allies. These were risks he *probably* would have been willing to take even while recognizing that the costs might be painful.[200]

To conclude, as this chapter does, that President John F. Kennedy would probably have yielded is also to acknowledge that it is *possible* that he would not. That possibility, even though slim, should be chilling to all who examine and assess the missile crisis. That possibility, as well as the various matters that went dangerously out of control during the crisis,[201] should be chastening to all analysts—and especially to those who would celebrate these 13 days as John F. Kennedy's "finest hour."

CONCLUSIONS AND IMPLICATIONS: RECONSIDERING THE MISSILE CRISIS

This chapter, while generally focusing on the Jupiters, has occasionally broadened to present a larger interpretation of the missile crisis: its causes, its dangers, and its settlement. In looking at the Jupiters, the chapter establishes that the Kennedy administration, not Eisenhower's, actually deployed the weapons in Turkey; that Eisenhower's had made the original agreement but seemed wary of sending the missiles; and that Kennedy himself was uneasy after, and probably before, the 1961 deployment decision but never gave an *order* before October 28, 1962, to remove these missiles. Well before the October crisis, some men in and near the Kennedy administration had privately likened the American emplacement of missiles in Turkey to a Soviet missile deployment in Cuba. Such private fears of a "double standard" were rejected uniformly by the administration in its public statements during the crisis, and the trusting national press, as well as most citizens, accepted this self-serving analysis. None knew that the president himself, at an early ExComm session, had both forgotten his role in sending the Jupiters to Turkey and had even seen similarities between such a deployment and the Soviet action in Cuba.

Khrushchev was deeply troubled by the American Jupiter deployment, complaining privately and publicly both before and after this extension of American missiles near his borders. That deployment, amid America's overwhelming strategic superiority, helped trigger Khrushchev's spring 1962 decision to place Soviet missiles in Cuba in order to narrow the imbalance and to defend Cuba. Ironically, he complained to the American ambassador about the Jupiters on the very day when President Kennedy learned, to his shock, of the Soviet MRBMs in Cuba.

Contrary to most early interpretations of the missile crisis, the problem of the Jupiters, and even the prospects of a deal involving them, periodically popped up within the administration during the early days of the crisis. Other advisers besides UN Ambassador Adlai Stevenson suggested, or flirted with, the possibility of a trade. (Kennedy would later skewer Stevenson by representing him as the dangerous, lone dove—JFK's words were, "Adlai wanted a Munich"—to trusting journalists, who blared the "news" and concealed the source.)[202] During the second week of the crisis, even before the Soviet demand of October 27, a trade received serious consideration within the administration. President Kennedy himself was even trying to prepare the way, in dealings with Turkey, to work out such possible arrangements.

On Saturday, October 27, after the Soviets made their public demand, some ExComm members, and most notably the president, were willing to make a trade—privately if possible, perhaps publicly if necessary. Even deceiving some ExComm members, the president, acting secretly with a small group of advisers, sent Robert Kennedy early in the evening of that fateful Saturday to offer Ambassador Dobrynin a private trade. That evening, concealing arrangements from most advisers, the president also agreed to preparations for a UN conduit for a public deal, if the proposed private one did not gain Kremlin approval.

These conclusions constitute an important reinterpretation of the October crisis, especially the nature of the final settlement. It was partly a private deal, with an important secret concession on the Jupiters. Thus, the settlement was not simply the triumph of a "tough" Kennedy policy. That was a myth promoted by President Kennedy, his brother, Sorensen, and other Camelot memoirists and aides, and accepted by many trusting journalists and others.

This new interpretation of Kennedy's handling of the settlement, and of the crisis, is based upon recent evidence. This *new* material underscores the important—indeed, the *essential*—relationship between evidence and analysis in understanding, explaining, and assessing historical events and their major actors. It also emphasizes, in such cases as the missile crisis, the heavy dependence of scholars and other analysts upon the American government, which controls and selectively releases crucial information, and upon key former participants, like Sorensen, Rusk, Bundy, McNamara, and Robert Kennedy, whose power to provide rich recollections (including "doctored" memoirs) can shape interpretations. Consider, once again, the significance of the revelation—long known only to these advisers and a few others—that a secret, firm deal on the Jupiters had helped settle the crisis.

The emergence of such information has taken some years, appearing at a time when the international political climate had changed and when presidential flexibility, rather than toughness, was more often admired in assessing Cold War presidents. Thus, just as the older image of Kennedy, as a man of resolute toughness, was once in line with the prevailing standards for the presidency, now the newly revealed Kennedy, a partly transformed handler of Soviet-American relations, is in line with the changed standards. Often controlling the evidence, the memoirists of Camelot and other aides have continued to serve the president well.

Recognition of the analysts' dependence upon evidence should make us aware of how interpretations might further change under the impact of new disclosures. Assume, for example, that Robert Kennedy, at his brother's behest but unknown to other ExComm members, had secretly suggested to the Soviets as early as midweek, say, October 24, a Turkey-Cuba missile trade. Or even on Friday night, for the first time, as Dobrynin now claims. Such evidence would further change the understanding of the ExComm (it would be a talking group with less influence), of the president's flexibility (he would seem more supple), of the use of back-channel negotiations (they would become even more important), of the reasons for the Kremlin's October 27 demand of a public trade (the puzzle might be the *public* demand and the failure to get an earlier agreement), and of the process (very secret negotiations spurred by the president's sense of growing peril) by which the crisis was settled.

Not only might the bureaucratic-politics analysis (at least as presented in Allison's dubious *Essence of Decision*) further crumble,[203] but the missile crisis might take on a new role in various theories of crisis management, bargaining, and compellence. Moreover, new foreign evidence, especially the recently released Castro-Khrushchev correspondence, also raises important questions about traditional interpretations of the crisis and the value of some established theories in helping to explain the suddenness of the settlement on Sunday morning, October 28. Khrushchev may well have settled so suddenly because events seemed to be hurtling dangerously beyond control, with Castro likely to direct more attacks against American surveillance planes, thus very likely provoking an American armed reprisal. The likelihood was a dangerous chain of escalation.

Focusing on the American side, the new evidence released in the last few years further affirms the need to see the president, at least in this crisis, as central in the decision making. His decisions were not a vector of bureaucratic and institutional forces. Not only did he define the agenda (doing nothing was unacceptable, and the MRBMs had to be speedily removed) and choose the main line of tactics (the quarantine), but he shaped the terms of settlement (trading the Jupiters). In the crisis, he was not the first among equals, but rather the first among aides and advisers, who knew they were subordinates. Though he frequently did not seem dominant in the ExComm transcripts and minutes, even when he was present at the sessions, he *decided* the major issues. True, he consulted, listened, learned, and tried out various notions. But in the most fundamental way, President John F. Kennedy was dominant: the key decisionmaker.

What is unclear, still, is how important the ExComm deliberations were in helping him decide. Did the group, or particular members, substantially influence him? Or were the sessions, whatever his early intentions, soon part of a larger, unstated presidential strategy to build a consensus for his policies? Perhaps additional evidence, including Robert Kennedy's crucial papers, may help resolve this interpretive problem. At present, the ExComm transcripts and minutes are valuable, at minimum, in revealing the thinking of various participants, especially on such crucial matters as Soviet motives, assessments of peril, possible deals with the Soviets, problems in the American alliance system, and the strategic significance of the Soviet missiles in Cuba. The transcripts reveal, for example, how McNamara initially interpreted the problem not as fundamentally a military threat but a domestic political threat to the president. Significantly, none in the ExComm that day dissented from this strategic analysis, and even the president seemed partly inclined, at least at times, to this political interpretation.

Surprisingly perhaps, at that first day of ExComm sessions, the president said that he wished that he had drawn the line differently in earlier public and private statements, so that the emplacement of the Soviet missiles would not seem a challenge to him and to America. For him, apparently, domestic politics easily coalesced with personal and international credibility to compel him to take action to get the Soviet missiles out of Cuba.

Despite occasional dissents from the Joint Chiefs and Paul Nitze, what dominated the ExComm discussions was the political, not the military, significance of the MRBMs and possible IRBMs in Cuba. In similar fashion, the earlier deployment of the Jupiters had been shaped by political, not military, considerations. Such matters were largely kept secret from the American people.

During the crisis, top-level administration members, despite their efforts to keep control of details and to manage the American effort, ran into various problems—some of which they did not discover until years later. At the time, they did learn, to their dismay, of some troubling matters: that an American U-2 had flown into Soviet air space on Saturday, October 27, but fortunately scampered back without provoking a Soviet attack; and that a CIA-sponsored small marauding expedition against Cuba was scheduled for the period, and apparently canceled only when Robert Kennedy learned of the plan before it was launched. But they undoubtedly did not know of the Air Force test of a long-range missile (located near *armed* nuclear missiles) in California, which could have looked to Soviet observers like the beginning of an American ICBM attack.[204] Imagine, even for a moment, how the Soviets might have responded if they had known of this missile launch and believed it was the early part of a large ICBM attack on the Soviet Union.

Whatever the best intentions of top-level American leaders, the defense system had become too complex for careful, effective management in crisis. Rooted in the hierarchy of authority and the complexities of communication were ambiguities, confusion, and misunderstanding. Yet, perhaps especially because of McNamara's naive faith at the time that he had brought new efficiency and substantial rationality to defense, the ExComm members did not generally worry, in defining major tactics (the quarantine) for the crisis, that matters might go dangerously out of control on the American side. They seemed, at least initially in the crisis, to believe that they could effectively manage American actions and that the only major problem was Soviet actions. In retrospect, the problems were far more complex—including also Cuban responses.

During the October crisis, the president—with his advisers—gained great benefits from secrecy. It enabled them to have more time for reflection and deliberation, and the terms of the ultimate settlement (including the hidden Jupiter trade) were certainly less troubling because secrecy, and attendant deceit, allowed them to misrepresent the final agreement. To paraphrase the president, appearances can shape reality.[205] Control over information can be politically, as well as personally, empowering.

In 1962-1963, by concealing the Jupiter trade, the administration avoided problems in NATO, though many key allies would undoubtedly have endorsed the deal as a comparatively small price to pay for settling the crisis peacefully. Secrecy also meant that the president, as well as the administration and the Democratic party, did not have to face problems with voters. The claims of a great triumph, as opposed to the reality of a victory with compromise, greatly helped the president and his administration both at home and abroad.

The October 1962 uses of secrecy and deceit raise fundamental questions about accountability in a democracy, about the public's understanding of policy and recent history, and about the lessons drawn, especially in the 1960s, from the missile crisis. The tactics that made the secret 1962 settlement easier for the president and his aides, and thus may have helped Kennedy and Khrushchev avoid war, may well have also ill-served Americans for at least a decade. Repeatedly told that, in this so-called "eyeball-to-eyeball" confrontation, "the other fellow blinked first,"[206] Americans were encouraged to believe in easy victory, not compromise, and to conclude that toughness and resolution were the guides to success in their nation's foreign policy.[206] That was part of the larger myth created by Kennedy and his close aides.

It was a burden of expectation, created by the myth of the crisis settlement, that Kennedy's successor, Lyndon B. Johnson, would bear in future years. What influence, analysts may profitably speculate, did the widespread belief in Kennedy's great victory in the missile crisis play as President Johnson struggled on, even against the counsel of advisers, for his own triumph in Southeast Asia in 1966-1968? Might he have felt psychologically, and even politically, more free to change policy if he had known, along with his fellow Americans, the truth of the October 1962 secret settlement?

And might not Americans have better understood Khrushchev's dangerous gamble of placing missiles in Cuba if they had known, contrary to official American statements at the time, of continuing CIA efforts, often presided over by Attorney General Kennedy, to overthrow Castro in various clandestine ventures? In turn, unnecessary Soviet secrecy even well after the crisis, by still concealing that the Soviets had possessed in autumn 1962 only about 20 land-based ICBMs, made Khrushchev's action seem strangely reckless and even irrational. But if his aim was substantially to stop the strategic imbalance from getting much worse, and if he viewed the Turkey and Cuban situations as roughly analogous, then for him the deployment in Cuba may well have seemed warranted and even reasonable.

It is too simple to explain the missile crisis primarily in terms of miscalculation, for that oversimplifies, treats different decisions almost equally, and strips this historical event of its formidable complexity. There were far more fundamental roots—of rival aims, of rival power, and of mutual suspicion. Amid deep-rooted Soviet-American antagonisms, the missile crisis must be understood substantially in the context of the events of 1961-1962, in which two powerful men—President Kennedy and Premier Khrushchev—made some crucial decisions that other men, if occupying the same office, might have handled differently. Each man operated within structures that provided constraints, but those constraints did not dictate, but only influenced, the crucial choices that were made.

Conceived this way, it is certainly plausible that a different president than Kennedy might well have chosen not to launch the Bay of Pigs venture, not to pursue clandestine activities against Cuba and Castro, not to build up the American nuclear arsenal well beyond the size of the Soviets',[208] and not to place the Jupiters in Turkey. And a different Soviet leader than Khrushchev, one using less bluster and more caution, might well have handled the Berlin crisis with fewer threats. Contingent on American behavior, such a leader, and even Khrushchev, might have felt no need to place missiles in Cuba. Such "might have beens," such plausible possibilities, are worth pondering in reconsidering the missile crisis.[209]

NOTES

The author expresses his gratitude to McGeorge Bundy, Alexander George, James Hershberg, David Holloway, Philip Nash, Scott Sagan, and Martin Sherwin for valuable discussions; to Laurence Chang and the National Security Archive, James Blight and David Lewis of Brown University's Center for Foreign Policy Development, Arthur Singer of the Sloan Foundation, Arthur Schlesinger, Jr., and David Welch for help with sources; and to the MacArthur Foundation and Stanford's Center for International Security and Arms Control for assistance. Parts of this chapter were presented in 1989-1992 at separate seminars of Stanford's Nuclear History group and the Peace Studies program, and also at the University of California (Santa Cruz), the University of Chicago, and the National Security Archive. Portions are drawn from Barton J. Bernstein, "The Cuban Missile Crisis: Trading the Jupiters in Turkey?" *Political Science Quarterly* 95 (Spring 1980), pp. 97-125. The present chapter constitutes a substantial revision, using new sources and reconsidering earlier materials, of that 1980 article (henceforth cited as "Trading the Jupiters.")

1. Chester Bowles to Kennedy, April 22, 1961 (marked "never sent"), Chester Bowles Papers, Yale University Library, New Haven, Connecticut.
2. "Off-The-Record Meeting on Cuba" (henceforth ExComm transcript), October 16, 1962, 6:30-7:55 P.M., p. 26, John F. Kennedy Library (henceforth JFKL), Boston, Massachusetts.
3. Robert Kennedy, *Thirteen Days* (New York: Norton, 1969), pp. 108-109.
4. See, for example, the studies by memoirists (sometimes scholars): Arthur Schlesinger, Jr., *A Thousand Days* (Boston: Houghton Mifflin, 1965), pp. 808-835; Theodore Sorensen, *Kennedy* (New York: Harper, 1965), pp. 673-717; Roger Hilsman, *To Move a Nation* (Garden City, NY: Doubleday, 1967), pp. 159-229; and Robert Kennedy, *Thirteen Days*. Or by independent scholars: Alexander George et al., *The Limits of Coercive Diplomacy* (Boston: Little, Brown, 1971), pp. 1-36, 86-143; and Albert and Roberta

Wohlstetter, "Controlling the Risks in Cuba," *Adelphi Paper* No. 17 (London, 1965). In recent work, Alexander George, "The Cuban Missile Crisis," in George, ed., *Avoiding War: Problems of Crisis Management* (San Francisco: Westview Press, 1991), pp. 222-268, seems more critical of the dangers than in his much earlier work. Like other scholars, he has profited from the careful research by Scott Sagan, "Nuclear Alerts and Crisis Management," *International Security* 9 (Spring 1985), pp. 107-122.

5. Barton J. Bernstein, "Their Finest Hour?," *Correspondent* 33 (August 1964), pp. 119-121; Bernstein, "The Cuban Missile Crisis," in Lynn Miller and Ronald Pruessen, eds., *Reflections on the Course of the Cold War* (Philadelphia: Temple University Press, 1974), pp. 111-42; Bernstein, "The Week We Almost Went to War," *Bulletin of the Atomic Scientists* 32 (February 1976), pp. 13-21; Bernstein, "Trading the Jupiters," *Political Science Quarterly* (Spring 1980); Bernstein, "Commentary: Reconsidering Khrushchev's Gambit—Defending the Soviet Union and Cuba," *Diplomatic History* 14 (Spring 1990), pp. 231-239; I. F. Stone, "The Brink" *New York Review of Books* 6 (April 14, 1966), pp. 12-16; Ronald Steel, "End Game," *New York Review of Books* 12, (March 13, 1969), pp. 15-22; Richard J. Walton, *Cold War and Counterrevolution* (New York: Viking, 1972), pp. 102-142; James Nathan, "The Missile Crisis: His Finest Hour Now," *World Politics* 27 (January 1975), pp. 256-281; and Bruce Miroff, *Pragmatic Illusions* (New York: David McKay, 1976), pp. 82-99.

6. McNamara in John F. Kennedy School of Government (Harvard) meeting, October 21, 1987, WGBH videotape, quoted in Marc Trachtenberg, "Commentary: New Light on the Cuban Missile Crisis," *Diplomatic History* 14 (Spring 1990), p. 242. Scott Sagan, "Organization, Accidents, and Nuclear Weapons" (forthcoming) adds significantly to earlier evidence on matters that went awry during the crisis.

7. James Blight and David Welch, *On the Brink: Americans and Soviets Reexamine the Cuban Missile Crisis* (New York: Hill and Wang, 1989), p. 100.

8. White House statement, October 27, 1962; and Kennedy letter to Khrushchev, October 27, 1962, both in *Public Papers of the Presidents: John F. Kennedy* 1962 (Washington, D.C.: USGPO, 1963), pp. 813-814.

9. Kennedy, *Thirteen Days*, pp. 94-95.

10. Arthur M. Schlesinger, Jr., *Robert Kennedy and His Times* (Boston: Houghton Mifflin, 1978), pp. 521-524, reached his conclusion partly on the basis of the Robert Kennedy Papers, JFKL, a collection to which he had privileged access. My own efforts to gain access to the major segments on the missile crisis have been unsuccessful despite various requests in 1979-1991, because the library has a policy of not processing these undeeded materials until other papers—more important in their judgment and deeded to the library system—are first processed. (Susan D'Entremont to Bernstein, December 17, 1990, January 15, 1991.) Though not formally defenders, see Graham Allison, *Essence of Decision* (Boston: Little, Brown, 1971), pp. 228-229; and Herbert Parmet, *JFK: The Presidency of John F. Kennedy*

(New York: Penguin, 1983), p. 297. For indications of such a bargain, also see Nikita Khrushchev, *Khrushchev Remembers: The Last Testament* (Boston: Little, Brown, 1974), p. 512.

11. Nathan, "Missile Crisis," pp. 268-270; and Steel, "End Game," pp. 15-17.

12. Bernstein, "Cuban Missile Crisis" (1974), pp. 120 and 135; and Bernstein, "Week We Almost Went to War," p. 19.

13. Dobrynin and Sorensen in Bruce Allyn, James Blight, and David Welch, eds., *Proceedings of the Moscow Conference of the Cuban Missile Crisis, January 27-28, 1989* (photocopy of typescript marked December 1989), pp. 50-51, 58, 90-92, courtesy of Astrid Tuminez; and Sorensen to Bernstein, August 17, 1990.

14. Harold Macmillan, *Riding the Storm, 1956-1959* (New York: Harper, 1971), pp. 245-246; and Michael Armacost, *The Politics of Weapons Innovation: The Thor-Jupiter Controversy* (New York: Columbia University Press, 1969), pp. 190-197.

15. Armacost, *Weapons Innovation*, pp. 175-211. Also see "Minutes of a Meeting Between the Secretary of State and the German Foreign Minister," November 21, 1957; and "IRBM Controversy at NATO Conference," *Los Angeles Times,* December 6, 1957, both from National Security Archive (hereafter NS Archives), Washington, D.C.

16. Memorandum of Conversation with the President, June 16, 1959, Dwight D. Eisenhower Library, summarized in NS Archives summary (June 16, 1959 entry), NS Archives. For evidence of earlier uneasiness in the Eisenhower administration about placing IRBMs in Turkey, see John Foster Dulles to General Robert Cutler, "Draft Letter to General Norstad," July 11, 1957, NS Archives; and George Kistiakowsky to James Killian, March 4, 1958, Killian folder, Ann Whitman Files, Dwight D. Eisenhower Library, Abilene, Kansas.

17. Compendium of Soviet Remarks on Missiles, March 2, 1961, summarized in NS Archives summary (July 26, 1959 entry), NS Archives.

18. William H. Brubeck, "Jupiters in Italy and Turkey," October 22, 1962, National Security files (NSF), Countries: Cuba, box 36, JFKL; W. W. Rostow to Bundy, "Turkish IRBM's," October 30, 1962, NSF: Regional Security Files (RSF): NATO-Weapons, box 226, JFKL; and *New York Times,* October 11, 1959, pp. 1, 11, and October 28, 1962, p. 31.

19. U.S. House of Representatives, Committee on Armed Services, *Hearings on the Military Posture,* 88th Cong., 1st Sess., pp. 277-281.

20. Ibid., pp. 277-285; Raymond Hare to Secretary of State, No. 587, October 26, 1962, NSF: NATO-Weapons, box 226, JFKL; cf. Sorensen, *Kennedy,* p. 3.

21. John Eisenhower, "Memorandum of Conference with the President, January 13, 1961," January 17, 1961, box 4, AEC files, Eisenhower Library.

22. Gary Tocchet, "Sending Nuclear Weapons to Europe, 1954-1961" (1985 unpub. paper delivered at Society for Historians of American Foreign Relations conference, Stanford University) contends—correctly, I think—that this was an example of what Fred Greenstein terms Eisenhower's

"hidden-hand" leadership. This paper was originally written in my graduate seminar at Stanford. Ironically, the Eisenhower administration had briefly feared, in July 1960, that Khrushchev might put missiles in Cuba. "Discussion of the 451st meeting of the NSC, July 15, 1960," July 18, 1961, Eisenhower Library.

23. Kennedy, *Thirteen Days*, pp. 94-95, implies that President Kennedy had been trying to remove them since 1961. Kenneth O'Donnell and David Powers, with Joe McCarthy, *Johnny, We Hardly Knew Ye* (Boston: Little, Brown, 1972), p. 333, states that the president had given the *order* five times. Also see Hilsman, *Move a Nation*, pp. 202-203; Elie Abel, *The Missile Crisis* (New York: Bantam, 1968), pp. 168-171; and Allison, *Essence*, pp. 44, 101, 142, and 226. Much of this "thwarting the president" interpretation has been refuted by George Ball, *The Past Has Another Pattern* (New York: Norton, 1982), pp. 500-502, which relies heavily for details upon Bernstein, "Trading the Jupiters."

24. James Grimwood and Frances Stroud, *History of the Jupiter Missile System* (U.S. Army Ordinance Command, July 1962), p. 104, NS Archives; cf. Jacob Neufeld, *Ballistic Missiles in the United States Air Force* (Office of Air Force History, 1990), pp. 225-227, which dates them as becoming operational in small groups between November 1961 and March 1962. No important argument in this chapter changes if the November 1961 date is accurate for the first few Jupiters.

25. Report, quoted in House, Armed Services, *Hearings on Military Posture*, 88th Cong., 1st Sess., pp. 279-280 (emphasis added). This report, also cited by Allison, *Essence*, pp. 311-312, should have led him and other scholars to dismiss the interpretation that Eisenhower's administration had installed the Jupiters and that Kennedy had inherited that situation. Additional information was available in the press that the missiles had not yet been deployed in Turkey by May 1961. On May 28, 1961, the *New York Times*, p. 8, reported that the Soviets had warned, in the words of the *Times*, against "*proposals* to base nuclear rocket stations in Turkey" (emphasis added).

26. Bowles, memorandum for the president, March 29, 1961, attached to Bowles to President, April 7, 1961, President's Official Files (POF), box 88, JFKL. In this memorandum, Bowles had erroneously referred to the Atomic Energy Commission as the Atomic Energy Committee. The Acheson study, "A Review of North Atlantic Problems for the Future," March 1961, stated, "First generation IRBM's are now deployed in the U.K. and Italy, and a squadron is *on order* for Turkey" (emphasis added), JFKL. Clearly, the IRBMs were not then in Turkey.

27. Report of Actions by the National Security Council, NSC Action 2405, March 29, 1961, JFKL.

28. Bowles to Kennedy, April 22, 1961 (marked "never sent"). For the danger of a double standard and also likening missiles in Turkey to Soviet missiles in Cuba, see Clairborne Pell, "Background Memo on Senator Pell's Thoughts Regarding Cuba," attached to Arthur Schlesinger, Jr., to President, May 13, 1961, NS Archives; and Senator Albert Gore (D-Tenn.) in

Executive Sessions of the Senate Foreign Relations Committee (Historical Series), 13 (1961), 87th Cong., 1st Sess., pp. 219-220.

29. Paul Nitze, with Ann Smith and Steven Rearden, *From Hiroshima to Glasnost* (New York: Grove Weidenfeld, 1989), p. 233 also implies that Kennedy never gave an order to remove the Jupiters. Rusk, *As I Saw It*, p. 239, incorrectly places the Jupiters already in Turkey, but also denies that there was a JFK order for their removal.

30. George McGhee to Bundy on "Turkish IRBM's" (emphasis added), June 22, 1961, NSF:RSF:NATO-Weapons (Cables-Turkey), box 226; and McGhee to Bernstein, February 19, 1979. Recently, in writing his memoirs, McGhee forgot about this June 1961 report and also mangled other matters involving the Jupiters. McGhee, *The US-Turkish-NATO Middle East Connection* (London: Macmillan, 1990), p. 166. At the Vienna summit in June 1961, Khrushchev had complained about the Jupiters and compared Turkey and Cuba. "Vienna Meeting Between the President and Chairman Khrushchev," June 3, 1961, 3 P.M., JFKL.

31. House Armed Services, *Hearings on Military Posture*, 88th Cong., 1st Sess., p. 283.

32. Hilsman, *Move a Nation*, pp. 202-3; Kennedy, *Thirteen Days*, pp. 94-5.

33. Hilsman, *Move a Nation*, pp. 202-3; Kennedy, *Thirteen Days*, pp. 94-5.

34. Bundy, National Security Action Memorandum, No. 181, August 23, 1962, Cunliffe-NSC box, Modern Military Records, National Archives, Washington, D.C. Item seven may have emerged from CIA director John McCone's fears, expressed to the president on August 21, that the Soviets might be putting "offensive" missiles in Cuba. Walter Elder to Elie Abel, December 17, 1965, Elie Abel Papers, Hoover Institution, Stanford, California.

35. Since some files are still classified, there may have been some action, but it is highly unlikely. Bundy does not recall that there was any action (interview with Bundy, July 31, 1979); and Bundy, *Danger and Survival*, pp. 436-437. At the meeting of August 31 or September 1, with JFK, on the points in this memo, there was, as Henry Rowen recalls, no discussion of items one or five (interview with Rowen, February 13, 1979).

36. Cf. Allison, *Essence*, pp. 101, 141-2, 225-6, who uncritically accepted recollections that JFK had given a clear order and then tries to explain, in terms of bureaucratic politics, why it was not carried out. A more subtle approach would acknowledge that a chief executive may often express preferences (not orders) for policies, and that he may sincerely reinterpret them as *orders* when his own inaction leaves him woefully unprepared in a crisis. In this way, a president can place blame on a subordinate, and other aides who listen to his charges tend to believe that the president actually issued an order, and not simply stated a wish or hope. In later memoirs and journalistic accounts, the president's interpretation dominates and becomes "fact." Practitioners of the bureaucratic politics model develop a vested interest in uncritically accepting such dubious evidence precisely because their model so nicely "explains" it. Thus, the model *first* helps define the

reliability of the evidence and *then* explains it—a dangerous, circular process. In view of the published evidence available to Allison, when he was writing, that the missiles were not deployed in Turkey at the time that Kennedy entered office, Allison should have been very suspicious of the recollections about these "orders." Such suspicions should have barred him from presenting a *firm* interpretation of thwarted presidential directives. Interviews with Ball, Bundy, and Nitze (which Allison implies but does not clearly assert that he conducted, though he refers to "conversations with most of the high-level participants") should have made him question his own interpretation. Did Allison perhaps develop such a powerful vested interest in advancing his interpretation that contrary evidence was not sought, or not pursued, or just easily dismissed? Also see Joseph Bouchard, "Use of Naval Forces in Crises: A Theory of Stratified Crisis Interaction" (Stanford University Political Science, Ph.D., 1988), II, pp. 618-628; and Forrest R. Johns, "The Cuban Missile Crisis Quarantine," *Naval History* 5 (Spring 1991), pp. 12-18. A number of scholars and others, apparently not knowing of contrary archival sources and some published literature, continue to cling to the belief that the missiles were placed in Turkey under Eisenhower and that President Kennedy, well before the October crisis, had given firm orders to remove these weapons. See Mark Falcoff, "Learning to Love the Missile Crisis," *National Interest* 16 (Summer 1989), p. 67; Robert Pollard, "The Cuban Missiles Crisis: Legacies and Lessons," *Wilson Quarterly* 5 (Autumn 1982), pp. 148-155; Richard Neustadt and Ernest May, *Thinking in Time: The Uses of History for Decision-Makers* (New York: Free Press, 1986), pp. 9-10; Wayne Smith, *The Closest of Enemies: A Personal and Diplomatic Account of U.S.-Cuban Relations Since 1957* (New York: Norton, 1987), p. 82; Richard Neustadt, *Presidential Power and Modern Presidents* (New York: Macmillan, 1990), p. 207; Michael Beschloss, *The Crisis Years: Kennedy and Khrushchev* (New York: HarperCollins, 1991), p. 8; and May to Bernstein, April 4, 1986. In contrast, the problem of the Jupiters is shrewdly treated in Philip Nash, "Nuisance of Decision: Jupiter Missiles and the Cuban Missile Crisis," *Journal of Strategic Studies* 14 (March 1991), pp. 1-26, an essay that I urged him to write.

37. Hilsman, *Move a Nation,* p. 170.

38. There was already evidence that recent Soviet deliveries probably included surface-to-air missiles (SAMs) and possibly planes.

39. I. M. Tobin, "Attempts to Equate Soviet Missile Bases in Cuba with NATO Jupiter Bases in Italy and Turkey," October 10, 1962, NSF: Countries, Cuba, box 36, JFKL. Also see Thomas Sorensen, USIA, "Information Policy Guidance on Cuba," October 22, 1962, Classified Subjects files (hereafter CSF), box 48, Theodore Sorensen papers, JFKL.

40. On the American arsenal, extrapolations from McNamara to president, "Military Strength Increases Since Fiscal Year 1961" (with SIOP), October 3, 1964, boxes 11-12, National Security Files, Lyndon B. Johnson Library (LBJL), Austin, Texas. On the Soviet arsenal, Dmitri Volkogonov, director

of military history, Ministry of Defense, in Allyn et al., eds., *Moscow Conference,* p. 34. I am assuming that a total of about 20 Soviet ICBMs could have been forecast by the Soviets in spring 1962. A spring 1962 arsenal of "about" 12 Soviet ICBMs is a rough calculation from the 20 that Volkogonov stated were in the Soviet arsenal in October 1962. The analysis in the text would not change if the numbers for the Soviet arsenal were somewhat larger or smaller.

41. Using publicly available sources in spring 1962, Michael Brower, "President Kennedy's Choice of Nuclear Strategy," *Council for Correspondence Newsletter* (June 1962) examined the American shift to counterforce. For Khrushchev's public response to McNamara's June 16, 1962, counterforce speech, see Khrushchev's speech, July 10, 1962, *Current Digest of the Soviet Press* 14 (August 8, 1962), pp. 3-4.

42. Raymond Garthoff, *Reflections on the Cuban Missile Crisis* (Washington, D.C.: Brookings, 1989, rev. ed.), pp. 10-19; and Bernstein, "Khrushchev's Gambit," pp. 232-235.

43. Khrushchev, *Khrushchev Remembers* (Boston: Little, Brown, 1970), pp. 493-494. Also see Khrushchev, *Khrushchev Remembers: The Glasnost Tapes* (Boston: Little, Brown, 1990), p. 170; and Andrei Gromyko, *Memoirs* (New York: Doubleday, 1989), p. 175. On many matters, though not on this subject, this most recent Khrushchev "memoir" may be suspect, because it is not clear that the tapes were voice-authenticated. Walter Schneir, "Time Bomb," *Nation* 251 (December 3, 1990), pp. 682-688; cf. Ronald Grele, letter, *New York Times* (West Coast ed.), December 24, 1990, p. 20. In a recent essay, Aleksandr Alekseev, former Soviet ambassador to Cuba, also stressed Khrushchev's motive of protecting Cuba. Alekseev, "The Caribbean Crisis: As It Really Was," *Ekho Planety,* No. 33 (November 1988), pp. 29-32 (used in translation). For powerful suggestive evidence about U.S. bellicose intentions toward Cuba, see James Hershberg, "Before 'The Missiles of Cuba,'" *Diplomatic History* 14 (Spring 1990), pp. 163-198. Despite claims by McNamara that the recently declassified evidence cited by Hershberg is evidence only of normal contingency planning, the evidence actually reaches far beyond the ordinary and is unnervingly suggestive—but not definitive—on U.S. intentions.

44. Garthoff, *Reflections on the Cuban Missile Crisis* (1989), pp. 12-16, and quotation on p. 13 drawn from Mikoyan, *Latinskaya Amerika* (January 1988), p. 79.

45. Khrushchev, speech, May 17, 1962, in *Current Digest of the Soviet Press* 14 (June 13, 1962), p. 3.

46. Khrushchev, speech, May 20, 1962, in ibid., p. 7. Also see a report on Soviet military doctrine, May 11, 1962, in ibid. (June 27, 1962), pp. 13-16.

47. Kennedy, *Thirteen Days,* p. 65.

48. *Tass,* September 11, 1953, reprinted in the *New York Times,* September 12, 1962, p. 16. In this statement, "designed" could also have been translated as "intended." See *Current Digest of the Soviet Press* 15 (October 10, 1962),

p. 14; and Ronald Pope, ed., *Soviet View on the Cuban Missile Crisis* (Washington, D.C.: University Press of America, 1982), p. 10.

49. *Tass,* September 11, 1962, reprinted in the *New York Times,* September 12, 1962, p. 16.

50. Tad Szulc, *Fidel: A Critical Portrait* (New York: Morrow, 1986), pp. 578-583, and Dorticós quoted on p. 583. In Szulc's interview with Castro, the Cuban leader likened the Soviet missiles to American missiles in Turkey and Italy, and claimed that he had expected the Soviet emplacement to create "a very tense situation" with the United States. It is highly unlikely that Castro foresaw the kind of crisis that developed. United States intelligence never had firm evidence that the warheads actually reached Cuba, but Soviet officials later claimed that they did arrive. Khrushchev, *Khrushchev Remembers: The Glasnost Tapes,* p. 172; and Volkogonov in Allyn et al., eds., *Moscow Proceedings,* p. 17.

51. Garthoff, *Reflections on the Cuban Missile Crisis* (1989), pp. 27-28. This meeting is not mentioned in Kohler's Calendar, Kohler Papers, University of Toledo, Toledo, Ohio.

52. McGeorge Bundy, *Danger and Survival* (New York: Random House, 1988), pp. 395-396 also adds a second reason for delaying: that night the president might have stirred up advisers by late calls and thus unintentionally encouraged leaks.

53. ExComm transcript, October 16, 1962, 11:50 A.M.-12:57 P.M., p. 14.

54. Ibid., pp. 14-15. The transcriber was not positive that the speakers were McNamara and Bundy.

55. ExComm transcript, October 16, 1962, 6:30-7:55 P.M., pp. 12-14. At the time, American analysts assumed that the Soviets had about 60-75 ICBMs in the Soviet Union, and not just 20, as was recently disclosed. Even if the Soviets had deployed 48 MRBMs and 32 IRBMs, there would probably have been only 24 MRBM launchers and 16 IRBM launchers, thereby allowing a first salvo of only 40 weapons. On the 16th, American analysts had not found all the MRBM and IRBM launchers, and therefore my conclusion of tripling or at least doubling the arsenal.

56. ExComm transcript, October 16, 1962, 6:30-7:55 P.M., pp. 15-16.

57. Ibid., pp. 17.

58. Ibid., pp. 14 and 22 (quotation).

59. Ibid., pp. 25 and 27 (quotation); cf. Kennedy, *Thirteen Days,* p. 31.

60. ExComm transcript, October 16, 1962, 6:30-7:55 P.M., p. 26.

61. Ibid.

62. Ibid.

63. Ibid., p. 32.

64. Hilsman, *Move a Nation,* pp. 196-197; and Sorensen, *Kennedy,* pp. 670-671.

65. ExComm transcript, October 16, 1962, 6:30-7:55 P.M., pp. 33-35.

66. Ibid., p. 36.

67. Ibid., p. 41-43.

68. Ibid., pp. 45-46, 48. This domestic politics theme has long been part of the revisionist critique of Kennedy's eschewal of negotiations and his choice of a public confrontation in the missile crisis. This line of analysis begins with Bernstein, "Their Finest Hour?" It is quite a leap from this analysis to the argument, which seems ill-founded, that Kennedy chose a public confrontation over the missiles *in order to enhance* his party's position in the forthcoming November 1962 elections. Rather, he may well have rejected private negotiations partly because of the domestic political dangers of such negotiations, and that made a public confrontation a *politically* safer course. Undoubtedly, JFK would have preferred not to have the Soviet missiles in Cuba. For discussions of politics and the crisis, see Thomas Paterson and William Brophy, "The Cuban Missile Crisis and American Politics," *Journal of American History* 73 (June 1986), pp. 86-119; and Richard Ned Lebow, "Domestic Politics and the Cuban Missile Crisis," *Diplomatic History* 14 (Fall 1990), pp. 471-492.

69. ExComm transcript, October 16, 1962, 6:30-7:55 P.M., pp. 46-47 (emphasis added).

70. This epigrammatic phrasing of bureaucratic politics apparently originated with Rufus Miles, but the general conception is now usually associated with Allison, *Essence,* a book with profound evidential and conceptual problems. It is dubious whether the "theory" can adequately explain shifts in people's positions on the same issues if bureaucratic interests remain constant. Of those giving advice during the course of the crisis (October 16-28, 1962), UN Ambassador Adlai Stevenson and the Joint Chiefs most closely conformed to the expectations that would reasonably be generated by the "theory" of bureaucratic politics. Secretary of Defense McNamara often seemed to fit poorly, and Robert Kennedy's oscillations (which are relevant to the "theory" if the Department of Justice has some vested interest in "rule of law") make him difficult to categorize or explain in such terms. CIA Director McCone probably fits the "theory" poorly, especially on October 27, Rusk is often elusive, and Bundy somewhat less so. In seeking to assess the value of bureaucratic politics as a "theory" to explain decision making in crisis, analysts might wisely compare the missile crisis to the decision making by the Truman administration, especially in June 25-26, 1950, leading to American military intervention in the Korean War. In that situation, the Joint Chiefs (with the exception of the Air Force chief of staff) and the secretary of defense, as well as the secretary of the army, were quite wary, especially of committing ground troops, but the secretary of state (Dean Acheson) was rather eager. In mid-October 1962, when Acheson had no formal position in the Kennedy government, he was also quite eager for bellicose action. On the Korean War decisions, see Bernstein, "The Week We Went to War: American Intervention in the Korean Civil War," *Foreign Service Journal,* part i (January 1977), pp. 6-9, 33-35; part ii in *Foreign Service Journal* (February 1977), pp. 8-11, 33-34. The theory of bureaucratic politics may be very useful in noncrisis situations, and especially on domestic issues, but the theory works poorly, at best, in foreign policy *crises*

involving decision making where the president is centrally involved. Of course, if the "theory" is broadened and thus is trivialized, as sometimes occurs, to the contention that, in foreign policy and other matters, advisers and agency chiefs do not always initially agree and that there are differences among participants, then the "theory" has simply restated what many *historians* of U.S. foreign and domestic policy have long understood and described in their writings. Such a process of rediscovery by bureaucratic-politics analysts is somewhat like finding the wheel, renaming it a "circular object item," closely examining its sizes, noting that it sometimes has spokes, and then offering a "spokes-circular object item" theory to describe that this item is round, appears on many vehicles, aids transportation, and sometimes breaks. Then, these analysts, if charged with restating the obvious, claim that they have aided others by stressing the importance of wheels and spokes in transportation.

71. Stevenson to President, October 17, 1962, Sorensen Papers.

72. Sorensen draft, October 18, 1962, Robert Kennedy Papers, courtesy of Schlesinger.

73. Leonard Meeker, memorandum of October 19, 1962, meeting of the Executive Committee of the National Security Council, Arthur Schlesinger Papers, quoted in Schlesinger, *Kennedy*, p. 515.

74. Minutes of NSC, October 20, 1962, 2:30-5:19 P.M., summarized in notes taken by Arthur Schlesinger, Jr., courtesy of Schlesinger.

75. Schlesinger, *Kennedy*, pp. 515-518; and Kennedy, *Thirteen Days*, p. 50. Also see: n.a. (probably Stevenson), "Political Program to Be Announced by the President," October 20, 1962, Sorensen Papers; n.a. (probably Stevenson), "Speech Insert on Political Program," n.d. (probably October 17 or 20), box 48, Sorensen Papers; and Stevenson, "Why the Political Program Should Be in the Speech," n.d. (probably October 21), in CSF, box 49, Sorensen Papers. The first memo called for sending UN observation teams to Turkey, Italy, and Cuba to "insure [against] surprise attack," and suggested discussions on NATO bases in Italy and Turkey. The last memo suggested trading Guantanamo but did not offer the bases in Turkey and Italy.

76. Minutes of NSC, October 20, 1962, quoted in Schlesinger, *Kennedy*, p. 515.

77. Schlesinger, *Kennedy*, p. 515.

78. Minutes of NSC, October 20, 1962, courtesy of Schlesinger.

79. Ibid.

80. Draft, no title (the first words are, "To restore the precarious balance . . ."), n.d. (probably October 20-22, 1962), box 49, Sorensen Papers.

81. Abram Chayes, *The Cuban Missile Crisis* (London: Oxford University Press, 1974), pp. 81-82

82. Harriman, "Memorandum on Kremlin Reactions," October 22, 1962, Harriman Papers, Library of Congress, Washington, D.C., and copy also at JFKL.

83. Schlesinger, *Thousand Days*, p. 811.

84. There is a small disagreement between two official histories about the exact date—October 19 or 22—when the first Jupiter launch position was turned over to the Turks. See HQ TUSLOG(USAFE) to HQ USAFE(OIHS), "Historical Date Record 1 July 1962-31 December 1962," February 20, 1963; and S. Sgt. Martin E. James, *Historical Highlights: United States Air Forces in Europe, 1945-1979* (Office of History, HQ US Air Forces in Europe, 28 November 1980), p. 61 (quotation), both sources in NS Archives. Curiously, *SAC Missile Chronology, 1939-1988* (Office of Historian, HQ SAC, May 1, 1990), p. 35, dates the turnover as May 1962, which seems to be an error. (Bernstein to Office of Historian, HQ, SAC, October 16, 1990; and Henry Narducci, Office of Historian, SAC, to Bernstein, October 23, 1990).

85. "Background Briefing on Cuban Situation," October 22, 1962 (6 P.M.), NSF, box 36, JFKL.

86. N.a., "Scenario," October 26, 1962, NSF: Countries, Cuba, JFKL. This memorandum also dealt with removal of the 30 Jupiters from Italy.

87. *New York Times,* October 30, 1962, p. 14; George Harris, *Troubled Alliance* (Washington, D.C.: Brookings, 1972), pp. 83-95.

88. Bromley Smith, "Summary Record of NSC Executive Committee Meeting, No. 7, October 27, 1962, 10:00 A.M.," NSF:NSC:ExComm Meetings, JFKL. (Hereafter cited as "Summary Record, ExComm," followed by number, date, and time.)

89. Secretary Rusk (drafted by Ball) to Ambassadors Hare and Finletter, October 24, 1962, NSF:RSF:NATO-Weapons, box 226, JFKL.

90. Ambassador Hare to Secretary of State, October 26, 1962, NSF:RSF:NATO-Weapons, box 226, JFKL.

91. Ibid.

92. Ambassador Finletter to Secretary of State, Polto 506, October 25, 1962, NSF:RSF:NATO-Weapons, box 226, JFKL.

93. N.a., "Political Path," October 25, 1962, NSF:NSC:ExComm Meetings, box 316, JFKL.

94. N.a., no title, n.d., but the document begins: "The following political actions might be considered." In Vice-Presidential Security File, Nations and Regions, Policy Papers and Background Studies on Cuba Affair, folder III, LBJL (this series will hereafter be cited as VP Security File: Cuba, followed by folder number).

95. Harriman to Under Secretary, October 26, 1962, NSF:Countries:Cuba, box 36, JFKL. Harriman's first choice was a resolution on denuclearization of Latin America, which excluded the problem of Europe. On the 24th, he had argues for the "Defanging Resolution." (Schlesinger to Stevenson, October 24, 1962, Schlesinger Papers, JFKL.)

96. CIA, "Readiness Status of Soviet Missiles in Cuba," October 23, 1962, had counted 23 (of the ultimate 24) MRBM launchers and 33 (of the ultimate 42) MRBMs, and 12 (of the ultimate 16) IRBM launchers, and was unsure whether the MRBM warheads were in Cuba (NSF:Countries:Cuba, JFKL). As a result, the American government also tried to get various nations to

bar over-flights from Russia that might be carrying the warheads (CIA, "The Crisis USSR/Cuba," October 26, 1962, NSF:NSC:ExComm meetings, JFKL, which is the location of all CIA, "The Crisis" reports). For an admission that some MRBMs were operational and probably had nuclear warheads, see McNamara's statement, *Washington Post,* October 25, 1962, p. A10. Generally newspapers, including the *Post,* disregarded this admission. For the implications on reassessing the crisis, see Bernstein, "Week We Almost Went to War," pp. 13-21. For a tendentious argument, which overlooks this essay and instead cites an abbreviated version, see Schlesinger, *Kennedy,* pp. 517-518, who charges suppression of evidence. His later paperback edition struggles to maintain much of this claim while squirming away from a candid admission that he failed to research his subject adequately and therefore had missed the original version of "Week We Almost Went to War." Neither private correspondence with Schlesinger in 1979 nor "Trading the Jupiters" (1980), p. 110, succeeded in persuading him to admit his error and adequately correct his book—even after a decade.

97. Harold Macmillan, *At the End of the Day, 1961-1963* (New York: Harper, 1973), pp. 209-211; "Summary Record, ExComm, No. 5, October 25, 1962, 5:00 P.M."; "Summary Record, ExComm, No. 6, October 26, 1962, 10:00 A.M."

98. Rusk to President, "Negotiations," with attached paper, October 26, 1962, NSF:Countries:Cuba, box 36, JFKL.

99. Rostow to Secretary et al., October 26, 1962, on "Alliance Missiles," with copy to Bundy in NSF:Countries:Cuba, box 36, JFKL, discussed trading the missiles in Turkey and Italy. Also see Rostow et al., to Secretary on "Cuba," October 25, 1962, NSF:RSF:NATO-Weapons, box 226, JFKL; Rostow to Secretary et al., "Negotiations about Cuba," NSF:Countries:Cuba, JFKL; and Rostow to Bundy, n.d. (October 25), with memorandum, "Summit," October 25, 1962, NSF, JFKL.

100. This conclusion is based partly on the fact that the reports are usually available in the NSF—actually the Bundy files—at the JFKL.

101. "Summary Record, ExComm, No. 6 October 26, 1962, 10:00 A.M." Also see Stevenson to Secretary of State, October 25, 1962, VP Security File: Cuba, III, LBJL.

102. "Summary Record, Excomm, No. 6, October 26, 1962, 10:00 A.M."

103. "Significantly, and contrary to expectations, Khrushchev did not seek to link the Cuba issue with . . . the Jupiters in Turkey and Italy." (N.a., "The Immediate Consequences," n.d. [late October 26 or early October 27, 1962], CSF, Sorensen Papers.) For a similar statement, also see Hilsman to Secretary, "Implications of the Soviet Initiative on Cuba," October 27, 1962, CSF, box 48, Sorensen Papers. In searching for a settlement, the ExComm and other advisers had usually dwelled more upon the American missiles in Turkey (and less upon those in Italy), possibly because those in Turkey were closer to the Soviet Union and had provoked more Soviet ire in the past.

104. Later, Edward Martin sent a telegram to "All ARA Diplomatic Posts," October 27, 1962, pointing out that the no-invasion pledge could be waived "if [Cuba's] breaking of accepted norms becomes flagrant, [for] US would feel . . . free to take whatever measures might be required" (CSF, box 48, Sorensen Papers). This telegram, as well as the ExComm minutes, indicates that the no-invasion pledge raised fewer problems for the president and the ExComm than did a trade involving removal of the Jupiters from Turkey.

105. "Summary Record, ExComm, No. 6, October 26, 1962, 10:00 A.M."; John McCone to Mac [Bundy], November 22, 1962, NSF:Countries:Cuba:General File, 11/21-11/30, JFKL.

106. Based on evidence presented for attitudes on Sunday, in Kennedy, *Thirteen Days*, p. 119. Alexander George has argued that a no-invasion pledge was a major concession that could protect Khrushchev from humiliation (George to Bernstein, May 18, 1979).

107. "Summary Record, ExComm, No. 6, October 26, 1962, 10:00 A.M."

108. Hilsman, *Move a Nation*, p. 220. The Soviet message of the 27th mentioned the missiles in Britain and Italy but specified only those in Turkey as a requirement for a trade. So far as the available materials indicate, no one in the ExComm speculated on why the Soviets added the Jupiters in Turkey to the deal and not *also* those in Italy.

109. Sorensen, memorandum, October 17, 1962, Cuba files, box 115, President's Official Files (POF), JFKL; Sorensen, *Kennedy*, pp. 680-82.

110. *New York Times*, October 28, 1962, p. 31; CIA, "The Crisis: USSR/Cuba," October 27, 1962.

111. Cyrus Sulzberger, *The Last of the Giants* (New York: Macmillan, 1970), pp. 20-22, 1004-06; Charles Bohlen, *Witness to History, 1929-1969* (New York: Norton, 1973), pp. 504-09.

112. Ambassador Bohlen to Secretary of State, No. 1970, October 27, 1962, VP Security File: Cuba, VI, LBJL.

113. Macmillan, *End of the Day*, pp. 187, 210-212, 213.

114. Cf. ibid., pp. 187, 210-212, 213. Perhaps Macmillan was more flexible about a Jupiter trade than he later acknowledged. More evidence awaits the likely opening of the British archives in 1993. For some indications (contrary to his memoir) that he had initial doubts about the quarantine strategy and that he may have preferred a less bellicose policy, see Minutes of 507th NSC Meeting, October 22, 1962, JFKL. There is evidence that some British officials did flirt with a Cuba-Turkey deal during the early days of the crisis. (Bohlen to Secretary of State, No. 2082, November 11, 1962, NSF:RSF:NATO-Weapons, JFKL.) For Labor and Liberal party responses, see *Manchester Guardian*, October 25, 1962, p. 2; the (London) *Times*, October 25, 1962, p. 8. For editorials suggesting a trade, see the (London) *Times*, October 24, 26, and 28 (accepting the Soviet offer) and *Manchester Guardian*, October 23, 24, and 25, 1962. On British press opinion, also see *Washington Post*, October 30, 1962, p. A8. Also see Roger Hilsman, "Trading US Missile Bases for Soviet Bases in Cuba," October 27, 1962, NSF, box 36, JFKL.

115. N.a., "Alliance Politics," n.d. (October 21-25?), 1962, NSF, JFKL; and Hilsman, "Trading US Bases in Turkey for Soviet Bases in Cuba," October 27, 1962.

116. *New York Times,* October 28, 1962, p. 31. The Norwegian officials approved the Soviet proposed deal *only* if removal of the Jupiters would not strategically impair NATO's defenses. Probably they knew that this criterion was clearly met, for the issue was international-psychological and -political, not strategic.

117. William Brubeck, through Bundy, to Schlesinger, on "Italy's Center-Left Government and the Cuban Crisis," November 20, 1962, with attachment of same title, November 26, 1962, NSF:Countries:Cuba, JFKL.

118. Robert Redford, *Canada and Three Crises* (Lindsay, Ontario: John Deyell, 1968), pp. 184-185; Peyton Lyon, *Canada in World Affairs* (Toronto: Oxford University Press, 1968), pp. 43, 53-55; and John Diefenbaker, *One Canada,* III, *The Tumultuous Years, 1962-1967* (Toronto: Oxford University Press, 1977), pp. 77-85. For Kennedy's later attitude toward Diefenbaker, see Benjamin Bradlee, *Conversations with Kennedy* (New York: Norton, 1975), pp. 182-183.

119. Sulzberger, *Last of the Giants,* pp. 921-22.

120. *New York Times,* October 28, 1962, p. 31. The Dutch, because of their role as a sea power, were very troubled by the blockade (*Manchester Guardian,* October 24, 1962, p. 15). Also see ibid. on the Turkey-Cuba equivalence.

121. *New York Times,* October 28, 1962, p. 31. Significantly, the NATO Council never officially broke ranks to support the trade of the Jupiters over American objections, and the Council actually endorsed JFK's *public* position. (Finletter to Secretary State, Polto 512, October 28, 1962, NSF:RSF:NATO-Weapons, JFKL.)

122. Ronald Hilton, "A Note on Latin America," *Council for Correspondence Newsletter,* No. 21 (October 1962), pp. 42-44. Also see *Manchester Guardian,* October 24, 1962, p. 15 and the (London) *Times,* October 27, 1962, p. 8.

123. These four nations did not support an OAS resolution to allow the use of force to remove the missiles (*Washington Post,* October 24, 1962, p. A1). For other evidence on negative Latin American attitudes, see: Rusk to Embassy, Rio de Janeiro, October 30, 1962, VP Security File: Cuba, III, LBJL; CIA, "The Crisis: USSR/Cuba," October 24, 1962; CIA, "The Crisis: USSR/Cuba," October 27, 1962; CIA, "The Crisis: USSR/Cuba," October 28, 1962; and *Hispanic American Report* 15 (October 1962), pp. 943-44, 957, 1964, 1064. Obviously, an analysis of the likely impact of an American deal might also consider the Central Treaty Organization (CENTO), which included Turkey but not the United States, but the declassified documents reveal little attention to this alliance. CIA, "The Crisis: USSR/Cuba," October 27, 1962, noted that two CENTO members—Iran and Pakistan— "have been slow to come out with public support of United States action." For implications that many noncommunist Asian governments initially supported the quarantine but would also have endorsed a deal on the

Jupiters, see Roger Hilsman, "The Cuban Crisis, Asian Reactions, and US Policy," October 27, 1962, NSF, 60 and 36, JFKL, which implied that Japan would have welcomed the deal involving Turkey.

124. Nitze, paraphrased in "Summary Record, ExComm, No. 7, October 27, 1962, 10:00 A.M." Also see ExComm transcript, October 27, 1962, pp. 2-3, courtesy of Bundy. A copy, sometimes with slightly different pagination, is also available at the Kennedy Library.

125. Ibid., pp. 2-3.

126. Ibid., p. 3.

127. Ibid., p. 4-5. For Bundy's later self-criticism and reflections on this matter, see Bundy, *Danger and Survival*, pp. 436-438. There was, of course, a guileful way of making the Jupiters trade: Keep the deal secret from the Turks and the rest of NATO. Nobody in the ExComm during the day's sessions suggested this strategy, though, curiously, Raymond Hare, America's ambassador in Turkey, had recently sent a cable to Washington outlining this scheme. Hare admitted that his proposal would depend on the Soviets keeping the matter secret. His cable was actually received and presumably being decoded at the very time that the ExComm was meeting that Saturday morning. Hare to Secretary of State. Part 2 of this telegram, with the proposal, was received in Washington at 10:17 A.M. on Saturday.

128. ExComm transcript, October 27, 1962, pp. 6-7.

129. Ibid., pp. 12-14.

130. "Summary Record, ExComm, No. 7, October 27, 1962, 10:00 A.M."; and ExComm transcript, October 27, 1962, p. 5.

131. Ibid., p. 10.

132. "Summary Record, ExComm, No. 7, October 27, 1962, 10:00 A.M."

133. Ibid.

134. Sorensen, memorandum, October 17, 1962, box 115, POF, JFKL; Bernstein, "The Week We Almost Went to War," pp. 16-20.

135. "Summary Record, ExComm, No. 7, October 27, 1962, 10:00 A.M."

136. White House press release, October 27, 1962. The statement was similar to Stevenson's proposal. (MVF [Forrestal] to President, October 27, 1962, NSF:Countries:Cuba, JFKL.) Stevenson, probably because of the hostility he had encountered in the ExComm meeting on October 20, was more wary of seeming "soft" on the 27th and thus he had somewhat backtracked from the 20th.

137. "Summary Record, ExComm, No. 7, October 27, 1962, 10:00 A.M." and Bundy, "NSC Executive Committee Record of Action, October 27, 1962, 10:00 A.M." both reveal that the statement was approved at the morning session.

138. ExComm transcript, October 27, 1962, pp. 16-19.

139. Ibid., p. 24.

140. Ibid.

141. Hilsman, *Move a Nation*, p. 223. Until the ExComm transcript was declassified, the authorship of this ploy was generally attributed to Robert Ken-

nedy. Such claims now seem dubious, despite Bundy's generous comments in *Danger and Survival*, p. 43. Bundy's efforts at generosity were more subdued in his oral history, with Richard Rusk, item CCC, Dean Rusk Project, University of Georgia Library.

142. ExComm transcript, October 27, 1962, p. 26.
143. Ibid., p. 28.
144. James Hershberg, "Before 'The Missiles of October': Did Kennedy Plan a Military Strike Against Cuba?" *Diplomatic History* 14 (Spring 1990), pp. 179-194; Thomas G. Paterson, "Commentary: The Defense-of-Cuba Theme and the Missile Crisis," ibid., pp. 252-256; and Bernstein, "Reconsidering Khrushchev's Gambit," ibid., pp. 234-235.
145. ExComm transcript, October 27, 1962, p. 29.
146. Ibid., p. 35-36.
147. Ibid., p. 36.
148. Ibid., p. 36-41.
149. Ibid., p. 42. One member, not identified in the transcript, wondered whether the Cubans might have controlled the SAM site. Ibid., pp. 45-46.
150. Ibid., pp. 42-44.
151. Ibid., pp. 47-51, 60.
152. Ibid., pp. 51-53.
153. Ibid., p. 51.
154. Ibid., pp. 58-59. Lippmann's suggestion appeared in his column in many papers, including the *Washington Post,* October 25, 1962, p. A25, and October 23, 1962, p. A10.
155. ExComm transcript, October 27, 1962, p. 58.
156. Ibid., p. 62.
157. Kennedy to Khrushchev, October 27, 1962, in *Public Papers of the Presidents: John F. Kennedy* (Washington, D.C.: USGPO, 1963), 1962, p. 814.
158. "Message to the North Atlantic Council and the Governments of all NATO Countries," n.d. (October 27, 1962), NSF:Countries:Cuba, box 36, JFKL. For an earlier interpretation based on severely limited evidence that exaggerated the importance of this draft message and apparently misconstrued attitudes at the end of Saturday's second ExComm session, see Bernstein, "Trading the Jupiters," p. 120. But also see Dillon's 1987 recollection in Blight and Welch, *On The Brink,* p. 72, a book resting heavily on a 1987 Florida conference with many major ExComm members. Unfortunately, that conference in effect barred all revisionists as well as McCone and thus very often followed a pattern of ardent deference. The result was that tough questions were seldom asked, contradictions seldom pursued, and various claims seldom probed. An occasionally snide article by J. Anthony Lukas, "Class Reunion: Kennedy's Men Relive the Cuban Missile Crisis," *New York Times Magazine,* August 10, 1987, describes a party flavor at this meeting, a flavor that *On The Brink* manages to omit in its generally uncritical use of ExComm members' stated recollections. *On The Brink*'s authors never seemed to have studied any other major U.S. foreign policy

crisis to determine the relationship of later recollections to documents created during the crisis itself; and thus the authors often lack an adequate basis for making judgments about undocumented claims in recollections. Often, the authors of *On the Brink* are remarkably trusting.

159. ExComm transcript, October 27, 1962, pp. 62-64.

160. Ibid., pp. 64-67.

161. Ibid., pp. 67-71.

162. Ibid., p. 71.

163. Ibid., p. 74.

164. Ibid., p. 65.

165. Rusk (drafted by Bundy and U. Alexis Johnson) to Finletter (with copies to U.S. ambassadors to all NATO nations), October 28 (12:21 A.M.), 1962, NSF, JFKL.

166. President to Bohlen, October 28, 1962, and President to Dowling, October 28, 1962, VP Security File: Cuba, VI, LBJL.

167. Sloan Foundation, "A Transcript of a Discussion About the Cuban Missile Crisis" (1983), pp. 54-55, courtesy of Arthur Singer.

168. Kennedy, *Thirteen Days*, pp. 107-08.

169. Robert Kennedy to Dean Rusk, October 30, 1962, quoted in Schlesinger, *Kennedy*, p. 522; and Kennedy, *Thirteen Days*, pp. 108-09; cf. O'Donnell and Powers, *Johnny . . .*, pp. 337-39. Robert Kennedy actually implied removal also of the 30 missiles from Italy (*Thirteen Days*, p. 109).

170. Discussions with Alexander George, 1970-1983.

171. Sloan Foundation, "A Transcript of a Discussion About the Cuban Missile Crisis," pp. 64-67; cf. Rusk, McNamara, Ball, Gilpatric, Sorensen, and Bundy, "The Lessons of the Cuban Missile Crisis," *Time* (September 27, 1982), p. 86.

172. Bundy, *Danger and Survival*, pp. 432-433 calls it a "unilateral private assurance." Also see Anatoly Gromyko, "U.S. Manipulations Leading to Cuban Missile Crisis" (trans. from *Voprosy Istorii*, No. 8, August 1971) in *USSR International Affairs*, September 7, 1971, p. G6-7, which cites *Thirteen Days* as the source but calls Kennedy's agreement to remove the Jupiters from Turkey and Italy "a specific promise." Khrushchev, *Last Testament*, p. 512, makes the same claim, as does Gromyko, "The Caribbean Crisis," V. V. Zhurkin and Ye M. Primakov, *Mezhdunarodnyye Konflikty* 70 (available in translation from Joint Publications Research).

173. Bundy, *Danger and Survival*, pp. 432-433; and Sloan Foundation, "A Transcript of a Discussion About the Cuban Missile Crisis," pp. 64-65.

174. Bundy, *Danger and Survival*, pp. 432-433.

175. Allyn et al., eds., *Moscow Proceedings*, pp. 50-52; cf. Khrushchev, *Khrushchev Remembers: The Glasnost Tapes*, p. 179.

176. Allyn et al., eds., *Moscow Proceedings*, p. 58 (quotation); and Sorensen to Bernstein, August 17, 1990. Sorensen's "six" or Bundy's "seven" at this meeting were in addition to the Kennedy brothers. My efforts to locate the actual manuscript copy of *Thirteen Days* (before Sorensen's editing) and

of Robert Kennedy's diary have been unsuccessful. The Kennedy Library has neither document, and Sorensen states that he does not know of their whereabouts; nor does the book's publisher, W. W. Norton. Susan D'Entrement, JFKL, to Bernstein, March 6, 1990; and Sorensen to Bernstein, August 17, 1990. In view of Sorensen's substantial work on *Profiles in Courage*, scholars may reasonably worry about how much of *Thirteen Days* was actually written by Robert Kennedy.

177. Allyn et al., eds., *Moscow Proceedings*, p. 58. According to Robert Kennedy's memo of October 30, Dobrynin on the 29th had brought the attorney general a letter from Khrushchev seeking to formalize the arrangement on the withdrawal of the Jupiters, but the attorney general denied there was a formal arrangement, consulted with Rusk and Thompson, met again with Dobrynin on the 30th, promised that the Jupiters would be removed within five months, and got Dobrynin to agree that there was no formal arrangement on the Jupiters. In view of Sorensen's recent admission, this October 30 memo seems to be an effort to rewrite the record by creating a somewhat false history. Robert Kennedy to Rusk, October 30, 1962, notes courtesy of Schlesinger. At the Moscow meeting in January 1989, Dobrynin incorrectly placed the meeting about Khrushchev's letter on October 28, and Sorensen said that a group of eight (those who had arranged the special Robert Kennedy Turkey-Cuba missile deal of the 27th) had met and decided to return Khrushchev's letter. *Moscow Proceedings*, p. 58.

178. See, for example, ibid., pp. 8, 43-44, and 97-98.

179. Castro to Khrushchev, October 26, 1962, in *Granma* (international English edition), December 2, 1990. For a slightly different translation, see *San Jose Mercury News*, December 2, 1990, p. C3, which, like many U.S. papers, relied upon a version in *Le Monde*.

180. Castro to Khrushchev, October 26, 1962, *Granma*, December 2, 1990. Some U.S. newspapers, drawing upon the *Le Monde* article and translation, omitted the possibly crucial "goal of occupying" phrase. How the Soviets could determine U.S. intentions during an attack remains unclear. Construed literally, the phrase would have required the Soviets to believe U.S. statements, or infer intentions from the size of the invasion force, or wait until after the invasion for actual U.S. occupation. Perhaps the phrase should not be taken literally.

181. Kennedy, *Thirteen Days*, p. 107. In January 1989, at the Moscow conference with former officials and some scholars, Dobrynin, in discussing his October 27 conversation with Robert Kennedy, did not mention this warning. My analysis assumes that such a warning was communicated to Khrushchev or that the Soviet leadership reached a similar conclusion without such a warning.

182. Castro's October 26 letter to Khrushchev did not specify Cuban attacks on American surveillance planes, but the message could have been plausibly interpreted by Khrushchev, amid the October 27 news of a shootdown of the U-2, to include such Cuban efforts. Khrushchev to Castro, October 28, 1962, *Granma*, December 2, 1990, makes clear that the Soviet leader

believed that the shootdown was by the Cubans. Which nation's forces actually shot down the U-2 is both interesting and important, but not essential to my analysis here. Castro's reply, October 28, in ibid., suggests Cuban responsibility but actually leaves unclear whose forces had shot down the plane. If it was not the Cubans, it is certainly curious that Castro did not act to set the record straight then, but perhaps he hoped to use Khrushchev's fear of such future Cuban actions as a bargaining ploy with the Soviets. Both the Cubans and Soviets have recently stressed that the Soviet forces shot down the U-2; *Granma*, December 2, 1990. The Soviets have also claimed that the act was ordered by a Soviet commander in Cuba who did not first check with the Kremlin; Allyn et al., eds., *Moscow Proceedings*, pp. 19 and 40. That claim of Soviet theatre responsibility remains somewhat puzzling in view of both Khrushchev's October 28 message and his later statements. Perhaps, in that period of dangerous crisis, other communications went awry and he was misinformed. Perhaps Khrushchev had somehow confused reports of Cuban *hopes* of destroying American "spy" planes with responsibility for the act. Also see John Newhouse, "A Reporter at Large: Socialism or Death?" *The New Yorker* (April 27, 1992), p. 70.

183. At the January 1989 Moscow meeting, Dobrynin also challenged Robert Kennedy's statement in *Thirteen Days* that he had given a virtual ultimatum to the Soviet ambassador in their Saturday evening meeting. Allyn et al., eds., *Moscow Proceedings*, pp. 53-54. According to Allyn and his two co-authors in their article, "Robert Kennedy soft-pedaled the danger of imminent American action, and Dobrynin claims that his cable to Moscow reporting the meeting was similarly low key on this point." Bruce Allyn, James Blight, and David Welch, "Essence of Revision: Moscow, Havana, and the Cuban Missile Crisis," *International Security* 14 (Winter 1989/90), p. 163. Strangely perhaps, no such statement by Dobrynin about a "low key" cable appears in the *Moscow Proceedings*, but Dobrynin did make such a statement in January 1989 to Blight and Welch outside the meeting. (Blight to Bernstein, February 10, 1991; Welch to Bernstein, February 15, 1991). Whether Dobrynin was accurate or not is another question. But even if his recollection was accurate, it is still quite possible, in view of Castro's messages to Khrushchev, that the Soviet leadership feared that events in Cuba were going out of control and that Castro might soon take action that would precipitate war with the United States. In January 1989, Dobrynin claimed that the issue of a Turkey-Cuba missile trade *first* came up in his conversation with Robert Kennedy on Friday, October 26, and that the attorney general, after making a quick phone call to the president that evening, said that it was a subject that the American government would consider. Dobrynin's recent claim of such a conversation on the 26th seems very dubious. If it had occurred, why then did both Kennedy brothers at the ExComm sessions on Saturday seem surprised and dismayed by Khrushchev's public demand for such a trade? Both brothers would have been far better prepared on the 27th for this Soviet demand even though it

was *public,* and they could have moved the ExComm rather speedily to endorse it. Or the brothers could have easily held an earlier meeting on Saturday with a small group, rather than the special evening meeting, to arrange for secret acceptance of a deal on the Jupiters. The fact that Robert Kennedy offered Dobrynin a missile trade before the final ExComm meeting on Saturday evening does mean that the president, his brother, and the six or seven others who knew about the offer were engaging that night, at the 9:00 P.M. ExComm meeting, in a kind of charade. At that 9:00 P.M. meeting, the president seemed to be seeking to legitimize the trade—without ever acknowledging his private offer, but not all the other knowledgeable ExComm members played fully complementary parts. Interestingly, Lyndon Johnson and McCone, both of whom were viewed as likely political enemies by the Kennedy brothers, were barred from the special Saturday meeting on the secret deal, but Johnson and McCone had said, near the end of the Saturday afternoon ExComm session, that they favored such a deal. For a partly fanciful version of Soviet events leading to Khrushchev's demand for a Jupiter-Cuba swap, see James Blight et al., eds., *Cuba Between the Superpowers, Antigua, 3-7 January 1991* (1991), pp. 65-69, courtesy of Blight. Scholars of the missile crisis will greatly benefit when the American and Soviet governments open the remaining documents on the crisis, and when the Cubans are also more forthcoming. Lamentably, even in cases where the Soviets have approved release of Khrushchev-Kennedy correspondence, the U.S. government delayed for nearly a year. Generally, however, the U.S. government has been the most forthcoming in releasing materials on this crisis.

184. Rusk to Embassy, Ankara and Paris, October 29, 1962, NSF:RSF:NATO-Weapons, JFKL.
185. U.S. House Appropriations Committee, *Department of Defense Appropriations for 1964,* 88th Cong., 1st Sess., 1963, part I, p. 57.
186. McNamara, in Sloan Foundation, "A Transcript of a Discussion About the Cuban Missile Crisis," p. 60.
187. Rusk to the President, "Political and Military Considerations Bearing on Turkish and Italian IRBM's," November 9, 1962, NSF:RSF:NATO-Weapons, box 226, JFKL.
188. Rusk had attached to his memorandum (ibid.) a seven-page double-spaced memorandum, "Significance to the US of Turkish and Italian IRBM's" (probably written by Raymond Garthoff), with which Rusk stated he agreed.
189. John F. Kennedy, n.t., n.d. (marked "Sunday afternoon" and probably October 28, 1962), Countries Series, Correspondence Subseries, POF, JFKL.
190. Komer to Mac [Bundy], November 12, 1962, NSF:RSF:NATO-Weapons, box 230, JFKL.
191. Komer to President, January 9, 1963, box 125, POF, JFKL. For Rusk's continuing strategy of assuring allies and especially Turkey that there had

been no deal on the Jupiters, see Rusk to Embassy Ankara and Embassy Paris, December 6, 1962, JFKL.

192. McNamara to President, April 25, 1963, POF 115, JFKL.

193. In addition to the men who knew about the deal, a few who did not know about it also energetically denied that there had been such an arrangement. See George McGhee, oral history (1964), p. 11; and W. W. Rostow, oral history (1967), pp. 106-107, JFKL. Rostow stated that President Kennedy had not agreed to any deal, because "the use of our allies' weapons as bargaining counters—to reduce the weight on us during a crisis—would have terribly damaged the Alliance."

194. Kennedy, *Thirteen Days*, p. 109; and Schlesinger, *Thousand Days*, p. 830; cf. Sorensen, *Kennedy*, pp. 715-716. Alexander George, "The Cuban Missile Crisis," in George et al., *The Limits of Coercive Diplomacy*, pp. 126-131, doubted that Kennedy would have attacked Cuba without first trying other tactics. Abram Chayes, *The Cuban Missile Crisis*, p. 100, leaned in this direction. More recently, McNamara and Bundy have stressed that Kennedy would first have tried other tactics, and Sorensen strongly leaned in that direction though he also emphasized the president's likely weakness if the crisis had not soon been resolved. "I have to remind you," Sorensen told the 1989 Moscow conference, "that John Kennedy was not a dictator, and General Smith is correct in saying that the pressures on him [JFK] from the military, and from others was rising, and one man alone is not able to hold out against that rising tide indefinitely." Allyn et al., eds., *Moscow Proceedings*, pp. 62-63, 66, 67 (Sorensen quotation).

195. ExComm transcript, October 27, 1962, p. 67. In discussion with me in the early 1980s, before this transcript was declassified, McGeorge Bundy emphasized this petroleum-oil-lubricant theme (which was mentioned in the then-available summary minutes) to argue that Kennedy would very probably have pursued this option before moving to a military attack. Bundy's counsel, citing the summary minutes, helped persuade me on this matter.

196. Rusk to Blight, February 25, 1987.

197. Rusk, *As I Saw It*, pp. 240-241. The claim that Rusk, not Kennedy, had initiated the idea of the Cordier-UN route was certainly not clear in Rusk's 1987 letter to Blight, and thus many analysts interpreted that letter to establish that Kennedy had *initiated* this strategy. For a brief treatment that does not rest on who initiated this strategy, see Neustadt, *Presidential Power and the Modern President*, pp. 307-308.

198. Rusk to Blight, February 25, 1987. In 1977, only 15 years after the crisis, Rusk seemed to imply a very different conclusion: that the two nations were very close to war on October 27, and that Kennedy would probably have taken military action against Cuba, with the likelihood of war against the Soviets, if the Soviets had not backed down on Sunday, October 28. Rusk, oral history #86, February 22, 1977, pp. 8-9, Richard Russell Collection, University of Georgia.

199. Cf. Bernstein, "Reconsidering Khrushchev's Gambit," p. 239. In 1987-1989, I had serious doubts about the general accuracy of Rusk's 1987 claim, but since then, after working more closely through the declassified materials for October 26-27, 1962, and after talking to Bundy and reading the *Moscow Proceedings,* I think that my earlier doubts were probably ill-founded. Rusk's 1990 version—that he *initiated* the idea—also helps to make his general recollection of a Cordier-UN route seem more plausible.

200. See Bundy, *Danger and Survival,* pp. 436-437 on political tactics that President Kennedy might have been able to employ to "sell" a missile trade in response to a UN proposal (though secretly initiated through the Cordier-UN route).

201. Analysts might also pay more attention to the post-crisis settlement and the dispute about whether Soviet bombers were included in the October 27-28 terms. See Bernstein, "Kennedy and Ending the Missile Crisis: Bombers, Inspections, and the No Invasion Pledge," *Foreign Service Journal* 56 (July 1979); Raymond Garthoff, "American Reaction to Soviet Aircraft in Cuba, 1962 and 1978," *Political Science Quarterly* 95 (Fall 1980), pp. 427-439; and Garthoff, *Reflections on the Cuban Missile Crisis* (1989), pp. 104-119. The recently declassified Kennedy-Khrushchev correspondence, especially for December 10 and 14, 1962, makes clear that the president, partly because of Cuba's refusal to allow on-site inspection of the missiles and related equipment, had backed away from a firm no-invasion pledge. For Khrushchev's later interpretation, see his letter to Castro, January 31, 1963, copy from James Blight.

202. For a fuller discussion, see Walter Johnson, ed., *The Papers of Adlai E. Stevenson* 8 (Boston: Little, Brown, 1979), pp. 348-352, which also reprints Kennedy's disingenuous December 1962 letter to Stevenson. Cf. Bundy, *Danger and Survival,* p. 459.

203. Generally, with the exception of a few pages, Allison's influential *Essence of Decision,* in developing and then applying a bureaucratic-politics model, treats the president and his decisions as virtually a vector of advisers' recommendations, amid the alleged pulling and hauling within the government. That model also has the profound liability of minimizing or ignoring domestic politics, which uneasily intrudes into the book in scattered places but not in a conceptually integrated way.

204. See Sagan, "Nuclear Alerts and Crisis Management," pp. 116-122. There is some possibility that Robert Kennedy may have failed to head off this planned expedition, or another similar one during the crisis. See Schlesinger in Blight et al., eds., *Cuba Between the Superpowers,* pp. 37-38. The information on the test-launch of a U.S. ICBM is in Scott Sagan, *Moving Targets: Nuclear Strategy and National Security* (Princeton: Princeton University Press, 1989), p. 146. At the level of implementing military orders and related communications, organizational theory can be useful in locating incidents and in helping to explain them. Such theory also requires that researchers mistrust many post-crisis official histories and similar documents, which may have been devised partly to paper over violated or

misunderstood orders. Organizations, by being allowed to sponsor and initially control their own history, are invited to shape their own past in self-serving ways. Well after writing this note, I read Sagan, "Organizations, Accidents, and Nuclear Weapons," which persuasively illustrates all three points—locating incidents, explaining them, and being critical of official history.

205. Kennedy, December 17, 1962, radio and TV interview, in *Public Papers: Kennedy,* 1962, p. 898.

206. The eyeball-to-eyeball confrontation, with the other guy blinking, was a characterization generally attributed to Dean Rusk, allegedly to his regret.

207. For a general discussion of presidential deceit and manipulation, see Barton J. Bernstein, "The Road to Watergate and Beyond: The Growth and Abuse of Executive Authority Since 1940," *Law and Contemporary Problems* (Spring 1976), pp. 58-86. Thomas C. Reeves, *A Question of Character: A Life of John F. Kennedy* (New York: Free Press, 1991), a best-selling, general indictment of Kennedy's "character," mostly a compilation of already known incidents and themes and based on little original research, praises JFK for his ultimate handling of the crisis and, strangely, notes but does not discuss the issue of deceit in the settlement.

208. This interpretation does not deny the political and bureaucratic influences on Kennedy in making these decisions, but it does stress in the case of the Bay of Pigs that those influences coalesced with *his* desires and hopes, and that in the case of the strategic buildup he again achieved basically what he desired. See Barton J. Bernstein, "The Bay of Pigs Invasion Revisited," *Foreign Service Journal* (March 1985), pp. 28-33; Fred Kaplan, *The Wizards of Armageddon* (New York: Simon and Schuster, 1983), p. 248-327; and Desmond Ball, *Politics and Force Levels: The Strategic Missile Program of the Kennedy Administration* (Berkeley: University of California Press, 1980), pp. 62-142, 180-201.

209. Counterfactuals can be fruitful in compelling analysts of nonreplicable events, as in history, to ponder, in a "thought experiment," the salience of various factors in shaping the result and thus in *explaining* the event under study. It may well be that counterfactual thinking is even necessary, though usually implicit, in analyses of such an event, for even a comparison with so-called similar events involves making a determination that the *apparent differences* between the two events (e.g., two revolutions or two beginnings of wars) are not the basic causal matters but, rather, marginal instead. Can this determination of difference as not basically involving causes be determined without at least some counterfactual thinking? For a more systematic discussion of these issues, see James Fearon, "Counterfactuals and Hypothesis Testing in Political Science," *World Politics* 43 (January 1991), pp. 169-195, which was brought to my attention by Scott Sagan after this comment-note had been drafted.

4

The View from Washington and the View from Nowhere: Cuban Missile Crisis Historiography and the Epistemology of Decision Making

Laurence Chang

In the three decades that have passed since the last Soviet freighters left Cuba in November 1962 carrying nuclear missiles back to the USSR, the Cuban missile crisis has emerged as perhaps the premier case study of U.S. national security decision making and crisis management. Hundreds of articles, books, and essays have been written on the missile crisis to date, and the attention given to the crisis by scholars in recent years has, if anything, increased rather than abated.[1]

For some scholars and former officials who took part in crisis deliberations in 1962, this continued academic fascination with the Cuban missile crisis is difficult to justify. Focusing so single-mindedly on one incident may obscure the meaning or "lessons" which might be drawn from other equally important historical events. Further, it has been suggested that the "uniqueness" of political conditions in 1962 means that the crisis, in the words of one political scientist, "offers precious little historical guidance for American statesmen today."[2] Or, as Douglas Dillon, the secretary of the treasury under President Kennedy, bluntly asserted at a retrospective conference on the crisis in 1987, "It is a totally different world today, and as far as I can see, the Cuban missile crisis has little relevance in today's world."[3]

Those skeptical about the academic industry surrounding the Cuban missile crisis are, of course, correct in noting that changes in political conditions since 1962 (such as the emergence of a rough nuclear parity between the United States and the USSR in the 1970s or, more fundamentally, the end of the Cold War) do make the missile crisis unique in many ways. And academics and political leaders who fail to appreciate these changes run the risk of drawing incorrect or anachronistic lessons from the crisis. One recent disclosure about the Reagan administration illustrates how the crisis can still serve still as an analogy, albeit a false one, for contemporary world events. Specifically, in 1984, some Reagan administration officials considered mobilizing support for its policies against the Sandinista government in Nicaragua by publicly portraying the shipment of relatively unsophisticated Bulgarian "L39" aircraft to the Nicaraguans a threat akin to deployment of nuclear weapons to Cuba in 1962.[4]

But the very "uniqueness" of the missile crisis argues for its continued importance as a historical case study. The crisis was, in fact, the most acute and dangerous confrontation in the Cold War. It was, and remains, the closest we ever came to a nuclear exchange. Hence, if we are to understand the dynamics of crisis escalation in the nuclear age, then there is no better—indeed, one might even argue no other—historical source than the Cuban missile crisis.[5] Perhaps most fundamentally, the missile crisis, for better or worse, has been and is likely to remain a significant historical paradigm. To the extent the crisis continues to be used as an historical analogy, it behooves scholars to create as accurate and balanced a rendering of the crisis as possible.

For the past 30 years, scholars have tried to amend and refine the history of the missile crisis primarily through the introduction of new information about the course and conduct of the crisis. But what exactly have the sources of information been? To what extent have these sources provided sufficient information for scholars to accurately evaluate the crisis, or, in other words, what epistemological limitations have these historical sources imposed on historians?[6] To what degree do the epistemological limitations of historians reflect the knowledge of the participants in the October 1962 drama?

HISTORICAL SOURCES OF THE CUBAN MISSILE CRISIS

When President Kennedy addressed the nation on the evening of October 22, 1962, he revealed that the United States was instituting a naval "quarantine" of Cuba in response to the discovery of Soviet nuclear missiles in Cuba. The dramatic, televised speech reflected a decision by President Kennedy to take public, unilateral action prior to opening any negotiations with the Soviet Union. Initiating secret discussions with Khrushchev, U.S. officials feared, would allow the Soviet leader to either stall until the missiles in Cuba became operational or publicly announce the deployment himself, thereby stripping the United States of the diplomatic initiative.[7]

Because the U.S.-Soviet confrontation was thus initiated in public, many of the major developments in the crisis were publicly known at the time: the discovery of the ongoing deployment of Soviet missiles in Cuba by a U.S. reconnaissance aircraft on October 14; the imposition by the United States of a massive naval "quarantine" of Cuba a week later; Nikita Khrushchev's demand for a trade of missiles in Cuba and Turkey on October 27; and the eventual backdown by the Soviet Union on the following day. But information on the underlying dynamics of the confrontation—how, for example, the U.S. decision to blockade Cuba was reached or why the Soviet Union abruptly agreed to withdraw the missiles on October 28—remained hidden from public view.

In the immediate aftermath of the crisis, newspapers and magazines scrambled to reconstruct events (particularly the role individual U.S. officials played in crisis deliberations) using information released by the U.S. government during the crisis and official and off-the-record interviews with Kennedy administration intimates. Additional information was gradually made public by the U.S. government in the following months, particularly through congressional hearings on the crisis and on continuing tensions between the U.S. and Cuban governments. Information about the size, composition, and timing of the Cuban military buildup and efforts to monitor the buildup by U.S. intelligence were also disclosed in an extraordinary February 1963 press conference by Secretary of Defense Robert McNamara and in a congressional study released three months later.[8]

More detailed narratives of the events of October 1962, however, appeared only years later, when inside accounts by top Kennedy administration officials and others involved in the crisis began to appear. These early accounts included an article by former State Department intelligence head Roger Hilsman in *Look* magazine in 1964 (as well as a similar account in his 1967 memoirs, *To Move a Nation*); Theodore Sorensen's memoir, *Kennedy* (1965); Arthur Schlesinger's *A Thousand Days* (1965); and Robert Kennedy's posthumously published memoir of the missile crisis, *Thirteen Days* (1969).[9]

Beginning in the 1960s, personal recollections by a variety of other U.S. officials were also collected under several oral history projects. In addition to making use of these first-hand accounts, some independent histories of the crisis written during this period, such as Elie Abel's 1966 book, *The Missile Crisis* or Edward Weintal and Charles Bartlett's, *Facing the Brink*

(1967), appear to have taken advantage of classified information or documentation which had been leaked by government officials. Several still-authoritative analyses of the crisis, including Graham Allison's 1971 work, *Essence of Decision,* were drawn exclusively from these early historical sources.

Nonetheless, other academic investigations have been greatly facilitated by the availability of key internal U.S. government documents which began with the opening of files at the John Fitzgerald Kennedy Library in Boston in the early 1970s. Although frustratingly slow and haphazard, the declassification process has led to the release of many of the contemporaneous documents read and generated by President Kennedy and his advisers during the crisis, the National Security Council Executive Committee (or "ExComm"). Currently, approximately 80 percent of all State Department records on the missile crisis have been publicly released in whole or in part, and documents from the National Security Council, Defense Department, and other agencies which played a significant role during the crisis have probably been released in comparable proportions.[10]

The declassified U.S. record has allowed scholars to highlight the inevitable distortions, limitations in perspective, and sheer inaccuracies in the narratives of individual memoirists. For example, the release of declassified documentation has shattered the long-standing myth that President Kennedy had ordered U.S. Jupiter missiles in Turkey withdrawn some time before the missile crisis. According to Robert Kennedy's memoir, President Kennedy was surprised and angered to learn during the crisis that his order to remove the obsolescent intermediate-range ballistic missiles (IRBMs) had never been carried out because of bureaucratic delays.[11] When Khrushchev insisted during the crisis that the United States withdraw its missiles in Turkey in exchange for the dismantling of Soviet missiles in Cuba, Robert Kennedy reportedly told Soviet ambassador to Washington Anatoly Dobrynin that the Jupiters could not be part of a U.S.-Soviet "deal," but that the United States nevertheless expected to execute its earlier decision to remove the Turkish missiles. However, historian Barton Bernstein was able to establish in a 1978 article that President Kennedy had not in fact ordered the Jupiters withdrawn prior to the onset of the crisis.[12] Bernstein's finding, which has been fundamental to more accurate evaluations of how a settlement to the missile crisis was achieved, was made possible only by the declassification of contemporaneous U.S. records which contradicted earlier first-hand accounts.

HISTORIOGRAPHY AND THE VIEW FROM WASHINGTON

As political scientists James Blight and David Welch have cogently argued, policymakers and academics approached the Cuban missile crisis in fundamentally different ways. Differences in the aims of each group—the scholar seeking explanations of behavior, and the policymaker concerned foremost with finding an appropriate course of action—color the analyses of each group. Scholars seek a value-free "view from nowhere," while politicians make decisions "somewhere" under specific psychological circumstances. The perspectives of academics and decisionmakers are, therefore, necessarily different. Thus, while scholars have debated whether the United States should have explored the possibility of simply accepting the Soviet missiles in Cuba or of seeking a private, diplomatic solution to the situation, the Kennedy administration officials who bore the responsibility of those actions have rejected these possibilities out of hand as politically impractical.

But if scholars and decisionmakers have differences in their analytical approaches to the missile crisis, they have nonetheless been profoundly linked in their epistemological perspectives. In particular, the fact that scholars have interpreted the crisis on the basis of the documents passing through the hands of high-level officials at the time has meant that histories of the crisis have necessarily reflected in some basic way the knowledge and information on the crisis held by those officials. Even in cases when historians were critical of U.S. actions or took exception to the ExComm's assessment of the crisis, their arguments and analyses were framed and supported almost exclusively by the *data* on the crisis used by U.S. decisionmakers. In short, the belief by scholars that they can begin to achieve a "view from nowhere" while studying the missile crisis (and often other contemporary international events) is illusory precisely because their sources of information have been severely limited in scope. In studying the missile crisis, the "view from nowhere" sought by historians and political scientists, in other words, has usually reflected the view from Washington in 1962.[13]

The problem in sharing this data base has become increasingly apparent as a result of new revelations indicating that the view from Washington in 1962 was in many respects incomplete or inaccurate. Recently, several sources of what might be called, for lack of a better term, "independent" information on the crisis—that is, information not known to U.S. decisionmakers at the time—has become available to scholars for virtually the first time. First, detailed data on U.S. military and covert operations related to Cuba has emerged. While President Kennedy and key members of his administration naturally directed and were kept apprised of major actions, many of the operational details of these actions were never reported to leaders in Washington. Researchers interested in operational aspects of the crisis have sought relevant information in official military histories and in the recollections of knowledgeable military officials.

The recent and unexpected disclosure of Soviet and Cuban information on the missile crisis represents a second source of historical data that has been hitherto unavailable to historians and was also unavailable to U.S. policymakers in 1962. Beginning with a 1987 retrospective conference on the crisis sponsored by Harvard University, knowledgeable Soviets officials have taken advantage of *glasnost* to offer the first detailed and candid accounts of Moscow's perspectives on the crisis. Prior to the testimony of these officials, the only sources for insight into Soviet actions and intentions during the crisis were the authenticated but often factually inaccurate memoirs of Nikita Khrushchev or less-than-frank accounts written by Soviet officials and commentators.[14]

Several other knowledgeable Soviets, joined by former Kennedy administration officials and, for the first time, Cuban officials, took part in a second retrospective conference held in Moscow in 1989.[15] Although varying in their knowledge and in their reticence, these officials, in the conferences and in subsequent interviews and articles, have provided insight into Soviet (and Cuban) decision making to a degree virtually unparalleled in the historiography of the Cold War.[16] A third Soviet-American-Cuban conference took place in Havana in 1992 and was attended by Fidel Castro. The Cuban leader's willingness to open the historical record on the crisis was evidenced by his recent release of several key documents, including correspondence between Khrushchev and himself during and after the October crisis.

These forms of "independent" information have begun to liberate historians from the "view from Washington." As a result, the full extent and effect of their earlier epistemological limitations—and those of U.S. decisionmakers in 1962—has become evident for the first time. These deficiencies in information and their effects on the U.S. decision-making process can be observed in several discrete areas: in interpretations of Soviet intentions, interpretations of Soviet actions, U.S. perceptions of its own actions, U.S. intelligence information, and in the uniformity of information among U.S. decisionmakers.

I. INTERPRETING SOVIET INTENTIONS: SOVIET MOTIVATIONS AND THE ORIGINS OF THE MISSILE CRISIS

On October 16, 1962, President Kennedy received word that a high-altitude U-2 reconnaissance mission had obtained hard evidence of Soviet medium-range ballistic missiles (MRBMs) in Cuba. Despite earlier intelligence indications pointing to such a possibility, the news came as a shock to President Kennedy and most U.S. leaders.[17] The surprise with which the discovery was received is indicative of the near-certainty in the U.S. intelligence community and among high-ranking Kennedy administration officials that Soviet leader Nikita Khrushchev would never attempt such a risky and potentially dangerous move. U.S. officials simply had no information regarding decision making in the Kremlin that would have led them to anticipate such a gamble on Khrushchev's part.

Lacking any hard information about the genesis of the Soviet missile deployment idea, President Kennedy and his advisers advanced several different speculative theories about Khrushchev's motivations. The Soviet missile deployment, members of the ExComm ventured in their first meeting on October 16, could have been seen by Khrushchev as, alternatively: a quick and inexpensive way to increase Soviet strategic missile strength; a bargaining chip to be traded away in exchange for Western concessions regarding the status of Berlin; a diversion which would allow the Soviets to take unilateral action on Berlin; a way to end the double standard which allowed the United States to deploy IRBMs on the Soviet periphery but not vice versa; or a test of U.S. resolve which would demonstrate U.S. irresolution and thus advance Soviet geopolitical power.[18]

President Kennedy tentatively explained Soviet motives by linking the issue of resolve and Soviet prestige to the long-festering issue of Berlin. The President told White House aide Arthur Schlesinger that he believed the move offered the Soviet Union several political advantages in its global struggle with the United States: It would deal the United States a blow to its international prestige and simultaneously strengthen the Soviet position in the Communist world and provide leverage for an eventual confrontation with the West over the status of Berlin.[19] State Department analysts also focused on the German question, notifying U.S. ambassadors abroad that they suspected the Soviet action to have been intended to bolster the Soviet position for a "showdown on Berlin."[20] All these explanations stressed the aggressive nature of Khrushchev's action. U.S. officials believed, as Schlesinger later wrote, that the Soviet decision "obviously represented the supreme probe of American intentions."[21]

One possible Soviet motivation which appears not to have been given much consideration by U.S. policymakers was that the deployment had been designed to prevent a U.S. attack on Cuba. Although historian Thomas Paterson has correctly pointed out that U.S. officials believed that Soviet shipments of conventional arms in 1962 stemmed from Cuban anxiety over a possible U.S. invasion,[22] this does not necessarily mean that the Kennedy administration saw the deployment of nuclear missiles as simply a continuation of the conventional military buildup and thus also the result of invasion fears. Indeed, the crisis's raison d'être, in the view of President Kennedy and the ExComm, was the qualitative difference that Soviet SS-4 and SS-5 nuclear missiles represented relative to the conventional arms which had been sent in earlier.

In the October 16 ExComm meeting, the defense of Cuba theme was notably absent among the possible Soviet motivations discussed. At one point in that meeting, McGeorge Bundy, Kennedy's adviser on national security affairs, read the September 12 *Tass* statement noting that the military equipment in Cuba was "designed exclusively for defense" and remarked, "Now there, it's very hard to reconcile *that* with what has happened."[23] Some months after the crisis, Nikita Khrushchev himself commented on his motivations in trying to establish missile bases in Cuba. Speaking before the Supreme Soviet on December 12, 1962, Khrushchev cast the move as an attempt to protect Cuba from U.S. aggression, stating, "Our purpose was only the defense of Cuba."[24] Khrushchev repeated his claim in his oral memoirs smuggled out of the Soviet Union and published in the West in the mid-1970s. However, in his memoirs, Khrushchev also admitted that additional Soviet concerns were involved in his decision. The installation of Soviet nuclear missiles in Cuba, he asserted, "would have equalized what the West likes to call the 'balance of power,' " and they would have given the United States, which had already established IRBM bases along the Soviet periphery, "a little of their own medicine."[25]

As part of the settlement to the missile crisis, the United States had offered assurances (albeit conditional ones)[26] that it would not invade Cuba if the Soviet missiles were dismantled. But until recently, Western scholars had been quick to discredit statements that Cuban defense was a real basis for moving Soviet rockets to that island, arguing that such an explanation was both improbable and self-serving. Khrushchev's insistence that the defense of Cuba was his primary motivation was widely seen as merely a belated attempt, after the fact, to put the best face on a Soviet foreign policy fiasco. Indeed, to accept Khrushchev's explanation at face value was tantamount, in Soviet specialist Arnold Horelick's words, to mistaking "salvage of a shipwreck for brilliant navigation."[27]

The defense of Cuba hypothesis, moreover, did not make sense as the sole explanation for the Soviet action. If Khrushchev really wanted to deter an invasion, some analysts have asked, why didn't he simply offer Cuba a contingent of Soviet troops to serve as a "tripwire" deterrent? If he believed nuclear forces to have been necessary to defend Cuba, why did he try to install SS-4 MRBMs and SS-5 IRBMs rather than less expensive and more easily deployed short-range tactical missiles?

Having dismissed Khrushchev's comments, however, historians have been left with little other direct evidence to shed light on the question of what Soviet and Cuban leaders sought to achieve in establishing missile bases in Cuba. In particular, the declassified U.S. record, a wealth of information to scholars in analyzing other aspects of the missile crisis, has provided little information on this issue, simply because U.S. decisionmakers themselves had little or no direct information about decision making in the Kremlin.

In looking at the origins of the missile crisis, then, scholars have labored under the same severe epistemological limitations as U.S. officials and have consequently adopted a similar approach. While perhaps more willing to firmly stake out their beliefs with regard to Soviet motivations than U.S. policymakers,[28] scholars have nonetheless viewed the different possible motivations as only tentative "hypotheses."[29] The inability of analysts to establish Soviet motivations with any certainty has prevented them from evaluating the effect *U.S.* policies had in giving rise to these motivations.

In the last few years, Soviet and Cuban officials have begun replacing much of the speculation surrounding Khrushchev's motivations with hard information. The idea of stationing Soviet missiles in Cuba reportedly first arose in an April 1962 conversation between Khrushchev and Soviet Defense Minister Rodion Malinovsky in the Crimea.[30] During their conversation, Malinovsky had pointed to the Black Sea and noted that the United States had installed IRBMs across the water in Turkey. Khrushchev was struck with the idea that if the United States could deploy missiles at the periphery of the Soviet Union, then the Soviets should be able to deploy similar weapons in Cuba, at the periphery of the United States.

In the following months, Khrushchev advanced his notion, initially with First Deputy Prime Minister Anastas Mikoyan, then with a group of close advisers, including Malinovsky; Soviet Foreign Minister Andrei Gromyko; Commander of the Strategic Rocket Forces Sergei Biryuzov; and Central Committee Secretary Frol Kozlov; and finally with the entire Soviet Presidium. In these discussions, Soviet sources have asserted, the idea gained momentum as a solution to three Soviet foreign policy problems. First, as Khrushchev had indicated to Malinovsky, Soviet medium-range missiles in Cuba would counterbalance U.S. missiles in Turkey, ending what the Soviets perceived as an intolerable double standard. Second, the deployment of missiles in Cuba was seen (particularly by the Soviet military) as a quick and effective means of redressing an egregious imbalance in nuclear forces favoring the United States. Third, the move would prevent what was otherwise seen as an inevitable invasion of Cuba by the United States.[31]

The Soviet missile initiative, rather than a bold initiative aimed at testing U.S. resolve, can now be seen, at least in part, as a Soviet reaction to what was perceived as provocative U.S. policies. With regard to the Soviet desire to counter U.S. IRBMs in Turkey, for example, even U.S. policymakers at the time of the Jupiter deployment decision recognized that the action could cause alarm and resentment in the Kremlin. In a meeting at the White House on June 16, 1959, President Dwight Eisenhower expressed discomfort with plans for the deployment of Jupiters overseas, arguing that "if Mexico or Cuba had been penetrated by the Communists, and then began getting arms and missiles from them . . . it would be imperative for us to take positive action, even offensive military action."[32]

The accelerating nuclear imbalance was an even more pressing Soviet concern in 1962. Soviet officials recently revealed that only about 20 Soviet ICBMs were operational in 1962. In contrast, the United States at the peak of the missile crisis had over 170 ICBMs and held a lopsided advantage in other strategic systems, such as manned bombers and submarine-launched ballistic missiles.[33] The U.S. advantage in nuclear weapons was largely dictated by erroneous intelligence estimates which, from 1957 until mid-1961, warned that the United States would be at the short end of a "missile gap" with the Soviet Union.[34] But well before the crisis materialized, the missile gap was known to favor the United States, not the Soviets.

The U.S. strategic advantage was underscored by several deliberate actions on the part of the Kennedy administration and had the effect of heightening Soviet strategic nuclear sensitivities. First, U.S. nuclear strategy under President Kennedy moved toward a "counterforce" policy, whereby enemy military installations rather than cities would be targeted. The possibility that the Soviet Union's fragile nuclear forces would be the primary target of the U.S. missiles must have raised Soviet fears of a possible U.S. first strike. These concerns may have been exacerbated by President Kennedy's remark in a March 1962 interview that "Khrushchev must *not* be certain that, where its vital interests are threatened, the United States will never strike first."[35] Furthermore, U.S. policymakers were not hesitant to use their nuclear superiority as a coercive political tool. U.S. officials, in the midst of the 1961 confrontation over Berlin, chose to underscore Soviet nuclear weakness in private meetings and in a dramatic public speech on October 21 by Deputy Secretary of Defense Roswell Gilpatric.[36] Lastly, even after a critical intelligence breakthrough in September 1961 revealed the extent of the United States' existing nuclear superiority,[37] the Kennedy administration called for the production of prodigious quantities of all forms of nuclear armaments, including the establishment of a force of 200 Minuteman I ICBMs in 1963.[38]

The controversial assertion that the defense of Cuba was one component of the Soviet decision has been advanced by several other Soviets, including Andrei Gromyko; former Soviet ambassador to Cuba Aleksandr Alekseev; Nikita Khrushchev's son, Sergei; and Sergo Mikoyan, the son of and aide to Anastas Mikoyan.[39] According to some of these sources, Khrushchev had been informed by Malinovsky that Cuba could withstand a full-scale U.S. invasion for only three to four days before being overwhelmed. In view of the apparent hopelessness of a conventional defense, and convinced that a U.S. attack was imminent, Khrushchev concluded that "there was no other path" to defending Cuba other than the installation of nuclear missiles.[40]

In light of these disclosures, most analyses of Soviet motivations appear to have been wrong in rejecting or downplaying the defense of Cuba theme. Many of the original objections to this motivation appear increasingly tenuous. An examination of the written record, for example, shows that the defense of Cuba explanation, as commonly asserted, was not offered as postcrisis rationalization. As early as October 23—before it became clear that a Cuban non-invasion assurance would become part of the crisis settlement—Khrushchev insisted that "the armaments in Cuba, regardless of the classification to which they belong, are intended solely for defensive purposes in order to secure [the] Cuban Republic from the attack of an aggressor."[41] The traditional argument that Khrushchev would have deployed tactical nuclear weapons instead of MRBMs and IRBMs if he wished to defend Cuba also seems somewhat hollow in light of the recent revelation that nuclear armed tactical weapons *were* in Cuba and recent Soviet assertions that both the defense of Cuba *and* the need to redress the strategic imbalance were motivating factors.[42]

The Soviet information has also opened new analytical perspectives into the origins of the crisis. By establishing Khrushchev's motivations with reasonable certainty, the new information has allowed scholars to shift their focus to secondary issues. Where did these motivations come from and to what extent did U.S. policies give impetus to the Soviet decision?[43]

The realization that the defense of Cuba was a contributing factor to the Soviet missile decision has focused attention on the possible role that the United States' aggressive policy toward Cuba may have had in instigating the missile crisis. In April 1961, 1,400 U.S.-trained anti-Castro émigrés attempting to storm a Cuban beachhead at the Bay of Pigs were quickly defeated by Cuban forces. Scholars have frequently suggested that Khrushchev regarded President Kennedy's unwillingness to commit U.S. forces to the foundering attack as a sign of U.S. weakness. However, it now seems likely that Khrushchev saw the Bay of Pigs episode primarily as a demonstration of the Kennedy administration's deep antagonism toward the Castro government.

U.S. policy and actions following the Bay of Pigs gave Cuban and Soviet leaders ample reason to believe that a new invasion would eventually occur, this time using U.S. military forces. Beginning in November 1961, the Kennedy administration renewed its efforts to overthrow the Castro government through a covert action program code-named "Operation Mongoose." Cuban and Soviet intelligence tracked subsequent U.S. activities directed against the Cuban government, including infiltration of the island by CIA agents; sabotage of Cuban ships and facilities; training and assistance provided to Alpha 66 and other violent anti-Castro Cuban émigré organizations; and assassination attempts against Cuban leaders.[44]

In light of these activities and overt actions such as the establishment of an economic embargo on Cuban goods, the successful effort of the United States to diplomatically isolate Cuba at the January 1962 meeting of the Organization of American States, and the staging of several large-scale military exercises in the Caribbean designed to test U.S. invasion plans, the conclusion reached in Havana and Moscow that U.S. troops would eventually storm Cuban beaches appears entirely reasonable. Robert McNamara has himself stated, "If I was a Cuban and read the evidence of covert American action against their government, I would be quite ready to believe that the U.S. intended to mount an invasion."[45] Perhaps even more relevantly, the United States may indeed have had those intentions. While claims that a firm decision had been made to invade Cuba before the missile crisis began seem overstated,[46] the Mongoose program did envision the use of U.S. forces as the ultimate answer to the Cuban problem. Recently declassified guidelines for Mongoose tacitly approved by President Kennedy in March 1962 noted that "final success" of the program would "require decisive U.S. military intervention."[47]

The "Actor-Observer" Fallacy:
My Actions Are Defensive—Yours Are Unprovoked

The purpose of the foregoing analysis is not to definitively examine the interaction between U.S. policies in 1961 and 1962 and Soviet motivations in deploying missiles to Cuba, but only to suggest that such a dynamic existed. Largely because of the absence of information about Soviet decision making, both U.S. decisionmakers and, until recently, Western analysts, seem to have succumbed to the "actor-observer" fallacy, whereby the actions of one's adversary appear to be unprovoked initiatives and one's own actions seem only defensive responses to those actions. New Soviet information suggests that while Khrushchev's gamble was indisputably a bold and irresponsible foreign policy initiative, it was at the same time a *reaction* to existing U.S. policies. The Soviet action thus appears to have been not so much the "supreme probe of American intentions"[48] perceived by Kennedy administration officials as an ultimately *defensive* measure aimed at restraining U.S. activity against Cuba and, in Raymond Garthoff's words, "prevent[ing] the United States from using its growing strategic superiority to compel Soviet concessions on various issues under contention."[49]

In the end, it is not clear how the misreading of Soviet motivations by U.S. policymakers affected their subsequent handling of the Cuban crisis. By perceiving the Soviet move as an aggressive test of U.S. resolve, the logic of taking strong action was certainly reinforced: if the United States did not stand up to the Soviet challenge in Cuba, President Kennedy and the ExComm feared an even more dangerous Soviet advance would be inevitable in the future. Nonetheless, it seems probable that other factors, such as President Kennedy's public assurances that Soviet missile bases in Cuba would not be tolerated, or the deceitful way in which the Soviet missiles were deployed, would have made the acceptance of missiles in Cuba extremely difficult.

II. U.S. INFORMATION ON SOVIET ACTIONS

But the question of Soviet motivations was only one of a multitude of areas in which relevant information about the missile crisis was severely limited. Moreover, while U.S. officials were quite aware of their lack of knowledge regarding Soviet motives, they did not recognize their own epistemological shortcomings in other areas which had a direct bearing on their handling of the crisis. One of these areas was the ExComm's interpretation of various Soviet diplomatic and military messages and "signals" during the crisis. Leaders in Havana, Moscow, and Washington sought to communicate their own posture and intentions through public statements, direct correspondence between Kennedy and Khrushchev, private exchanges and meetings between other U.S. and Soviet officials, messages to allied nations which were possibly intended to leak to the other side, and changes in military posture and alert status.[50]

The ExComm did not have access to any information which would allow them to differentiate between deliberate actions ordered by Khrushchev and Castro and inadvertent or unauthorized actions which did not actually reflect official Soviet or Cuban posture. When attempting to interpret developments in the crisis, U.S. decisionmakers therefore generally assumed that the actions of their adversaries were the result of conscious decisions reached in Moscow and Havana. Historians following the paper trail generated by U.S. policymakers usually have not had access to any additional information which would allow them to question these judgments. However, with the recent release of detailed Soviet and Cuban accounts on their roles in the missile crisis, it now appears that several key developments previously assumed to have been the result of deliberate decisions by Soviet leaders were in fact the result of unauthorized actions by subordinate officials.

One means of communication employed during the missile crisis was a somewhat improbable diplomatic channel opened between Aleksandr Fomin, the KGB head in Washington, and John Scali, a reporter for ABC News. Fomin had contacted Scali on October 26 and had urged him to pass on to his "high-level friends" in the Kennedy administration a possible formula for ending the missile crisis: The Soviet Union would withdraw its missile bases under United Nations inspection in exchange for a U.S. guarantee not to invade Cuba. When President Kennedy received a long, emotional letter from Khrushchev later that same day, the ExComm noted that the missive seemed in a vague manner to make the same proposal, but without mentioning the issue of UN inspection. The ExComm decided that the Fomin message and the Khrushchev letter complemented each other and could be interpreted as a single, coherent offer on the part of the Soviet Union.[51]

In fact, the two proposals were *not* coordinated with each other. Soviet officials have now disclosed that Fomin, in making the offer to Scali, had acted strictly on his own initiative. While Fomin had been given approval by the Soviet embassy in Washington to feel out the American position, his specific proposal was authorized by neither the Soviet embassy nor the Kremlin. Without Fomin's unauthorized comments, it seems unlikely that the ExComm would have treated Khrushchev's October 26 letter as a serious negotiating position. Secretary of Defense Robert McNamara remarked in a meeting the following day that "when I read [Khrushchev's October 26 letter] . . . I thought, My God, I'd never . . . base a transaction on that contract. Hell, that's no offer . . ."[52]

An even more startling revision regarding the ExComm's interpretation of Soviet actions in the crisis involves the downing of an American U-2 aircraft over Cuba on October 27. On the morning of October 27, the ExComm received word of a new, public letter from Khrushchev demanding that the United States remove its Jupiter missiles from Turkey as part of an agreement to get the Soviet missiles out of Cuba. On top of the new hard-line negotiating position adopted by Khrushchev, the ExComm received another piece of bad news: an American U-2 aircraft on a morning reconnaissance mission over Cuba had been shot down and destroyed by a Soviet SA-2 surface-to-air missile (SAM) battery near Banes, Cuba. Although some historians have argued that U.S. officials did not hold Khrushchev personally responsible for the U-2 shoot-down,[53] the ExComm meeting transcript indicates that in the absence of direct information suggesting otherwise, most members of the ExComm assumed that the attack had been authorized by political leaders in the Kremlin. At one point in their discussions, for example, State Department Undersecretary U. Alexis Johnson noted: "You could have an undisciplined . . . Cuban anti-aircraft fire, but to have a SAM-site and a Russian crew fire is no accident."[54]

The ExComm perceived the U-2 downing as a part of an attempt on the part of the Soviet Union to up the ante in the crisis. Llewellyn Thompson, the ExComm's Soviet specialist, appeared to express concern over both the new letter from Khrushchev and the U-2 incident, remarking that the Soviets had "done two things. They've put up the price, and they've escalated . . . the action." Moments later, Vice-President Lyndon Johnson appears to argue that the U-2 shoot-down was the primary escalatory action: "You just ask yourself what made the greatest impression on you today, whether it was his [Khrushchev's] letter last night or whether it was his letter this morning. Or whether it was his [words unclear] U-2 . . . ?" After Thompson replies, "The U-2," Johnson remarks, "That's exactly right." President Kennedy himself, upon hearing that the U-2 was downed by a Soviet SAM, grimly noted, "This is much of an escalation by them, isn't it?"[55]

Soviet and Cuban sources have now revealed that the attack on the U-2 was ordered by local Soviet air defense commanders without direct authorization from Moscow (or even from the overall Soviet military commander in Cuba, General Issa Pliyev).[56] While the action did not technically violate Soviet standing orders (since Khrushchev had apparently never given explicit orders not to open fire), the attack was not ordered by the Kremlin, as most members of the ExComm and most scholars have believed. The ExComm's misinterpretation of the U-2 incident, while understandable if not inevitable given the fragmentary nature of available information, was nonetheless dangerous.

By interpreting the action as a deliberate Soviet provocation, the ExComm read political significance into what in reality was only a Soviet command and control failure. In addition, the ExComm's interpretation of the incident as a deliberate action heightened the possibility of a U.S. retaliatory strike on portions of the air defense system in Cuba or even the missile sites themselves. Robert Kennedy recorded in his memoirs that upon learning of the Soviet attack on the U-2, "there was almost unanimous agreement that we had to attack early the next morning with bombers and fighters and destroy the SAM sites."[57]

While transcripts of the October 27 ExComm meeting suggest that many ExComm members were actually reluctant to call an air strike on the SAM sites, the possibility that the United States would take some form of military action in response to the shoot-down nonetheless existed since, four days earlier, the ExComm had decided that in the event a U.S. aircraft was shot down, an attack on the responsible SAM site would be executed. President Kennedy's decision to refrain from ordering such a strike was thus a reversal of established policy and was reportedly met with strenuous objections by some military officials.[58]

In each of these cases, the misperceptions of U.S. officials cannot be attributed to failures in analysis or in logic. The assumptions that Fomin had been authorized by Khrushchev to float a possible solution to the crisis or that Khrushchev had directed Soviet forces to shoot down the U-2 seem understandable as informational failings. Essentially, there was not the knowledge base, nor was there an ability to traverse the gap of empathy that might have given events an alternative interpretation in the minds of U.S. decisionmakers at the height of the crisis.

III. INFORMATION ON U.S. MILITARY ACTIONS

Another epistemological gap in the ExComm's understanding of the missile crisis lay in its information regarding the United States' own military actions. In analyzing the military aspects of the crisis, scholars have also tended to highlight episodes in the crisis in which political authority intervened to prevent potentially inflammatory or hazardous military actions. In *Essence of Decision*, for instance, Graham Allison describes how President Kennedy ordered a U.S. intelligence-gathering vessel away from the Cuban coast to avoid possible capture by Cuban forces and how Secretary of Defense McNamara and Navy Admiral George Anderson clashed over McNamara's insistence on establishing political control over quarantine interception procedures.

U.S. officials believed at the time that they were generally successful in orchestrating and controlling military activities. President Kennedy and Secretary of Defense McNamara were highly conscious of the close linkage between political and military developments in the crisis and sought to exercise extremely tight control over U.S. military actions in order to avoid the danger of having the Kremlin regard unauthorized actions as intentional "signals." A classified November 14, 1962, postmortem on the crisis reinforced the belief that Kennedy had managed to establish "continuous, intense, central control" over both U.S. military actions and the overall direction of the crisis.[59]

The focus on successful political micromanagement of military actions during the crisis seems to have been the result of scholars using memoirs and the declassified documents of *political* leaders as their primary historical sources. Recent research into operational aspects of the crisis, using military records and the recollections of military officials, has revealed several examples of potentially dangerous activities which members of the ExComm and other political leaders never learned about. For example, on October 22, General Thomas Powers, the head of the U.S. Strategic Air Command, decided to conduct the U.S. nuclear alert process "in the clear" rather than with customary encryption.[60] Power's high-profile advertising of U.S. nuclear strength was apparently noted by the Soviet military and Soviet intelligence, but never reported to the ExComm. In another case, U.S. political leaders did not know that a U.S. test intercontinental ballistic missile (ICBM) located nearby actual alerted ICBMs was launched during the crisis, an action which could conceivably have been misconstrued by Soviet intelligence as the launching of an armed U.S. missile.[61]

Military actions undertaken by covert operation teams also took place without the knowledge of U.S. political leaders. During the missile crisis, the ExComm contemplated working with anti-Castro Cuban émigrés, but ultimately rejected proposals to employ these assets. On October 28, with a crisis settlement apparently at hand, Secretary McNamara gave orders for U.S. military forces to prevent any sabotage or harassing raids by anti-Castro groups which might reignite tensions. Robert Kennedy gave similar orders to prevent any actions by CIA covert action teams working under Operation Mongoose which, unknown to the ExComm, had been infiltrated into Cuba during the crisis. Unfortunately, recalling the groups was more difficult than dispatching them. One of the six infiltrated teams carried out its planned mission and blew up a Cuban industrial facility on November 8, at the same time delicate tripartite negotiations over the removal of the Soviet missiles and bombers in Cuba were underway. As with the other incidents cited, the ExComm never knew that the action had taken place.[62]

The ExComm knew some, but not all, of the details in two other un-anticipated incidents arising from U.S. military operations.

The first happened shortly before the announcement of the U.S. blockade on October 22. President Kennedy ordered the Navy to give "the highest priority to tracking [Soviet] submarines and to put into effect the greatest possible safety measures to protect" U.S. vessels.[63] As Scott Sagan has noted, U.S. forces took these instructions as virtual carte blanche to take any and all measures necessary to flush Soviet submarines to the surface. While the antisubmarine warfare (ASW) activities, including the use of low-level depth charges, were thus authorized, U.S. officials at the time did not know that one Soviet submarine was actually crippled by U.S. naval forces.[64]

The second incident occurred on October 27, when an American U-2 plane on a "routine" air sampling mission near the Arctic Circle lost its bearings and strayed over Soviet territory. Soviet MiG fighters and U.S. interceptors based in Alaska converged on the errant U-2. The U-2 was eventually able to make its way out of Soviet airspace without any shots fired. Khrushchev heatedly alluded to the incident in his October 28 letter to Kennedy: "Is it not a fact that an intruding American plane could easily be taken for a nuclear bomber, which might push us to a fateful step . . . ?"[65] Neither Khrushchev nor U.S. officials, however, were fully aware of how potentially hazardous the incident might have been. According to research conducted by Scott Sagan, the U.S. fighter aircraft that escorted the wandering U-2 back to base appear to have been armed with low-yield nuclear air-to-air defense missiles.[66] This new piece of information raises the issue of whether nuclear armaments might, but for chance, have been detonated along the Soviet periphery at the height of the crisis.

The ExComm's lack of information about U.S. military actions allowed some of these unsettling incidents to occur. Given the complexity of military operations during the missile crisis, it was not possible for Kennedy and McNamara to have had full knowledge about all ongoing U.S. military actions. The ability of the national civilian command to prevent inadvertent and possibly provocative accidents was correspondingly limited by the sheer complexity and extensiveness of deployments and operations. Thus, in response to the question of why during the crisis he did not cancel "routine" U-2 air sampling missions like the one just mentioned, Robert McNamara recently replied that "we just didn't know [the U-2] was up there collecting samples.[67] Similarly, in the case of the Mongoose sabotage effort, the ExComm simply did not learn about the infiltration of assets into Cuba until it was too late to recall the teams.

IV. FAILURES IN U.S. INTELLIGENCE

Fundamental information about Soviet and Cuban military capabilities, diplomatic maneuvers, and other developments in the crisis was furnished to President Kennedy and the ExComm by the U.S. intelligence community. Some intelligence concerns, such as the question of whether warheads for Soviet MRBMs were present in Cuba, were recognized at the time as being unanswerable from the standpoint of U.S. intelligence. The ExComm simply believed it prudent to "assume" that warheads were in fact on the island.[68] But other intelligence estimates were not openly questioned and yet formed the basis for U.S. decision making. For example, U.S. intelligence estimated during the crisis that some 8,000 to 10,000 Soviet troops were present in Cuba.[69] U.S. military planners using these figures calculated that U.S. forces could successfully overwhelm these forces and seize the island, but at the cost of an estimated 18,500 U.S. casualties.[70]

Scholars have tended to treat these figures as empirical fact rather than possibly inaccurate estimates. In Graham Allison's study of the crisis, for example, he simply states that "there were some 22,000 Soviet soldiers and technicians in Cuba to assemble, operate, and defend" the Soviet missile installations. Allison does not qualify the 22,000 figure as being only an estimate, nor does he note that U.S. officials weighing the pros and cons of a U.S. invasion used a substantially lower number.[71] But Cuban and Soviet sources have now revealed that some 42,000 to 44,000 Soviet troops and 270,000 Cubans were armed and prepared to defend against a U.S. invasion.[72]

Even more shockingly, recent Soviet evidence suggests that the belief of U.S. officials that no nuclear warheads existed for Soviet short-range tactical missiles was wrong. According to Anatoly Gribkov, a Soviet military officer in Cuba in 1962, some nine nuclear warheads for tactical missiles were on the island. Moreover, local Soviet commanders were astonishingly given authority to fire the missiles without further orders from the Kremlin in the event of a U.S. invasion. If true, a U.S. attack on Cuba might have escalated into a nuclear exchange far faster than any U.S. official could have anticipated. U.S. officials trying to weigh the costs of an invasion were clearly ill-served by the underestimate of Soviet troop strength and by the failure of

U.S. intelligence to warn that Soviet *tactical* missiles were capable of starting a nuclear war.[73]

V. UNIFORMITY OF INFORMATION AMONG U.S. DECISIONMAKERS; THE JUPITER DEAL AND THE SIGNIFICANCE OF THE EXCOMM GROUP

The central decision-making body for the U.S. government during the missile crisis was by all accounts an extraordinary group: Composed of individuals from both within the administration and outside government, the ExComm wrestled with various U.S. policy options without reference to each member's position or rank.[74] While President Kennedy's political autonomy has never seriously been questioned, ExComm members clearly saw their role as a crucial part of the decision-making process. Scholars have generally followed this approach, treating the American handling of the missile crisis as being as much a result of the dynamics of small-group decision making as it was a manifestation of President Kennedy's own personality.

One of the most surprising recent disclosures about the missile crisis concerns diplomatic initiatives undertaken by President Kennedy without the full, or in some cases, even partial knowledge of his advisers on the ExComm. In 1987, former Secretary of State Dean Rusk disclosed contingency planning for one such initiative, describing it as a "postscript only I can furnish." Rusk revealed that on the evening of October 27, President Kennedy asked him to contact Andrew Cordier, a former UN Undersecretary, in order to lay the groundwork for a possible public trade of U.S. IRBMs in Turkey and Soviet missiles in Cuba. Upon receipt of a further signal from Rusk, Cordier was instructed to ask UN Secretary-General U Thant to propose such a trade, which the United States would then presumably accept. No such signal was ever given, but the approach to Cordier, made without the knowledge of any other ExComm members, suggests that President Kennedy was at least seriously considering ending the crisis through a public deal involving the Turkish missiles.[75]

Even more startling evidence of President Kennedy's own inclination to end the crisis through negotiations, even if it meant trading away the U.S. Jupiters in Turkey, was presented at the 1989 Moscow conference by former Soviet ambassador to the United States Anatoly Dobrynin. According to Dobrynin, Robert Kennedy, with President Kennedy's direct approval, volunteered in a secret meeting at the Soviet embassy on October 26 that the United States was ready to "examine favorably the question of Turkey."[76] No U.S. official aside from the president and his brother knew of this meeting with Dobrynin or the fact that Robert Kennedy himself raised the possibility of having the Jupiters play a part in a crisis settlement.

Secret U.S. diplomatic initiatives unknown to some ExComm members also took place the following night. Following the ExComm meeting on the afternoon of October 27, a smaller group of dovish advisers met and decided that Robert Kennedy should meet with Ambassador Dobrynin that evening to discuss the deepening crisis.[77] At Dean Rusk's suggestion, it was agreed that Robert Kennedy would tell Dobrynin that the United States intended to remove the Jupiter missiles from Turkey as soon as the crisis ended.

While the other, more hawkish ExComm members were informed of the Kennedy-Dobrynin meeting, they were not told that Robert Kennedy intended to offer limited assurances on the Jupiter missiles.[78] Further, even the group of dovish ExComm members who had originally decided that Robert Kennedy should meet with Dobrynin may have been slightly misinformed about Kennedy's actual intentions. Rusk and the other U.S. officials knew that Robert Kennedy would provide assurances that the Jupiters would be eventually withdrawn, but at the same time they believed that the younger Kennedy would emphasize that the Jupiters were, in essence, "irrelevant" to the Cuban question and thus could not be part of any formal deal. Dobrynin has recently asserted, however, that in his meeting with Robert Kennedy the night of October 27, the attorney general pursued the idea of an explicit arrangement involving the Jupiters and suggested to the Soviet ambassador that the U.S. position was a significant diplomatic concession.[79]

These new details, beyond dramatically altering historical understanding of how the missile crisis was settled, also highlight the degree to which most ExComm members were kept in the dark about U.S.-Soviet negotiations during the crisis. The fact that information about the status of crisis negotiations was withheld in varying degrees from members of the ExComm does suggest that the body was becoming increasingly peripheral to the decision-making process. On the other hand, the influence of the ExComm on President Kennedy's perceptions and actions cannot be dismissed altogether. Even late in the crisis, the ExComm exerted considerable psychological pressure on the president and was able to sway some of his actions. For example, on October 27, Kennedy initially hesitated in going along with the idea of ignoring Khrushchev's public demand for a Turkey-Cuba trade and instead "accepting" the earlier Soviet "offer" to remove its missiles in return for a U.S. pledge not to invade Cuba. Kennedy's eventual agreement was the result at least in part of the agreement among nearly all members of the ExComm that such a tactic might work.[80]

It seems likely that the resistance to an outright Turkey-Cuba deal expressed by nearly all members of the ExComm would not have been so strong if they had known that Robert Kennedy had himself introduced the possibility of such a trade in his secret talks with Dobrynin. The growing split between an increasingly dovish president and his advisers edging toward further U.S. military action was thus in part the result of their differing sets of information on the crisis. If Khrushchev had not promptly backed down on the morning of October 28, the recommendations of the ExComm would likely have been based on an understanding of the crisis quite different from that of President Kennedy. As a U.S. postmortem on the crisis noted, "While it is not a cardinal necessity that all advisers whom the President consults have the same information, it is highly undesirable that their advice diverge merely because some lack certain key facts."[81] Details of secret negotiations over a major stumbling block to a crisis settlement clearly qualify as "key facts."

CONCLUSION

At the outset of this essay, the question of whether it was worth continuing to study the Cuban missile crisis was raised. The recent wave of new disclosures, particularly from Soviet officials, has demonstrated how much there was, and very likely still is, to learn about the crisis. Earlier attempts by historians to present a full account of the Cuban missile crisis appear incomplete or inaccurate in several areas in light of these new revelations. But perhaps more significantly, the new information has suggested that many of these previous historical deficiencies existed only because they reflected inaccuracies in the views of U.S. officials at the time of the crisis.

Misinformation and lack of information—in short, the epistemological limitations of U.S. officials—represented a severe flaw in the U.S. decision-making process during the crisis. President Kennedy's handling of the crisis ("so brilliantly controlled, so matchlessly calibrated" as Arthur Schlesinger once described it)[82] was in fact crippled by the lack of accurate data on developments in the crisis. It seems safe to assume that decision making in Moscow and in Havana were distorted in similar ways.

To some historians, the new facts about the crisis suggest that it was more "manageable" and less dangerous than previously believed. As Mark Trachtenberg notes, the most important point to emerge from these new sources is that President Kennedy was much more willing to compromise on the issue of the Jupiter missiles in Turkey than had been previously thought. The implication he teases from this is that there was more of a "cushion," more room for diplomatic settlement, and thus less risk, than had earlier been assumed.[83] But the epistemological limitations hinted at in this paper suggest that severe crises in general are less manageable than they usually are believed to be. Although it is true that in the case of Cuba, President Kennedy now appears to have been prepared to offer significant concessions to end the crisis peacefully, one cannot assume that in future crises, political leaders will be so prone to seeking a settlement through political accommodation. What is certain, however, is that decisionmakers on all sides of intense crises will be forced to act without having a full and accurate understanding of the situation, and that they will largely underestimate the incompleteness and inaccuracy of their available information and operating assumptions.

In addition, such a sanguine assessment of crisis manageability rests upon new information on U.S. decision making. New information from the Cuban and Soviet sides, such as the revelation that Castro called on Khrushchev to strike a preemptive nuclear blow on the United States in the event of a Cuban invasion, certainly makes the crisis seem a far more dangerous incident that earlier believed.[84]

The study of contemporary U.S. history has been aided immeasurably by the Freedom of Information Act and other statutes which have sought to make internal U.S. government records public as quickly as possible, given legitimate national security concerns. However, scholars have not been sufficiently aware of the limits on their knowledge that exist in spite of the availability of declassified U.S. documents. Many sensitive U.S. records take several decades to be released, and perhaps more importantly, the information contained in those documents is often incomplete or inaccurate. The understandable tendency of Western scholars to equate Washington's knowledge, estimates, and assumptions with the totality of empirical fact has led to underestimation of the extent to which decision making in the Cuban missile crisis was conducted in the dark. Now, to the extent that new information has begun to liberate analysts from the "view from Washington" in the Cuban incident, policymakers and scholars alike should be more aware of their limits to understanding of other confrontations.

NOTES

1. See the bibliography published in Laurence Chang, ed., *The Cuban Missile Crisis, 1962* (Alexandria, Va: National Security Archive/Chadwyck-Healey, 1990), vol. 1, pp. 155-169. Document numbers cited in the endnotes

correspond to the declassified and unclassified documents published in this collection.

2. Eliot A. Cohen, "Why We Should Stop Studying the Cuban Missile Crisis," *National Interest* (Winter 1986): 6.

3. James G. Blight and David A. Welch, *On the Brink: Americans and Soviets Reexamine the Cuban Missile Crisis* (New York: Hill and Wang, 1989), p. 23. At the same conference, Theodore Sorensen concurred with Dillon, saying, "We need to be very careful about making easy judgments about the present and the future based on a very different past."

4. According to minutes of a National Security Planning Group meeting on November 11, 1984, Secretary of Defense Caspar Weinberger argued that the delivery of these aircraft could be publicly portrayed as "like the Cuban missile crisis" by virtue of their having "crossed the line of what we can accept." U.S. Ambassador to the UN Jeane Kirkpatrick took issue with Weinberger, suggesting that the missile crisis was not in fact analogous to the situation in Nicaragua. See National Security Planning Group (NSPG) Meeting (document no. 03316).

5. Some factors in the missile crisis, such as the dynamics of small-group decision making, remain relevant today. See James G. Blight, Joseph S. Nye, Jr., and David A. Welch, "The Cuban Missile Crisis Revisited," *Foreign Affairs* 66, no. 1 (Fall 1987):171.

6. The "epistemological limitations" referred to in this paper consequently refer to limitations in accurate information and empirical data which may have affected the analyses and beliefs of historians or policymakers.

7. See comments by McGeorge Bundy and Theodore Sorensen in Blight, *On the Brink*, p. 245.

8. See Press Briefing by Robert McNamara, February 6, 1963 (document no. 02909) and "Interim Report by the Preparedness Subcommittee on the Cuban Military Buildup," May 9, 1963 (document no. 03102).

9. Other published first-hand accounts have since been contributed by Ex-Comm members such as McGeorge Bundy, George Ball, U. Alexis Johnson, and Maxwell Taylor, as well as other officials such as former CIA analyst Raymond Cline and State Department officials Abram Chayes and Robert Hurwitch.

10. This estimate is derived from State Department responses to requests filed under the Freedom of Information Act for the release of all classified State Department records on the crisis.

11. Robert F. Kennedy, *Thirteen Days: A Memoir of the Cuban Missile Crisis* (New York: W.W. Norton, 1969), p. 95.

12. Barton Bernstein, "The Cuban Missile Crisis: Trading the Jupiters in Turkey?" *Political Science Quarterly* 95, no. 1 (Spring 1980): 97-125.

13. Perhaps the only significant way in which historians have had access to more information than U.S. officials during the crisis is in their use of information which became known to U.S. officials *after* the crisis.

14. See the collection of Soviet commentaries in Ronald R. Pope, ed., *Soviet Views on the Cuban Missile Crisis: Myth and Reality in Foreign Policy*

Analysis (Lanham, Md.: University Press of America, 1982). Khrushchev's memoirs were published in the West in two volumes in 1970 and 1974, with a third volume, containing previously withheld material, published in 1990.

15. Information on the Soviet side of the crisis has been furnished by several Soviet officials, including former Soviet ambassador to Washington, Anatoly Dobrynin; Sergei Khrushchev, Nikita Khrushchev's son; Sergo Mikoyan, the son of Soviet Deputy Premier Anastas Mikoyan; Aleksandr Alekseev, the Soviet ambassador to Cuba in 1962; Fyodor Burlatsky, a speechwriter and aide to Khrushchev, and General Dimitri Volkogonov, the head of the Soviet Ministry of Defense Institute of Military History. For a listing of recently published Soviet accounts on the crisis, see Bruce J. Allyn, James G. Blight, and David A. Welch, "Essence of Revision: Moscow, Havana, and the Cuban Missile Crisis," *International Security* 14, no. 3 (Winter 1989/1990):136-137.

16. Some historians have called into question the value of these Soviet testimonials. For example, historian Marc Trachtenberg, in a 1990 article commenting on a published interview with Sergo Mikoyan, the son of former Soviet Deputy Premier Anastas Mikoyan, argued that nearly all significant new historical information has come from American documentation and that "Soviet sources, even in this era of *glasnost*, have not provided us with much hard evidence" about the crisis. However, Trachtenberg's article was written before the 1989 Moscow conference and the subsequent publication of Soviet and U.S. articles which draw on more knowledgeable Soviet sources. See Marc Trachtenberg, "Commentary: New Light on the Cuban Missile Crisis?" *Diplomatic History* 14, no. 2 (Spring 1990): 241.

17. Robert Kennedy wrote that the "dominant feeling" at the first ExComm meeting was one of "stunned surprise." Kennedy, *Thirteen Days,* p. 24. However, some high-ranking officials, most notably CIA Director John McCone, had anticipated the Soviet move.

18. Graham Allison's analysis of possible Soviet motivations suggests that the ExComm considered the possibility of Cuban defense in the first ExComm session, but meeting transcripts do not appear to bear this out. Cf. Graham T. Allison, *Essence of Decision* (Boston: Little, Brown and Co., 1971), pp. 42, 47-50 and "Off-the-Record Meeting on Cuba, October 16, 1962, 11:50 A.M.-12:57 P.M." (document 00622).

19. Arthur M. Schlesinger, Jr. *A Thousand Days: JFK in the White House* (Boston: Houghton Mifflin, 1965), p. 811.

20. State Department circular telegram 744, October 24, 1962 (document no. 01153).

21. Schlesinger, *A Thousand Days,* p. 796.

22. Thomas G. Paterson, "Fixation with Cuba: The Bay of Pigs, Missile Crisis, and Covert War against Castro," in Thomas G. Paterson, ed., *Kennedy's Quest For Victory: American Foreign Policy, 1961-1963* (New York: Oxford University Press, 1989), p. 141.

23. "Off-the-Record Meeting on Cuba, October 16, 1962, 11:50 A.M.-12:57 P.M." (document 00622), p. 15.

24. *Current Digest of the Soviet Press,* January 16,1963.

25. Nikita S. Khrushchev, *Khrushchev Remembers,* trans. and ed. Strobe Talbott (Boston: Little, Brown & Company, 1970), p. 494.

26. The United States never provided public, unconditional "guarantees" that it would not invade Cuba as the Soviet Union and Cuba wished. Although non-invasion assurances were explicitly mentioned in Kennedy's October 27, 1962 letter to Khrushchev and Khrushchev's reply on October 28, the U.S. government never consummated the agreement, noting that the Soviet Union had failed to allow the United Nations to verify the dismantling of the missiles and establish safeguards against their reintroduction, as specified in the U.S.-Soviet agreement. In closed congressional testimony several months after the crisis, Secretary of State Dean Rusk acknowledged that "an unadorned commitment" not to invade Cuba did not exist. See "Briefing on the World Situation," January 11, 1963 (document no. 02847). The declassification in 1992 of all previously withheld correspondence between Kennedy and Khrushchev from the crisis period has also confirmed the lack of any formal non-invasion agreement. Kennedy side-stepped Khrushchev's repeated demand that the two governments "write down" their mutual commitments and submit them to the UN. Despite the lack of a formal pledge from the U.S. government, Khrushchev apparently believed that he had sufficient personal assurances from Kennedy that Cuba would note be attacked. In a January 31, 1963 letter to Castro, he notes, " . . . [W]e have prevented the North [American] invasion. . . . Perhaps for one or two years, and we think that even for five or six, the situation will be more favorable for Cuba than before the crisis." See letter from Nikita Khrushchev to Fidel Castro, January 31, 1963; letter from Khrushchev to John Kennedy, November 14, 1962 (State Department FOIA request).

27. Arnold L. Horelick, "The Cuban Missile Crisis: An Analysis of Soviet Calculation and Behavior," World Politics 16 (1964): 365.

28. See Blight, *On the Brink,* pp. 117-121.

29. In addition to the Soviet motivations considered by the ExComm, Sovietologists have since advanced several others, including the possibility that Khrushchev had been pressured by domestic considerations, the need to reassert Soviet hegemony in light of the growing Sino-Soviet split, or the desire to use missiles in Cuba as a bargaining chip to force the withdrawal of U.S. IRBMs from Turkey. See for example Blight, *On the Brink,* pp. 116-118.

30. Raymond L. Garthoff, *Reflections on the Cuban Missile Crisis,* 2nd edition, (Washington, D.C.: The Brookings Institution, 1989), p. 13.

31. Soviet sources have offered differing assessments of the relative importance of the three motivating factors, with most of the disagreement centered on whether the defense of Cuba or the strategic imbalance was Khrushchev's foremost concern. Many of these differences possibly reflect differing interpretations of the deployment idea held by Soviet officials in 1962. The totality of new Soviet information in any case suggests that each of the three motives first mentioned by Khrushchev in his memoirs—the defense of

Cuba, the need to rectify the strategic imbalance, and the desire to give the United States a "taste of its own medicine" with respect to the deployment of forward-based MRBMs and IRBMs—did play some role in driving the Soviet decision in the spring of 1962.

32. "Memorandum of Conference with the President," June 17, 1959 (document no. 00011).
33. Garthoff, *Reflections*, pp. 206-208 and Allyn, "Essence of Revision," p. 142.
34. Memo from Lawrence McQuade to Paul Nitze, "But Where Did the Missile Gap Go?" May 31, 1963 (document no. 03119).
35. Stewart Alsop, "Kennedy's Grand Strategy," *Saturday Evening Post,* March 31, 1962. U.S. military officials were not reticent about the possibility of a U.S. first strike, either. See Robert McNamara's comments in Blight, *On the Brink,* p. 29.
36. Soviet military weakness was underscored in a meeting between Paul Nitze and Soviet Ambassador Mikhail Menshikov and possibly in a talk between President Kennedy and Soviet Foreign Minister Andrei Gromyko on October 6, 1961. See Richard K. Betts, *Nuclear Blackmail and Nuclear Balance* (Washington, D.C.: Brookings Institution, 1982), pp. 104-105. For Gilpatric's speech, see, "Address by Roswell Gilpatric," October 21,1961 (document no. 00115).
37. Memo from Lawrence McQuade to Paul Nitze, "But Where Did the Missile Gap Go?" May 31, 1963 (document no. 03119).
38. Desmond Ball, *Politics and Force Levels: The Strategic Missile Program of the Kennedy Administration* (Berkeley, University of California Press, 1980), p. 135. See also "Recommended Long Range Nuclear Delivery Forces," September 23, 1961, (document no. 00109), pp. 2, 11. Besides the Minuteman, the continued production of Atlas and Titan ICBMs was also authorized.
39. Allyn, "Essence of Revision," p. 139.
40. Ibid., p. 140. Khrushchev's belief in the inevitability of a U.S. invasion of Cuba is captured in his January 1963 letter to Castro: "It was clear to us that the North [Americans], having been defeated once [at the Bay of Pigs], would . . . change tactics and *repeat* the invasion. However, it would be a much better prepared invasion, and therefore a lot more dangerous. . . ." Letter from Nikita Khrushchev to Fidel Castro, January 31, 1963.
41. Letter from Nikita Khrushchev to John Kennedy, October 23, 1962 (document no. 00896). See also Thomas G. Paterson, "Commentary: The Defense-of-Cuba Theme and the Missile Crisis," *Diplomatic History* 14, no. 2 (Spring 1990): 254-255.
42. Khrushchev apparently allowed the Soviet military to choose the exact composition of nuclear forces sent to Cuba. Conversation with Sergo Mikoyan, January 29, 1989. See also Garthoff, *Reflections,* p. 20.
43. Even before new Soviet information became available, some scholars noted that analyses of the origins of the crisis had paid excessive attention to first-order questions involving Soviet motivations and policies, without

considering how U.S. policies may have affected those policies. For example, at a 1987 historical conference, Marc Trachtenberg commented: "[M]ore attention has to be paid . . . to basic issues of [U.S.] policy before you get into a crisis." Graham Allison echoed these sentiments, noting that "we weren't thinking about the effects of our actions on the Soviets [before the crisis]. Clearly, this is an aspect of American policy that needs much more thought." See Blight, *On the Brink,* p. 110.

44. Details of many of these activities were first revealed in a congressional report entitled, "Alleged Assassination Plots Involving Foreign Leaders," November 1975 (document no. 03272). The study was prepared by the Senate Select Committee to Study Governmental Operations with Respect to Intelligence Activities (better known as the "Church Committee").

45. Allyn, "Essence of Revision," p. 145.

46. See for example the thesis presented by James Hershberg, "Before 'The Missiles of October': Did Kennedy Plan a Military Strike against Cuba?" *Diplomatic History* 14, no. 12 (Spring 1990): 163-199 and this collection.

47. "Guidelines for Operation Mongoose," March 14, 1962 (document no. 00187).

48. Schlesinger, *A Thousand Days,* p. 796.

49. Garthoff, *Reflections,* p. 21.

50. For instance, Robert McNamara recommended in a November 12 ExComm meeting that U.S. nuclear alert status not be reduced because such an action would send the wrong "signal" to the Soviet Union. See "Summary Record of NSC Executive Committee Meeting No. 24," November 12, 1962 (document no. 02264).

51. Elie Abel, *The Missile Crisis* (Philadelphia: Lippincott, 1966), p. 183.

52. "Transcript of October 27 Cuban Missile Crisis ExComm Meetings," (document no. 01544), p. 57.

53. In particular, see Trachtenberg, "New Light on the Missile Crisis?", pp. 245-246.

54. "Transcript of October 27 Cuban Missile Crisis ExComm Meetings," (document no. 01544), p. 49. Mark Trachtenberg claims that it was not universally assumed in the ExComm that Moscow had ordered the attack, citing Lyndon Johnson's comment that "some crazy Russian captain" might "pull a trigger." However, Johnson was somewhat confusedly talking about possible future attacks on low-altitude reconnaissance, not the downing of the U-2 earlier in the day by a SAM battery.

55. "Transcript of October 27 Cuban Missile Crisis ExComm Meetings," (document no. 01544), p. 45.

56. The Soviet commanders have been identified as Lt. Gen. Stepan N. Grechko, Gen. Leonid S. Garbuz, and Gen. Georgy A. Voronkov. See Allyn, "Essence of Revision," pp. 160-161.

57. Kennedy, *Thirteen Days,* p. 98.

58. Allison, *Essence of Decision,* p. 140.

59. Draft Memo (declassified in 1990) from U.S. Department of Defense, Assistant Secretary for International Security Affairs, entitled, "Some Lessons from Cuba," November 14, 1962 (document no. 02296), p. 6.
60. Garthoff, *Reflections,* pp. 61-62.
61. Barton J. Bernstein, "Commentary: Reconsidering Khrushchev's Gambit—Defending the Soviet Union and Cuba," *Diplomatic History* 14, no. 2 (Spring 1990): 238.
62. Garthoff, *Reflections,* p. 122.
63. Kennedy, *Thirteen Days,* pp. 61-62.
64. Blight, *On the Brink,* p. 63.
65. Letter from Nikita Khrushchev to John Kennedy, October 28, 1962 (document no. 01570).
66. See U.S. Alaskan Air Defense Command report, "Air Defense Operations," December 1962 (document no. 02655).
67. Ibid., pp. 62-63.
68. Some Soviet sources have indicated that warheads for the MRBMs were in fact on the island. See Garthoff, *Reflections,* pp. 39-42.
69. See Raymond L. Garthoff, "Cuban Missile Crisis: The Soviet Story," *Foreign Policy* 72 (Fall 1988): 67.
70. "Summary of Items of Significant Interest Period 010701-020700 November 1962" (document no. 1890).
71. Allison, *Essence of Decision,* p. 105. The 22,000 figure was a retroactive estimate arrived at in early 1963. See Raymond L. Garthoff, "Cuban Missile Crisis: The Soviet Story," *Foreign Policy* 72 (Fall 1988): 67.
72. Allyn, "Essence of Revision," pp. 151-152.
73. For Gribkov's claim, see Arthur M. Schlesinger, Jr., "Four Days with Fidel: A Havana Diary" *New York Review of Books,* March 26, 1992, p. 23.
74. Kennedy, *Thirteen Days,* p. 46.
75. Letter from Dean Rusk to James Blight, February 2, 1987 (document no. 03322).
76. Allyn, "Essence of Revision," pp. 158.
77. This group included President Kennedy, Robert Kennedy, Robert McNamara, McGeorge Bundy, Theodore Sorensen, Dean Rusk, and Llewellyn Thompson. See McGeorge Bundy, *Danger and Survival: Choices about the Bomb in the First Fifty Years* (New York: Random House, 1988), p. 342.
78. Conversation with Douglas Dillon, June 15,1989. In contrast, many accounts report that some ExComm members were not even aware of the planned meeting between Robert Kennedy and Anatoly Dobrynin. See, for example, Allyn "Essence of Revision," p. 159.
79. Cf. Dobrynin's account as reported in Allyn, "Essence of Revision," p. 164, with McGeorge Bundy and Dean Rusk's comments in Bundy, *Danger and Survival,* pp. 432-433 and Letter from Dean Rusk to James Blight, February 2, 1987 (document no. 03322).

80. Bundy, *Danger and Survival*, p. 430. See also "Transcript of October 27 Cuban Missile Crisis ExComm Meetings," (document no. 01544), p. 38.

81. Draft Memo from U.S. Department of Defense, Assistant Secretary for International Security Affairs, entitled, "Some Lessons from Cuba," November 14, 1962 (document no. 02296), p. 10.

82. Schlesinger, *A Thousand Days*, p. 841.

83. Trachtenberg, "New Light on the Missile Crisis?" p. 243.

84. See Nikita S. Khrushchev, *Khrushchev Remembers: The Glasnost Tapes*, trans. and ed. Jerrold L. Schecter with Vyacheslav V. Luchov (Boston: Little, Brown and Company, 1990), pp. 176-177, 182-183; and Jean Edern-Hallier, "The Castro-Khrushchev Letters," San Jose *Mercury News*, December 2, 1990.

5

The Traditional and Revisionist Interpretations Reevaluated: Why Was Cuba a Crisis?

Richard Ned Lebow

INTRODUCTION:
THE REVISIONIST CRITIQUE

For more than a quarter of a century, there have been two diametrically opposed points of view about why Cuba was a crisis and why it was resolved. The traditional interpretation, enshrined in the writings of Theodore C. Sorensen, Arthur M. Schlesinger, Jr., and Elie Abel, describes the Cuban missiles as an intolerable provocation.[1] President John F. Kennedy had to compel the Soviet Union to withdraw the missiles to defend the balance of power, preserve NATO, and convince Nikita S. Khrushchev and the world of American resolve. Sorensen, Schlesinger, and Abel laud the "quarantine" as the optimal strategy, depict the outcome of the crisis as an unqualified American triumph, and attribute it to Kennedy's skill and tenacity. The revisionist interpretation, primarily associated with the writings of I. F. Stone, Ronald Steel, and Barton J. Bernstein, contends that Kennedy needlessly risked war for domestic political gain. Revisionists condemn the blockade as irresponsible and explain the resolution of the crisis as the result of Soviet moderation and American good luck.[2]

The new evidence that has become available in the last several years compels us to reevaluate the competing claims of these divergent interpretations. This evidence indicates that there are important truths—and errors—

in the arguments of both sides. It dictates a more complex and nuanced assessment of Kennedy's motives and policies. This article attempts to demonstrate the need for such a reconstruction and to take a first step in that direction.

Traditionalists offer compelling documentation to support their contention that Kennedy was very concerned with the international implications of the missiles. He worried that the Soviets would become emboldened by a successful missile deployment. If they get away with it, the president warned the Executive Committee (ExComm) on the first day of the crisis, "then they would start getting ready to squeeze us in Berlin."[3] He also emphasized this concern in his televised speech announcing the blockade, comparing Khrushchev's testing of American resolve to Adolf Hitler's testing of France and Britain on the eve of World War II. The 1930s, he told the American people, "taught us a clear lesson: aggressive conduct, if allowed to go unchecked and unchallenged, ultimately leads to war."[4]

The transcripts of the ExComm tapes and the writings of administration officials indicate that Kennedy also worried about the impact of Khrushchev's challenge on public opinion in Europe and Latin America. According to Theodore Sorensen, the president was concerned that "The Soviet move had been undertaken so swiftly, so secretly and with so much deliberate deception—it was so sudden a departure from Soviet practice—that it represented a provocative change in the delicate status quo."[5] Arthur Schlesinger conceded that

> while the missiles might not have had much effect on the overall U.S.-Soviet military balance, they had a considerable effect on the world *political* balance. The emplacement of nuclear missiles in Cuba would prove the Soviet ability to act with impunity in the very heart of the American zone of vital interest—a victory of great significance for the Kremlin, which saw the world in terms of spheres of influence and inflexibly guarded its own.[6]

Some years after the crisis, Sorensen reaffirmed his belief that Kennedy had no choice but to oppose the missiles. "Soviet long-range missiles in Cuba," he maintained, "represented a sudden, immediate and more dangerous and secretive change in the balance of power, in clear contradiction of all U.S. commitments and Soviet pledges. It was a move which required a response from the United States, not for reasons of prestige or image but for reasons of national security in the broadest sense."[7]

Sorensen, Schlesinger, and more recent defenders of the traditional interpretation vociferously deny that Kennedy was influenced by domestic political considerations. They insist that domestic politics never entered into the ExComm's deliberations.[8] "I've listened to the tapes of the October 27th meetings," McGeorge Bundy explained, "and I can say with a high degree of confidence that I don't think there was any worry of that kind whatsoever. I have no recollection of anyone voicing any fear of being lynched over the affair in Cuba."[9] Sorensen goes a step further and argues that Kennedy opted for the blockade in full knowledge that it would adversely affect his political standing. "JFK," he contends, "was convinced that his course of action would hurt his party in the elections." He recognized that the air strike would "be a swifter and more popular means of removing the missiles before Election Day."[10] Dean Rusk's revelation about Kennedy's willingness late in the crisis to consider a public missile swap has been taken by traditionalists as additional evidence of his willingness to incur severe domestic political costs.[11]

The traditional interpretation views the blockade as the appropriate response to the threat posed by the missiles. It was sufficiently threatening to communicate American resolve to Khrushchev but avoided the violence of the air strike, which might have compelled a Soviet military response. In Sorensen's judgment, Kennedy's policy represented "a carefully balanced and precisely measured combination of defense, diplomacy, and dialogue." He chose the quarantine in preference to an air attack because it demonstrated resolve without violence and thereby provided the Soviets room to maneuver and a peaceful way out of the crisis.[12]

Sorensen is also effusive in his praise of Kennedy's ability to keep his emotions in check. "Despite his anger at being deceived and his awareness that one misstep meant disaster, he remained cool at all times. He refused to issue any ultimatum, to close any doors, or to insist upon any deadlines, noting only that continued work on the missile sites would 'justify' (not necessarily ensure) further U.S. action."[13] When the Soviets agreed to remove the missiles, the president "refused to crow or claim victory. He was at each step firm but generous to his adversaries and candid with his major allies, with the American public, and with Congressional leaders, although he gave advance information to no one and sought advance approval from no one."[14]

In contrast to Sorensen's fulsome depiction of Kennedy, revisionists accuse the president of being misled by his emotions, of overreacting to the Soviet missile deployment, and of willingly risking the peace of the world for the sake of his political career. According to I. F. Stone, the most prominent early revisionist, there was a clear divergence between American national interests and the president's political interests. The former dictated a secret overture to Khrushchev in the hope of resolving the conflict diplomatically. Kennedy decided on a confrontation because it was more likely to compel Khrushchev to remove the missiles before the November congressional election. "There was no time for prolonged negotiation, summit conference, or U[nited] N[ations] debates if the damage was to be undone before the election. Kennedy could not afford to wait."[15] Stone insists that the president was also attracted to the blockade because of his personal need to display machismo. The "eyeball to eyeball" confrontation that ensued "was the best of therapies for Kennedy's nagging inferiority complex."[16]

Ronald Steel, another influential revisionist, made essentially the same argument. He stressed Kennedy's political vulnerability on Cuba and corresponding need to get the missiles out before Election Day. Steel also emphasized the importance of Kennedy's obsession with his image and fear that Khrushchev would never again take him seriously if he backed down on Cuba. For both of these reasons, Kennedy decided against making any kind of private overture to Khrushchev before he proclaimed the blockade. Steel believes that such an overture would have led to resolution of the conflict and avoided the crisis.[17]

Within the scholarly community, the revisionist interpretation has received its fullest expression in the writings of Stanford historian Barton Bernstein. In a series of carefully researched articles in the mid-1970s and early 1980s, Bernstein portrayed Kennedy and his most intimate advisers as men driven to impress Khrushchev and other Soviet leaders with American resolve. "A public confrontation and a public triumph would allow him dramatically to . . . persuade various 'constituencies'—citizens at home, allies abroad, and the Soviets—of his decisiveness and commitment."[18] According to Bernstein, the Cuban confrontation was the most far-reaching expression of the "potentially fatal paradox behind American strategic policy: that the country might have to go to war to affirm the very credibility that is supposed to make war unnecessary."[19] Like Stone and Steel, Bernstein argued that Kennedy should have tried negotiations instead of confrontation.[20]

THE DOMESTIC FACTOR NOW

On the first of the three issues dividing traditionalists from revisionists, the evidence, direct and inferential, supports the revisionist claim that Kennedy was very concerned about the domestic consequences of the Cuban missiles and his response to them. Some former administration officials are now willing to acknowledge this truth.

John Kenneth Galbraith, Kennedy's ambassador to India, is quite blunt about the role domestic politics played in influencing Kennedy's choice of the blockade. "Once they [the missiles] were there," he insists, "the political needs of the Kennedy administration urged it to take almost any risk to get them out."[21] Roger Hilsman, head of intelligence at the State Department and later assistant secretary of state, acknowledged the irony in the fact that Kennedy's largely successful attempt to exploit Cuba in the presidential election ultimately came back to haunt him. "He had used it in his campaign against Nixon to great effect, asking over and over why a Communist regime had been permitted to come to power just ninety miles off our coast. Then came the Bay of Pigs, and now the Soviets were turning Cuba into an offensive military base. . . . The fact of the matter," Hilsman admits, "was that President Kennedy and his administration were peculiarly vulnerable on Cuba."[22] Hilsman is quick to point out that Kennedy was influenced by more than electoral considerations. If the administration tolerated the missiles, he argues, it would be faced with a revolt from the military, from the hardliners in other departments, both State and CIA, from not only Republicans on Capitol Hill but some Democrats, too; that it would be faced with all this opposition at home just at the time that it would be undergoing deep and very dangerous challenges from the Soviets brought on by the alteration in the balance of power wrought by their successful introduction of missiles in Cuba, and which might well put the United States in mortal danger. This was why the Kennedy administration was in trouble.[23]

For Hilsman, domestic politics was only one component, albeit an important one, of Kennedy's decision to seek a showdown with Khrushchev. Theodore Sorensen now acknowledges the existence of these political influences but downplays their significance. He maintains that the pressures pushing Kennedy toward a confrontation were always offset by those pulling him in the opposite direction.[24]

Public opinion was indeed divided in its response to the blockade; there were some Americans who believed that Kennedy was needlessly courting nuclear war. But the overwhelming majority supported the president. There was also a sizable minority who believed he was not being tough enough. Kennedy heard complaints to this effect from the senators, some of them prominent Democrats, with whom he met prior to his announcement of the blockade.[25] Richard Russell (D-GA), criticized the blockade as a halfway measure that would arouse allied opposition without doing any real harm to the Russians. J. William Fulbright (D-AK), chairman of the Senate Foreign Relations Committee, joined with Russell in calling for an invasion of Cuba.[26]

President Kennedy and his brother Robert, the attorney general, also gave vivid testimony to how they were affected by the long shadow of domestic politics. On Wednesday morning, the day the quarantine went into effect, intelligence reports indicated that Soviet ships were steaming steadily toward the blockade line. Robert Kennedy reported that en route to that morning's ExComm meeting his brother confided: "'It looks really mean, doesn't it? But then, really there was no other choice. If they get this mean on this one in our part of the world, what will they do on the next?' 'I just don't think there was any choice,' I said, 'and not only that, if you hadn't acted, you would have been impeached.' The President thought for a moment and said, 'That's what I think—I would have been impeached.'"[27]

The president's remarks indicate that two concerns were foremost in his mind: teaching the Soviets that neither he nor the United States could be pushed around and avoiding domestic political loss. Did Kennedy really believe he would have been impeached? His unguarded comment can certainly be read as a frank admission of his feelings of vulnerability. But it can also be interpreted as an example of postdecisional rationalization. Kennedy had committed himself to a risky course of action, one that he realized could lead to war.

Almost any leader in this situation would experience anxiety and harbor second thoughts about the wisdom of his policy. Psychologists find that people often resort to bolstering to cope with their lingering doubts and the residual anxiety they generate.[28] One manifestation of bolstering consists of "spreading the alternatives." People convince themselves that the rewards of their chosen policy will be much greater than they had originally thought and the costs of rejected alternatives much higher. The president's comment to his brother may have been a form of bolstering. If so, we must be cautious about accepting it at face value.

Even if Kennedy's concern about impeachment was exaggerated, it points to a very real concern for the domestic political implications of his Cuban policy. McGeorge Bundy suggests that critics like Senator Kenneth B. Keating (R-NY)—and, much more damaging, Dwight D. Eisenhower and Richard M. Nixon—would have brought a triple indictment against the administration. They would have complained: "You said it wouldn't happen, and you were wrong; you said you would know how to stop it if it did happen, and you don't; and now you say it doesn't matter, and it does."[29] Faced with such criticism, which might have been fanned by public grumbling by dissatisfied generals, the administration would have been dead in the water.

Some defenders of the traditional interpretation argue that the ExComm's failure to discuss domestic politics indicates that Cuban decisions were made entirely in response to strategic and foreign policy considerations.[30] This argument fails to take into account the composition of the ExComm, which consisted of national security officials and advisers, not politicians. It was hardly the forum for Kennedy to air his domestic political concerns. It seems more likely that he would have deliberately refrained from doing so to encourage his advisers to speak their minds freely and to evaluate their options solely with regard to their security implications. He could then have factored in the political element himself, or have done so in consultation with his most trusted political advisers.[31]

There was an even more important reason why the president might have thought it prudent to refrain from discussing politics in the ExComm. As Ronald Steel points out, "It would have been political folly for Kennedy to have broached the subject of the elections before the Executive Committee where it would have fallen on a good many unsympathetic ears."[32] The president was an astute enough politician to be sensitive to the possibility that any comment he made about the election might later be used against him or even leaked by ExComm members opposed to the blockade. This was probably why, when he discussed the possibility of making concessions to Khrushchev on 27 October he did so outside the ExComm and with a small group of officials—Sorensen, Bundy, Rusk, and his brother—whose personal loyalty he did not doubt.

The assertion that domestic politics were never referred to in the ExComm is in any case incorrect. On 16 October, the first day the ExComm met, Defense Secretary Robert S. McNamara volunteered his view that the missiles were "primarily a domestic political problem."[33]

Some ExComm members disagreed strongly with McNamara, insisting that the missiles did have strategic significance.[34] But no one challenged his assertion that the president confronted a serious political problem. Bundy's comment, and that of the unidentified speaker, indicated agreement. As Roger Hilsman, not a member of the ExComm, put it: "The United States might not be in mortal danger but . . . the administration most certainly was."[35]

Domestic politics entered into the ExComm's deliberations again on 27 October, the climactic day of the crisis. In that afternoon's meeting, Kennedy alluded to the political dilemma he faced. He worried aloud that "when the blood starts to flow" that public opinion in Europe and at home would turn decisively against a president who had gone to war on behalf of obsolescent missiles that he had wanted out of Turkey in any case. How could he convince the American people that a missile trade was a sensible action *before* the fighting began? He feared that it would be seen as a sellout to the

Communists.[36] "If we take no action or if we take action," Kennedy complained, "they're all going to be saying we should have done the reverse."[37]

Kennedy's comments indicate that the problem posed by public opinion was more complex than either traditionalists or revisionists acknowledge. Both interpretations address only the expected costs to the president of *not* challenging the Soviets in Cuba. They ignore the possible political costs of pursuing such a challenge. The president did not. He was sensitive to the likelihood that the Republican opposition—and Democrats like Senators Russell and Fulbright, who wanted an invasion of Cuba—would almost certainly turn on him the moment American military operations met with serious resistance.

Kennedy would have remembered the fate of his Democratic predecessor, Harry S. Truman. Ohio Senator Robert A. Taft, leader of the Republican opposition, was initially full of praise for Truman's decision to come to the aid of South Korea. But within weeks, he and other Republican senators were derisively referring to the conflict as "Truman's War."[38] Truman's subsequent decision to cross the thirty-eighth parallel and occupy North Korea was primarily a response to domestic political pressures.[39] But as soon as Douglas MacArthur's advancing forces ran into the Chinese and were forced into an ignominious and costly retreat, the Republicans turned on Truman and successfully made his conduct of the Korean War a major campaign issue.[40]

Kennedy's desire to avoid this kind of political trap was probably one important reason why he shied away from an air strike and sent his brother to tell Soviet Ambassador Anatoly A. Dobrynin on Wednesday evening of 24 October, the day after the blockade went into effect, that he was prepared to pull the Jupiter missiles out of Turkey.[41] It may also have influenced his apparent willingness to consider further concessions if they became necessary to resolve the crisis.

Defenders of the traditional interpretation have also argued that Kennedy's willingness, late in the crisis, to consider further concessions indicates that he was not constrained by domestic political considerations. This is an unwarranted inference. That the president contemplated concessions at the height of the crisis in the hope of avoiding war reveals nothing about his motives for insisting on the withdrawal of the Soviet missiles at the outset of the crisis.

Analysts need to distinguish between the role domestic politics played early on in the crisis and at its denouement. At the beginning, it seems clear, it helped to push the president into a confrontation. Later on, it was one of several considerations pulling him back from the brink.

THE QUESTION OF RESOLVE

The second issue dividing revisionists from traditionalists is Kennedy's concern for demonstrating resolve. Traditionalists contend that it was essential to convince Khrushchev that the United States, and the Kennedy administration in particular, could not be pushed around. Revisionists insist that Kennedy's concern for his resolve was neurotic and had little to do with any objective foreign policy need.

Revisionists are undoubtedly correct in seeing something extraordinary about Kennedy's thoroughly documented propensity to see Khrushchev's assessment of his resolve as an important component of all of his foreign policy initiatives. From the very beginning of his presidency, Kennedy felt the need to convince Khrushchev of his resolve. His concern intensified dramatically during his first year in office. The Bay of Pigs, the Vienna summit, and the Berlin Wall, all convinced Kennedy that Khrushchev viewed him as a "pushover." For the president and his advisers, the Cuban missiles were confirmation of their worst fears.

Soviet testimony indicates that Kennedy's understanding of Soviet foreign policy expectations was wrong in two fundamental respects. Khrushchev's provocations were neither opportunity driven nor prompted by his lack of respect for Kennedy's resolve. Khrushchev's foreign policy was a response to Soviet fears about the consequences of their own strategic and political weakness, fears that were only intensified by American efforts to demonstrate strength and resolve. It was not Kennedy's performance in Vienna, acceptance of the Berlin Wall, or failure to commit troops to the Bay of Pigs that led to the Cuban missiles but rather his deployment of Jupiters in Turkey, proclamations of strategic superiority, and political-military pressures against Castro.[42]

Kennedy's failure to grasp Khrushchev's motives was due in large part to the conceptual biases he and most of his advisers brought to the analysis of Soviet foreign policy, biases that were derived from the experience of the 1930s. At the outset of the Cold War, American policymakers treated Stalin's Russia as the lineal descendant of Hitler's Germany. The lessons they had belatedly learned about Hitler and his regime were now held to apply to Stalin and the Soviet Union. Like Nazi Germany, Communist Russia was assumed to be ideologically motivated and hell-bent on world domination. And like Hitler, Stalin and his successors were thought to be consummate opportunists, constantly probing for weak spots in their adversaries' defenses that could be exploited to extend their influence and territorial control.

Kennedy gave every indication of viewing the Soviet Union through the prism of the 1930s. It is probably not an exaggeration to describe his world view as largely shaped by the fiasco of appeasement. He also played a direct hand in exposing its political and moral bankruptcy. His father, ambassador to the Court of St. James's on the eve of the war, had been an outspoken supporter of appeasement. The 23-year-old Kennedy, who spent time with his father in England, used the opportunity to expand his senior thesis, published under the title *Why England Slept*. It was a stunning indictment of England's lack of preparedness and the policy of appeasement associated with it.[44] The young Kennedy's personal involvement in the issue, his father's commitment on the other side, and the death of his older brother in the war that followed made him even more committed to the so-called lesson of Munich and its relevance to Soviet-American relations.

In fairness to Kennedy, we must recognize that whatever predisposition he had to see parallels between Nazi Germany and the Soviet Union was undeniably abetted by Khrushchev's bullying speeches, boasts of superiority, and crude displays of force. All of this evoked memories of Hitler and had the effect of legitimizing the hold of the lessons of the 1930s on American minds. We know today that Khrushchev's bellicose posturing was primarily designed to mask Soviet inferiority. But Kennedy did not know this and his analogical reasoning led him to put the worst possible interpretation on Khrushchev's rhetoric and behavior.

Khrushchev's admittedly threatening behavior cannot in itself account for Kennedy's doubts about his own reputation for resolve. Kennedy's comments to advisers and newsmen are revealing for their one-sided fixation on events and policies that he believed conveyed an impression of weakness to Khrushchev.[45] The Bay of Pigs was admittedly ambiguous in its implications, but Vienna and the Berlin crisis could only be interpreted this way by someone prepared to distort reality to confirm his unjustified fears.

By all accounts Kennedy had been tough at the Vienna summit; even Khrushchev had come away impressed by his bravura performance.[46] He had also been firm in Laos and Berlin. In Berlin, he had remained firm in the face of Khrushchev's threats and had successfully exposed as bluff the Soviet threat to allow East Germany to deny the Western powers access to the city. It bordered on the neurotic for him to interpret his refusal to tear down the Berlin Wall as a sign of cowardice. Its construction was a confession of Soviet political weakness and its toleration by Kennedy a statesmanlike decision to eschew a confrontation that risked provoking a war in the heart of Europe.

One explanation for Kennedy's fixation on his resolve is cognitive. Its starting point is his use of the images and lessons of the 1930s as his organizing principles for understanding international relations. These images and lessons led him to draw analogies between the 1930s and the 1960s and to predict that Khrushchev would behave aggressively if he had a military advantage or doubted the resolve of his adversaries. Another explanation is motivational. It directs our attention to Kennedy's personal insecurities and the ways in which they might have distorted his understanding of Khrushchev's motives. To the extent that Kennedy had deep-seated doubts about his own courage and capability he may have projected them on to Khrushchev and interpreted his actions in terms of them.[47]

Whichever explanation is correct—and perhaps they both are—the effect was the same. Kennedy's analysis of his successive encounters with Khrushchev in terms of the assumptions he made about both himself and Khrushchev only served to confirm the validity of those assumptions in his mind and to tighten their grip on him. This process blinded him to the possibility that Khrushchev might be motivated by any defensive reason, or combination of reasons.

To this point, our review of the evidence offers considerable support for the revisionist interpretation of the origin of the crisis. Kennedy unquestionably misunderstood Soviet motives and had an exaggerated and largely counterproductive concern for demonstrating resolve. He was also deeply influenced by domestic political considerations. His vulnerability on Cuba and Republican efforts to exploit it led him to define the introduction of ballistic missiles into Cuba as unacceptable. Theodore Sorensen has made a remarkable admission about the calculations that entered into Kennedy's warnings to the Soviets. The president had no qualms about his warnings, according to Sorensen, because he did not believe that Khrushchev had any intention of introducing missiles into Cuba. "Let me say," he announced at the Hawk's Cay Conference,

> that the line between offensive and defensive weapons was drawn in September, and it was not drawn in a way which was intended to leave the Soviets any ambiguity to play with. I believe the President drew the line precisely where he thought the Soviets were not and would not be; that is to say, if we had known that the Soviets were putting forty missiles in Cuba, we might under this hypothesis have drawn the line at 100, and said with great fanfare that we would absolutely not tolerate the presence of more than 100 missiles in Cuba. I say that believing very strongly that that would have been an act of *prudence,* not

weakness. But I am suggesting that one reason the line was drawn at zero was because we simply thought the Soviets weren't going to deploy any there anyway.[48]

Whether Kennedy would have drawn the line at 100 missiles—and there are good political reasons for doubting this—Sorensen's remarks indicate the extent to which the president conceived of the missiles as a domestic political, not a military threat.

Domestic politics also played an important role in shaping Kennedy's response to the discovery of Soviet missiles in Cuba. His expectation of public outrage—directed against himself as much as Khrushchev—convinced him of the need to secure the missiles' withdrawal and to seize the initiative before knowledge of the missiles became public. Kennedy asked the ExComm to help him formulate the best means of attaining this end; but the end itself was not subject to debate. He adopted a hard-line policy in the hope of avoiding political loss, *not* in the expectation of making political gains. It is simply not true, as some revisionists allege, that Kennedy risked the peace of the world to improve his political standing and the electoral prospects of the Democratic party.

The difference between avoiding loss and seeking gain is not merely semantic. Sorensen's remarks indicate that Kennedy had tried his level best to avoid a situation in which he would have to choose between a war-threatening confrontation and political loss. His desire to finesse this unpalatable choice motivated his public and private warnings to Khrushchev. By drawing the line at the introduction of ballistic missiles, Kennedy was telling Khrushchev that he would not oppose the ongoing Soviet conventional buildup in Cuba.

This was a major concession given the American public's opposition to that buildup. It stands as a clear indication of the president's willingness to incur real political costs in the hope of forestalling a more serious confrontation. To seek such a confrontation in the hope of gain would have been as anathema to Kennedy as it is to the revisionists.

Revisionists also err in ignoring or dismissing the strategic and foreign policy implications of tolerating the Cuban missile deployment. It is by no means clear that their military consequences were so minimal—the evidence indicates otherwise—but this was not why Kennedy opposed the missiles.[49] In addition to the domestic costs of acquiescence, he feared that Khrushchev would become even more aggressive in the future if his missile ploy went unchallenged. Revisionists are unpersuaded by this argument; they insist, and with reason, that Kennedy exaggerated the importance of demonstrating resolve. But in evaluating the importance of resolve we must make a fundamental distinction between Soviet-American relations *before* and *after* the introduction of missiles into Cuba.

Even if Khrushchev's decision to deploy the missiles had little or nothing to do with his assessment of Kennedy's resolve, Kennedy's failure to oppose them could have raised doubts about that resolve. In this respect, Cuba was different from the Bay of Pigs or the Vienna summit. The implications of those incidents for the president's credibility were at best marginal because it was not at all obvious how, if at all, his credibility had been engaged.[50] But in Cuba, Kennedy had publicly drawn the line and had staked his reputation on defending it. To have tolerated the introduction of Soviet missiles into Cuba would have revealed his well-publicized commitment to have been a bluff. This could have had serious, detrimental consequences for the future.

Khrushchev's apparent failure to take this dimension of the problem into account when formulating his policy does not mean that he would have remained blind to it in its aftermath. The domestic political consequences of tolerating a Cuban missile deployment would have been enormous. Kennedy's presidency would have been crippled and the Republicans might even have won control of Congress in November. Kennedy's willingness to accept these losses in preference to the risks of a Soviet-American crisis would have communicated a clear and dangerous message to Khrushchev. It could have emboldened him, as Kennedy feared, to embark upon further provocations. The revisionists are wrong to dismiss the serious international implications of the deployment just as the traditionalists err in ignoring their domestic political consequences.

DIPLOMACY OR A BLOCKADE?

The third issue on which the traditionalists and revisionists disagree is Kennedy's decision to impose a "naval quarantine" of Cuba as the preferred means of compelling the Soviets to withdraw their missiles. Traditionalists view the blockade as a judicious and successful choice. Revisionists believe that it unnecessarily risked war for a goal that might have been achieved by purely diplomatic means. Here the evidence seems to support the traditionalists, but not necessarily for the reasons they advance.

Traditionalists insist that quiet diplomacy was ruled out by the need to act before the missiles became operational which would make military action against them immeasurably more costly. But we know that the pressure on the president to act had little to do with the status of the missiles. The CIA reported that *some* of the missile sites in Cuba were *already operational at the time* of their discovery but that most would not become operational until well into December.[51] The pressure on the president to resolve the crisis was internal and generated by his political need to maintain a consensus within the ExComm.[52]

Kennedy rejected a secret overture to Khrushchev because he did not believe it would succeed in halting work at the missile sites or in securing the removal of the missiles. To gain these ends, Kennedy and his advisers believed they would have to threaten military action. If so, they reasoned, it was better to present Khrushchev with a fait accompli than an ultimatum that would allow him time to prepare a countermove.[53]

Kennedy also viewed a secret overture as too pusillanimous. Khrushchev needed to be taught a lesson, not just rebuffed. Otherwise, he might have been tempted to renew his challenge of the U.S. position in Berlin. Even if private diplomacy succeeded in convincing Khrushchev to withdraw his missiles, it would not have conveyed American resolve in the dramatic way Kennedy believed essential to moderate future Soviet behavior.[54] For this reason, he opted for a full-fledged confrontation even though he recognized that it raised a serious and undesired risk of war.

The evidence indicates that Kennedy acted from a combination of motives. He was troubled by both the foreign policy and domestic political implications of the Cuban missiles. He chose the blockade because it conveyed resolve without violence and was less likely than an air strike to lead to runaway escalation. The blockade represented a tradeoff between the imperatives for action, which pushed him up the ladder of escalation, and the risks of a confrontation, which pulled him down.[55]

The ExComm's Soviet experts, Charles "Chip" Bohlen and Llewellyn "Tommy" Thompson, argued unsuccessfully for a private overture to Khrushchev. During the ExComm discussions on 17 and 18 October, Bohlen proposed that Kennedy write a letter to Khrushchev asking him to withdraw the missiles and then decide whether to proceed with a blockade, air strike, or invasion on the basis of Khrushchev's response. "No one can guarantee," he wrote to Kennedy, "that withdrawal can be achieved by diplomatic action—but it . . . seems essential that this channel be tested before military action is employed."[56]

Revisionists fault Kennedy for not following the advice of these two experienced diplomats. Ronald Steel asserts that Kennedy should have "used traditional diplomatic channels to warn the Russians that he knew what they were up to, and thus give them a chance quietly to pull back." He suggests that Kennedy could have communicated directly with Khrushchev via the hot line, or alternatively, through Soviet Foreign Minister Andrei A.

Gromyko, who visited the White House on 18 October, three days after the president had learned about the Cuban missiles.[57] Walter Lippmann also believes that Kennedy should have confronted Gromyko with the facts, giving "Mr. Khrushchev what all wise statesmen give their adversaries—the chance to save face."[58]

The question is not Kennedy's ability to communicate with Khrushchev but the likelihood that a purely diplomatic initiative would have convinced the Soviet leader to withdraw his missiles. None of the revisionists offers any reasons to support the contention that Khrushchev would have responded positively. One argument that could be made, and it seems implicit in Lippmann's formulation of the problem, is that backing down in response to a private rather than a public ultimatum would have been less costly for Khrushchev, and hence more attractive. It might also be argued that a secret overture would have changed Moscow's estimate of the risk involved in continuing with the missile deployment. Khrushchev's speechwriter, Fyodor Burlatsky, is convinced that a crisis could have been avoided if Kennedy had told Gromyko that the United States had discovered the Soviet missiles and would tolerate them. Khrushchev, he told the Cambridge conference, would have realized "that he would need now to negotiate about a *new* situation."[59] Burlatsky expanded on his view in an article in *Literaturnaya Gazeta*. "I am almost 100 percent certain," he wrote, "that if J. Kennedy had sent such a notification to Moscow, the further escalation of the conflict would have been prevented. There would have been an opportunity to resolve the problem by diplomatic means."[60]

We will never know if secret negotiations could have prevented a crisis. It is certainly possible that Khrushchev might have been persuaded by a combination of threats and promises to dismantle his missile bases in Cuba. But it seems more probable that Khrushchev would have rejected Kennedy's demand to withdraw the missiles on the grounds that they were necessary to protect Cuba from an American invasion. He would also have tried to drag out his exchange of notes with Kennedy as long as possible to gain time for the Cuban missiles to become fully operational.

When deciding to go ahead with the deployment, Khrushchev had not considered the domestic political pressures that would make the missiles intolerable to Kennedy. Nor is there any evidence that he considered the important differences between openly deploying missiles in Turkey and secretly installing them in Cuba after giving assurances to the contrary. I have previously argued, and knowledgeable Soviets now agree, that Khrushchev's failure to grasp these realities and their implications was the result of anger and wishful thinking.[61] Khrushchev's emotional commitment to his initiative also made it unlikely that any letter, or exchange of letters, would have opened his eyes to these critical political facts. We know that he was entirely unaffected by Kennedy's public and private warnings of 4 and 13 September which should have made it clear that the administration would not tolerate the introduction of ballistic missiles into Cuba.[62] Is there any reason to expect that he would have responded any differently to subsequent warnings and threats that were not backed by observable military preparations or dramatic public revelations?

An even more serious impediment to a purely diplomatic accommodation was the cost of concessions for both leaders. The revisionists are correct in asserting that the public foreign policy costs to Khrushchev of backing down in an "eyeball to eyeball" confrontation could have been avoided by a private accommodation. But this was by no means the only or the most important price to Khrushchev of withdrawing the missiles. Evidence from the Soviet side indicates that the two most critical constituencies for Khrushchev were Fidel Castro, and the Soviet political and military officials upon whom he relied for internal political support. Castro welcomed the missiles and bitterly opposed their withdrawal.[63] Marshal Rodion Yu. Malinovsky and other Soviet hard-liners felt the same way and almost certainly would have accused Khrushchev of cowardice and of selling out Castro had he agreed to dismantle the missile sites and withdraw the missiles in response to a secret ultimatum from Kennedy. The crisis was probably necessary to convince both Castro and Soviet hard-liners that Khrushchev had absolutely no choice but to remove the missiles or face war with the United States. The crisis also softened the blow for Khrushchev politically by allowing him to secure a noninvasion pledge from Kennedy and a private commitment to withdraw the American Jupiter missiles from Turkey.

It is conceivable that Kennedy would have agreed to a noninvasion pledge in the absence of a crisis but extremely unlikely that he would have consented to withdraw the Jupiters. The Jupiter concession was made by the president because he believed that another superpower could not be expected to back down in a public confrontation without some kind of quid pro quo. In retrospect, it seems apparent that Kennedy also needed a war-threatening crisis to alter the psychological context in which his concessions were evaluated by Congress and the American public. Because the promise to remove the Jupiters was not publicly revealed until years later, most Americans did not view the pledge as a craven accommodation but as a statesmanlike gesture to end the confrontation by allowing a defeated adversary to save face.

There is also the important question of Kennedy's objectives to consider. These were not limited to removing the missiles. Kennedy also sought to teach Khrushchev a lesson, something he did not believe he could accomplish by quiet diplomacy, even if it led to the withdrawal of the missiles. Rightly or wrongly, the president sought a dramatic public confrontation as the only means of accomplishing this end. Like every other aspect of the Cuban crisis, its significance for the subsequent course of Soviet-American relations has been hotly debated.

The traditional interpretation views Cuba as a notable American victory with long-term beneficial consequences for Soviet-American relations. Revisionists agree that Kennedy imposed his will on Khrushchev but insist that his victory was a pyrrhic one because it prompted the subsequent Soviet strategic arms buildup. They further contend that Kennedy's successful use of coercive diplomacy led ineluctably to American intervention in Vietnam. Once again, there is truth to the arguments of both sides.

Kennedy's immediate reaction to the resolution of the crisis was relief, not triumph. Robert Kennedy writes: "After it was finished, he made no statement attempting to take credit for himself or for the Administration for what had occurred. He instructed all members of the ExComm and government that no interview should be given, no statement made, which would claim any kind of victory. He respected Khrushchev for properly determining what was in his own country's interest and what was in the interest of mankind."[64]

The media and academic commentators were less restrained than the president. Typical of their self-congratulatory analyses was Zbigniew Brzezinski's arrogant assertion in 1967 that Cuba reaffirmed American strategic supremacy. "Faced with a showdown," he wrote in the State Department *Bulletin*, "the Soviet Union didn't dare to respond. . . . The U.S. is today the only effective global military power in the world."[65] Such claims of unalloyed American triumph were an exaggeration. The outcome of the crisis was closer to a compromise than to a one-sided American victory. In addition to a public noninvasion pledge, the president privately agreed to withdraw the American Jupiters from Turkey and considered making a public declaration to that effect. Had Khrushchev "hung tough" for another day or two, Kennedy might have invoked and responded favorably to an appeal from UN Secretary-General U Thant to end the crisis on the basis of a missile swap.[66] The public appearance was deceiving; the U.S. victory was a very near thing. Kennedy knew this, and his sensible desire to allow Khrushchev to save face aside, it may have been another reason for his instructions not to gloat over the outcome.

Claims that the missile crisis succeeded in moderating Soviet foreign policy by demonstrating American resolve are highly questionable. But such claims are standard fare among students of the crisis. McGeorge Bundy believes that "it was a tremendously sobering event with a largely constructive long-term result."[67] Walt W. Rostow, chief of the State Department's Policy Planning Council, called Cuba the "Gettysburg of global conflict"— with the Soviets presumably cast in the role of the Confederacy.[68] Perhaps the most self-conscious formulation of this position is that of the noted deterrence theorist Thomas Schelling, who maintains that "the Cuban missile crisis was the best thing to happen to us since the Second World War. It helped us avoid further confrontations with the Soviets; it resolved the Berlin issue; and it established new basic understandings about U.S.-Soviet interaction." Schelling, who made these remarks at the Hawk's Cay conference, hastened to add that "I don't think the Cuban missile crisis should be repeated, but I do think it was a good crisis."[69]

Underlying many of the assertions that the missile crisis was worth whatever risk of war it entailed are the twin assumptions that Khrushchev was motivated by the prospect of offensive gain and that he perceived an opportunity to act because Kennedy had failed to demonstrate adequate resolve. The evidence indicates little support for either assumption. Soviet testimony reveals that Khrushchev was acting in response to his own country's perceived weakness and seeking to prevent loss. Kennedy's bargaining reputation, considered the most important determinant of credibility by deterrence theorists, seems to have been largely irrelevant to Khrushchev's expectation that his provocation would succeed. If the missile deployment was neither triggered nor abetted by Soviet doubts about American resolve, then a demonstration of resolve was unnecessary to forestall this or other challenges. Indeed, such demonstrations helped to bring it about.

Bundy, Rostow, and Schelling are nevertheless right in seeing Cuba as an important turning point in Soviet-American relations. Since the denouement of the missile crisis, neither Khrushchev nor any of his successors has tried again to ride roughshod over a commitment that an American president has publicly defined as vital. But the explanation for this must be traced to other attributes of the crisis.

The most fundamental reason why there has been only one Cuba has to do with the origins of the crisis. Khrushchev acted out of a sense of desperation. He was willing to embark on a high-risk challenge to the United States because he believed that the consequences of inaction would be more detrimental to Soviet strategic and foreign policy interests. We have never had another crisis of the magnitude of Cuba because neither superpower has ever felt as threatened by the other as the Soviets did in the spring and summer of 1962.

The closest we have come is the superpower crisis of 1973 arising out of the war in the Middle East. Western analysts generally agree that the Soviet "ultimatum" that triggered that crisis was issued in response to Soviet fears that a continued Israeli advance would result in a humiliating defeat of their client state Egypt and the possible overthrow of its leader.[70] It is the absence of acute needs, not of opportunities, that has been responsible for the lack of acute crises.

In 1962, Khrushchev also acted out of anger. His emotional arousal clouded his judgment and made empathy with President Kennedy and the constraints under which he operated all but impossible. It also ruled out a thorough and dispassionate evaluation of the likely repercussions of a Cuban missile deployment. We have only spotty evidence about the emotions of subsequent Soviet leaders, but it supports the supposition that the combination of anger and threat are a potent catalyst for risky and aggressive foreign policies. Brezhnev's decision in October 1973 to threaten intervention in the Middle East was made in such circumstances, as was his decision in 1978 to invade Afghanistan.[71]

To put the Cuban crisis in its proper perspective it is also necessary to consider the personality of Nikita Khrushchev. No student of Soviet affairs has suggested that Khrushchev was a prudent man. He was attracted to grand gestures and acted impulsively. He gambled often with little apparent chance of success. Cuba fits this pattern of behavior. It should be seen in the same light as his bluff about the potency of Soviet strategic forces, his Berlin challenges, and his virgin lands program. Together with Cuba, these initiatives were the "harebrained schemes" that his Politburo colleagues referred to at the time of his dismissal.

The Cuban missile crisis unquestionably had an effect on Soviet policy toward the United States. Soviet pronouncements after the crisis indicated a clear interest in reducing Cold War tensions. It may be, as Raymond L. Garthoff has speculated, that "the crisis opened up a degree of greater belief in the possibility of mutual accommodation."[72] This was true for Washington as well. Many Kennedy administration officials have testified to the way in which their long look down the barrel of the nuclear gun rekindled their fervor for finding some way to reduce the chances of war. "The effect," Theodore Sorensen observed, "was to purge their minds, at least temporarily, of cold-war cliches."[73] The chastened attitude on both sides facilitated the test ban treaty and the agreement to install the hotline telephone, and sparked renewed interest in arms control. It was also a catalyst of détente. "If there had been no Cuban missile crisis," Sergo Mikoyan observed, "we should perhaps have organized it."[74]

To the degree that Cuba lowered the subsequent risks of war it might be seen as worth the risk of war it entailed. But this judgment must be tempered by recognition of the ways in which Cuba also encouraged recklessness. Here, the link between Cuba and Vietnam is both striking and tragic.

That Cuba was the precedent for Vietnam there can be no doubt. The crisis encouraged the belief that Communist challenges could most effectively be dealt with by a policy of military threat and intimidation. "After Cuba," one student of American foreign policy has observed, " 'escalation' became the *idée fixe* of academics and policy-makers—a vision of a ladder of force with rungs separated by equivalent spaces of destruction, each with its own 'value,' running out toward darkness."[75]

The Cuban experience paved the way to Vietnam in other ways as well. James Nathan, who has traced the impact of the missile crisis on Vietnam policy, has identified four "lessons" of the crisis that disposed American policymakers to intervention in Southeast Asia. These are

> that success in international crisis was largely a matter of national guts; that the opponent would yield to superior force; that presidential control of force can be "suitable," "selective," "swift," "effective," and "responsive" to civilian authority; and that crisis management and execution are too dangerous and events move too rapidly for anything but the tightest secrecy—all these inferences contributed to President Johnson's decision to use American air power against Hanoi in 1965.[76]

From the perspective of a quarter of a century, Cuba increasingly has the air of a lost opportunity. It created the mood and determination that were necessary for the test ban and hot line agreement. But this momentum did not carry the superpowers much further along the road to accommodation. Perhaps this was because Kennedy was assassinated in November 1963 and Khrushchev was removed from power in October 1964. Their successors had neither their commitment to bury the Cold War hatchet nor their special intimacy, both of which were essential prerequisites for this objective.

American and Soviet officials agree that the missile crisis created a unique bond between the two superpower leaders. It was based in part on having guided the destinies of their respective nations through the most acute confrontation of the nuclear age. Only Kennedy and Khrushchev really knew what it was like to make decisions that might determine the survival of their countrymen. More important still was the personal relationship the two men had developed during the course of the crisis. By its end, they had become as much allies as adversaries, struggling against their own hawks and the mounting pressures pushing them toward a military showdown. It is no exaggeration to say that through the mechanism of a public-private deal, they went so far as to conspire with each other against their respective internal opponents.

Kennedy emerged from this crisis with a very different view of Khrushchev. His image of the Soviet leader as bellicose, opportunistic, and willing to risk the peace of the world for the sake of expanding communism's sphere of influence was replaced by respect for his adversary as a man who was as concerned as he was with the lives and well-being of his countrymen and motivated by many of the same fears and insecurities that moved him. Soviet officials report that Khrushchev's image of Kennedy underwent a similar transformation.[77] If there was a silver lining in the stormy Cuban cloud, it was the breakthrough these two men achieved in their understanding of one another. Perhaps a better understanding of the crisis will help today's leaders take up where Kennedy and Khrushchev left off.

NOTES

1. Theodore C. Sorensen, *Kennedy* (New York, 1965); Arthur M. Schlesinger, Jr., *A Thousand Days: John F. Kennedy in the White House* (Boston, 1965); Elie Abel, *The Missile Crisis* (Philadelphia, 1966).
2. The best revisionist critiques are I. F. Stone, "The Brink," *New York Review of Books*, 14 April 1966; Ronald Steel, "End Game," review of *Thirteen Days* by Robert Kennedy, *New York Review of Books*, 13 March 1969; James A. Nathan, "The Missile Crisis: His Finest Hour Now," *World Politics* 27, no. 2 (January 1975): 265-81; Barton J. Bernstein, "The Week We Almost Went to War, in *Bulletin of the Atomic Scientists* 32, no. 2 (February 1976): 12-21; and idem, "The Cuban Missile Crisis: Trading the Jupiters in Turkey?" *Political Science Quarterly* 95, no. 1 (1980): 97-125. See Garry Wills, *The Kennedy Imprisonment: A Meditation on Power* (Boston, 1982), 235-74, for a more recent revisionist critique.
3. ExComm meeting, 16 October 1962, 6:30-7:55 P.M., *Presidential Recordings: Transcripts,* Cuban Missile Crisis Meetings, 16 October 1962, John F. Kennedy Library, Boston, Massachusetts.
4. Kennedy speech, 22 October 1962, in *Public Papers of the Presidents: John F. Kennedy, 1962* (Washington, 1963), 806-80.
5. Sorensen, *Kennedy,* 683.
6. *Proceedings of the Hawk's Cay Conference on the Cuban Missile Crisis,* Marathon, Florida, 5-8 March, 1987, Final Version (Center for Science and International Affairs, Harvard University, April, 1988), mimeograph, 22.

7. Theodore C. Sorensen, *The Kennedy Legacy* (New York, 1969), 187.

8. For a recent argument to this effect see David A. Welch and James G. Blight, "An Introduction to the Excomm Transcripts," *International Security* 12 (Winter 1987-88): 25.

9. *Hawk's Cay Conference*, 115. In his book, *Danger and Survival* (New York, 1989), 394, 411-12, Bundy acknowledges the importance of domestic political factors in Kennedy's thinking.

10. Sorensen, *The Kennedy Legacy*, 190; Bundy, *Danger and Survival*, 412.

11. Welch and Blight, "An Introduction to the Excomm Transcripts," 25.

12. Sorensen, *The Kennedy Legacy*, 188.

13. Ibid.

14. Ibid., 189.

15. Stone, "The Brink," 12-16.

16. Ibid., 12.

17. Steel, "End Game," 15-22.

18. Bernstein, "The Week We Almost Went to War," 17. See also idem, "The Cuban Missile Crisis: Trading the Jupiters in Turkey?"

19. Bernstein, "The Week We Almost Went to War," 20.

20. Ibid., 13-21.

21. Quoted in Steel, "End Game", 119.

22. Roger Hilsman, *To Move A Nation: The Politics of Foreign Policy in the Administration of John F. Kennedy,* (Garden City, NY, 1967), 196.

23. Roger Hilsman, "An Exchange on the Missile Crisis," *New York Review of Books,* 16 March 1969.

24. *Hawk's Cay Conference,* 115.

25. *New York Times,* 23 October 1962.

26. Abel, *The Missile Crisis,* 119.

27. Robert Kennedy, *Thirteen Days: A Memoir of the Cuban Missile Crisis* (New York, 1969), 67.

28. Irving L. Janis and Leon Mann, *Decision Making: A Psychological Analysis of Conflict, Choice, and Commitment* (New York, 1977), 74-95. For its application to foreign policy see Richard Ned Lebow, *Between Peace and War: The Nature of International Crisis,* (Baltimore, 1981); and Robert Jervis, Richard Ned Lebow, and Janice Gross Stein, *Psychology and Deterrence* (Baltimore, 1985), chaps. 3-4,9.

29. Bundy, *Danger and Survival,* 394, 411-12.

30. Welch and Blight, "An Introduction to the Excomm Transcripts," 25.

31. C. Douglas Dillon offers this argument to explain why the ExComm did not discuss politics. "I don't accept the premise that we were swayed by the question of public opinion or how our choices would fly politically or anything else like that. Obviously, every President has to consider that sort of thing, but that wasn't *our* job." See *Hawk's Cay Conference,* 116.

32. Steel. "End Game," 16.

33. Transcript of ExComm meeting, 6:30-7:55 P.M., 16 October 1962, 45-48.

34. On 17 October, Theodore Sorensen submitted a memorandum to the president, widely quoted after the crisis, in which he reported that it was "generally agreed that these missiles, even when fully operational, do not significantly alter the balance of power—i.e., they do not significantly increase the potential megatonnage capable of being unleashed on American soil, even after a surprise American nuclear strike." See Sorensen, "Memorandum for the President," 17 October 1962, box 48, folder Cuba. General, Sorensen Papers, Kennedy Library. But in the previous evening's Excomm meeting, Chairman of the Joint Chiefs Maxwell Taylor had warned that the Cuban missiles "*can* become a, very, a rather important adjunct and reinforcement to . . . the strike capability of the Soviet Union." See Transcript of "Off-the-Record Meeting on Cuba, October 16, 1962, 6:30-7:55 P.M." The general discussion that ensued made it apparent that neither the president nor his advisers was at all certain about the military importance of the missiles.

McNamara told the ExComm that he had put the question to the Joint Chiefs and found them perturbed by the military threat the missiles would pose. He did not believe that the missiles would make no military difference. The United States could be attacked by ICBMs stationed in the Soviet Union and Moscow would significantly augment the size of this force in the course of the next few years whether or not it was able to keep its shorter-range missiles in Cuba. The only advantage of the Cuban deployment was that it allowed the Soviets to close the missile gap a few years earlier than they would in any case. "A missile is a missile," McNamara exclaimed, "It makes no difference whether you are killed by a missile fired from the Soviet Union or from Cuba." Transcript of "Off-the-Record Meeting, October 16"; Hilsman, *To Move A Nation,* 195. Deputy Secretary of Defense Roswell Gilpatric concurred. After the crisis, he told the *New York Times* that "the military equation was not altered" by the Cuban missiles. "It was simply an element of flexibility introduced into the power equation that the Soviets had not heretofore possessed." *New York Times,* 12 November 1962.

In the ensuing week, two memorandums on the missiles were submitted to the president and secretary of state. See Theodore C. Sorensen, Memorandum, October 19, 1962." Sorensen Files, box 49, 1-4; and W.W. Rostow, "Memorandum to the Secretary of State, October 22, 1962," National Security Files, box 36A-37, 3, Kennedy Library. But the first serious evaluation of their military implications only became available to the ExComm on 27 October in the form of a memorandum, prepared by Raymond L. Garthoff, special assistant for Soviet bloc politico-military affairs in the State Department. Raymond L. Garthoff, *Reflections on the Cuban Missile Crisis,* rev. ed. (Washington, 1989), 202-03. Garthoff argued that 24 MRBM launchers and 12 to 16 IRBM launchers would increase Soviet first-strike capability against targets in the continental United States by over 40 percent. This advantage would be in part offset by the missiles' vulnerability to a United States first strike. Garthoff's memorandums are of academic interest only because by the time they were submitted the decision in favor of the blockade had already been made and implemented.

35. Hilsman, *To Move A Nation*, 197.
36. Ibid., 34, 47-48, 120; McGeorge Bundy, interview with author, 22 July 1987.
37. Transcript of ExComm meeting, 27 October 1963, 48.
38. Hilsman, *To Move A Nation*, 197, also notes the analogy to Korea.
39. Lebow, *Between Race and War*, 169-84.
40. John Spanier, *The Truman-MacArthur Controversy and the Korean War*, rev. ed. (New York, 1965); Ronald J. Caridi, *The Korean War and American Politics: The Republican Party as a Case Study* (Philadelphia, 1969).
41. See Richard Ned Lebow and Janice Gross Stein, *We All Lost the Cold War* (forthcoming), Chap. 6, for details of this meeting.
42. Richard Ned Lebow, "Provocative Deterrence: A New Look at the Cuban Missile Crisis," *Arms Control Today* 18 (July-August 1988), 15-16; Raymond L. Garthoff, *Reflections on the Cuban Missile Crisis*, rev. ed. (Washington, 1989), 6-42; Richard Ned Lebow and Janice Gross Stein, *We All Lost the Cold War* (forthcoming), chap. 4.
43. Ernest R. May, *Lessons of the Past: The Use and Misuse of History in American Foreign Policy* (New York, 1973), for the relevance of the 1930s to American intervention in Vietnam; and Richard Ned Lebow, "Generational Learning and Foreign Policy," *International Journal* 40 (Autumn 1985): 556-85, for a broader treatment of the lessons of the 1930s and their relevance to postwar American foreign policy.
44. John F. Kennedy, *Why England Slept* (New York, 1940).
45. *New York Herald-Tribune*, 16 March 1966; Stone, "The Brink"; Schlesinger, *A Thousand Days*, 391; Reston, *New York Times Magazine*, 15 November 1964, 126.
46. Sorensen, *Kennedy*, 549; Hugh Sidey, "What the K's Really Said To Each Other," *Life*, 16 June 1961, 48-49; Nikita S. Khrushchev, *Khrushchev Remembers: The Last Testament*, trans. Strobe Talbott (Boston, 1974), 491-98.
47. Sigmund Freud, "The Neuro-Psychosis of Defense," (1894) and "Further Remarks on the Neuro-Psychoses of Defense," in *The Standard Edition of the Complete Psychological Works of Sigmund Freud* (London, 1962), 3, 43-68, 159-85.
48. *Hawk's Cay Conference*, 51; *Proceedings of the Cambridge Conference on the Cuban Missile Crisis*, Final Version (Cambridge, Massachusetts, Center for Science and International Affairs, Harvard University, April 1988), 60-61.
49. See the source cited in footnote 33.
50. For a fuller discussion of these incidents and a critique of the argument that they influenced Khrushchev's judgment of Kennedy's resolve, see Richard Ned Lebow, "The Cuban Missile Crisis: Reading the Lessons Correctly," *Political Science Quarterly* 98, No. 3 (Autumn 1983): 431-58, and Lebow

and Stein, *We All Lost the Cold War*, chap. 4, which makes use of the latest Soviet sources.

51. "Report on the Construction of Missile Sites in Cuba," 19 October 1962, 2 (the word "now" is penned in after the printed phrase "sites operational"). Central Intelligence Agency, "Report on Readiness Status of Soviet Missiles in Cuba," 21 October 1962; Central Intelligence Agency, "Readiness Status of Soviet Missiles in Cuba," 23 October 1962; Central Intelligence Agency, Memorandum, *The Crisis: USSR/Cuba*, 27 October 1962, Summary and I-1. National Security Archive, Washington, DC.

52. For a discussion see Lebow and Stein, *We All Lost the Cold War*, chap. 6.

53. Comments of McGeorge Bundy, *Cambridge Conference*, 54-55.

54. Several Kennedy advisers spent two days trying unsuccessfully to draft a letter. They were unable to find a way of expressing American indignation and the demand that the missiles be removed in a manner that would not provoke the kind of crisis the letter was meant to avoid. Theodore C. Sorensen's notes of the 18 October 1962 ExComm meeting, 1, and "Memorandum," 17 October 1962, 1-4; Sorensen, *Kennedy,* 683; Arthur M. Schlesinger, Jr., *Robert Kennedy and His Times* (Boston, 1978), 513.

55. This point is also made by Fen Osler Hampson, "The Divided Decision-Maker: American Domestic Politics and the Cuban Crises," *International Security* 9, no. 3 (Winter 1984-85): 130-65.

56. Charles E. Bohlen, *Witness to History, 1929-69* (New York, 1969), 491-92; Sorensen's notes of the 18 October 1962 ExComm meeting, 1, and "Memorandum," 17 October 1962, 1-4; Sorensen, *Kennedy,* 683; Schlesinger, *Robert Kennedy and His Times,* 513.

57. Steel, "End Game," 18-19.

58. *Washington Post,* 25 October 1962.

59. *Cambridge Conference,* 49-53, for Burlatsky's views and the reactions of the American participants.

60. Fyodor Burlatsky, "The Caribbean Crisis and Its Lessons," *Literaturnaya Gazeta,* [Literary Gazette], 11 November 1987. For a bad English translation see Foreign Broadcasting Information Service, *Soviet Union* 1987, no. 221, pp. 21-24.

61. Lebow, "The Cuban Missile Crisis"; and Lebow and Stein, *We All Lost the Cold War*, chap. 4.

62. See Lebow and Stein, *We All Lost the Cold War*, chap. 4, for a discussion of these warnings.

63. See the testimony of the Cuban officials, *Proceedings of the Moscow Conference on the Cuban Missile Crisis, January 27-28, 1989,* ed. Bruce J. Allyn, James G. Blight, and David A. Welch, Center for Science and International Affairs, Harvard University, 1990; Lebow and Stein, *We All Lost the Cold War*, chap. 2.

64. Kennedy, *Thirteen Days,* 128.

65. Zbigniew Brzezinski, "The Implications of Change for United States Foreign Policy," *Department of State Bulletin* 52 (3 July 1967): 19-23.

66. For a discussion of Kennedy's state of mind from 27-28 October, see Lebow and Stein, *We All Lost the Cold War*, chaps. 6 and 13.
67. *Hawk's Cay Conference*, 175-76.
68. Walt W. Rostow, *The View From the Seventh Floor* (New York, 1964), 19.
69. *Hawk's Cay Conference*, 173-74
70. See Lebow and Stein, *We All Lost the Cold War*, chaps. 8 and 12 for a discussion of this case.
71. Ibid.
72. Raymond L. Garthoff, *Reflections on the Cuban Missile Crisis* (Washington, 1987), 87.
73. Sorensen, *The Kennedy Legacy*, 192.
74. *Cambridge Conference*, 130.
75. Nathan, "The Missile Crisis," 258.
76. Ibid., 280-81.
77. Author's interviews with Fyodor Burlatsky and Georgy Shaknazarov (Cambridge, Massachusetts, 11 October 1987), Sergei Khrushchev (Moscow, 15 May 1989), and Aleksei I. Adzhubei (Moscow, 17 May 1989).

6

Thirteen Months:
Cuba's Perspective on the Missile Crisis

Philip Brenner

The Cuban missile crisis may be the most studied confrontation in our history. Yet until recently, Cuba has been left out of the Cuban missile crisis.[1] The traditional view focused attention on the fabled 13 days in October 1962, from the time President John F. Kennedy learned that the Soviets were constructing sites for intermediate-range ballistic missiles in Cuba, until Chairman Nikita Khrushchev ordered the sites dismantled and the missiles removed. From this perspective, the crisis was a showdown between the two superpowers, and Cuba was merely the location where the confrontation occurred.

New evidence, however, demonstrates that the crisis cannot be understood adequately—that appropriate lessons cannot be drawn—unless Cuba is placed back in the study of the missile crisis.[2] Once a Cuban perspective is addressed, the crisis is no longer merely 13 days. It begins in November 1961 and does not end until November 1962, 13 months later.

CUBA'S APPREHENSIONS AND
THE ACCEPTANCE OF SOVIET MISSILES

Cuban leaders believed in 1962 that the Kennedy administration had reacted to the April 1961 Bay of Pigs debacle by preparing for a much larger invasion of Cuba, one that would have the full intent of overthrowing the Cuban government and would rely on U.S. military forces. Fidel Castro reflected on this in 1974 when he remarked: "If the United States had not been bent on liquidating the Cuban revolution there would not have been an October [missile] crisis. . . . Were we right or wrong to fear direct invasion? Didn't the United States invade the Dominican Republic? . . . How could we be so sure that we would not be invaded?"[3] Soviet leaders seem to have shared the Cuban judgment, though it is not clear if the Soviets arrived at this view independently or largely as a result of Cuban intelligence and analyses.[4] This belief framed the Cuban interpretation of each hostile U.S. action during the 18 months after the Bay of Pigs and led inexorably to the conclusion that an invasion was coming.

One major action that fueled Cuban suspicions was the January 1962 suspension of Cuba's membership in the Organization of American States (OAS). Sergo Mikoyan, son of the late Soviet first deputy premier Anastas Mikoyan, explained that this was seen in Havana as "a preparatory diplomatic action taken for the invasion."[5] Shortly thereafter, Castro received a report from Aleksei I. Adzhubei, the editor of *Izvestia* and Premier Nikita Khrushchev's son-in-law, about an interview Adzhubei had had with President Kennedy. The Soviet editor reportedly derived a strong impression from the interview that an invasion was being planned.[6] A few weeks later, in April, Miro Cardona, head of the Cuban Revolutionary Council (the would-be government-in-exile), told journalists that President Kennedy had indicated to him in a White House meeting that the administration wanted to invade Cuba with an exile army headed by Cardona.[7] At about the same time, the United States undertook two large military exercises in the Caribbean near Cuba. The first, "Lantphibex 1-62," involved a marine assault using the island of Vieques off the coast of Puerto Rico. The second, called "Quick Kick," was a massive set of naval maneuvers—with 79 ships and more than 40,000 troops—off the southeastern U.S. coast. Cuban leaders watched these events with growing concern.[8]

Meanwhile, the United States attempted to extend its economic embargo by threatening to cut off aid to countries that traded with Cuba, by refusing to purchase goods that had the possibility of containing any Cuban materials and by pressuring U.S. allies to end commercial ties with Cuba.[9] A recently declassified progress report about the economic campaign against Cuba confirmed that "diplomatic means were used to frustrate Cuban trade negotiations in Israel, Jordan, Iran, Greece, and possibly Japan."[10] These activities were interpreted by Cuban officials as part of a well-developed plan to destabilize and destroy their government. In fact, the efforts were coordinated by an interagency working group chaired by a State Department representative.[11]

Cuban unease was reinforced by the campaign that may have been the most threatening portent of an invasion. The Kennedy administration was engaged in a well-orchestrated, multifaceted plan—named "Operation Mongoose"—to "bring about the revolt of the Cuban people . . . [which] will overthrow the Communist regime and institute a new government with which the United States can live in peace."[12] Recently declassified documents about Operation Mongoose reveal that the planners recognized that the ultimate success of destabilizing the Cuban government would probably have required the use of U.S. military forces.[13] In an amazing historical irony, the target date for the revolt was set as October 1962, when the missile crisis did occur. Notably, though, planning for the revolt began before either the Cubans or Soviets ever discussed missiles. President Kennedy authorized the covert war against Cuba in November 1961. From a Cuban view, this might be seen as the start of the missile crisis.

Operation Mongoose was the largest operation that the CIA had ever undertaken. Four hundred agents, and many more "assets" and operatives, were assigned the task of destroying the Cuban government. Run out of headquarters in Miami, it deployed paid Cuban exiles on raids into Cuba from south Florida, Puerto Rico, and Central American. General Edward Lansdale, chief of operations for Mongoose, reported that their actions included "blowing up bridges to stop communications and blowing up certain production plants."[14] It also involved the destruction of sugar mills and fields, oil facilities and transportation equipment; the sabotage of machinery and replacement parts; damage to sugar and tobacco exports; and the supplying of anti-government guerrillas. By the end of July 1962 the CIA claimed to have infiltrated 11 teams into Cuba to support "guerilla forces," and that "guerrilla warfare could be activated with a good chance of success, if assisted properly."[15] Their efforts were supported by clandestine radio broadcasts to Cuba on a station called Radio Americas, the successor to Radio Swan, which had supported exiles in the Bay of Pigs invasion. The Cubans viewed the exile attacks as integrally coupled to the several attempts that were made during this period to assassinate Castro.[16]

Sergo Mikoyan explained the logical link in 1988 by arguing that there would have been no reason to assassinate Castro only to have him replaced by Che Guevara. The logic was that Castro's death would be followed by an invasion of U.S. troops.[17] Cuban officials did not believe that the exiles themselves would overthrown the Cuban government, because Cuba was far better armed in 1962 than it had been in April 1961.[18] If the United States was unaware of this fact, and there is little evidence that Cuba believed U.S.

planners were so badly informed, Castro underlined it with an interview in *Pravda* in January 1962.[19]

Cuban officials recently verified that Cuban agents had infiltrated the Mongoose sabotage teams and that Cuba was aware of the common talk among the exile groups about plans for an invasion. Division General Fabian Escalante summarized the Cuban perspective in 1991 by asserting that after the Bay of Pigs "the government of the U.S. and its agencies gave support to the internal counterrevolution: it revived its hopes, provided resources, and reaffirmed its promises to intervene directly in order to prod it towards a new battle against the revolution."[20]

Escalante detailed Cuban information about a large number of sabotage actions, and said that Cuba had calculated there were more than 5,000 separate incidents related to the clandestine war. However, it is not known how Cuban officials assessed each aspect of Operation Mongoose: the sabotage, the psychological operations, the radio transmissions, the diplomatic offensive, and the various military maneuvers, some of which may have been intended only as psychological ploys. What we know is that Cuban leaders generally anticipated an invasion, that Mongoose activities were a significant factor in shaping this assessment, and that events in early 1962 likely stimulated the Cuban decision in May to accept Soviet ballistic missiles on the island.

Cuban fears of a U.S. invasion in the weeks just before the United States discovered the missiles may have been related to what now appear to be real threats posed by the United States. The recently declassified *CINCLANT Historical Account of Cuban Crisis 1962* describes a series of actions taken by the U.S. Atlantic Command beginning on 1 October that "accelerated planning and preparations to increase force readiness posture for the execution of CINCLANT[21] OPLAN 312-62."[22] We do not know how aware Cuban leaders were of the preparations for OPLAN 312-62 that were undertaken before Cuba decided to accept ballistic missiles.[23] Presumably, the accelerated activity contributed to Cuban statements between 1 October and 22 October that invasion preparations were under way. Indeed, on 6 October U.S. forces were directed to increase "readiness to execute the 314 and 316 Plans as well as 312."[24] This apparently prompted the 8 October speech by Cuban president Osvaldo Dorticós at the United Nations, in which he warned the United States that an invasion could have ominous consequences, and he obliquely hinted that there were nuclear weapons on the island.[25]

However, other factors may have led the Cubans to believe an invasion was imminent before the end of 1962. An important one could have been Defense Department publicity about large-scale military exercises off the coast of Puerto Rico planned for October. Named "Phibriglex-62," it included an "invasion" of Vieques in a mock overthrow of a leader named Ortsac, or "Castro" in reverse.[26] On 24 August, an émigré terrorist group named the Cuban Student Directorate strafed a hotel near Havana and killed several Soviet technicians and Cubans.[27] The attack may have been viewed with greater importance than similar previous actions by the group, because on that day President Kennedy stated in a press conference that "I am not for invading Cuba at this time." He thereby left the impression that he would be for it in the near future. At about the same time, British historian Hugh Thomas notes, the Defense Department "announced that Cubans enrolled in the U.S. army could be used against Cuba."[28] Cuban officials were probably sensitive to the announcement, because they had been troubled when the United States began drafting Cuban exiles in late 1961.[29]

Clearly, Cuban leaders knew about the strident calls throughout September and early October, in the media and by members of Congress, for an attack against Cuba.[30] The weekly magazine *Bohemia* declared in an editorial on 9 September, "Never has the international situation been so full of danger for Cuba. The Yankee *metropoli*, that has lost in the island the most precious jewel of its empire, has designed very precise schemes for the great assault. . . . It has reproduced, after 18 months, the outward conditions that preceded the Bay of Pigs invasion."[31] Castro said in 1974 that before 22 October "we saw certain movements in Washington . . . which we understood not only by instinct and smell, but by our experience with the way in which Kennedy had imposed the blockade [economic embargo]. We declared a state of alarm and mobilized our anti-aircraft weapons."[32]

WHAT WERE THE CUBANS THINKING WHEN THEY ACCEPTED THE MISSILES?

There are now may versions of why and how Cuba came to have Soviet missiles. But a consensus has emerged that the idea originated with the Soviets, and that it was accepted by the Cubans as an act of "socialist solidarity" and as a means of deterring a U.S. invasion. There is also a good indication of some of the key actions taken by Cuba before 22 October and the decisions made by the Cuban leadership.

However, there is little information about Cuban perceptions of the way in which U.S. officials viewed Cuba's behavior. It may be that Cuban leaders did not care about what the United States perceived, but it would seem more likely that they would have needed to familiarize themselves with the attitudes of U.S. leaders because of the potential threat posed by the United

States. Yet, we do not even know how Cuban officials imagined the United States would react to the Second Declaration of Havana. In that 4 February 1962 speech Castro asserted, "The duty of every revolutionary is to make the revolution," and he provided the basis for a policy of supporting armed struggle in Latin America.[33] What interpretation would be placed on the obviously increased military ties to the Soviet Union in 1962 and the stationing of IL-28 (Beagle/Mascot) light jet bombers and Komar patrol boats? The Cubans may have calculated that the United States would accept their presence in Cuba with equanimity, because the Soviets had sent them elsewhere without much reaction.[34] In addition, Cuban leaders seem to have surmised that their behavior did not matter to the United States anymore since U.S. policy was fixed on a course of overthrowing the Cuban government regardless of what Cuba did. In all, Cuba seems not to have considered that U.S. policy might be accelerated by their actions and declarations.

What of the missiles themselves? Cuban leaders believed that these new weapons would deter a U.S. invasion.[35] But what precisely did they expect the U.S. reaction would be? Castro told journalist Tad Szulc that he expected "a very tense situation would be created, and that there would be a crisis."[36] Still, the Cubans had no contingency plans for a crisis.[37] They do seem to have been surprised by President Kennedy's 22 October revelation about the missiles, although apparently they were not as complacent about the secret as the Soviets.

Indeed, Castro's 26 July speech, in which he said that Cuban weapons would be able to cause untold casualties in the United States, and Dorticós 8 October UN speech indicate that they assumed the United States would or did know about the missiles, and that they were offering a warning to the United States. Yet military preparations appear to have been made only to counter the feared U.S. invasion that Cuban leaders had seen coming many months earlier. There is no evidence that they connected the seeming invasion plans to their own introduction of ballistic missiles. Cuban leaders seem to have assumed, then, that the United States would accept the presence of missiles once they were operational, as the Soviets had accepted U.S. missiles in Turkey.[38] Yet if this were the case, it would be important to know why they misinterpreted President Kennedy's two September warnings against the introduction of offensive capabilities in Cuba.[39]

CUBA AND THE SOVIETS BEFORE THE CRISIS

While we have a partial picture of Cuban perceptions of U.S. views about Cuban behavior, our portrait of Cuba's perceptions about Soviet views is cloudy. We do know that relations between the two countries were strained in the early part of 1962 and that Soviet military aid was provided at a reduced level until June.[40] The Cuban leadership may have surmised that acceptance of the missiles would strengthen the relationship. On the other hand, they may have viewed the missiles as an offer they could not refuse on pain of straining the relationship even further. We know that the Cubans wanted to be included under the Soviet nuclear umbrella in 1962, and were seeking a way to sharpen Khrushchev's vague 1960 threat to let missiles fly if the United States were to attack Cuba.[41] They may have seen emplacement of the missiles as an acceptable alternative to joining the Warsaw Pact.

That Castro viewed the placement of missiles in Cuba as akin to a military alliance is reinforced by an explosive letter he wrote to Khrushchev on 26 October.[42] Castro observed first that he anticipated U.S. military aggression "within the next 24 to 72 hours." The most likely form of action, he surmised, would be air attacks against specified targets. But it was also possible, he reasoned, that there could be an invasion. If an invasion were to occur, he said, it would pose a danger for all humanity. The implication of an invasion, he suggested, was that the United States would also carry out a "first nuclear strike against [the Soviet Union]." Under the circumstances of an invasion, then, he warned that the Soviet Union would need to launch a preemptive first strike.[43] The logic of Castro's warning became clear at a January 1992 meeting in Havana of U.S., Soviet, and Cuban officials who were involved in the crisis. Soviet General Anatoly Gribkov revealed that the Soviet commanding general in Cuba had the authority to fire nuclear-tipped tactical rockets in the event of a U.S. invasion. Former Defense Secretary Robert S. McNamara remarked that such a nuclear strike would have resulted in a U.S. nuclear strike against Cuba.[44] With a possible escalation, it is logical to imagine a U.S. nuclear strike, as well, against the Soviet Union.

Castro's explanation of Cuban motives has varied since 1963. In a speech toward the end of a six-week visit in the Soviet Union, the Cuban leader said that "Cuba saw a danger to its security, and with an absolute right . . . adopted the measures that would fortify its defense."[45] Yet a few months earlier he told journalist Claude Julien that "because we were receiving important aid from the socialist camp we estimated that we could not slink away [from the offer of missiles]." He added then, "It was not to assure our own defense, but first to reinforce socialism at an international scale."[46] This theme has been repeated since. Yet in a 1974 interview he revived the matter of Cuban defense, as he pointed to the missiles as "an effective guarantee against a direct attack." Since then the defense of Cuba has been included as a second Cuban motive.[47]

Indeed, at the 1992 Havana meeting Castro said that "when the issue of missiles was first brought up, we thought that it was something beneficial to the consolidation of the defense power of the entire socialist bloc. . . . We did not want to concentrate on our problems. Subsequently, it represented our defense." The Cuban leader went on to explain that if the missiles had been intended primarily for Cuban defense, "we would not have accepted the missiles," because the missiles made Cuba into a "Soviet military base" and so they posed "a high political cost for our country's image, which we valued so highly."[48] Still, the Cuban leadership did lack sophistication about nuclear weapons, and placed great faith in the Soviet military judgments about nuclear strategy. Carlos Franqui reports that Castro "seemed to have a blind belief in the Soviet military machine." The Cuban leader himself acknowledged in 1984 that "it did not occur to me to ask the Soviets how many missiles each of the superpowers possessed."[49] At the 1992 Havana conference Castro observed that he was unaware of the extent to which the United States had missile superiority over the Soviet Union. "If we had that information," he remarked, "and if they had talked to us in strategic terms, we would surely have advised prudence."[50]

Whatever military significance he attached to the notion of strengthening the socialist camp, the Cuban leader meant it in a political sense as well. Castro understood the missiles as part of the U.S.-Soviet equation, in which the Cuban-based weapons might have enabled Khrushchev to bargain more effectively for socialist gains elsewhere, such as in Europe.[51] In addition, for Cuba to stand up to the United States would weaken the U.S. image as an invincible power, and in a zero-sum world the missiles would have strengthened the non-Western camp.

Castro is likely to have believed that if an avowedly socialist country were able to resist U.S. attacks, then it would encourage similar resistance elsewhere. This construction would have been consistent with the Second Declaration of Havana.[52] However, the Soviet Union did not endorse Cuba's enthusiasm for Third World revolution, especially in Latin America.

There is also uncertainty about the way Cuban leaders calculated how the missiles would contribute to the defense of Cuba. The weapons sent to Cuba (and those intended for delivery) were a weak second-strike deterrent. Liquid propelled and requiring eight hours to fuel and arm with a nuclear warhead, they would have been of little use in responding to a nuclear attack, and of uncertain use in response to a conventional one. As historian Barton Bernstein observed about the U.S. Jupiter missiles in Turkey, it would be more likely that they "would draw, not deter, an attack."[53]

Cuban officials may have understood this because Castro remarked in 1974 that Cuba had an obligation, in effect, to make itself as much of a target as other socialist countries. "If we expected them [the socialist camp] to take a chance for us," he said, "we had to be willing to do likewise for them."[54] Yet it is most likely that the Cuban leaders had a relatively unsophisticated understanding about the missiles. Jorge Risquet Valdes, a member of the Cuban Communist party's Political Bureau, observed in 1989 that the Cuban leadership felt vulnerable with the few arms available in early 1962, and reasoned simply that Cuba would be better able to repel U.S. aggression with more arms. From their viewpoint, he suggested, missiles were better still, and were a reasonable means of defense.[55] Whatever use was intended for the missiles, they would have been a deterrent, because their very presence in Cuba would have meant that a conventional U.S. attack would run the risk of escalating into a nuclear confrontation.

Still, there is the possibility that Cuban leaders did expect that the missiles might be used. They may have anticipated that a direct invasion by U.S. forces would trigger the missiles. Castro has said that he drew little distinction between a conventional assault on Cuba and a nuclear retaliation, because from the Cuban perspective a conventional attack would cost Cuba millions of lives and would thus affect Cuban society much the way a nuclear attack would ravage the United States.[56]

While there have been conflicting reports in the past over who initiated the plan to bring missiles to Cuba, Castro's accounts are consistent with other evidence that indicates the idea was first raised by the Soviets in May 1962.[57] Emilio Aragones Navarro reported in 1989 that six Cuban officials were involved in the decision, and that they unanimously agreed to accept the offer: Fidel Castro, Raúl Castro, Che Guevara, Blas Roca, Osvaldo Dorticós, and Aragones. The six formed the Secretariat of the Integrated Revolutionary Organizations (ORI), the ruling party at the time.[58]

A trip to Moscow by Raúl Castro in July served to develop details of the plan and during those two weeks a formal agreement was drafted and initialled.[59] However, the agreement was never finalized. Fidel Castro amended the July draft, he explained in January 1992, because the initial "draft was erratic, in the sense that there was no clear foundation set about the matter."[60] The new draft emphasized that Cuba and the Soviet Union were "guiding themselves by the principles and objectives of the United Nations Organization Charter," and were "taking into account the urgency of taking measures to assure mutual defense in the face of possible aggression against the Republic of Cuba and the USSR." The agreement did not make any mention of missiles, or any other equipment to be delivered to Cuba.[61]

It appears that the decisions to send IL-28 bombers, MiG-21s, other military equipment, and Soviet troops, were made in Havana in May, in discussions with Marshall Sergei S. Biryuzov, commander of the Soviet Strategic Missile Forces.[62] The Soviets controlled the surface-to-air missiles (SAMs) throughout the crisis, because the Cubans had not been sufficiently trained at the time to use them.[63] Cuban pilots had been trained to fly the IL-28s, but Cuba never took full possession of the bombers.[64] The IL-28s were considered to be virtually obsolete as an offensive weapon, but would have been useful in defending Cuba against commando raids or in attacking commando bases.[65]

By the end of October there were more than 40,000 Soviet military personnel on the island, about half of whom were troops. We do not know if the Cubans requested this large number, whether they sought even more, or how they considered the troops would be used. Such a significant Soviet military contingent in itself would likely have prompted a U.S. attack, because it would have made Cuba a major Soviet base.[66] With such a large contingent, the Soviet stakes in a U.S. attack would also have been enormous. Were the Soviet troops overrun by U.S. forces, Premier Khrushchev might not have survived the ensuing humiliation.

Che Guevara and Aragones traveled to Moscow on 27 August to finalize the missile agreement, after Castro had made amendments to the July draft. Aragones asserted in 1989 that he sought to make the agreement public immediately. The missile deployment was badly camouflaged, and there was Cuban concern as to whether the missiles could be kept secret from the United States.[67] Cuba also reasoned that an announcement about the missiles would gain it more security than the secret installation of offensive weapons.[68] Indeed, former White House official Theodore Sorensen reflected at the 1989 Moscow conference that it would have been more difficult for the United States to compel withdrawal of the missiles had the agreement been made public, because then the situation would have paralleled U.S. agreements with countries on the Soviet periphery.[69] Castro suggested a similar line of argument in 1992, when he recalled that he had opposed installing the missiles in secret. "The secrecy of the military agreement did harm," he said. There would have been significant protests against the United States for initiating a quarantine, he explained, "if we had done things openly. All of this is true because we were within our most absolute right to do so [deploy the missiles]. And how, if we had the right, were we going to act in a way that made it seem that we did not have this right, that made it seem that we were doing something wrong."[70]

From the Cuban perspective, a public agreement in itself would have had a deterrent effect, similar to membership in the Warsaw Pact, by making an attack against Cuba equivalent to an attack against the Soviet Union. Cuba did not take Soviet protection for granted, and it sought to maneuver the Soviet Union into an embrace at the same time Cuba sought to protect itself from the United States. Such an alliance was precisely what the Soviets had resisted, because of the difficulties that would be entailed in sustaining a conflict with the United States so far from the Soviet Union. Khrushchev refused to make the agreement public, and proposed to announce the accord in November, once the missiles were operational.[71] It was never signed formally by the Cuban or Soviet heads of state.

Journalist Herbert Matthews argues that to exclude Cuba from the missile crisis is akin to "saying that *Hamlet* can be played without a stage."[72] The metaphor unfortunately suggests that Cuba played a passive role, that it was no more than the inanimate stage for the superpower players. While the review of the period before 22 October already has invalidated the metaphor, the notion that Cuba had little impact on events during the height of the crisis may have been the most serious oversight in earlier studies.

The response in Cuba to President Kennedy's 22 October announcement of the quarantine was apparently, in Matthews's phrasing, "a curious mixture of exhilaration and calm." As filmmaker Adolfo Gilly observed, "It was as if a long-contained tension relaxed, as if the whole country had said as one, 'at last.' "[73] Castro himself was reportedly quite calm, perhaps because he had experienced the possibility of total defeat several times before. "For Kennedy and the United States," political scientist Herbert Dinerstein reasoned, "this was the first time."[74]

The exhilaration undoubtedly came from the full-scale mobilization announced by Castro as President Kennedy spoke on 22 October.[75] With a seeming certainty that the United States would launch a major invasion of the island, the official government newspaper *Revolucion* was emblazoned by a headline on 23 October that read: "The Nation on a War Footing." Sergio del Valle Jímenez, then Cuban army chief of staff, recalled in 1989 that the Cuban leaders anticipated there would be massive U.S. bombing with an invasion, and they had ordered the erection of ramparts and the digging of trenches. He said that 270,000 people were placed under arms within days.[76] *The CINCLANT Account* reports that "Cuban Army units mobilized and assumed defensive positions quickly and with a minimum of confusion."[77] Interestingly, it seems that there was not a roundup of suspected counterrevolutionaries and dissidents, as there had been during the Bay of Pigs invasion.[78] This may have been due to the sense that the danger to Cuba this time was from a direct U.S. attack, not from subversive forces.

Sergo Mikoyan remarked in an interview in 1989 that he found it "incredible that the Cubans and Soviets in Cuba were ready to die to the last man" during the crisis.[79] Indeed, there appears to have been an atmosphere of defiance and toughness throughout the country, in part stimulated by the Cuban media. The headlines in *Revolucion* on 24 October screamed defiantly: "The Blockade: We Will Resist It"; "Direct Aggression: We Will Repel It"; "Those That Unleash Nuclear War Will Be Exterminated." The party newspaper *Hoy* on 24 October featured a large drawing of Castro, with his rifle raised high, declaring "To the struggle, victory will be complete." Posters quickly went up throughout the country with the phrase "On a War Footing."[80]

Had the United States invaded Cuba—there are indications that an invasion was being prepared for 29 or 30 October in order to resolve the crisis[81]—military preparations by Cuba would have made the ensuing conflict different from the one anticipated by U.S. planners. The U.S. expectation was that the main fighting would have been over in ten days, and that U.S. forces would sustain 18,484 casualties.[82] However, in Moscow in 1989, Cuban Political Bureau member Jorge Risquet argued that major guerrilla warfare would have gone on for years, and del Valle estimated that there would have been 100,000 civilian and military casualties in the short term.[83] More important, as indicated above, the United States was unaware that there were nine Soviet tactical nuclear missiles (*Lunas*) on the island that were armed with warheads of between 7,000 and 12,000 tons of TNT equivalent. (This was comparable to the bombs that destroyed Hiroshima and Nagasaki.) Moreover, the Soviet general in command on the island had the authority to fire these missiles in the event of a U.S. invasion. Such a nuclear strike on the 140,000 invading U.S. forces would have resulted in tens of thousands of deaths and a near certain retaliatory U.S. nuclear strike. It would have been difficult to contain the likely ensuing escalations.

One indication of the ferocity of the Cuban position, and the willingness to throw caution to the wind, was Castro's order on 27 October to open fire on any hostile aircraft in Cuban airspace.[84] That morning a Soviet officer, who may have been responding to Castro's general command instead of following instructions from Moscow to avoid provocations, fired a SAM that downed a U-2 surveillance aircraft.[85] On the afternoon of the 27th, at the height of the crisis, Cuban 37 mm guns hit a low-flying F8U-1P plane that was on a reconnaissance mission.[86] (Cuban forces controlled the island's antiaircraft batteries, which apparently became operational between 24 October and 27 October.)

Had the F8U-1P been unable to return to base, it is likely that the threatened U.S. attacks would have commenced. There already was pressure on President Kennedy from several of his advisers and from the Joint Chiefs of Staff to launch an attack, at least against the surface-to-air and ballistic missiles.[87] With a second reconnaissance plane down on the 27th, the pressure would have been irresistible. Attorney General Robert Kennedy reportedly said in a 1964 interview that after the downing of the U-2 on 27 October, Ambassador Anatoly Dobrynin was warned that "if one more plane was destroyed, we would hit all the SAMs immediately, and probably the missiles as well, and we would probably follow that with an invasion."[88] Former Treasury Secretary C. Douglas Dillon recalls that when the U-2 was shot down, it added enormously to the pressure to act. By Saturday the 27th, there was a clear majority in the ExComm in favor of taking military action.[89]

The Soviet ambassador to Cuba, Aleksandr Alekseev, recounts that there were daily communications between Castro and Khrushchev from 23 to 27 October. Castro, he recalls, encouraged the Soviets to remain firm in keeping the missiles in Cuba.[90] But it is not clear whether the Cubans were informed fully about Soviet deliberations and intentions, or even whether the Soviets may have misinformed the Cubans intentionally or inadvertently. For example, on 24 October Soviet General Issa A. Pliyev reportedly responded to Castro's inquiry about the state of Soviet forces by telling the Cuban leader that "everything is ready." (Pliyev was overall commander of the Soviet forces in Cuba.) Castro seems to have interpreted this answer to mean that all of the missiles were operational, and that each missile was configured with a warhead ready to be fired. It is not clear what he understood "all the missiles" to mean at the time. By 22 October, 42 missiles had arrived in Cuba; 80 had been planned for delivery. All 42 were "medium range" (SS-4) ballistic missiles, with a range of 1,020 miles. Six undelivered missiles were also SS-4s, and 32 were "intermediate range" (SS-5) missiles, with a range of 2,200 miles.[91] Soviet participants at the 1992 Havana conference said that the 36 warheads for the ballistic missiles on the island were at some distance from the missiles, and that it would have required eight hours to fuel and prepare a missile for firing. Moreover, by 24 October only nine missiles reportedly were in place and fully assembled.

The nature of the communications between Castro and Khrushchev take on added significance because of the way Khrushchev may have interpreted them, and how that influenced his behavior. An indication of why this is important comes from the controversy surrounding the most publicized cable, sent on 26 October by Castro. In Khrushchev's most recently released memoirs, he recalls that "Castro suggested that to prevent our nuclear missiles from being destroyed, we should launch a pre-emptive strike against the U.S. My comrades in the leadership and I realized that our friend Fidel totally failed to understand our purpose."[92]

This communication from the Cuban leader, Khrushchev indicates, was an important factor in his decision to withdraw the missiles. Yet Soviet participants at a 1991 meeting of former officials from Cuba, the United States, and the Soviet Union, held in Antigua, explained that Castro's cable did not reach Khrushchev until 1:10 A.M. on 28 October, after he had decided to withdraw the missiles.[93] Moreover, as indicated earlier, Castro's call for a preemptive attack was qualified by his assessment that the likely U.S. action would be an air strike, and that only a U.S. invasion should be met with a Soviet first strike. Still, in a letter to Castro on 30 October, Khrushchev provided evidence that he may have missed the subtlety in the Cuban's cable, because he writes: "In your cable of October 27 you proposed that we be the first to launch a nuclear strike against the territory of an enemy. You, of course, realized where that would have led. Rather than a simple strike, it would have been the start of a thermonuclear world war. Dear Comrade Fidel Castro, I consider this proposal of yours incorrect, although I understand your motivation."[94]

What Khrushchev may have based his judgment on was a 27 October cable from the Soviet ambassador to Cuba, previewing the Castro cable that was to arrive later. It may have been on the basis of the ambassador's report that Khrushchev believed Castro was highly agitated, fearing an imminent invasion (although that would contrast with the several reports about Castro's general calmness). Alternately, the ambassador may merely have reported his assessment that an invasion was imminent, and an excited Khrushchev interpreted this in an extreme manner. Whatever the case, Castro's cable or its preview by the ambassador may have contributed to the Soviet leader's calculation that a speedy termination of the crisis was essential to avoid a major conflagration.

In short, it is certain that Cuba was more than a passive stage during the height of the crisis, although both the White House and the Kremlin focused almost exclusively on the opposing superpower. Neither appreciated that Cuba would perceive, for example, that low-level reconnaissance flights would be more threatening than U-2 surveillance flights. Low-level operations are intended to establish precise targets just prior to an invasion. As Castro noted in the 1992 conference, it was this purpose that made the low-level flights dangerous to Cuba. The U-2s, he said, had already seen all there was to see, and no longer posed a real threat.

AFTER THE BRINK:
28 OCTOBER TO 20 NOVEMBER

What Americans call the "Cuban missile crisis," and the Soviets call the "Caribbean crisis," the Cubans call the "October crisis." This nomenclature is used to signify that the period in October, when the United States and Soviet Union were on the brink of nuclear catastrophe, was only one of several crises that took on catastrophic proportions for the Cubans.

In reality, the crisis did not end on 28 October for either the United States or the Soviet Union. The Kennedy-Khrushchev agreements had to be implemented and Cuba became very much a part of that process. Until 20 November, the U.S. Strategic Air Command remained on alert at Defense Condition (DefCon) 2 (the state of full readiness for war); other forces were held at DefCon3, and the naval quarantine was maintained in place. Just as any of several incidents before 28 October might have led to an escalating exchange, so too the situation until 20 November remained very dangerous.

The United States asserted that the Kennedy-Khrushchev agreement required an on-site UN inspection in Cuba to assure that the offensive weapons were being dismantled and returned to the Soviet Union. Included in the list of weapons were all the Il-28 bombers.[95] Cuba, in turn, insisted that it would not permit inspection on its soil, and that the IL-28s were Cuban property, given to Cuba by the Soviet Union. Castro asserted that the Soviet Union had no authority to negotiate with the United States about inspection procedures or about the return of the bombers. Instead, he announced, Cuba would be willing to negotiate on the basis of five demands: that the United States end the economic embargo, cease subversive activities against Cuba, end the "pirate" attacks from bases in the United States and Puerto Rico, cease violations of Cuban airspace, and return Guantanamo Naval Base.[96]

Cuba maintained this position until 20 November, in the face of appeals by Acting UN Secretary-General U Thant and Anastas Mikoyan, both of whom traveled to Cuba. U Thant found that Castro was insistent that "any formula adopted by the Security Council must guarantee the full sovereignty of Cuba." On-site inspection violated Cuba's sovereignty and insulted Cuba, said Castro, because the crisis was not rooted in Cuba's efforts to defend itself but in U.S. "provocations" and "threats to peace." Yet there was no equivalent demand, the Cuban leader told U Thant, that the U.S. pledge not to invade Cuba be verified. Indeed, the secretary-general reported Castro declaring, "The United States would not give up their intention of launching another aggression. He [Castro] said that high officials in Washington publicly declared . . . that they would invade Cuba again."[97] To assuage Cuba's concern, U Thant offered a "UN presence" in Cuba for three weeks, "to eliminate the danger of aggression," but President Dorticós rejected the offer. He declared that "the danger of war would renew itself, because the conditions that propitiated North American [U.S.] aggression against Cuba would endure."[98]

Cuban negotiations with Mikoyan led the Soviets to back down on their initial willingness to remove all 40,000 troops. Apparently at Cuban insistence, the Soviets agreed to maintain 3,000 troops in Cuba. Sergo Mikoyan said that in a sense these were an offering to Castro, "to show that we were still supporting him." He added that they also provided a continued measure of deterrence against a U.S. invasion, functioning, in effect, as a kind of "trip-wire."[99]

There is no question that Castro was furious about the Kennedy-Khrushchev agreements. Early in November, at a University of Havana meeting, the Cuban prime minister described the Soviet premier as lacking "*cojones*" and encouraged public chanting of a song: "Nikita, Nikita, Indian giver, You don't take back what you once deliver."[100] For the week after the agreement, *Revolucion* printed stories that glorified Cuban patriotism and suggested the Soviets were traitors. Castro refused to meet with Ambassador Alekseev for several days after 28 October, despite Alekseev's repeated attempts to see him.

When Anastas Mikoyan arrived in Havana on 2 November, Castro grudgingly met him at the airport, but then did not meet with him again for nearly a week. During their negotiations, Castro "disappeared" for days at a time, or allegedly came to an agreement one evening only to renege on it the next day.[101] Even in January 1963 his fury was such that he told journalist Claude Julien that Khrushchev "should not have returned the missiles without consulting us . . . I cannot accept that Khrushchev promised Kennedy to return the missiles without making the least reference to the indispensable agreement by the Cuban government . . . Had Khrushchev come himself [to Cuba, instead of Mikoyan], I would have boxed him."[102]

The graphic stories of Castro's anger have tended to enshrine a conventional wisdom that his response to the Kennedy-Khrushchev agreements was rooted primarily in personal pique. His fury is said to have been the result, in the first instance, of learning about the agreement over the radio, not through a direct communication from Moscow. Moreover, the Soviets acted without consulting Cuba, and such disregard was seen as a "blow to the Cuban leader's pride."[103] In the second instance, the agreement was seen as an insult to Cuban sovereignty and dignity, as if Cuba were "a pawn" in a great power chess game, because the Soviet leader had acquiesced in a demand for inspection on Cuban territory "without relying on Cuba."[104]

Beyond such psychological explanations are those that relate to Cuba's vulnerability. Castro asserted in a letter to U Thant on 15 November that despite the removal of the missiles, U.S. officials "do not consider themselves bound by any promise."[105] Indeed, as early as November 1962, the United States did back away from the 27 October pledge contained in President Kennedy's letter to Premier Khrushchev. Kennedy had qualified the initial pledge with two conditions: a) that the "weapons systems" would be removed "under appropriate United Nations observation and supervision"; and b) that the Soviets would "undertake, with suitable safeguards, to halt the further introduction of such weapons systems into Cuba." Then, in a letter on November 6, he emphasized that his "assurances against an invasion of Cuba" were predicated on the "verified removal of the missile and bomber systems, together with real safeguards against their reintroduction." But the President added a new element now: "that Cuba can never have normal relations with the other nations of this hemisphere unless it ceases to appear to be a foreign military base and adopts a peaceful course of non-interference in the affairs of its sister nations" (see chapter 9 in this volume). The Soviets appear not to have reported to the Cubans how weak the U.S. assurances were. Castro's distrust of the United States was not based on specific knowledge of the U.S. position.

Castro's sense at the time was that the bargain was struck too readily, without adequate assurances, and that the United States would take advantage of loopholes to undermine Cuban security. This apparently was confirmed for him when the United States included the IL-28s in the demand for removal of offensive weapons, and later when Komar patrol boats were on the list Ambassador Adlai Stevenson presented to Anastas Mikoyan.[106]

Similarly, on 8 November a Mongoose terrorist squad bombed a Cuban factory. Its action was supposedly unauthorized, because Mongoose activities had been suspended on 30 October.[107] Apparently the group had been dispatched to Cuba before the official suspension of activities, and could not be recalled. The attack undoubtedly reinforced the Cuban belief that the United States could not be trusted. Their first inclination would have been to conclude that the U.S. destabilization campaign was still at work. It is also possible that they viewed the attach as a ploy in the U.S.-Soviet negotiations concerning the removal of the IL-28s and on-site inspection. However, since Cuba was not a party to the negotiations, Cuban officials would have been unlikely to interpret the Mongoose bombing merely as a negotiating tactic.

In part it was concern over Mongoose raids that led Cuba to be adamant about the violation of airspace, because U.S. surveillance planes had been used to support sabotage operations. In his 15 November letter to U Thant,

Castro observed that "photographs taken by the [U.S.] spying planes serve for guidance in sabotage."[108] He also asserted that low-level flights went over "our military defences and photograph not only the dismantled strategic missile installations but in fact our entire territory." Clearly, Cuba saw the flights as continued preparation for an invasion and Castro warned that surveillance craft would be destroyed.[109]

Notably, Cuba did make an offer—on 25 November, after the crisis ended—to allow UN inspection on its soil. But it was based on the pointed condition of a reciprocal inspection of alleged émigré training camps in the United States and Puerto Rico, to assure that they were being dismantled.[110]

The agreement with Kennedy left no room for Cuban participation and offered Cuba no opportunity to bring the United States to the bargaining table over matters of vital Cuban interest. A simple demand that the United States talk to Cuba at the moment when the world stood at the brink would have been difficult for Kennedy to reject. Castro no doubt found it difficult to fathom why Khrushchev would not include such a demand in his deal.[111] This contributed to Castro's anger as much as the fact that Khrushchev did not notify him before announcing that the missiles would be removed.

Had Castro been involved in negotiations, there is little doubt that a resolution of the crisis would have been more difficult. Some argue that his "adventurism" led to the very placement of the missiles of Cuba,[112] and from this point of view he would have been an irascible negotiator. Personality aside, though, if Cuba had been included in negotiations, its interests would then need to have been taken into account. But the Kennedy-Khrushchev agreements left Cuba feeling quite vulnerable. Not only were the missiles to be removed, non-offensive weapons, such as the IL-28s and Komar patrol boats, as well as all Soviet troops, were also to be withdraw. Cuba viewed the bombers and patrol boats as key weapons in the fight against terrorist attacks. In this light, Cuban resistance to the accords must be seen as rather more than mere obstinacy or pique.

Still, we do not know much about the negotiations between Anastas Mikoyan and the Cuban leaders, whether the Soviet leader provided details on Soviet negotiations with the United States,[113] or how Cuba assessed the alleged Soviet commitment to continue defending Cuba. The extent of Cuba's attentiveness to its hemispheric setting during the crisis is also unknown. Castro was contemptuous of the OAS's unanimous endorsement of the U.S. position on 24 October, but Cuba must have been aware of the rumors that the Latin Americans' support was coerced.[114] Cuba also sought at the time to maintain good relations with several countries in the hemisphere, such as Brazil and Mexico, which had publicly opposed a U.S. attack against Cuba.[115] But it is unclear what advice the Latin American countries offered Cuba, and how the advice was received.

RETHINKING THE CRISIS

"The final lesson of the Cuban missile crisis," Robert Kennedy observed in his memoir, "is the importance of placing ourselves in the other country's shoes." He went on to note that President Kennedy wisely "instructed all members of the ExComm and government that no interview should be given, no statement made, which would claim any kind of victory."[116] Yet, at the same time, there seems to have been, if not delight taken over Cuba's sense of vulnerability, at least an enormous blind spot about it. Indeed, though there were CIA analyses that pointed to Cuba's fear of a U.S. invasion, there is no evidence that the ExComm considered offering a no-invasion pledge to Cuba during the legendary thirteen days as a way of defusing the crisis. The only negotiating ploy contemplated was vis-à-vis Soviet concerns, namely the missiles in Turkey.[117] Perhaps this orientation was due to the assumption that dominated thinking about Cuba, that it was no more than a pawn of the Soviet Union.[118] One conclusion from this investigation is that, on the contrary, Cuba had its own interests and acted on them. Cuban decisions and assessments had a bearing on the way in which the crisis developed, evolved, and ended, and on how close it brought the world to oblivion.

There has been considerable analysis about the consequences for the superpowers,[119] but little detailed analysis about Cuba and the crisis aftermath. The general view is that the crisis led to significant strains between Cuba and the Soviet Union.[120] Even during Castro's 1963 trip to the Soviet Union—which followed on the heels of a favorable trade agreement that signified that the Soviet Union recognized that Cuba was fully in the socialist camp[121]—Prime Minister Castro implicitly chided the Soviets for abandoning armed struggle. Castro mixed his gracious appreciation for Soviet willingness to risk nuclear war in defense of "a small nation" with references to the necessity for the socialist camp to struggle "against the colonial yoke of imperialism."[122] One consequence of the strain, which was still in evidence as late as 1971, three years after the Soviet invasion of Czechoslovakia, may have been that Cuba began to choose to underscore its support for Third World insurgency as a way of maintaining its "own version of influence against the Soviets."[123]

Cuba stepped up its revolutionary activity after the missile crisis. But Castro's rationale may not have been to thumb his nose at or compete with the Soviets. After all, Cuba still relied heavily on the Eastern bloc for economic support. The rationale may have been more closely related to Cuba's sense of national security. Cuban officials seem to have concluded that the Soviet Union would not risk its own security "for the sake of Cuba," as Anastas Mikoyan reportedly admitted to Warsaw Pact ambassadors on 30 November 1962.[124] Hence, if Cuba could no longer count on the Soviet Union for its defense, and it still feared a hostile United States, then the development of an allied bloc of Third World countries, especially in Latin America, might have been one way to provide for its defense.[125] Castro also calculated that if the United States were confronted with insurrection in several Latin American countries, the efforts to suppress these revolutions would "overextend" the United States and undermine its ability to strike at Cuba.[126]

On the surface, Cuba had good reason to fear the United States. When President Kennedy met with the recently freed Bay of Pigs veterans in December 1962, he promised to return the brigade's flag to them in a "free Havana."[127] While Operation Mongoose was discontinued early in 1963, terrorist actions were reauthorized by the president. In October 1963, 13 major CIA actions against Cuba were approved for the next two months alone, including the sabotage of an electric power plant, a sugar mill and an oil refinery. Authorized CIA raids continued at least until 1965, as did CIA attempts on Castro's life.[128] The Cuban leader pointed to these menacing signs in 1963 when he first made his often repeated comment that "war was avoided, but peace was not gained."[129] From the Cuban perspective, the October crisis was just one of many.

For several years after the Cuban missile crisis there was a conventional wisdom, articulated by Arthur Schlesinger, Jr., that the crisis was resolved through a "combination of toughness and restraint, of will, nerve and wisdom, so brilliantly controlled, so matchlessly calibrated."[130] Yet we have come to realize now that luck may have been just as important, because so much was uncontrolled and so many incidents may have precipitated a clash inadvertently. By adding a Cuban perspective to the picture of missile crisis decision making, it becomes even clearer that the potential for miscalculation was great. Cuban leaders were new to "high" politics, as one Cuban delegate to the Moscow conference said in a 1989 interview. They did not have experience in dealing with matters that had global implications. None of the leaders involved in the crisis wanted a nuclear war, but none was able to be the fully rational actors that some would believe they could have been.[131] Because they lacked considerable information necessary for rational action, Cuban officials were probably the worst informed of any of the actors in the crisis.

The emerging view about how the missile crisis was managed has led to a new dictum. As Robert McNamara said in 1987, "Crisis management is a very uncertain and very difficult thing to do, and therefore, you've got to avoid the crises in the first place."[132] The first step in such an effort is improvement in communications between adversaries. This was appreciated at the time, and the so-called hotline was installed soon after the crisis. But what could the United States have communicated honestly to Cuba about Operation Mongoose and the attempted assassinations of Prime Minister Castro that would have assuaged Cuba's fears? Improved communications can reduce misunderstanding; but Cuba seems to have understood U.S. intentions quite well.

This suggests a lesson from the crisis that has been overlooked, because prior analyses have focused only on the two superpowers. For a small power, conventional warfare may be as threatening as nuclear warfare is to the United States. And a small power is likely to take whatever steps are necessary to reduce the threat. Thus, when the United States deals with small countries, the use of force or the threat of force to achieve political ends can have "exaggerated" consequences.

In reviewing recent scholarship about the missile crisis, political scientist David Bobrow aptly concluded that "narratives should include . . . all those actors with latitude to act," as well as "the context of the story as construed by each of those actors."[133] The validity of his recommendation is clear from the analysis here: Only by reintroducing Cuba into the Cuban missile crisis can we hope to develop a picture of the full significance of the crisis itself.

NOTES

Preparation of this chapter was made possible by an American University Summer Research Award.

1. See, for example, Graham T. Allison, *Essence of Decision* (Boston, 1971); Arthur M. Schlesinger, Jr., *A Thousand Days: John F. Kennedy in the White House* (Boston, 1965), chaps. 30-31; Roger Hilsman, *To Move a Nation* (New York, 1967); Lester H. Brune, *The Missile Crisis of October 1962* (Claremont, CA, 1985); Herbert S. Dinerstein, *The Making of a Missile Crisis: October 1962* (Baltimore, MD, 1976); T. Szulc, *Fidel: A Critical Portrait* (New York, 1986); Herbert L. Matthews, *Revolution in Cuba* (New York, 1975).
2. For example, James G. Blight and David A. Welch, *On the Brink* (New York, 1989); Raymond L. Garthoff, *Reflections on the Cuban Missile Crisis*, rev. ed., (Washington, D.C., 1989); Jorge I. Dominguez, *To Make*

the World Safe for Revolution: Cuba's Foreign Policy (Cambridge, 1989);
Thomas G. Paterson, "Fixation with Cuba: The Bay of Pigs, Missile Crisis,
and Covert War Against Castro," in Thomas G. Paterson, ed., *Kennedy's
Quest for Victory* (New York, 1989), pp. 136-41. Much new data has
become available because of five major conferences on the missile crisis.
Edited transcripts and analyses of the first two conferences can be found in
Blight and Welch, *On the Brink*. The first included nearly all of the living
members of the ExComm (Executive Committee of the National Security
Council, formed by President Kennedy on 16 October 1962), and the second
included many of these men and three Soviet experts. A transcript of the
third conference—held in Moscow in January 1989, with participation by
U.S., Soviet, and Cuban delegates—is available in Bruce J. Allyn, James
G. Blight and David A. Welch, eds., *Back to the Brink: Proceedings of the
Moscow Conference on the Cuban Missile Crisis, January 27-28, 1989,*
Center for Science and International Affairs, Harvard University (Lanham
MD: University Press of America, 1992). The transcript from the fourth
conference, "Cuba Between the Superpowers"—held in Antigua in January
1991 with U.S., Soviet, and Cuban participants—is available from the
Brown University Center for Foreign Policy Development. It is edited by
James G. Blight, David Lewis, and David A. Welch. The fifth conference
was held in Havana, Cuba in January 1992 and was attended by former
policymakers from the United States and the former Soviet Union, and
former and current policymakers from Cuba, including President Fidel
Castro. A transcript will be available from the Brown University Center for
Foreign Policy Development.

3. Frank Mankiewicz and Kirby Jones, *With Fidel* (New York, 1975), pp.
    150-1.

4. Allison, *Essence of Decision*, p. 239; Blight and Welch, *On the Brink*, pp.
    249-50, 294-5; Garthoff, *Reflections* (1989), pp. 6-10; H. L. Matthews,
    Fidel Castro (New York, 1970), p. 227; Szulc, *Fidel*, pp. 578-9.

5. Sergo Mikoyan, "La Crisis del Caribe, en retrospectiva," *America Latina*,
    no. 4 (April 1988), p. 45; also comments made by Jorge Risquet, head of
    the Cuban delegation at the Moscow conference, 27 January 1989 (during
    the conference). Certainly, Soviet leaders relied on several sources of
    intelligence to develop their analysis of an impending U.S. invasion. While
    the Soviet conclusion seems to have coincided with the Cuban assessment,
    it is not clear how much influence the Cuban view had. See Soviet com-
    ments in Blight and Welch, *On the Brink*, pp. 238, 249, 258. On the
    expulsion, see W. Smith, *The Closest of Enemies* (New York, 1987), p. 80;
    M. H. Morley, *Imperial State and Revolution: The United States and Cuba,
    1952-1986* (New York, 1987), pp. 155-8.

6. Carlos Franqui, *Family Portrait With Fidel*, trans. Alfred MacAdam (New
    York, 1984), p. 185, claims that Adzhubei gave Castro the report in person.
    Matthews, *Revolution in Cuba*, p. 208, writes that Castro received
    Adzhubei's information from a copy of a report submitted to Khrushchev
    that was sent to Havana.

7. H. Thomas, *The Cuban Revolution* (New York, 1977), p. 607; Matthews, *Revolution in Cuba*, p. 208. For a report of earlier comments by Cardona see Dinerstein, *Making of a Missile Crisis*, p. 141.

8. Garthoff, *Reflections* (1989), p. 6; Laurence Chang, ed., *The Cuban Missile Crisis, 1962* (Washington, D.C.: National Security Archive, 1990), vol. I, p. 43; interviews with Cuban officials; Allyn et al., *Back to the Brink*, pp.15-18.

9. Morley, *Imperial State and Revolution*, pp. 191-202; D. Rich, *The U.S. Embargo Against Cuba: Its Evolution and Enforcement*, A Study Prepared for the Commonwealth Countries (Washington, D.C., July 1988), pp. 24-37.

10. Brig. Gen. Lansdale, "Memorandum for the Special Group (Augmented)— Review of Operation Mongoose," 25 July 1962, p. 5; classified Top Secret, partially declassified 5 January 1989; available at the National Security Archive, Washington, D.C., which obtained it through the Freedom of Information Act. Hereafter cited as "25 July 1962 Memorandum."

11. Ibid., p. 4.

12. Brig. Gen. E. G. Lansdale, "The Cuba Project," 18 January 1962 (program review for the president and ten others), p. 1; classified Top Secret, partially declassified 5 January 1989; available at the National Security Archive, Washington, D.C., which obtained it through the Freedom of Information Act; hereafter cited as "The Cuba Project." Also see Select Committee to Study Governmental Operations with Respect to Intelligence Activities, *Alleged Assassination Plots Involving Foreign Leaders*, An Interim Report, no. 94-465, U.S. Senate, 94th Cong., 1st sess., 20 November 1975, p. 139; hereafter cited as *Assassination Report*.

13. The Cuba Project, p. 2.

14. Quoted in *Assassination Report*, p. 146; also see ibid., pp. 139-47.

15. 25 July 1962 Memorandum, p. 5. Also see Morley, *Imperial State and Revolution*, pp. 149-50; A. M. Schlesinger, Jr., *Robert Kennedy and His Times* (New York, 1978), pp. 512-17, 575; N. Fuentes, *Nos Impusieron La Violencia* (Havana, 1986); Paterson, "Fixation with Cuba," pp. 137-8.

16. *Assassination Report*, pp. 71-135. Also see Schlesinger, *Robert Kennedy*, pp. 517-37.

17. Mikoyan, "La Crisis del Caribe," p. 45.

18. Allyn, et al., *Back to the Brink*, p.42.

19. Dinerstein, *Making of a Missile Crisis*, p. 161.

20. Blight, et al., "Cuba Between the Superpowers," pp. 2-3.

21. R. L. Dennison, *CINCLANT Historical Account of Cuban Crisis 1962*, Serial: 000119/J09H, 29 April 1963, The Atlantic Command, Norfolk, Virginia, p. 153; available at the National Security Archive. Hereafter cited as *CINCLANT Account*.

22. Ibid., pp. 17, 39-40. For an insightful article about the significance of the CINCLANT Account, see James G. Hershberg, "Before the 'Missiles of October': Did Kennedy Plan a Military Strike Against Cuba?" in this

volume. Also see his "Before the Missiles of October," *Boston Phoenix*, 8 April 1988.

23. There is no evidence that they knew about any of the contingency plans, two of which—OPLAN 314 and 316—described an invasion by U.S. forces that "would lead to the overthrow of the Castro Government." *CINCLANT Account*, pp. 20-1.

24. Ibid., p. 40.

25. "Dorticós en la ONU: En Defensa de Cuba," *Bohemia*, 12 October 1962, pp. 48ff.; "Excerpts From Cuban President's Speech in the UN," *New York Times*, 9 October 1962, p. 14.

26. Allison, *Essence of Decision*, p. 47; E. Abel, *The Missile Crisis* (Philadelphia, 1966), pp. 102-3; N. L. Cotayo, *El Bloqueo a Cuba* (Havana, 1983), pp. 314-15. The exercises began on 21 October, at which point they were in reality no longer exercises but prepositioning for a possible invasion.

27. Garthoff, *Reflections* (1989), pp. 30-1.

28. Thomas, *Cuban Revolution*, p. 621.

29. Allyn, et al., *Back to the Brink*, p. 15.

30. Cotayo, *El Bloqueo*, pp. 308-13. For a description of some of the press and congressional demands, see Thomas G. Paterson and William J. Brophy, "October Missiles and November Elections: The Cuban Missile Crisis and American Politics, 1962," *Journal of American History* 72 (June 1986); Thomas, *Cuban Revolution*, pp. 621-2; Abel, *Missile Crisis*, pp. 12-13; Allison, *Essence of Decision*, p. 188; A. Chayes, *The Cuban Missile Crisis* (New York, 1974), pp. 8-10.

31. "Cuba Està Lista Para La Batalla Decisiva," *Bohemia*, 9 September 1962, pp. 58-9.

32. Mankiewicz and Jones, *With Fidel*, p. 148. Exile writer Carlos Franqui, then editor of Revolucion, recounted that Cuba had reports on 20 October that "all US troops in Florida were on full alert, and there was a general mobilization." Franqui, *Family Portrait*, p. 189.

33. F. Castro, "The Duty of a Revolutionary Is to Make the Revolution: The Second Declaration of Havana," in Martin Kenner and James Petras, eds., *Fidel Castro Speaks* (New York, 1969), pp. 85-106 (esp. p. 104); Dominguez, *To Make the World Safe for Revolution*, pp. 115-16; H. M. Erisman, *Cuba's International Relations* (Boulder, CO, 1985), pp. 20-1.

34. Garthoff, *Reflections* (1989), pp. 111.

35. Blight, et al., "Cuba Between the Superpowers," pp.71-72. Dinerstein, *Making of a Missile Crisis*, p. 152.

36. Szulc, *Fidel*, p. 582.

37. Blight and Welch, *On the Brink*, pp. 238, 251, 252, 297-9; Dinerstein, *Making of a Missile Crisis*, p. 152; Schlesinger, *A Thousand Days*, p. 820.

38. Castro told Tad Szulc that "in the same way that the United States had missiles in Italy and Turkey . . . we had the absolutely legal right to make use of such measures in our own country." Szulc, *Fidel*, p. 582.

39. In a statement on 4 September he cautioned against the introduction of "offensive ground-to-ground missiles in Cuba." On the 13th he warned against Cuba becoming "an offensive military base of significant capacity for the Soviet Union." See Hilsman, *To Move a Nation,* p. 171; "The President's News Conference of September 13," *Public Papers of the Presidents of the United States: John F. Kennedy 1962* (Washington, D.C., 1963), pp. 674-5. One authoritative Soviet view of President Kennedy's statements—by Anatoly Gromyko, the son of the Soviet foreign minister at the time—focused only on the aspects of bellicosity in what Kennedy said, and ignored any mention of the implicit warning against placing ballistic missiles or combat troops in Cuba. See Anatoly Gromyko, "The Caribbean Crisis, Part 1," in Ronald R. Pope, ed., *Soviet Views on the Cuban Missile Crisis* (Lanham, MD, 1982), pp. 165-7.

40. R. L. Garthoff, *Reflections on the Cuban Missile Crisis* (Washington, D.C., 1987), p. 8, fn. 9; Dominguez, *To Make the World Safe for Revolution,* p. 36.

41. Dinerstein, *Making of a Missile Crisis,* pp. 80-1, 166-8; Mankiewicz and Jones, *With Fidel,* p. 152.

42. In November 1990, Cuba released a series of letters between Castro and Khrushchev that had been the basis of speculation about whether Castro had demanded the Soviet Union unleash a first strike on the United States. "1962 October Crisis: Letters Between Fidel and Khrushchev," *Granma International Edition,* 2 December 1990.

43. Blight, et al., "Cuba Between the Superpowers," pp.85-86.

44. McNamara's comment was made at a press conference in Havana, January 12, 1992.

45. "Balance del Primer Encuentro con La Realidad Sovietica," 23 May 1963, reprinted in F. Castro, *La Revolucion de Octubre y La Revolucion Cubana: Discursos 1959-1977* (Havana, 1977), p. 91.

46. Claude Julien, "Sept Heures Avec M. Fidel Castro," *Le Monde,* 22 March 1963, p. 6. Also see Matthews, *Fidel Castro,* p. 225.

47. Mankiewicz and Jones, *With Fidel,* p. 152; Szulc, *Fidel,* p. 580; Carlos Cabrera, "The October 1962 Crisis: 'It's Ridiculous to Claim That We Wanted to Provoke a Nuclear War'" (interview with Rafael Hernandez), *Granma Weekly Review,* 26 February 1989, p. 9. Hereafter cited as "Hernandez interview."

48. Fidel Castro, "Castro Remarks at Missile Crisis Conference," as translated by U.S. Foreign Broadcast Information Service (FBIS), Latin America, 4 March 1992.

49. Franqui, *Family Portrait,* p. 188; Szulc, *Fidel,* p. 583.

50. Castro, "Castro Remarks at Missile Crisis Conference."

51. Thomas, *Cuban Revolution,* p. 610; Hilsman, *To Move a Nation,* pp. 164-5, 201-2; Schlesinger, *A Thousand Days,* pp. 796-7.

52. This was how Aleksandr Alekseev, who was soon to become the Soviet ambassador to Cuba, claims to have understood Castro. See Aleksandr

Alekseev, "Karibskii Krizis: kak eto bylo [The Caribbean Crisis: As It Really Was]," *Ekho Planety*, no. 33 (Moscow, November 1988).

53. Barton J. Bernstein, "The Cuban Missiles Crisis: Trading the Jupiters in Turkey?" *Political Science Quarterly*, vol. 95 (Spring 1980), p. 99. The estimate of time necessary to prepare a missile for firing was made by Soviet military officials at the 1989 Moscow conference.

54. Mankiewicz and Jones, *With Fidel*, p. 152.

55. Allyn, et al., *Back to the Brink*, p. 18.

56. Dominguez, To Make the World Safe for Revolution, pp. 39-40. Rafael Hernandez describes the Cuban intention graphically: "From our point of view, the crisis signified for Cuba an act of asserting our claim, to the extent that the world was presented a vision of holocaust precisely the perspective that faced Cuba in its unequal confrontation with the United States." Rafael Hernandez, "La Crisis de Octubre de 1962: Leccion y Parabola," *America Latina*, no. 4 (April 1988), p. 36.

57. Matthews, *Revolution in Cuba*, p. 209-10; Thomas, *Cuban Revolution*, pp. 613-14; Szulc, *Fidel*, pp. 578-80; Blight and Welch, *On the Brink*, pp. 238-9.

58. Allyn, et al., *Back to the Brink*, p. 51. (The ORI was the precursor of the Cuban Communist Party and was formed out of Castro's 26th of July Movement, the university-based Revolutionary Directorate, and the old Communist Party or Partido Socialista Popular.) Also see Alekseev, "Karibskii Krizis." Franqui (*Family Portrait*, p. 189) recalled that there were only five Cuban officials involved. Four on his list are the same as on Aragones's, but Franqui's list deletes Aragones and Blas Roca and includes Ramiro Valdes.

59. Garthoff, *Reflections* (1989), p. 17; Thomas, *Cuban Revolution*, p. 609.

60. Castro, "Castro Remarks at Missile Crisis Conference."

61. Draft agreement, released by the Cuban government on 21 January 1992. English language version provided by Cuba.

62. Garthoff, *Reflections* (1989), p. 18.

63. Dominguez, *To Make the World Safe for Revolution*, p. 40; Szulc, *Fidel*, p. 583; interviews with Cuban officials in 1988 and 1989. At the 1992 Havana meeting Castro said the SAM missiles were ultimately given to Cuba.

64. There are discrepancies in reports of how many bombers arrived in Cuba and were operational. According to the *CINCLANT Account*, p. 15, 42 bombers were shipped to Cuba, and 11 were completely assembled and 2 were partially assembled when Cuba agreed to return them on 20 November. But former Cuban Army Chief of Staff Sergio del Valle recalled in an interview on 18 May 1989 with Bruce Allyn, James J. Blight, and David A. Welch that there were only 12 bombers in Cuba: 3 unassembled ones in Cuban hands and 9 assembled ones controlled by the Soviets.

65. Interviews in January 1989 with Cuban delegates at the Moscow conference. Castro noted on 19 November 1962 that "owing to their [the IL-28s] limited speed and low flight ceiling, they are antiquated equipment in relation to modern means of anti-aircraft defence." "Text of Communica-

tion dated 19 November 1962 from Primer Minister Fidel Castro of Cuba to Acting Secretary-General U Thant," Office of Public Information, United Nations, Press Release SG/1379 20 November 1962, p. 2. Also see Garthoff, *Reflections* (1989), p. 104, fn. 183. Sergo Mikoyan said in an interview on 30 January 1989 that none of the nuclear warheads on the island could have been refitted as bombs for the IL-28s, and that there were no nuclear bombs delivered to Cuba.

66. In his 4 September statement, President Kennedy warned that if there was any evidence of "any organized combat force in Cuba from any Soviet bloc country . . . the gravest issues would arise." Hilsman, *To Move a Nation*, p. 171. Also see Garthoff, *Reflections* (1989), pp. 120-21.

67. Interestingly, Soviet military experts had calculated that the missiles could be obscured by "dense palm tree forests" in Cuba. Reportedly, Soviet officials were shocked when they ultimately observed the way in which palm trees in Cuba are grown on sparsely scattered plots. See Blight, et al., "Cuba Between the Superpowers," p. 77.

68. Allyn, et al., *Back to the Brink*, pp. 51-52.

69. On this point also see Garthoff, *Reflections* (1989), pp. 24-5.

70. Castro, "Castro Remarks at Missile Crisis Conference."

71. Allyn, et al., Back to the Brink, pp. 51-52, 71. The agreement, which was to be a five-year renewable pact, stipulated that "in the event of aggression against the Republic of Cuba...," the Soviet Union and Cuba "will take all necessary measures to repel the agression."

72. Matthews, *Revolution in Cuba*, p. 208.

73. A. Gilly, *Inside the Cuban Revolution*, trans. Felix Gutierrez (New York, 1964), p. 48, as quoted in Thomas, *Cuban Revolution*, p. 630.

74. Dinerstein, *Making of a Missile Crisis*, p. 217. Also see Mankiewicz and Jones, *With Fidel*, pp. 149-50; Alekseev, "Karibskii krizis."

75. *Hoy*, 23 October 1962.

76. Allyn, et al., *Back to the Brink*, pp. 106, 155. Also see, Blight, et al., "Cuba Between the Superpowers," pp. 121-122.

77. *CINCLANT Account*, p. 13.

78. Based on interviews with the Cuban delegates to the 1989 Moscow conference. Also see Matthews, *Fidel Castro*, p. 232.

79. Interview on 30 January 1989. Also see Mario H. Garrido, "General of the Army Dimitri Yazov: I Have My Uniform, Ready to Fight," *Granma Weekly Review*, 23 April 1989, p. 8.

80. *Hoy*, 25 October 1962.

81. R. F. Kennedy, *Thirteen Days* (New York, 1969), p. 109; Abel, *Missile Crisis*, pp. 194-95.

82. *CINCLANT Account*, pp. 55-6.

83. Allyn, et al., *Back to the Brink*, pp. 42, 156. Interestingly, at the Moscow conference del Valle's estimate was translated initially as "800,000," and this was readily accepted by U.S. participants as credible once they learned that there were 40,000 Soviet military personnel in Cuba. During the crisis,

the U.S. estimate of Soviet military strength on the island ranged from 10,000 to 16,000. See Garthoff, *Reflections* (1989), p. 356.

84. Szulc, *Fidel,* p. 584; Garthoff, *Reflections* (1989), p. 84; "Documentos de la Crisis Mundial," *Bohemia,* 2 November 1962, p. 52.

85. The officer seems to have been Lieutenant General (then Major General) G. A. Voronkov. See Adela Estrada Juarez, "The General Who Gave the Order to Fire," *Granma Weekly Review,* 23 April 1989, p. 8. Another officer, Major General Igor Statsensko, has also been cited as the local Soviet commander responsible for the shoot-down. See Garthoff, *Reflections* (1989), pp. 82-5. Also Blight and Welch, *On the Brink,* pp. 310-11.

86. Chang, *The Cuban Missile Crisis,* vol. I., p. 72. *The CINCLANT Account,* p. 14, reported that the guns were 57 mm, and that no low-level plane had been hit.

87. "October 27, 1962: Transcripts of the Meetings of the ExComm," *International Security* 12, no. 3 (Winter 1987/88), pp. 63, 65, 68; Kennedy, *Thirteen Days,* pp. 107-8.

88. Daniel Ellsberg, "The Day Castro Almost Started World War III," *New York Times,* 31 October 1987, p. 27.

89. Blight and Welch, *On the Brink,* p. 72. In contrast, McGeorge Bundy and Robert McNamara argued that the likely response to a continued stalemate would have been a "turning of the screw," an extension of the quarantine to include nonmilitary items. See ibid., pp. 83-4, 189-90.

90. Alekseev, "Karibskii krizis."

91. Garthoff, *Reflections* (1989), pp. 36-7 (fn. 63), 207-9.

92. Nikita Khrushchev, "Khrushchev's Secret Tapes," *Time,* 1 October 1990, p. 75.

93. Notably, the 26 October letter was not transmitted from Havana until the morning of 27 October, and it reached Khrushchev on 28 October because of the problems in communication and decoding. See Blight, et al., "Cuba Between the Superpowers," pp. 75, 85.

94. "1962 October Crisis: Letters Between Fidel and Khrushchev."

95. "Message to Chairman Khrushchev Calling for Removal of Soviet Missiles from Cuba, October 27, 1962," *Public Papers of the Presidents of the United States: John F. Kennedy 1962* (Washington, D.C., 1962), pp. 813-14; Garthoff, *Reflections* (1989), pp. 106-14.

96. "Fija Fidel Las Cinco Garantias Contra La Agresion a Cuba," *Revolucion,* 29 October 1962. Also see U Thant, "Summary of my meeting with President Dorticós, Premier Castro of Cuba and Foreign Minister Roa in [Havana] 10:00 A.M., October 31, 1962," UN Archives, DAG-1/5.2.2.6.2:1, unpaginated.

97. U Thant, "Summary of my meeting, October 31, 1962."

98. "Nuestro Derecho a la Paz se Está Abriendo Paso en El Mundo," *Verde Olivo,* 11 November 1962, pp. 14, 15. This speech by Castro included a transcription of the 30 October meeting with U Thant. In his notes of that meeting, U Thant said that the remarks were those of Castro, not Dorticós. See U Thant, "Summary of my meeting with President Dorticós, Premier

Castro and Foreign Minister Roa in Havana, October 30, 1962," UN Archives, DAG-1/5.2.2.6.2:1, unpaginated.

99. Interview, 30 January 1989.

100. Thomas, *Cuban Revolution*, p. 636; Abel, *Missile Crisis,* p. 213; Franqui, *Family Portrait*, p. 196.

101. Alekseev, "Karibskii krizis"; Mikoyan, "La Crisis del Caribe," p. 55; interview with Mikoyan, 30 January 1989; Blight and Welch, *On the Brink*, pp. 267-8.

102. Julien, "Sept Heures Avec M. Fidel Castro," pp. 1, 6.

103. Matthews, *Fidel Castro*, p. 232; C. A. Robbins, *The Cuban Threat* (New York, 1983), p. 211. Also see Franqui, *Family Portrait*, pp. 194-5. Castro himself suggested this interpretation in 1974 by saying: "We felt very passionate. . . . We were annoyed by matters of form, by certain formalities in the conduct of the negotiations." See Mankiewicz and Jones, *With Fidel*, p. 152. At the 1989 Moscow conference, Cuban participants acknowledged that the necessity of time made the lack of consultation understandable, but they argued that even then Khrushchev should have qualified his acceptance of Kennedy's proposal with a requirement that Cuba's security demands be satisfied; Allyn, et al., *Back to the Brink*, p. 72.

104. Ibid., p. 73. Szulc, *Fidel*, pp. 585-8; Thomas, *Cuban Revolution*, p. 636; Julien, "Sept Heures Avec M. Fidel Castro," p. 6.

105. Letter from Prime Minister Fidel Castro to UN Secretary-General U Thant, 15 November 1962, unofficial UN translation, U.S. Department of State incoming telegram no. 802, 15 November 1962, 7:00 P.M., classified Secret, now declassified, p. 2.

106. Mikoyan, "La Crisis del Caribe," p. 55; Blight and Welch, *On the Brink*, pp. 267-8.

107. Garthoff, *Reflections* (1989), p. 122; Schlesinger, *Robert Kennedy*, pp. 574-5; *Assassination Report*, pp. 147-8.

108. Castro letter to U Thant, 15 November 1962, p. 3.

109. Ibid., pp. 3, 4.

110. Garthoff, *Reflections* (1989), p. 122.

111. These ideas were expressed by Jorge Risquet and Emilio Aragones at the 1989 Moscow conference. Also see Hernandez interview. Notably, the Soviet Union did propose direct U.S.-Cuban negotiations "regarding the removal of the Guantanamo naval base," in a joint Cuban-Soviet protocol offered on 15 November to settle the November crisis. See U.S. Department of State incoming telegram no. 1798, 15 November 1962, 6:00 P.M., p. 3.

112. For example, Theodore Draper, "Castro and Communism," *The Reporter*, 17 January 1963; Matthews, *Fidel Castro*, pp. 230-2.

113. It appears that Cuba was unaware until 1963 of the implicit agreement between the Soviet Union and the United States over removal of the Jupiters in Turkey. See Szulc, *Fidel*, pp. 586-7.

114. "Nuestro Derecho a la Paz se Está Abriendo Paso en El Mundo," p. 14; Bernstein, "Trading the Jupiters in Turkey," pp. 116-17.

115. William LeoGrande, "Uneasy Allies: The Press and the Government During the Cuban Missile Crisis," Occasional Paper No. 3, Center for War, Peace and the News Media, New York University, 1987, p. 31.

116. Kennedy, *Thirteen Days*, pp. 124, 127-8.

117. On the awareness of Cuba's fears, see Paterson, "Fixation with Cuba," p. 141. On the discussion about Turkish missiles, see Bernstein, "Trading the Jupiters in Turkey," pp. 104-11; "October 27, 1962: Transcripts of the Meetings of the ExComm." Notably, the ExComm was sensitive to Turkish and NATO concerns about a withdrawal of missiles without consultation, but U.S. officials did not extrapolate this sensitivity to the parallel circumstance of the Soviet Union and Cuba.

118. This view of Cuba was most evident in President Kennedy's 22 October address to the nation, in which he said: "Finally, I want to say a few words to the captive people of Cuba. . . . Now your leaders are no longer Cuban leaders inspired by Cuban ideals. They are puppets and agents of an international conspiracy which has turned Cuba against your friends and neighbors in the Americas." See "Radio and Television Report to the American People on the Soviet Arms Buildup in Cuba, October 22, 1962," *Public Papers of the Presidents of the United States: John F. Kennedy 1962* (Washington, D.C., 1962), p. 809. An alternative explanation, of course, is that the Kennedy administration did not want to abandon its hope of destroying the Cuban revolution.

119. For a good discussion of these, see James A. Nathan, "The Missile Crisis: His Finest Hour," *World Politics* (January 1975), pp. 272-6. Also see Blight and Welch, *On the Brink*, pp. 93-111.

120. P. Bonsal, *Cuba, Castro and the United States* (Pittsburgh, PA, 1971), p. 187; Cole Blasier, *The Giant's Rival: The USSR and Latin America* (Pittsburgh, PA, 1983), pp. 104-7; Garthoff, *Reflections* (1989), p. 138; Matthews, *Fidel Castro*, p. 199; Szulc, *Fidel*, pp. 585-6.

121. R. Duncan, *The Soviet Union and Cuba* (New York, 1985), p. 44.

122. "Balance del Primer Encuentro con La Realidad Sovietica," pp. 92, 93.

123. Duncan, *The Soviet Union and Cuba*, p. 43.

124. Quoted in Garthoff, *Reflections* (1989), p. 23. Also see Nathan, "The Missile Crisis," pp. 279-80.

125. Erisman, *Cuba's International Relations*, p. 18.

126. "*Playboy* Interview: Fidel Castro," *Playboy*, January 1967, p. 70.

127. Schlesinger, *A Thousand Days*, p. 839.

128. *Assassination Report*, pp. 170-7. Also see Schlesinger, *Robert Kennedy*, pp. 590-602; Paterson, "Fixation with Cuba," pp. 152-3.

129. *Revolucion*, 16 January 1963, p. 9.

130. Schlesinger, *A Thousand Days*, p. 841.

131. For example, see Ray S. Cline, "Commentary: The Cuban Missile Crisis," *Foreign Affairs* (Fall 1989).

132. Blight and Welch, *On the Brink,* p. 281. Also see Davis S. Bobrow, "Stories Remembered and Forgotten," *Journal of Conflict Resolution* 33, no. 2 (June 1989), pp. 197-201.
133. Bobrow, "Stories Remembered and Forgotten," p. 203.

7

President Kennedy's Decision to Impose a Blockade in the Cuban Missile Crisis: Building Consensus in the ExComm After the Decision[1]

Elizabeth Cohn

INTRODUCTION

According to most accounts of the Cuban missile crisis, President John F. Kennedy's decision to blockade Cuba in response to the discovery of medium-range ballistic missiles (MRBMs) on October 16, 1962 was based on the debate and consideration given the matter by the Executive Committee of the National Security Council (ExComm). Newly released documentation of the decision-making process, however, raises doubts about the traditional analyses.[2] These declassified documents show, first, that well before President Kennedy's announcement on October 22 to initiate a blockade, the U.S. government had already developed contingency plans for military actions against Cuba. These actions, known as OPLAN 312, OPLAN 314, and OPLAN 316, included a blockade, invasion, or air strike. In addition, the declassified documents indicate that a decision was made as early as October 1, 1962 to reconfigure the Atlantic Fleet in preparation for a blockade, ordered to be complete by October 20. Two days later, on October 3, the ships began to be moved into position.[3] Thus, as of October 3 the necessary ships were already moving into place for a possible blockade against Cuba.

Traditional accounts of the role of the ExComm are challenged further because the ExComm was still discussing the air strike, invasion, and blockade options for at least three days after the president had decided on a blockade. On the morning of October 18 the president asked Robert Kennedy and Theodore Sorensen to pull the group together for a blockade. The ExComm continued to debate the subject until the afternoon of the 20th, even though Sorensen had given them the message that the president had settled on the blockade response.

This new information suggests that the president may have been predisposed toward a blockade before the ExComm even began its deliberations. In fact, it is now apparent that the decision to impose a blockade was a feasible option only because the necessary military planning and the Navy's implementation of the plans had already been put in motion before the ExComm began to meet concerning the missile crisis. Thus, the new evidence, along with the reinterpretation of old accounts that tout the ExComm as central to the president's decision-making process, suggests that the ExComm's role was mainly to reinforce and validate decisions reached by the president outside of the ExComm context.

BEFORE "THE CRISIS"

The Cuban missile crisis is considered to have begun when President Kennedy was informed on October 16, 1962 that offensive Soviet missiles were sighted in Cuba. Conventional accounts state that the crisis lasted 13 days, until October 28, when Khrushchev offered to remove the missiles in Cuba and Kennedy promised not to invade Cuba. However, events before October 16 should be factored into any analysis of the decision-making process.

Dealing with the Castro government in Cuba remained a priority of the Kennedy administration after the failed Bay of Pigs invasion in April 1961. For example, on November 30, 1961 the president authorized "Operation Mongoose," a covert operation to "use our available assets . . . to help Cuba overthrow the Communist regime."[4] In February 1962 the Joint Chiefs of Staff (JCS) "established a first priority for the completion of all Cuban contingency plans."[5] Kennedy's concern with Cuba intensified in the late summer and early fall of 1962, in response to a Soviet military buildup there.

According to U.S. intelligence, "a large scale increase in Soviet ship movements to Cuba became apparent in July 1962," and in early September Cuba obtained surface-to-air missiles (SAMs).[6] In late August, 55 Soviet ships arrived in Cuba—more than quadruple the August 1961 figure. In September the number peaked at 66.[7] As a result of this increased activity, contingency operations against Cuba were planned.[8]

In response to the general military buildup in Cuba, CINCLANT, the commander in chief of the Atlantic Command, had developed several plans of action. The CINCLANT report on the missile crisis recalled that "[t]hese plans were either tentatively or fully approved by the JCS and provided for various degrees of response and reaction for Cuban operations."[9] The most limited action, OPLAN 312, included air strikes against single targets, such as SAM sites, or large-scale attacks on Cuba. Both OPLAN 314 and OPLAN 316 called for an invasion by combined air force, navy, and army forces, although OPLAN 316 demanded a shorter time period between the initial air strikes and invasion forces. A blockade was also considered, although only in conjunction with an air strike or invasion, and not as an isolated measure.

Indeed, as early as August 23, 1962 President Kennedy, in National Security Action Memorandum No. 181, had ordered the Department of Defense to study the various options the U.S. government could take against potential Cuban installations capable of launching a nuclear attack against the United States.

Contingency planning does not necessarily mean implementation of the plans. However, in this case the plans were put into effect. On October 1, Secretary of Defense Robert McNamara and the Joint Chiefs of Staff received a briefing by the Defense Intelligence Agency claiming that there was evidence to indicate that offensive Soviet missiles had arrived in Cuba.[10] One of the decisions made at that meeting was "to alert Admiral Dennison, Commander-in-Chief of the Atlantic Fleet, to be prepared to institute a blockade of Cuba."[11] Two days later Admiral Dennison gave the orders to prepare his forces for a blockade.[12] The navy took advantage of a previously scheduled amphibious assault exercise called Phibriglex 62.[13] "To mask widespread preparations for the actions proposed, Admiral Dennison suggested that we announce that our forces were preparing for an exercise. PHIBRIGLEX 62 . . . provided a cover for our Caribbean preparations."[14]

On October 3, 1962, the Atlantic Fleet began to be reconfigured for a blockade of Cuba. "On 3 October, CINCLANTFLT promulgated an OpOrder for blockade of Cuba. . . ."[15] To "promulgate an OpOrder" is to execute or carry out a particular operation. James Hershberg states that "the actual prepositioning of supplies, weapons, and troops—all these seem to transcend 'routine contingency planning' and suggest that something more serious was afoot."[16] As an extensive Pentagon evaluation of the missile crisis summarized, "For the public, the President's address [October 22] was the first alarm bell of danger. *But for many days the Commander in Chief Atlantic (CINCLANT) had been preparing* to counter this newest aspect of the Russian buildup in Cuba."[17]

THE ROLE OF THE EXCOMM

On the morning of October 16, 1962, a Tuesday, President Kennedy was briefed on the existence of MRBMs in Cuba. Immediately, he called his brother Robert to the White House for consultation. He kept his scheduled appointments, but within three hours convened key members of his administration into an ad hoc group that was later to be called the ExComm.[18] Kennedy liked the ad hoc committee format for seeking advice on specific matters.[19]

At the first ExComm meeting, 11:50 A.M. on the 16th, Secretary of State Rusk, Secretary of Defense McNamara, and Chairman of the Joint Chiefs of Staff General Maxwell Taylor were the first three to present possible courses of action. Conversation quickly centered on the air strike option. Robert McNamara cautioned that if there were to be an air strike, it must occur before the missile sites became operational. The strikes, he argued, should be broadened to include airfields and aircraft and "all potential nuclear storage sites."[20] One of the problems was lack of intelligence identifying all of the sites, but General Taylor described some of the technical air strike possibilities.

At this first ExComm meeting General Taylor mentioned a blockade, but only as a proposed second stage after an air strike, to halt Cuba's receipt of further materiel.[21] President Kennedy, already concentrating on the details of a blockade, pointed out that a blockade might be run by submarines and could prove dangerously confrontational. None of the other participants gave serious consideration to the blockade idea, and conversation centered on an air strike or invasion.

Robert Kennedy raised moral and political considerations, reminding the president he would "kill an awful lot of people and . . . take an awful lot of heat on it."[22] His brother, who had expressed little of his own thoughts during the meeting, summarized the discussion and asked in a non-specific manner that preparations be made for an air strike, a general air strike, and an invasion.

I think we ought to . . . meet tonight again at six, consider these various, uh, proposals. . . . [G]o ahead with . . . whatever is needed from the [surveillance] flights. . . . Maybe just have to just take them [the MRBMs] out, and continue our other preparations if we decide to do that. . . . [W]e're going to take out these, uh, missiles. Uh, the questions will be whether, which, what I would describe as number two, which would be a general air strike. That we're not ready to say, but we should be in preparation for it. The third is the, uh, the general invasion.

At least we're going to do number one, so it seems to me that we don't have to wait very long. We, ought to be making those preparations.[23]

At this moment McGeorge Bundy, highly respected by Kennedy who had recruited him to be special assistant for national security affairs, queried the president: "You want to be clear, Mr. President, whether we have *definitely* decided *against* a political track. . . ."[24] But the discussion that morning was dominated by the military men who had discovered Soviet missiles in Cuba, and political or limited responses were not explored. The president was noncommittal except that he was clear that he wanted the missiles out, that some action should be taken quickly, and that discussions should be kept from the public.

In another ExComm meeting later that day, Dean Rusk, Robert Kennedy, and Robert McNamara attempted repeatedly to refocus the conversation on political issues. Secretary of State Rusk commented for the first time that "any course of action involves heavy political involvement. . . . it's going to affect all sorts of policies, positions. . . ."[25] Robert Kennedy raised long-term concerns, such as what would keep Cuba from rebuilding the sites six months later.[26] McNamara later argued that it was not a military problem but a "domestic, political problem," because the president had publicly announced that action would be taken if Cuba possessed offensive weapons it could use against the United States.[27]

Later in the meeting, as he had done earlier, McNamara summarized the possible U.S. responses as: (1) diplomatic/political, (2) blockade, or (3) "variants of military action."[28] McNamara had introduced the idea of a blockade as a singular act that the United States could take against Cuba. This is in contrast to the options summarized at the morning ExComm meeting: (1) limited air strike, (2) general air strike, (3) invasion, (4) blockade after options 1, 2 or 3. Whereas the first ExComm meeting was dominated by discussion of air strike or invasion, by evening the proposals were more judicious.

Graham Allison cites the next day, Wednesday, October 17, as the critical day for the blockade option, because on that day the president's closest advisers—a "triple alliance" of Robert McNamara, Robert Kennedy, and Theodore Sorensen—came to support a blockade. These were the men the president admired most. Similarly, the group advocating the air strike option consisted of CIA Director McCone, Assistant Secretary of Defense Nitze, and former Secretary of State Acheson—the president's unnatural allies.[29] As President Kennedy was to remark later in the crisis about the military's advocacy for an invasion, "the military are mad."[30]

BUILDING CONSENSUS IN THE EXCOMM

By October 18, "the President had already moved from the air strike to the blockade camp," according to Theodore Sorensen's account.[31] When Kennedy met with the ExComm that evening, discussion was still weighted toward an air strike, although a consensus was beginning to form for a blockade. David Detzer, in one of the many volumes written on the missile crisis, reported that a vote during an early evening meeting on October 18 was six for an air strike and eleven for a blockade. However, under the president's questioning "ExComm's resolution [for a blockade] began to collapse."[32] Unhappy with the group's indecision, the president asked ExComm members to rethink the issues, and then informed them that he had tentatively chosen the blockade option.[33] At this meeting the president was particularly hostile to the air strike advocates. Afterward he told Kenneth O'Donnell, "These brass hats have one great advantage in their favor. If we listen to them, and do what they want us to do, none of us will be alive later to tell them that they were wrong."[34]

On Friday, October 19, according to a State Department postmortem report, "it was apparent to most of the insiders that a 'rolling consensus' was moving towards the notification—defensive quarantine [blockade] track." However, some members of the ExComm thought "the final decision was not at that stage a foregone conclusion. . . . [and] that there was a hedge on the decision against an air strike until Sunday morning."[35] Kenneth O'Donnell recalls that on Friday morning Kennedy "had definitely made up his mind to start his action against Khrushchev with a naval blockade of Cuba. . . . Even though he had made his decision, he still wanted a consensus of support from the ExComm members."[36]

On that Friday morning the president met with the Joint Chiefs of Staff, who again were pushing for an air strike or invasion. Frustrated, the president instructed Sorensen and Robert Kennedy "to pull the group [ExComm] together quickly"—that is, to form a consensus in favor of a blockade.[37] Sorensen recalls:

> [The President] had just met with the Joint Chiefs, who preferred an air strike or invasion; and other advisors were expressing doubts. In retrospect it is clear that this delay enabled us all to think through the blockade route much more thoroughly, but at the time the president was impatient and discouraged. He was counting on the Attorney General and me, he said, to pull the group together quickly—otherwise more delays and dissension would plague whatever decision he took. He wanted to act soon, Sunday if possible—and Bobby Kennedy was to call him back when we were ready.[38]

Curiously, Sorensen is much more guarded in his phrasing than O'Donnell and Powers. Sorensen is more protective of the president's image, whereas O'Donnell and Powers are clearer about the dynamic: the president had made up his mind but wanted his advisory group to share the same opinion.

When the ExComm met on that Friday morning, Sorensen tried to keep the participants from continuing the discussion of the different options, yet they broke into two working groups to analyze the two options. One participant thought a decision had been reached for a blockade the night before, but General Taylor disagreed.[39] Sorensen later wrote that he complained to those assembled that they were "not serving the president well."[40] Despite the fact that the ExComm did not reach a clear decision, Sorensen told them he would go off and write a draft of a speech announcing a blockade. No one objected to this.[41] Though some may argue that Sorensen was only preparing for when a final decision was made, it is worth noting that he never wrote a speech for the president announcing an invasion or air strike.

Thus, by Sorensen's own account, President Kennedy had moved from air strike to blockade by the morning of Thursday the 18th. Nevertheless, the ExComm was still debating the topic as late as the afternoon of Saturday, October 20. On the 20th, long considered the "day of decision,"[42] the ExComm, including the president, met again in the morning to consider the options "before his decision became final," according to Sorensen.[43] By then the majority of members of the ExComm had been persuaded to support the blockade option, although the decision still was not unanimous.

The ExComm, including the president, met again on Saturday, ostensibly to make a final decision. Kennedy informed the group that a blockade against Cuba would be announced on October 22, and placed in effect on October 24. The president, as if to narrow the divisions and build unity, said, "The ones whose plans we're not taking are the lucky ones."[44] At the 10:00 A.M. ExComm meeting on October 21, each participant had ready for the president a written statement of his recommendation, pursuant to a previous request by Robert Kennedy. The president nevertheless refused to collect these reports.[45] Perhaps he did not want to confirm or make a record of opposition to his decision, or perhaps he wanted to instill in all participants a mentality of "we're all in this together." He did not want to undermine the notion of consensus that he badly wanted at a time of crisis.

Sorensen wrote that after the ExComm meeting on the 20th, the president said he was "keeping his decision open until he had one last talk with the Air Force."[46] On Sunday October 21, at 11:30 A.M., Kennedy met with his key military advisers to hear their arguments for an air strike one more time.[47] However, he had already met with Rusk and McNamara at 10:00 A.M. that day, and had given final approval for the blockade at the time.[48]

Points from this historical record show a different role for the ExComm than previously presented. At least one-half of the ExComm discussions on which option to support occurred after the president asked Robert Kennedy and Sorensen to pull the group together for a blockade. And, as the ExComm broke into two groups to explore the scenarios, Sorensen went off to write a speech announcing a blockade. Whether it was leaving ExComm meetings early, not attending ExComm meetings at all, or not collecting written recommendations, it seems that the president was not as open and eager for the ExComm's advice as previous accounts suggest. It appears that one of the main purposes of the ExComm was to have a forum to build consensus for a decision the president had already made. While the president did react strongly to the discovery of Soviet missiles in Cuba at the first ExComm meeting on the 16th, even at this meeting he was exploring the details of a blockade when others present focused on an air strike or invasion.

ANALYSIS

The exact moment when President Kennedy decided to initiate a blockade against Cuba, rather than to invade or to carry out an air strike, will probably never be known. It is clear, however, that the ExComm was still debating the issue at least three days after the president's mind was made up. It is also now known that the president's decision in favor of a blockade came some two weeks after the Atlantic Fleet was being reconfigured for a blockade, and at least two months after contingency operations against Cuba had begun.

Thus, the events before October 16 suggest that ExComm discussions were not as significant as previously thought. As shown here, by the time the ExComm began to meet, much planning and preparation had already taken place. On October 19, in fact, when President Kennedy asked his military advisers for blockade plans, the plans were already well formed:

On October 19, Admiral Dennison completed his command arrangements for the execution of contingency plans, and established his Cuban contingencies communications. Late that evening, the President decided that Admiral Dennison, acting for the Joint Chiefs of Staff, should prepare a plan for the limited blockade of Cuba. In fact, as already indicated, *such plans already existed,* although not designed specifically for the situation at hand. These plans, however, provided a firm base line and contributed substantially to the prompt preparation of detailed cohesive plans to meet the requirement.[49]

Indeed, the events before October 16 may have led the president to favor the blockade option. That is, as President Kennedy considered his options, he knew that a naval blockade was feasible because the Navy had already determined how many ships they needed, and had even begun to make the ships available by reconfiguring the Atlantic Fleet. Clearly the existence of these contingency plans made the blockade option a meaningful one.

Even at the time there was one member of the ExComm who questioned the centrality of the group. Former Secretary of State Dean Acheson, who eventually excused himself from the ExComm, charged that "after a couple of sessions [ExComm meetings] seemed to me repetitive, leaderless, and a waste of time. I was happy, therefore, when the President asked me to meet with him at 3:45 pm on Thursday, October 18. He received me alone for about an hour, listening to my views. . . ."[50] Acheson's criticism has been wrongly discounted as sour grapes since he was not an advocate of a blockade.[51]

The president acted as a "president-in-sneakers," rather than a "president-in-boots," actively but informally inducing advisers to come on board.[52] The ultimate decision, as organizational process highlights, lay with the president, and the options were available because standard operating procedures called for planning. This raises questions about analyses of the missile crisis that consider the ExComm to have been the key or single instrument for the president in making decisions. Paul Anderson's "Decision Making by Objection and the Cuban Missile Crisis," for example, reexamines the missile crisis based only on minutes from the ExComm.[53] These analyses assume that the President made his decision only after the ExComm recommended a blockade over an air strike, and only after lengthy discussions in which the pros and cons of each option were weighed.[54] Robert Kennedy, in his portrait of the missile crisis, characterizes the role of the ExComm as: "From this group came the recommendations from which President Kennedy was ultimately to select his course of action."[55]

The events of October 1-3 and October 18-20 described in preceding sections suggest an alternative proposition not presented in previous decision-making literature about the Cuban missile crisis: that President Kennedy formed the ExComm not to help him decide what to do, but instead to ensure that he would have consensus within his administration to support the final decisions taken.

Additional support for this proposition may be found in subsequent events as well. It has been shown, for example, that the ExComm was excluded from decision making at the tensest moments of the crisis, on October 27. In one case, unknown to the ExComm, Robert Kennedy gave Soviet Ambassador Anatoly Dobrynin assurances that the United States would withdraw its Jupiter missiles from Turkey—a position that the ExComm had not supported in its discussions. In addition, the president bypassed the ExComm in a move later called the "Cordier maneuver." On the 27th, Dean Rusk asked Columbia University Dean of the School of International Affairs Andrew Cordier to be prepared, if called upon, to contact Acting UN Secretary General U Thant to propose a public trade of the U.S. missiles in Turkey and the Soviet missiles in Cuba. Cordier had recently left the UN where he had served for over 15 years as executive assistant to the Secretary General. As far as Rusk knew, only he, the President, and Andrew Cordier were aware of this diplomatic move. This plan was never executed.[56]

Scholars Bruce Allyn, James Blight, and David Welch argue that "the ExComm had become largely irrelevant to the president's decision-making at the height of the crisis. Crucial decisions were being made by the president and a few close advisers, well away from—and unknown to—the ExComm as a whole. The group that had played a central role in the early option-formation phase of the crisis seems to have been left out of important aspects of decision-making at its climax."[57] This author questions further whether the ExComm was central to the decision-making process even in the early part of the crisis.

Perhaps because there are minutes and recordings for researchers to analyze, much emphasis has been given to the ExComm meetings. But the ExComm was by no means the president's only forum for gathering information. Indeed, he consulted with Soviet expert Charles Bohlen, former Secretary of Defense Robert Lovett, former Secretary of State Dean Acheson, and John McCloy, a Republican and special adviser to Kennedy on disarmament, among others. More important were his informal discussions with his brother and with Ted Sorensen. There are no records of these conversations, so we will never know what was said.[58] He also set up channels unknown to the ExComm, such as the Robert Kennedy–Dobrynin negotiations and the unused Cordier ploy.

But this is not to suggest that ExComm meetings were unnecessary. Rather, they were essential for the president in building consensus for his decision to impose a blockade. Presidents do not rule alone. They need support within the bureaucracy, as well as the appearance of support in the eyes of the public and Congress.

Kennedy understood this. As one official government account of the missile crisis reported, on Monday, October 22, the "President cautioned the group [ExComm] against the dangers that could flow from any appearances of disunity within the government. It was essential that all support the course of action that had been adopted, and, for public purposes at least, to 'sing one song.' "[59]

In a time of crisis, the need for consensus is especially great. With the discovery of nuclear missiles in Cuba, the possibility of nuclear confrontation with the Soviet Union had grown more ominous. President Kennedy had to face much greater risks for the nation, himself as leader, and his political party—and all this just before congressional elections. The president had to contend with the Republican leadership, who had highlighted Cuba in the 1962 campaign, and with New York Senator Kenneth Keating, who had urged Kennedy, beginning in late August, to take some action in response to the Soviet military buildup in Cuba.[60]

Thus, with a military leadership advocating a strong military response, and political leadership less eager for an invasion or air strike, but not ruling them out, the president sought to use the ExComm to bring together his administration. In an ExComm meeting before his speech on October 22 announcing the blockade, the president reminded his advisers that "the course adopted was to be viewed as the consensus which all had helped reach."[61]

IF NOT THE EXCOMM, THEN HOW WERE DECISIONS REACHED?

In light of the preceding analysis, the following question arises: If the ExComm was not the principal instrument of presidential decision making during the missile crisis, how were decisions made? Why, despite pressure from the Joint Chiefs for an air strike or invasion, did the president opt for a blockade?

The answer may lie partly in the fact that Kennedy did not want to be remembered unfavorably by history. The much-repeated comment by Robert Kennedy on October 16 best represents this concern: "I now know how Tojo felt when he was planning Pearl Harbor."[62] Clearly, fear of condemnation from world opinion was a factor in limiting the U.S. response.

The president had learned several lessons from the Bay of Pigs. According to traditional accounts, the president recognized the need for advisers who would give a variety of opinions and who would not necessarily agree with him just because he was the president.[63] For example, John Kennedy praised

Adlai Stevenson when others condemned him: "He's [Stevenson] not strong enough or tough enough to be representing us at the UN at a time like this," Robert Kennedy complained to his brother at one point.

"Now wait a minute," the president replied. "I think Adlai showed plenty of strength and courage, presenting that viewpoint at the risk of being called an appeaser. It was an argument that needed to be stated, but nobody else had the guts to do it. . . . I admire him for saying what he said."[64]

Kennedy's decision-making style might be summarized as one in which opinions from different quarters were sought, but with more emphasis on seeking those with which the president agreed. One must remember that Stevenson advocated the most prudent of actions, an inclination the president shared. The president asked Stevenson on October 16 to remain in Washington and also urged Charles Bohlen to postpone his trip to France. Both of these men advocated caution and were skeptical of the air strike or invasion proposals. In contrast, while the president consulted on the 16th with former Assistant Secretary of War John McCloy, who urged drastic action, the president did not ask McCloy to change his plans to leave for Germany.[65]

Kennedy also learned from the Bay of Pigs not to trust his military advisers, and this showed in the missile crisis. The president was "choleric" after Air Force Chief of Staff Curtis LeMay's presentation on the 18th calling for an air attack.[66] Just after the Cuban missile crisis Kennedy said, "The advice I'm going to give my successor is to watch the generals and to avoid feeling that just because they were military men their opinions on military matters were worth a damn."[67] But not trusting the experts meant that he relied more on himself and a few close advisers.

Kennedy was not afraid to make his own decisions. By choosing the blockade first, he acted prudently, as a politician, but reserved the right to invade, as his military men were advising. A State Department report on the crisis commented on the ExComm deliberations: "The President listened, asked questions, probed replies—and gave directions. One participant observed that at the close of a session the President issued orders firmly. They were *his* decisions and he expected them to be obeyed."[68] By not leaving the decision-making process to his advisers, and using his brother and Sorensen as his proxies, the president could sustain a presence in tense deliberations, even when his demanding schedule required him to be elsewhere.

John F. Kennedy used his brother Robert and Ted Sorensen as his "engineers of consensus."[69] Some members of the ExComm were aware of this. "McNamara has affirmed that it was Robert Kennedy 'acting with his brother's consent, who did so much to organize the effort, monitor the results and assure the completion of work on which recommendations to the

President were based.'"[70] Another participant said, "We all knew little brother was watching; and keeping a list of where everyone stood."[71] The roles that Robert Kennedy and Sorensen played are not accounted for in bureaucratic politics, yet they were essential in the missile crisis decision-making process. These two men enabled the president to build consensus, and to justify a decision already made, so that policy could be implemented.

President Kennedy was not shy about making decisions. When asked on October 19 by his assistant Kenneth O'Donnell, "What if you can't get a consensus?" Kennedy replied, "I'll make my own decision anyway. I'm the one who has the responsibility, so we'll do what I want to do."[72] Nonetheless, the ExComm meetings indicate that achieving a consensus in support of his decisions was highly important to him.

Active presidents like Kennedy tend to use advisory bodies to serve them, and specifically to provide support for their decisions.[73] Other analyses of governmental decision making place too much emphasis on group process, the bureaucracy, and presidential advisers. The missile crisis illustrates a process where the top decisionmaker makes a decision and then seeks support from key government officials, and ultimately from the American people, to justify a decision already made.

We will never know the exact moment when President Kennedy made a final decision on how to respond to the Soviet placement of missiles in Cuba in 1962. Decision making is a process that involves considering the alternatives, making a decision, reevaluating the options, and announcing a decision and implementing it. But, as this chapter suggests, October 20 was not the "day of decision" and the ExComm was not the agent of decision making that it has previously been portrayed to be. As shown, the preplanning for contingency operations against Cuba, including the reconfiguration of the Atlantic Fleet, had occurred much earlier, making the blockade a very viable option. Moreover, as early as the 18th the president asked Ted Sorensen and Robert Kennedy to pull the ExComm together to support a blockade. Furthermore, the president relied on advisers outside of the ExComm and ignored its advice when it did not reflect his thinking.

NOTES

1. The author would like to thank Philip Brenner, Laurence Chang, and the National Security Archive for assistance in preparation of this chapter.
2. The documents, obtained by the National Security Archive and WGBH-Boston through the Freedom of Information Act, include: Commander in

Chief, U.S. Atlantic Command, "CINCLANT Historical Account of Cuban Crisis—1963," April 29, 1963; Adam Yarmolinsky, "Department of Defense Operations During the Cuban Crisis," Department of Defense Memo, February 12, 1963; and Frank Sieverts, "The Cuban Crisis, 1962," Department of State, August 22, 1963.

3. Secretary of State Dean Rusk, however, in an interview 25 years after the crisis, stated that he knew nothing of these contingency plans. "'I don't recall any [U.S. military preparations] that preceded the location of the missiles in Cuba,' Rusk said. He added that he presumed the readiness steps outlined in the CINCLANT report represented 'normal contingency planning' but that it was 'theoretically possible' that the State Department was deliberately excluded from military planning that took place 'outside of cabinet channels.'" (James G. Hershberg, "Before 'The Missiles of October,'" *Diplomatic History* 14, no. 2, Spring 1990, p. 192).

4. Kennedy to Rusk, et al., November 30, 1961, in *Alleged Assassination Plots Involving Foreign Leaders*, an interim report of the Senate Select Committee to Study Governmental Operations with Respect to Intelligence Activities, Senate Report 94-465, p. 139.

5. Jean R. Moenk, *USCONARC Participation in the Cuban Crisis 1962*, p. 17, cited in Hershberg, p. 174.

6. "CINCLANT Historical Account," pp. 5, 8.

7. "CINCLANT Historical Account," p. 5.

8. For the most complete account see James G. Hershberg, "Before 'The Missiles of October': Did Kennedy Plan a Military Strike Against Cuba?" *Diplomatic History* 14, no. 2, Spring 1990, pp. 163-198. Hershberg argues that what prompted U.S. contingency operations was the Kennedy administration's eagerness for Castro's downfall, not the Soviet military buildup.

9. "CINCLANT Historical Account," p. 17.

10. Colonel Wright of the Defense Intelligence Agency later stated that the report that the Soviets were installing strategic missiles in Cuba was given, but only as a hypothesis. ("Letter from Wright to Elie Abel in Oral History with Abel, March 18, 1970, cited in Laurence Chang and Donna Rich, editors, "Draft: September 8, 1988, Chronology of the Cuban Missile Crisis," Washington, DC: National Security Archive, 1988.)

11. Adam Yarmolinsky, "Department of Defense Operations During the Cuban Crisis," Department of Defense Memo, February 12, 1963, p. 1. See also "CINCLANT Historical Account," pp. 39-40.

12. "Department of Defense Operations During the Cuban Crisis," p. 1; "Personal History or Diary of Vice Admiral Alfred G. Ward, U.S. Navy While Serving as Commander Second Fleet," p. 2.

13. Phibriglex-62 was the third major set of military exercises to be conducted near Cuba that year. Obviously intended to send a direct message to Fidel Castro, the exercises included a marine landing on Vieques to liberate an island run by "Ortsac"—Castro spelled backwards.

14. "Department of Defense Operations During the Cuban Crisis," p. 1.

15. "Personal History or Diary of Vice Admiral Alfred G. Ward," p. 2.

16. Hershberg, p. 192.

17. "CINCLANT Historical Account," p. 1. Emphasis added.

18. The Excomm was composed of President Kennedy, Secretary of State Dean Rusk, Secretary of Defense Robert McNamara, Attorney General Robert Kennedy, Chairman of the Joint Chiefs of Staff General Maxwell Taylor, CIA Director John McCone, Secretary of the Treasury Douglas Dillon, Special Assistant for National Security Affairs McGeorge Bundy, Presidential Counsel Theodore Sorensen, Undersecretary of State George Ball, Deputy Secretary of Defense Roswell Gilpatric, Soviet expert Llewellyn Thompson, Deputy Undersecretary of State for Political Affairs U. Alexis Johnson, Assistant Secretary of Defense Paul Nitze, Assistant Secretary of State Edwin Martin, and others brought in on occasion such as Vice-President Lyndon Johnson, UN Ambassador Adlai Stevenson, Special Assistant to the President Kenneth O'Donnell, and former Secretary of State Dean Acheson.

19. Kennedy preferred advice from ad hoc groups, rather than from an established bureaucracy. Kennedy thought of himself as decisive, able to make his own decisions. For more on this see David Detzer, *The Brink* (New York: Thomas Y. Crowell, 1979), pp. 101-102.

20. "ExComm Minutes," October 16, 1962, 11:50 A.M., p. 11.

21. Ibid., p. 12.

22. Ibid., p. 21.

23. Ibid., p. 27.

24. Ibid.

25. "ExComm Minutes," October 16, 1962, 6:30 P.M., p. 10.

26. Ibid., p. 24.

27. Ibid., p. 46.

28. Ibid., p. 9, 44-49.

29. Graham T. Allison, *Essence of Decision* (Boston: Little, Brown and Co., 1971), pp. 203-204.

30. Arthur M. Schlesinger, Jr., *A Thousand Days: John F. Kennedy in the White House* (Boston: Houghton Mifflin Company, 1965), p. 831.

31. Theodore C. Sorensen, *Kennedy* (New York: Harper and Row, 1965), p. 691. Roger Hilsman corroborates this impression. See Roger Hilsman, *To Move a Nation* (New York: Dell, 1964), p. 204.

32. David Detzer, p. 145. See also Robert Kennedy, *Thirteen Days* (New York: W. W. Norton, 1971), pp. 21-22, and Frank Sieverts, "The Cuban Crisis, 1962," August 22, 1963, p. 60.

33. Allison, p. 205; Sieverts, p. 60; Detzer, p. 145.

34. Kenneth O'Donnell and David Powers, *Johnny, We Hardly Knew Ye* (Boston: Little, Brown and Co., 1972), p. 318.

35. Frank Sieverts, "The Cuban Crisis, 1962," pp. 65-66. Frank Sieverts, Special Assistant to the Assistant Secretary of State for Public Affairs,

based his report on documents from the departments of Defense and State, CIA, and the White House, including ExComm minutes, as well as personal interviews and private notes.

36. O'Donnell and Powers, p. 319.

37. Sorensen, *Kennedy,* p. 692.

38. Ibid.

39. "ExComm Minutes," October 19, 1962, p. 4. See also Sieverts, p. 64.

40. Sorensen, *Kennedy,* p. 692.

41. "ExComm Minutes," October 19, 1962, p. 9.

42. Allison, p. 208.

43. Sorensen, *Kennedy,* p. 694.

44. Elie Abel, *The Missile Crisis* (Philadelphia: Lippincott, 1966), p. 94.

45. Abel, p. 104.

46. Sorensen, *Kennedy,* p. 3. Hilsman writes "It seems likely that the President was waiting to make his decision final mainly because of this continued opposition of the JCS to blockade and preference for more violent action.... Even as late as Saturday, he said that before making his decision on a blockade final he wanted to talk personally with the Air Force Tactical Bombing Command to make very sure that a limited air strike could not be successful," p. 205.

47. Robert McNamara, "Notes on October 21, 1962 Meeting with the President."

48. Graham Allison, in the bureaucratic politics tradition, calls this "preparation of the record." (Allison, p. 249.)

49. "Department of Defense Operations during the Cuban Crisis," p. 9. Emphasis added.

50. Dean Acheson, "Dean Acheson's Version of Robert Kennedy's Version of the Cuban Missile Affair," *Esquire,* vol. 71, no. 2, February 1969, p. 77.

51. See O'Donnell and Powers, p. 322.

52. Richard E. Neustadt, "White House and Whitehall," *The Public Interest,* no. 2, Winter 1966, p. 64.

53. *Administrative Science Quarterly* 28, June, 1983, pp. 201-222.

54. A complete listing of books on the missile crisis is unnecessary here, but others that emphasize the importance of the ExComm are Robert F. Kennedy, *Thirteen Days* (New York: W. W. Norton, 1971); Graham T. Allison, *Essence of Decision* (Boston: Little, Brown and Co., 1971), pp. 57, 200; David Detzer, *The Brink* (New York: Thomas Y. Crowell, 1979); and Roger Hilsman, *To Move A Nation* (New York: Dell, 1964), pp. 194-206.

55. Robert F. Kennedy, *Thirteen Days,* p. 9.

56. Bruce J. Allyn, James G. Blight, David A. Welch, "Essence of Revision," *International Security* 14, no. 3 (Winter 1989/1990), p. 159. See also David A. Welch and James G. Blight, "The Eleventh Hour of the Cuban Missile Crisis," *International Security* 12, no. 3 (Winter 1987/1988), pp. 15-16.

57. Ibid.

58. The written record, such as Robert Kennedy's *Thirteen Days* and Ted Sorensen's *Kennedy,* emphasize certain factors that reflect positively on the president. If one lesson from the missile crisis is clear, it is that history is in the hands of the recorder.

59. Sieverts, pp. 95-96.

60. Schlesinger, Jr., pp. 800-801; Hilsman, p. 177.

61. Sieverts, p. 96.

62. Robert F. Kennedy, *Thirteen Days,* p. 9.

63. See Irving L. Janis, *Groupthink: Psychological Studies of Policy Decisions and Fiascoes* (Boston: Houghton Mifflin, 1982.

64. O'Donnell and Powers, p. 323.

65. The way that Robert Kennedy recounts it in *Thirteen Days,* "It was to obtain an unfettered and objective analysis that he frequently, and in critical times, invited Secretary of the Treasury Douglas Dillon, for whose wisdom he had such respect; Kenny O'Donnell, his appointment secretary; Ted Sorensen; and, at times, former Secretary of State Dean Acheson, former Secretary of Defense Robert Lovett, former High Commissioner of Germany John McCloy, and others. They asked the difficult questions; they made others defend their position; they presented a different point of view; and they were skeptical," p. 96.

66. Arthur M. Schlesinger, Jr., *Robert Kennedy and His Times* (Boston: Houghton Mifflin Company, 1978), p. 511.

67. Detzer, p. 137.

68. Sieverts, p. 48.

69. Allison, p. 207.

70. Allison, p. 207.

71. Abel, p. 58.

72. O'Donnell and Powers, pp. 319-320.

73. See Richard E. Neustadt, *Presidential Power* (New York: Wiley and Sons, 1960). Kennedy was a great admirer of Neustadt's ideas about the qualities of a good president.

8

Before "The Missiles of October": Did Kennedy Plan a Military Strike Against Cuba?

James G. Hershberg

Was the Kennedy administration moving toward a military attack on Cuba in the fall of 1962, even before it discovered Soviet strategic missiles on the island? Recently declassified evidence and fresh controversy compel a new look at this infrequently examined question. While not offering a definitive answer, this chapter presents new information, interpretations and hypotheses regarding U.S. behavior in the period leading up to the Cuban missile crisis. It is now clear that throughout the first ten months of 1962, Operation Mongoose, the Kennedy administration's secret program of covert operations against Cuba, was closely coordinated with enhanced Pentagon contingency planning for possible U.S. military intervention to bring about Castro's downfall. During this period, U.S. officials actively considered the option of sparking an internal revolt in Cuba that would serve as a pretext for open, direct military action. Top officials in the U.S. government initially "shied away from" the idea of overt military involvement in Cuba prior to the missile crisis. But the Pentagon, acting at the direction of the president and the secretary of defense, dramatically accelerated contingency planning for military action against Cuba in late September and early October 1962, just as the president was ordering a sharp increase in anti-Castro covert operations. Although the ultimate purpose of these intensified military preparations remains unclear, the possibility that, under domestic political pressure and even before they learned in mid-October that Soviet nuclear-capable missiles were in Cuba, top U.S. policymakers seriously considered conventional military action—including, if necessary, a full-scale invasion—to overthrow the Castro regime, has to be considered.

The new evidence suggests that Moscow and Havana were justified in suspecting that Washington was considering an invasion of Cuba, although it does not confirm that a decision to order an invasion was, in fact, ever made. And it raises the possibility that large-scale U.S. conventional military maneuvers in the Caribbean in the spring of 1962, heretofore ignored in most analyses of the crisis, may have influenced the Soviet perception that an American invasion was in the offing.

Until very recently, the issue of precrisis U.S. military measures aimed at Cuba remained virtually untouched by historians, who have largely confined themselves to the dynamics, consequences, and "lessons" of the superpower confrontation that took place between 16 October 1962, when President John F. Kennedy learned of the presence of Soviet medium-range ballistic missiles (MRBMs) in Cuba, and 28 October, when Premier Nikita S. Khrushchev agreed to remove the missiles under American pressure.[1]

Relatively scant attention[2] has been given to the events preceding the detection of the Soviet missiles and the question of whether U.S. military action against Cuba was already under consideration.[3] This issue of whether the U.S. government had planned direct military action against the Castro regime prior to the crisis garnered renewed attention as a result of a flurry of Soviet-American exchanges made possible by glasnost. Brief bursts of press attention surrounded an October 1987 conference held to mark the 25 anniversary of the events of October 1962, and a Soviet-American-Cuban gathering in Moscow in January 1989. Soviet participants cited Moscow's fear of a U.S. attack on Cuba as one of two principal motives behind Khrushchev's decision to deploy the missiles, the other being a desire to dent Washington's massive nuclear superiority.[4]

Although these statements had merely echoed Moscow's traditional version of the events surrounding the crisis, high-ranking former Kennedy administration officials expressed profound surprise at them.[5] They admitted having been frustrated with Castro, and acknowledged the existence of previously revealed covert operations aimed at undermining him, but they vehemently denied that serious consideration had been given to invading Cuba between the failed Bay of Pigs invasion in April 1961 and the detection of the Soviet surface-to-surface missiles 16 months later.

"Nothing of that sort was in our heads," insisted McGeorge Bundy, Kennedy's national security adviser, who voiced "astonishment" at the Soviet claim. In "the summer and early fall of 1962," Bundy said, invading

Cuba was "180 degrees away from what the Kennedy Administration was thinking at the time." Although Washington was "in trouble" with Castro and unsure of its next move, Bundy recalled that "the only thing we really *did* know was that we *did not want* an enlarged version of the Bay of Pigs. We were not going to repeat that exercise by adding a zero and throwing in the American Army."[6] Robert S. McNamara, the then-secretary of defense, was equally emphatic. *"We had absolutely no intention to invade Cuba,"* he said, "and I guarantee you that President Kennedy would not have invaded, and I am certain that Mac [Bundy] and [Kennedy aide] Ted [Sorensen] and I would have strongly recommended against it . . . If we had recommended, 'Do it,' he [Kennedy] would not have done it. *There was absolutely no chance of it."*[7]

Newly declassified documents raise questions about these categorical assertions. The new evidence does not resolve the question of whether Kennedy actually intended to attack Cuba. It does suggest that preparations for military action, including active steps to ready an air strike or invasion, had reached a more advanced stage before the 16 October revelation to Kennedy of the Soviet missile deployments than previously known or acknowledged.

Among the most important of these newly declassified documents is a 174-page Pentagon postmortem of the crisis prepared by the office of the commander in chief of U.S. Atlantic (CINCLANT) forces, Admiral Robert Lee Dennison, who directed all U.S. military activities in the Caribbean during the crisis.[8] Although dated 29 April 1963, the CINCLANT report quotes and paraphrases memoranda and directives contemporaneous with the crisis. Portions of the document remain classified.[9] Nevertheless, the CINCLANT report fleshes out what had been a skeletal account of advanced preparations derived from previously released documents, most notably a far less detailed report on "Department of Defense Operations During the Cuban Crisis" prepared by McNamara aide Adam Yarmolinsky and declassified in 1979.[10]

Also pertinent are several hundred pages of documents declassified in January 1989 in response to a Freedom of Information Act suit filed by the National Security Archive, a Washington-based foreign policy research institute. Although congressional investigations in the mid-1970s revealed much of the essential information relating to "Operation Mongoose"—the covert war against Castro—previously hidden links between the Kennedy administration's covert operations plotting and U.S. military plans for a full-scale invasion have now come to light as well.[11]

Several cautionary notes are in order. First, one must be careful to distinguish planning from intent. The driving force behind some of the actions to enhance military readiness toward Cuba remains unclear. It could as easily reflect a prudent—indeed prescient—response to mounting concern about the already-detected Soviet bloc military buildup in Cuba. That, at any rate, is the stance taken by several Kennedy administration officials interviewed for this chapter.[12]

By the same token, however, it should be possible to sort out routine, dog-day-afternoon contingency planning of the "Suppose Canada goes Communist?" variety from the far more serious brand of planning that leads to concrete actions such as redeployments of forces and equipment that might implement an established policy objective. Much of the Cuban contingency planning, the denials of former officials notwithstanding, clearly falls into this second category.[13]

It is also important to keep in mind the chronological and cognitive relationship between U.S. and Soviet actions. Threatening U.S. actions toward Cuba in September 1962, for example, obviously cannot be viewed as explaining Soviet actions taken in April or May of that year, when Khrushchev reports that he made the decision to ship the missiles to Cuba.[14] Evidence of internal U.S. discussions or plans to invade Cuba may vindicate Soviet contentions that Washington harbored thoughts of overthrowing Castro, but only information known to Soviet leaders can be cited as having the potential to influence the decision to deploy the missiles.[15]

The events of October 1962 unfolded against a backdrop of mounting U.S. public and government concern over Soviet aid to Cuba. Cuba had become a political hot potato.[16] The Republican leadership had vowed early on that Cuba would be "the dominant issue of the 1962 campaign,"[17] and Republicans in Congress—particularly Senator Kenneth Keating of New York—lambasted Kennedy for permitting a Soviet military buildup in Cuba and urged him to blockade the island.[18] "The Congressional head of steam on this [issue] is the most serious that we have had," a worried Bundy told the president on 13 September.[19]

The Republican claims put Kennedy on the defensive. Kennedy had seen his tough image battered by the Bay of Pigs debacle in April 1961, by a tense summit in Vienna two months later, and by right-wing criticism of Washington's acquiescence to the erection of the Berlin Wall that August 1961. Moreover, Kennedy had promised to shoulder any burden to defend liberty, not only in Berlin but around the world, from Laos to the Congo. When an

East-West flashpoint arose so close to home, both domestic political and foreign policy considerations compelled him to demonstrate resolve.

On 4 September 1962, Kennedy publicly warned Moscow that introducing "offensive" weapons into Cuba would have the "gravest" consequences.[20] Heeding Bundy's warning that he risked appearing "weak and indecisive" unless he provided "a very clear and aggressive explanation" of U.S. policy toward Cuba and took control of the situation, Kennedy issued another stern public warning at a press conference on 13 September. The United States, he said, would do "whatever must be done" to prevent Cuba from being converted into an offensive military base.[21]

Such warnings elicited a private assurance from Khrushchev that no deployment would take place.[22] Inside the administration, however, ominous yet ambiguous reports of increasing military activity in Cuba prompted continuing concern. U.S. intelligence recorded a sharp increase in Soviet shipping to Cuba and in early September confirmed the presence of Soviet surface-to-air (SA) antiaircraft missiles in Cuba for the first time.[23]

With the exception of CIA Director John McCone, however, virtually every U.S. official who was privy to this information concluded that the Soviets would not deploy strategic missiles in Cuba, and a National Intelligence Estimate ratified this conclusion on 19 September.[24]

Nevertheless, as partisan charges continued to fill the air, on 4 October the White House secretly directed more, and more aggressive, covert sabotage operations against Castro. A decision was also made to step up U-2 reconnaissance flights over western Cuba.[25] Yet as late as Sunday, 14 October, Bundy and other U.S. officials were still discounting rumors of Soviet MRBMs in Cuba.[26] Ironically, the same day that Bundy was uttering reassuring comments on national television, a U-2 was taking photographs of the Soviet strategic missile sites. CIA analysts detected the preparations the next afternoon and briefed Kennedy on Tuesday morning, 16 October.

That, in rough outline, is the traditional account of the steps the United States took before learning the shocking news of the Soviet deployment. According to this account, the United States limited its actions during the precrisis period to diplomatic warnings, reconnaissance overflights and other intelligence collection efforts.

Usually ignored in this rundown of events are the measures that were taken by the U.S. military to prepare for possible military action against Cuba and the personal interest taken by President Kennedy in those plans. The CINCLANT report recounts that in the weeks preceding the discovery of the missiles the United States had prepared two principal military options: air strike or invasion, either together or in sequence. Steps were also taken to ready a blockade. Although the documents refer to "contingency" measures, they make clear that the Kennedy administration wanted the option of hitting Castro with military force and wanted it ready by late October.[27] The administration had paid increasing attention to developing military plans for dealing with Cuba that were coordinated with the highly secret (to Americans, at least) Mongoose program initiated by President Kennedy in late 1961. The secret preparations facilitated overt military pressure on Cuba once the crisis became public on 22 October. A review of Pentagon planning measures undertaken in conjunction with Mongoose makes it clear that the idea that the United States might deliberately provoke events in Cuba that could serve as a pretext for U.S. intervention represented a possible course of action, frequently evoked, rather than an unthinkable libel emerging from the paranoid delusions of Havana and Moscow.

PRE-1962 PLANNING FOR CASTRO'S UNDOING

The emergence of a leftist revolution in Cuba, supplanting the pro-Washington rule of dictator Fulgencio Batista, led to the initiation, in November 1959, of interservice planning for possible U.S. military operations on the island. Taking the lead in developing those plans in the office of the Joint Chiefs of Staff was Admiral Dennison,[28] assisted by Army, Air Force, and Marine representatives. Of course, the Eisenhower and Kennedy administrations at first hoped to overthrow Castro covertly, without resorting to open intervention, although various ideas were bandied about in search of a plausible casus belli, including one that called for staging a bogus Cuban attack on the American base at Guantanamo Bay.[29]

But after the disastrous failure of the landing at the Bay of Pigs by CIA-backed anti-Castro Cuban exiles in April 1961—a failure that was especially galling to Kennedy and his advisers when contrasted to the success of the Eisenhower administration seven years earlier in using the CIA to overthrow the leftist Arbenz government in Guatemala, the covert operation upon which the ill-fated "Operation Zapata" had been modeled[30]—there was renewed planning for direct U.S. military intervention. A July 1961 meeting between Secretary of Defense McNamara and the Joint Chiefs produced enlarged Army and Air Force support for a CINCLANT Joint Task Force charged with detailing a "fast reaction air strike" (Operation Plan 312, or OPLAN 312) or an actual invasion (OPLAN 314 and OPLAN 316).[31]

The fall of 1961 brought new presidential pressures to accelerate military contingency planning. On 5 October 1961, Kennedy issued a cryptic directive ordering preparations for the possibility of Castro's removal.[32] In late

October, the Joint Chiefs approved a revised version of Operational Plan 316, the contingency plan for an invasion after five days' notice that was ultimately partially implemented during the missile crisis.[33] And, on 30 November 1961, Kennedy authorized the creation of Operation Mongoose, a top-secret covert action campaign to "use our available assets . . . to help Cuba overthrow the Communist regime."[34]

Employing paramilitary subversion, sabotage, economic, political, and psychological warfare, Mongoose opened a new phase in U.S.-sponsored operations aimed at Castro's downfall. Although run by the CIA, Mongoose was overseen by a high-level panel made up of CIA, State, Defense, and White House aides, along with Attorney General Robert F. Kennedy. The panel, known as the Special Group (Augmented) or SGA, operated in great secrecy. SGA mingled the caution of the once-burned with frustration and fury toward the upstart revolutionaries that gripped the Kennedy administration's senior levels.[35] (McNamara himself later acknowledged that "we were hysterical about Castro at the time of the Bay of Pigs and thereafter.")[36]

To accomplish the objective of exorcising Castro, President Kennedy tapped a man with a reputation as a covert operations miracle-worker, appointing Brigadier General Edward G. Lansdale as Mongoose's chief of operations. Landsdale was responsible for devising the Mongoose strategies, marshaling its troops and resources, and implementing its program on a day-to-day basis. Counterinsurgency specialist and jack-of-all-trades covert operator, Lansdale had masterminded anticommunist campaigns in the Philippines and Vietnam. Though a cloak-and-dagger man, Lansdale had already earned considerable attention as the archetypal American spy abroad, inspiring central roles in such well-known novels as Graham Greene's *The Quiet American* and Eugene Burdick and William Lederer's *The Ugly American*.

MONGOOSE AND THE MILITARY OPTION IN 1962

Now, given a new secret mission to advance U.S. interests in the Third World, Lansdale set up shop at the Pentagon in the Office of the Secretary of Defense. Echoing President Kennedy's initial charge to Mongoose, his first major planning document, dated 18 January 1962, defined the program's objective as to "help Cubans overthrow the Communist regime from within Cuba and institute a new government with which the United States can live in peace." Most of Lansdale's plans aimed at inciting Cubans themselves to rise against Castro, with U.S. support, but they also included preparations for possible direct U.S. military force—which Lansdale described as even more important "as a positive political-psychological factor in a people's revolt" than for its military contribution to the climactic struggle.

Lansdale got right to the business of notifying the Pentagon that it, too, had a part to play in overthrowing the Castro government. Of the 33 tasks parceled out to various government agencies and departments to get Mongoose off the starting block, the Defense Department was given the job of "preparing a contingency plan for U.S. military action, in case the Cuban people request U.S. help when their revolt starts making headway." Lansdale also requested that the Defense Department define under what conditions such a plan could both achieve Castro's downfall yet at the same time "not necessarily lead to general war." He recognized, however, that these military preparations were preliminary to "obtaining a policy decision on the major point of U.S. intentions"—that is, whether Washington was willing to intervene directly to push an anti-Castro uprising over the top. (This question would emerge as a sticking point in the months to come.) Within five weeks, Lansdale expected the Pentagon to provide a full analysis of the conditions necessary for a successful military intervention, as well as plans for assisting CIA efforts and "'special operations' use of Cubans enlisted in the U.S. armed forces."[37]

Per Lansdale's instructions, the Pentagon moved military preparations for a possible invasion of Cuba to the top of its agenda. A formerly top secret history of Army participation in the Cuban missile crisis, written in 1963 and declassified in October 1988, relates, without explicitly referring to Mongoose, that "the seriousness of planning" for a possible invasion of Cuba "was emphasized by the Joint Chiefs of Staff in February 1962 when they established a first priority for the completion of all Cuban contingency plans." The report notes that the Joint Chiefs were also directed to prepare new plans that would cut by more than half any advance notice required for a successful invasion.[38]

These new plans were nominally contingency measures. But the imperative to raise military readiness appears to have been deadly serious. A pep talk by Robert Kennedy to the SGA on 19 January left no doubt, at least in Lansdale's mind, that overthrowing Castro was an "unreserved requirement." "It is untenable to say," the president's brother was quoted as telling the group, "that the United States is unable to achieve its vital national security and foreign policy goal re Cuba." Lansdale exhorted those working on Mongoose to "put the American genius to work on this project," and added forcefully: "[W]e are in a combat situation—where we have been given full command."[39]

By 20 February 1962 Lansdale had formulated and submitted an ambitious schedule for overthrowing the Castro government through a carefully programmed six-phase operation that would culminate in October 1962 with a "popular revolution" against Castro—an "open revolt and overthrow of the Communist regime." The existence of this schedule, first revealed in a passing reference in the 1975 Senate report, was closely guarded within the government. Lansdale classified it "eyes only" and distributed a total of ten copies, one to the president and each member of the SGA. It consumed almost 30 pages of text and appendices. Lansdale wrote that he considered his scenario for sparking a successful overthrow of Castro to be "realistic," but also noted that it reflected "the maximum target timing which the operational people jointly considered feasible." Hinting at the importance he placed upon direct U.S. intervention, if needed, he included among the plan's seven central elements a "military support" component.[40]

Despite Lansdale's evident enthusiasm for his detailed "projection of actions to help Cubans recapture their freedom," Mongoose's overseers preferred a far less grandiose scheme; and, in March 1962, the SGA endorsed an initial phase concentrating on gathering intelligence inside Cuba, the better to evaluate prospects for proceeding to a second, more active phase at some point during the summer of 1962. To complement overt U.S. diplomacy aimed at isolating and weakening Castro, they also sanctioned political, economic, and covert actions against Castro "short of those reasonably calculated to inspire a revolt within the target area, or other development which would require U.S. armed intervention."[41]

At least for the moment, then, both President Kennedy and the SGA had seemingly recoiled from committing the United States to military action to overthrow Castro. Yet the official guidelines for Mongoose that were handed down on 14 March—and were *not* published in full in the 1975 Senate report[42]—also show clearly that a U.S. invasion was central to hopes for Mongoose's success and that the covert program was intended to have the capacity to produce a pretext for direct U.S. intervention. The guidelines, which were discussed in Kennedy's presence and apparently received his "tacit" approval,[43] stated that Mongoose would "be developed on the following assumptions":

> a. In undertaking to cause the overthrow of the Castro government, the U.S. will make maximum use of Cuban resources, internal and external, but recognizes that final success will require decisive U.S. military intervention.

    b.   Such Cuban resources as are developed will be used to prepare for and justify this intervention, and thereafter to facilitate and support it.[44]

The somewhat limited mandate that President Kennedy and the SGA appear to have given Mongoose by no means signified an attenuation of the administration's determination to oust Castro, only uncertainty about the means to be employed in doing so. Testifying to the seriousness of the effort was the scale of Mongoose itself. Largely administered out of the Miami CIA station, which was headed by Thomas Clines and Theodore Shackley, Mongoose rapidly burgeoned into the largest postwar U.S. covert operation yet undertaken in terms of resources expended (upwards of $50 million per year, according to one estimate)[45] and agents involved. An official assessment of the CIA unit that ran Mongoose, Task Force W, put its strength at approximately 400 CIA officers divided between headquarters and the Miami station, which had become the agency's largest outpost in the world. These case officers, in turn, allegedly controlled thousands of Cuban agents, a huge secret fleet of ships and aircraft, bank accounts, and other resources.[46]

The SGA's initial concentration on intelligence meant insinuating agents into Cuba, and frequent attempts were made throughout the spring to infiltrate anti-Castro Cuban exiles onto the island, with mixed results. Several teams disappeared, presumably intercepted and captured by Castro's forces.[47] Only three teams were reported to be in place by May 1962, but by mid-summer Lansdale could proudly cite as evidence of the CIA's "splendid effort" the presence of 45 agents "in the Havana area alone" along with an unspecified number of "agents and teams" in the provinces.[48]

Military contingency planning proceeded apace during the first phase of Mongoose, which lasted from March 1962 through the end of July. One of the principal tasks to be accomplished during this period was, in Lansdale's words, to "continue JCS planning and essential preliminary actions for a decisive U.S. capability for intervention."[49] In late March 1962, the Joint Chiefs issued instructions to add forces to CINCLANT's resources for carrying out contingency plans.50 In April 1962 the Defense Department prepared a study on how to impose a "total blockade" of Cuba, and the CIA analyzed that action's likely impact on Castro's regime.

The Defense Department established a "working group" for Cuban contingency plans, with Joint Chiefs of Staff (JCS), service, and Defense Intelligence Agency (DIA) representation, and appointed a full-time senior liaison to Mongoose, Brigadier General Benjamin T. Harris. By late July, Harris could report that steps to date had included:

i. Contingency Plan for Overt US Military Intervention in Cuba. In order to insure a decisive US military capability for overt military intervention in Cuba, CINCLANT's regular contingency plan has been updated. Attempts are being made to reduce the reaction time required for implementation of this plan, without piecemeal commitment of US forces.

j. Alternate Contingency Plan for Overt US Military Intervention in Cuba. CINCLANT has developed an alternate plan which accomplished a reduction in reaction time but requires piecemeal commitment of forces. In order to reduce the risk inherent in such an operation CINCLANT is seeking means for reduction of the reaction time without piecemeal commitment.

k. Cover and Deception plan. This plan has been developed for the purpose of [*4 lines deleted*]

l. Air Strikes Against Cuba. A plan has been developed for the use of airpower only following a national policy decision to suppress and/or neutralize Cuban forces pending the execution of an assault—or to be executed in support of an internal revolt.

m. Air and Sea Blockade of Cuba. A plan has been developed for the complete air and sea blockade of Cuba within [*two-digit number deleted*] hours after decision.

n. Civil Affairs and Military Government. An outline plan providing guidance for the conduct of civil affairs and for a provisional military government for Cuba has been prepared.

o. DOD's Position as to its Stake and Proposed Role in the Removal of the Communist Regime from Cuba. This paper included a statement of conditions under which Defense believes that overt military intervention in Cuba could be accomplished without leading to general war and without serious offense to public opinion.51

The Mongoose documents establish that this extensive array of increased planning stemmed not from any enhanced threat from Cuba but from the covert program's internal momentum and perhaps from the increased hopes of the program's overseers that they might get an opportunity to assist an anti-Castro revolt in Cuba. The latter is the explanation given by Lansdale in a secret memorandum to the SGA in early July: "Rumors in mid-June of a Cuban uprising led to my tasking Defense for further contingency planning including an inter-departmental plan. Defense reports that this planning is progressing well."52

In memorandums written later that month, Lansdale made a point of noting that the revolt allegedly planned inside Cuba was to occur "without U.S.sponsorship."[53]

Since declassified portions of a CIA estimate produced around this time fail to mention any uprisings in Cuba, U.S.-sponsored or otherwise, and indeed, argue strongly against the likelihood that a sullen and largely "indifferent" populace would revolt against Castro any time in the near future, Lansdale's explanation that an expected uprising in June accounted for ordering stepped-up military readiness seems puzzling.[54]

My own suspicion, based on circumstantial evidence, is that what Lansdale really had in mind was the possibility that one of several assassination plots against Castro set in motion by the Kennedy administration might succeed. The 1975-1976 Senate investigation disclosed that between 1960 and 1965 U.S. officials hatched a host of conspiracies to kill Castro, involving methods as varied as Mafia hit men, poison cigars and pills, mercenary sharpshooters, exploding seashells, and a germ-infested gift diving suit.[55] (The investigators were unable to determine conclusively whether President Kennedy directly ordered or knew of these schemes.)[56] The United States intensified its efforts to arrange Castro's murder in the spring of 1962, around the time of Lansdale's call for increased military readiness.

The official in charge of trying to put the hit on Castro was William King Harvey, chief of the CIA's Task Force W, acting with the knowledge and approval of CIA Deputy Director Richard Helms. Harvey oversaw the Miami station's activities and reported frequently and in detail to Lansdale. In April and May 1962, Harvey passed poison pills, explosives, detonators, rifles, handguns, and other equipment to underworld figure John Rosselli for use by Cubans against Castro. In mid-June, Rosselli told Harvey that a Cuban contact had "dispatched a three-man team to Cuba" for the purpose of killing Castro. When hauled before Senate investigators 13 years later, Harvey denied telling Mongoose supervisors of his efforts to arrange Castro's assassination, and Lansdale strongly disclaimed any knowledge of them.[57]

Even Lansdale's admiring biographer doubts this flat denial, however. It "would have been 'highly unusual' had he *not* known what was planned," writes Cecil B. Currey, "given his grasp of detail, his tight control over Task Force W, and his insistence on staying on top of current activity."[58] Moreover, even if Harvey and Helms had kept Lansdale in the dark as to the details of their actions, it seems highly likely that Lansdale was at least alerted to the possibility that an assassination plot of some kind, to be carried out by anti-Castro Cubans, was in progress and might be nearing fruition.

Although Lansdale's hopes for a mid-June anti-Castro uprising, possibly in response to the death of Castro, went unfulfilled, by late July, at the close of Mongoose's first phase, he could take comfort from the fact that military planning for a possible intervention had significantly advanced. In a 25 July 1962 progress report, Lansdale told the SGA that the JCS had "fully met its responsibility, under the March guidelines," for "planning and undertaking preliminary actions for a decisive U.S. capability for intervention in Cuba."[59]

Pressing for a political decision on what Mongoose's next phase would entail, Lansdale presented the SGA with a new contingency plan for military intervention in Cuba on 31 July 1962. In a cover memo he explained that the plan, already approved by McNamara and the Joint Chiefs and known as "United States Contingency Plan No. 2, Cuba(S)," had been "developed as a result of reports in mid-June 1962, that the Cuban people were about to revolt against the Castro-communist regime, without U.S. sponsorship, and [as a result of] the desire expressed by the Special Group that the U.S. be ready for such a contingency."[60] Details of the plan apparently remain classified, but its purpose seems clear. It was meant to give the United States the capacity to use military force in a decisive manner to impose a pro-Washington government on the island. General Harris, the Pentagon's and Joint Chiefs' liaison to Mongoose, summarized the plan's general outlines in a secret memorandum in early August. "In concept," Harris stated, "initial military operations [would] commence with an air and naval blockade, concentrated air strikes, and coordinated naval gunfire to effect destruction of enemy airpower and to neutralize and destroy as much as possible of the enemy armor, artillery and anti-air capability."[61]

It is important to note that although Cuban Defense Minister Raúl Castro, Fidel Castro's brother, had visited Moscow between 2 and 17 July, there is no indication at this point that concern about renewed Soviet shipments to Cuba had motivated these new contingency plans or proposals for increased sabotage efforts. Indeed, Lansdale had scoffed at the idea of citing Soviet aid to convince Latin American leaders to cooperate in U.S.-backed "plans by Cuban patriots to attack Castro by bombing key installations in Havana from a third country." It was, Lansdale wrote U. Alexis Johnson, "'digging pretty deep' to use 'increased Soviet aid to Raúl Castro' as an argument by U.S. officials with foreign governments."[62]

Soviet shipments in the late summer and early autumn of 1962 eventually did cause genuine concern among U.S. officials. But the evidence shows that serious planning for the use of direct military force to topple Castro, perhaps in support of a U.S.-backed internal revolt or assassination plot, predated concern about Soviet weapons deliveries.

THE SOVIETS AND AMERICAN PLANS:
DID THE SOVIETS REACT TO AMERICAN PLANS?

Although the declassified documents do not disclose any obvious increase in U.S conventional military preparations aimed at Cuba prior to Moscow's decision in the spring of 1962 to deploy nuclear missiles on the island, that does not mean that Soviet leaders had no reason to suspect that the United States may have been considering a conventional military strike against Castro. The Kennedy administration's hostile rhetoric, its political and diplomatic efforts to isolate Cuba, and Mongoose's sporadic sabotage and psychological warfare operations undoubtedly contributed to Soviet concerns. In addition, in April and early May 1962 the United States staged massive and well-publicized military maneuvers, some personally observed by President Kennedy, which may have served, however unwittingly, to feed the fears of Soviet leaders that the United States was building toward another invasion of Cuba.

The first series of maneuvers covered the period between 9 and 24 April, stretched from North Carolina to the Caribbean, engaged 40,000 Marines and Navy personnel and hundreds of ships and aircraft. Code-named "Lantphibex 1-62," the exercise culminated in a dramatic landing of a 10,000-man attack force on the tiny island of Vieques off Puerto Rico.[63] When that mock assault ended, the military announced that another exercise of comparable size, dubbed "Quick Kick," would begin on 7 May.[64] Like Lantphibex 1-62, Quick Kick was devoted to coordinated air and marine assaults. Declassified Pentagon documents note that, as the Soviets and Cubans probably suspected, Quick Kick and "Whip Lash," another multiservice military exercise slated for 8 to 18 May, were designed to test procedures that would be used by CINCLANT during an actual invasion of Cuba.[65]

Although Lantphibex 1-62 and Quick Kick received significant notice at the time in the American press, they have been largely dismissed, ignored, or overlooked by later analysts of the crisis.[66] Yet these large-scale military maneuvers presumably attracted intense scrutiny from Soviet intelligence analysts reporting to the Kremlin from embassies in Washington and Havana, and they could indeed have heightened the suspicions of Khrushchev and Soviet military authorities concerning U.S. intentions toward Cuba at precisely the moment when the Soviet leader is reported to have made up his mind to send the nuclear missiles. At least one senior Soviet military commander, General Igor D. Statsenko, who was in Cuba at the time of the crisis, has explicitly stated in a little-noticed 1977 article that U.S. military exercises undertaken in the spring of 1962 helped to trigger the missile deployment decision by raising fears of an invasion.[67]

SUMMER 1962:
PRESSURE TO INTENSIFY MONGOOSE

In the late summer of 1962, Mongoose's first phase, largely devoted to intelligence collection and small-scale sabotage and psychological warfare, drew to a close. Pressure mounted among those informed of the operation to escalate the administration's private campaign against Castro. Still limited by Mongoose's charter to instigating actions that would fall "short of inspiring a revolt in Cuba or developing the need for U.S. armed intervention," Lansdale again implored his superiors to commit themselves to military involvement, if such involvement should become necessary to assure the project's ultimate success. A "firm U.S. intention to help free Cuba" he asserted to the SGA on 25 July, "is the key factor" in motivating Cubans to revolt. "[T]ime is running out" for Washington to act. If anti-Castro Cubans became convinced that the United States was "not going to do more than watch and talk," they would "make other plans for the future" and "start getting serious about settling down for life in the U.S."

Lansdale offered his overseers four options for Mongoose's next phase:

a.   Cancel operational plans; treat Cuba as a Bloc nation; protect Hemisphere from it, or

b.   Exert all possible diplomatic, economic, psychological, and other pressures to overthrow the Castro-Communist regime without overt employment of U.S. military, or

c.   Commit U.S. to help Cubans overthrow the Castro-Communist regime, with a step-by-step phasing to ensure success, including the use of U.S. military force if required at the end, or

d.   Use a provocation and overthrow the Castro-Communist regime by U.S. military force.[68]

In August there were several weeks of internal wrangling about moving beyond Mongoose's initial phase. The covert program's reassessment came at a time when, as Bundy has recently recalled, the dominant emotion within the administration in its dealing with Cuba was frustration.[69] That frustration surfaced when the SGA met to consider Lansdale's alternatives on 10 August 1962. At that meeting the idea of assassinating or "liquidating" Castro and other Cuban leaders was openly raised, allegedly by McNamara, who suffered an acute memory loss about the occasion when later questioned by Senate investigators.[70]

Three currents converged to produce greater pressures for action against Cuba. The first was Operation Mongoose's internal momentum, which was propelling plans for a second, stepped-up phase of operations. The second was new and alarming information on Soviet bloc aid to Cuba, which reinforced earlier beliefs that the Castro regime's continued existence presented an intolerable affront to U.S. prestige and interests. And finally, the domestic political cost of appearing unable to act effectively against Castro grew as the congressional election campaign began to dominate the agenda and Republicans pounced on the reports of renewed Soviet shipments as evidence that the Democrats were incapable of handling the Communist menace. Between mid-August and mid-October, all three of these considerations increasingly reinforced each other in the administration's deliberations concerning more, and more effective, action against Castro.[71]

President Kennedy's National Security Action Memorandum 181 (NSAM-181) of 23 August 1962 gave new impetus both to Operation Mongoose and to the military contingency planning aimed at Cuba. Anxious to see more results from the covert program, yet still reluctant to commit the U.S. government to decisive military intervention, Kennedy ordered Maxwell Taylor, his military adviser and chairman of the SGA, to develop "with all possible speed" various activities "projected for Operation MONGOOSE Plan B plus." Unlike phase one, with its more restrictive guidelines, plan "B plus" would allow the administration to deliberately seek to provoke a full-scale revolt against Castro that might require U.S. intervention to succeed.[72]

As Kennedy directed a stepped-up covert action program, he also set into higher gear the process of military contingency planning. Kennedy's August 23 directive, NSAM-181, requested the Defense Department to "study . . . the various military alternatives which might be adopted in executing a decision to eliminate any installations in Cuba capable of launching [a] nuclear attack on the U.S. What would be the pros and cons, for example, of pinpoint attack, general counter-force attack, and outright invasion?" Kennedy's motives here appear to have been twofold. He wanted a continuing complement to Mongoose, for he explicitly specified that only "senior officers already informed of MONGOOSE" should be assigned to draw up contingency plans for a possible attack on Cuba.[73] He also wanted an active response to the reports of increased Soviet shipments to Cuba.[74]

Planning for the "pinpoint attack" option, at least, began quickly. The scenarios ranged from the destruction of individual surface-to-air missile sites to "large scale air strikes against Cuba."[75] As early as 7 September 1962, the CINCLANT report states, the Air Force's Tactical Air Command "established a planning group charged with the task of developing an air plan; its objective was to achieve the complete destruction of the Cuban air order of battle."[76]

THE FALL OF 1962: WAS THE UNITED STATES ABOUT TO UNDO CASTRO ANYWAY?

On 14 September, President Kennedy, McNamara, and the Joint Chiefs of Staff met to discuss a possible aerial attack against Cuba, leaving Kennedy perplexed by varying estimates as to the extent of likely losses the United States would sustain in an assault against the Soviet SA-2 batteries on the island.[77] Four days later, the Air Force "initiated extensive training exercises . . . [including] flight profiles which closely approximated planned combat missions."[78] Detailed, revised blueprints for proposed air strikes were completed and approved by Air Force officials on 27 September and ratified by CINCLANT Dennison the next day. The Air Force set a target date of 20 October for the completion of all preparations.[79]

By late September, with reports of a Soviet buildup in Cuba continuing and with Republican charges of presidential vacillation filling the air, Kennedy had expressed additional interest in military readiness for action against Cuba, and specifically in the details of planning for a possible air attack against the surface-to-air missile installations. In a recently-declassified 21 September 1962 memorandum to McNamara, Kennedy suggested building a model SA-2 site against which practice air strikes could be conducted. Perhaps recalling the unfortunate results of his previous approval of a military operation against Cuba on the basis of general assurances from subordinates (the Bay of Pigs), the erstwhile commander of PT-109 proposed that the efficacy of any such exercise be judged by "an objective and disinterested party" that should be sure to include in its calculations "the addition of anti-aircraft guns to protect the site." More broadly, the president requested the secretary of defense to "assure that contingency plans with relation to Cuba are kept up-to-date, taking into account the additions to the armaments resulting from the continuous influx of Soviet equipment and technicians."[80]

In the last week of September and the first week of October, preparations for a variety of alternatives for military action against Cuba accelerated. OPLAN 312 detailed air strike specifications while OPLAN 314 and OPLAN 316 set the requirements for larger-scale military options, such as a full-scale invasion and occupation of Cuba. The latter invasion scenarios envisioned "joint military operations in Cuba by combined Navy, Air Force and Army forces . . . [and] a simultaneous amphibious and airborne assault in the Havana area by a Joint Task Force"—in sum, a "projection of U.S. military force" that "would lead to the overthrow of the Castro Government."[81]

Both the air strike and invasion plans began receiving more serious attention after McNamara met on 1 October 1962 with the Joint Chiefs of Staff "to discuss intensified Cuban contingency planning . . . in light of the latest intelligence."[82] At the meeting, the hypothesis that the Soviets were emplacing surface-to-surface missiles on the island was presented to McNamara but "carefully explained as a theory only," according to a DIA representative in attendance.[83] Strikingly, the meeting produced directives to attain "maximum readiness" for either an air strike or invasion by a deadline of 20 October. At 7:22 on the evening of 1 October, the documents relate, Admiral Dennison at the JCS directed fleet commanders to "take all feasible measures necessary to assure maximum readiness to execute CINCLANT OPLAN 312 [air strike] by October 20" and ordered the "[p]repositioning of the necessary aviation ordnance and support material."[84] And according to the CINCLANT report, army commanders received from CINCLANT "an indication as early as 1 October 1962 concerning the imminence of a possible implementation of CINCLANT OPLAN 316-62 [for a full-scale invasion of Cuba]." At 4:42 P.M. on 2 October, in response to an inquiry from subordinate commands, CINCLANT explained that its directive "was not intended to establish 20 October as an operational date on which all involved forces assumed DEFCON 1 posture [i.e., war footing] but rather a date by which CINCLANT desired the maximum readiness of plans, personnel and logistical support to include the prepositioning of all classes of required supplies." In the same 2 October message CINCLANT specified that its directive to commence prepositioning included "combat forces."[85]

Finally, according to the Defense Operations Report prepared by Yarmolinsky, the 1 October meeting also produced a decision "to alert Admiral Dennison, Commander-in-Chief of the Atlantic Fleet, to be prepared to institute a blockade of Cuba." Two days later, on 3 October, Dennison "took the initial steps to prepare his forces, and directed his subordinate commands to prepare for the formation of a blockade force."[86]

"To mask widespread preparations for the actions proposed," the report continues, "Admiral Dennison suggested we announce that our forces were preparing for an exercise. PHIBRIGLEX 62, a large-scale amphibious assault exercise provided a cover for our Caribbean preparations."[87] The

Phibriglex exercises were to be the third major series of U.S. military training operations in the Atlantic region that year, and would afford the Marines yet another opportunity to storm the beaches of Vieques. In a sophomoric bit of psychological warfare, the Pentagon informed reporters that the exercises, scheduled to begin on 15 October, involved practice landings by a force of 7,500 Marines to liberate Vieques from a mythical despot named Ortsac—Castro spelled backwards.[88]

On 2 October 1962, the day after his conference with the military leaders, McNamara sent the Joint Chiefs a strongly worded directive that triggered a further intensification of preparations for the implementation of "any or all" of the contingency plans for attacking Cuba.[89] This directive offers perhaps the strongest new evidence that before discovering the missiles, officials at the highest level of the Kennedy administration showed increasing interest in improving the ability of the U.S. military to take overt and covert action against Cuba.

The "political objective" of a U.S. military strike, McNamara wrote, would be either, first, the "removal of the threat to U.S. security of Soviet weapons systems in Cuba," or, second, the "removal of the Castro regime and the securing in the island of a new regime responsive to Cuban national desires."[90] McNamara added that "inasmuch as the second objective is the more difficult objective and may be required if the first is to be permanently achieved, attention should be focused upon a capability to assure the second objective."

In his directive McNamara listed six possible "contingencies under which military action against Cuba may be necessary and toward which our military planning should be oriented." These included, in order, the following:

1. A Soviet move against Western interests in Berlin

2. Evidence of Soviet offensive weapons in Cuba

3. A Cuban attack on the U.S. forces at Guantanamo Bay or elsewhere

4. "A substantial popular uprising in Cuba, the leaders of which request assistance in recovering Cuban independence from the Castro Soviet puppet regime" (i.e., the Mongoose scenario)

5. Cuban armed aid "to subversion in other parts of the Western Hemisphere"

6. "A decision by the President that the affairs in Cuba have reached a point inconsistent with continuing U.S. national security"[91]

It is interesting to compare these conditions for possible U.S. intervention in Cuba, propounded secretly by McNamara, with those offered publicly by President Kennedy just a few weeks earlier. On 13 September 1962, Kennedy publicly rejected unilateral U.S. military intervention in Cuba. He vowed, however, that the United States would "do whatever must be done" to safeguard its security and that of its allies

> [i]f at any time the Communist buildup in Cuba were to endanger or interfere with our security in any way, including our base at Guantanamo, our passage to the Panama Canal, our missile and space activities at Cape Canaveral, or the lives of American citizens in this country, or if Cuba should ever attempt to export its aggressive purposes by force or the threat of force against any nation in this hemisphere, or become an offensive military base of significant capacity for the Soviet Union.[92]

Notably absent from Kennedy's extensive list of potential *casus belli* are several of McNamara's: a Soviet move in Berlin, the possibility of an internal revolt against Castro, and the catch-all category of a presidential determination that the situation in Cuba was no longer compatible with U.S. national security.

It is not clear whether Kennedy personally reviewed McNamara's 2 October directive, but on 3 October the president again expressed interest in intensified military contingency planning, and requested that the defense secretary and the Joint Chiefs "war-game the effectiveness" of a proposed air strike against the Soviet SAMs in Cuba.[93]

On 4 October McNamara responded to Kennedy on the status of the air attack plans. While the SA-2s themselves were unlikely to down attacking U.S. planes, McNamara told Kennedy, Air Force and Navy leaders predicted that losses from antiaircraft artillery fire were possible during any attempt to wipe out the SAM sites. McNamara pointed out, however, that those losses could be minimized by a surprise attack. Noting that the Air Force had built a model target for pilots to practice against, McNamara summarized for Kennedy the plans for destroying the ostensibly defensive antiaircraft installations:

> The Navy plans to attack SA-2 targets at low levels using 4 divisions of A-4D's (4 aircraft per division) armed with 250#, 500#, and 2000# low level drag bombs and napalm. All crews are proficient in the delivery techniques planned. Similarly, the Air Force plans primary use of napalm and 20mm cannon delivered at low level, and crews are proficient. Both have made detailed target studies; target folders are in the hands of crews; and crews are familiar with their assigned

targets. As new missile sights are located, they are picked up in the target and attack plans within a few hours of receipt of photographs.[94]

Perhaps alluding to his 1 October meeting with the Joint Chiefs and to his follow-up directive to them the next day, McNamara also assured Kennedy that he had "taken steps to insure that our contingency plans for Cuba are kept up to date."[95] Kennedy read McNamara's memorandum "with interest" and, in an acknowledgment by an aide that was passed to the defense secretary on 5 October, urged further coordination with the Joint Chiefs.[96] McNamara ordered the Joint Chiefs to raise the level of conventional military preparedness vis-à-vis Cuba, and the president's brother passed the word that covert operations should also be sharply increased. The president still did not feel that the Mongoose operators were responding quickly or aggressively enough. At a 4 October 1962 meeting of the SGA, Robert Kennedy loudly sounded his brother's message, taking "sharp exception" to CIA director McCone's claim that he detected a "hesitancy" to authorize direct actions attributable to Washington. There ensued, McCone's notes record, "a sharp exchange which was clarifying inasmuch as it resulted in a reaffirmation of a determination to move forward." Official minutes of the meeting record that Robert Kennedy urged the group to approve "massive activity" against Castro, declaring that the president felt "that more priority should be given to mount[ing] sabotage operations."

From this meeting a consensus quickly emerged that the previously approved phase two "was now outmoded," and "that more dynamic action," such as mining Cuban harbors and capturing pro-Castro forces for interrogation, "was indicated." In response to Robert Kennedy's strong words, the covert planners approved "considerably more sabotage" and endorsed "all efforts . . . to develop new and imaginative approaches" to the goal "of getting rid of the Castro regime." They also decided that the president's brother should chair subsequent SGA meetings.[97]

Meanwhile, following up on his memorandum to the Joint Chiefs, McNamara continued to give full support for measures to increase military readiness to implement contingency plans against Cuba. On 6 October McNamara discussed the situation with the Joint Chiefs and Admiral Dennison. At the meeting Dennison "called attention to the requirement for relocation and prepositioning of troops, aircraft, ships, equipment and supplies" and specifically proposed relocating armored units stationed at Fort Hood, Texas, to Fort Stewart, Georgia, where they would be closer to the ports that would be used in the event of a seaborne invasion of Cuba. Dennison hesitated to take such far-reaching steps in light of budgetary restrictions, but McNamara allayed his concerns, assuring him forcefully at one point that where the movement of troops and materiel was concerned, "cost was no object."[98]

Armed with McNamara's support, Admiral Dennison on 6 October "directed the development of the highest state of readiness" to "execute the 314 and 316 [invasion] Plans as well as 312 [air strike plans]."[99] On that same day the Joint Chiefs also requested Dennison to enlarge CINCLANT's contingency plans for invading Cuba to include forces that might be required for a long-term military occupation.[100]

The Defense Operations Report notes that between 6 and 16 October 1962 "preparatory actions were taken that did much to insure that we were in a balanced posture when the crisis came to a head." Included among these actions were the "prepositioning of bulk supplies (POL [petroleum, oil, and lubricants] and ammunition) at Florida bases, completion of plans to reinforce Guantanamo, the reinforcement of our air defense capabilities in the southeastern United States, and advanced preparation for the transfer of the 5th Marine Expeditionary Brigade, with its associated amphibious shipping, from the West Coast to the Caribbean area."[101] The last of these moves was explained by the Joint Chiefs on 10 October as required "in view of the serious threat developing and high level of national interest concerning Cuba."[102]

Other military redeployments carried out before the missiles were discovered in mid-October included the dispatching of a Military Assistance Group, a squadron of F4H fighters (on 8 October) and aviation equipment ("on a priority basis") to the navy base at Key West, Florida.[103] "High gear" military airlift operations began on 10 October, and on 11 October the Navy aircraft carrier *Independence* departed from Norfolk for southern waters.[104] In addition, a recently declassified Air Force history states that by 10 October, Tactical Air Command forces "had already commenced training exercises at McCoy, MacDill, and Homestead AFB's and the build-up of war readiness materiel at these bases had begun."[105]

By then, covert diplomatic overtures to underpin the invasion planning had also begun to bear fruit. On 8 October the Joint Chiefs informed CINCLANT that the British government had "agreed the US may proceed with prepositioning of supplies and equipment at Mayaguana" in the Bahama Islands, then a British colony. Obviously sensitive to the implications of the U.S. plans, London had insisted on two conditions: first, that "nothing is to be put in writing," and second, that the facilities would not "be put to active use" without Britain's prior approval.[106]

In a further response to McNamara's memo, which had requested urgent comments on the contingency plans, the Joint Chiefs called a conference of "operations and logistics planners" at the Pentagon on 12 October to develop "specific actions to be taken to increase readiness and reduce reaction time" for an invasion option.[107] At this conference the operations planners made further contingency preparations and fine-tuned the air strike and invasion options. Among the actions the Army reported taking to increase readiness for the invasion plan were the prepositioning of 64 "units" (of unspecified size) "with equipment, supplies and increments of resupplies" in a "D-5 posture," 56 units in a "D-8 posture," and the "restationing of selected units to reduce movement time from home station to POE [port of embarkation]."[108] The CINCLANT report does not specify when this prepositioning of forces took place, but the somewhat ambiguous wording suggests that it was either underway by the time of the 12 October meeting or ordered as a result of it.

Both the early stages of the U.S. buildup and the planning behind it remained a tightly guarded secret, even inside the military.[109] "Within the Staff the information relating to reconnaissance operations and the build up was extremely closely held, being disclosed on a strict 'need to know' basis," the CINCLANT report notes. "During this period [between 1 and 19 October] normal command and staff activity continued and served in many instances to provide 'cover' for initial functions in our build up."[110]

In conclusion, the timing and nature of the directives and preparations outlined in the documents support the interpretation that U.S. military action of some kind was under active consideration prior to mid-October 1962. Secretary of Defense McNamara's memorandum to the JCS in the first week of October directing that "attention should be focused" on attaining a capability to invade Cuba; the repeated directives, perhaps as early as 1 October and certainly by 6 October, ordering the military to attain "maximum readiness" or "the highest state of readiness" by 20 October; and the actual prepositioning of supplies, weapons, and troops—all these seem to transcend "routine contingency planning," and suggest that something more serious was afoot.

THE DOMESTIC FACTOR

That the target date for "maximum readiness" was October 20—two weeks before hotly contested mid-term congressional elections—inevitably raises the question of whether domestic political considerations, as well as concern about a possible Soviet threat, may have prodded the Kennedy administration to consider a military strike. After all, a successful preelection military strike promised substantial political gains for Kennedy, who had come under heavy pressure from Republican critics for failing to take firm action against Castro. "The Kennedy people wanted to be known as people with balls, and this was a chance to show whether they had them or not," commented retired Lieutenant General Samuel V. Wilson, who in 1962 was working on covert operations in the office of the secretary of defense. "I don't think McNamara intended any [military action], he was more cautious than that, but there were members of the Kennedy Administration who were keenly aware of the upcoming elections and domestic political pressures, and might have set off some Roman candles to enhance their position at the polls."[111]

Thomas G. Paterson and William J. Brophy, in an article published in the *Journal of American History,* have implicitly discounted this possibility. Although politics had "preoccupied" Kennedy in the fall of 1962 and the Republicans had succeeded in "making Cuba a troublesome political issue for the Democrats," Paterson and Brophy write, before 16 October the Democrats "had no political need to manufacture a war scare and Kennedy did not welcome a new Cuban crisis."[112] To justify this assertion they cite polling data that appears to show the Democrats were headed for victory despite Republican charges of Kennedy administration weakness toward Cuba.

The Paterson-Brophy argument, however, does not negate the deep concern in the White House about the volatility of the Cuban issue during the remainder of the campaign. On 4 October, for example, presidential pollster Louis Harris advised Kennedy that 62 percent of voters had a negative view of his handling of the Cuban issue.[113] Nor does it obviate the fact, which they acknowledge, that Kennedy, like other presidents, permitted domestic political considerations to influence, at times decisively, his actions in the foreign policy realm.[114] McGeorge Bundy, in his recently published account of the missile crisis, says that congressional pressure, which expressed a "strong national conviction" that a threatening Soviet-backed military presence in Cuba would be unacceptable, "forced [Kennedy's] hand" in taking a tough line before and at the outset of the crisis.[115]

I think, then, it is fair to say that by mid-September Cuba had cast a shadow over the domestic political landscape and that as a result Kennedy and his associates worried that the issue posed at least the potential to inflict severe damage at the polls, even if their worst fears had not yet been realized. Therefore, the Paterson-Brophy analysis leaves open the possibility that the enhanced contingency measures may have stemmed at least in part from the desire of John F. Kennedy or those around him to lay the groundwork for a demonstration of U.S. and presidential firmness toward Cuba. Whether a demonstration of this sort would ultimately be required depended upon national security and/or domestic political considerations, and from the standpoint of Kennedy and his advisers those considerations were not necessarily incompatible or contradictory.

WAS THE CONCESSION NOT TO ATTACK MEANINGFUL?

It is important to keep two points in mind when considering U.S. military actions before the crisis. First, the historical issue under examination is not merely the yes-or-no question of whether the United States intended to invade Cuba; it is also the determination of just how much attention and consideration were given to the option of military action, whether as mere muscle flexing or as a means of toppling Castro, harassing him, or pressuring him, and to what extent, if any, these U.S. plans and actions contributed to a perception by other parties that military action was a real possibility.[116] Second, the risks involved in contemplating military action against Cuba changed completely once the missiles were discovered. Previously, the United States could flirt with military action against Cuba with relative impunity, although the possibility of a Soviet response elsewhere, particularly in Berlin, and a negative impact on international public opinion could not be discounted. The risk of thermonuclear war, however, almost certainly did not factor into precrisis calculations. The Soviet missiles utterly transformed the situation. Suddenly, attacking Cuba entailed the theoretical danger (assuming the missiles were operational and armed) of causing the prompt nuclear destruction of American cities and the deaths of millions of their inhabitants.

The evidence of heightened U.S. military preparations, as well as the broad range of contingencies mentioned in McNamara's directive to the JCS, raises doubts about subsequent assertions by U.S. officials to the effect that Washington's promise at the close of the crisis not to invade or countenance the invasion of Cuba did not represent a concession because no such action had been contemplated in any case. Military action clearly was an option prior to 16 October, even if it was not necessarily the preferred option at that time. Thus, it is misleading to suggest, as some former officials have, that Washington would have gladly issued a no-invasion pledge even if the Soviets had never deployed nuclear-capable missiles.[117] Again, this does not mean that such an action would necessarily have been ordered, only that the U.S. government retained the option of direct military action to topple

Castro's regime until 28 October 1962 (and perhaps beyond, as Washington did not formally bind itself to the pledge not to invade Cuba until 1970).[118]

THE COVERT AND MILITARY PLANNING NEXUS

That the United States significantly and urgently increased its preparations for possible military action against Cuba before detecting the Soviet surface-to-surface missiles and, indeed, initiated heightened planning prior to receiving indications of the Soviet buildup in Cuba in the late summer of 1962, can be seen as lending credibility to Moscow's oft-stated claim that Washington had not entirely banished the notion of launching a post-Bay of Pigs military strike to overthrow the Havana government or to at least give Castro a bloody nose. That the United States carried out a covert operations program against Castro has been public knowledge since the mid-1970s. The CINCL-ANT report and other declassified documents, however, show that precrisis covert operations were accompanied by and synchronized with an acceleration of preparations for possible direct U.S. military intervention. The conjunction of the two takes on added significance because of the renewed controversy over U.S. intentions toward Cuba prior to the crisis.

Admiral George W. Anderson, Jr., who was chief of naval operations at the time of the missile crisis, stated in a 1987 interview that he and Maxwell Taylor believed McNamara ordered the increased readiness in early October in the hope that U.S.-sponsored covert operations would spark an upheaval on the island, thus providing a pretext for overt military action to oust Castro. "I think he was prepared to exploit any developments that took place," Anderson said, recalling that he felt the military and Mongoose actions were "generally coordinated" and that McNamara "was hoping" that the covert action would ultimately lead to Castro's downfall and was positioning the U.S. military to be ready to finish the job should the necessity arise. Anderson conceded, however, that he never actually heard McNamara express the hope that Mongoose operations would lead to a decisive U.S. military intervention, but rather inferred the defense secretary's view from his actions and comments.[119]

Informed of Anderson's remarks, McNamara "absolutely" rejected the idea that Mongoose actions were aimed at sparking a revolt that would facilitate a U.S. invasion—as did several other members of the SGA contacted for this chapter.[120] Reiterating previous denials that the United States sought to intervene militarily in Cuba, McNamara maintained that he and other senior policymakers never viewed the covert anti-Castro operation as capable of leading to actions that would endanger Castro's rule or require

Washington to use overt force. "Mongoose wasn't worth a damn," he declared.[121]

Evidence on Anderson's hypothesis seems mixed. On the one hand, the declassified documents explicitly link Mongoose and conventional military planning concerning Cuba in 1962. They show that Kennedy and other high-level U.S. policymakers and military officials who were informed of both activities viewed them as offering complementary means of pressuring Castro that could be alternated or combined as parts of a coordinated strategy. Evidence for this conclusion ranges from the March 1962 Mongoose guidelines stating that covert operations were intended to "prepare for and justify" U.S. military intervention, to internal Pentagon documents pointing to a "priority" on Cuban contingency planning from early 1962, to Kennedy's August 1962 presidential directive stipulating that Pentagon officers informed of Mongoose should draw up military plans for Cuba, to McNamara's October 1962 memo to the Joint Chiefs citing a "popular uprising" in Cuba as a potential trigger for U.S. intervention. Most important, the president's approval in August of a stepped-up "Plan B plus" meant that Washington was ready to risk inciting a full-scale revolt in Cuba that might require U.S. intervention to assure a victory for anti-Castro forces.

In fact, according to another senior Navy official involved in planning the precrisis buildup of U.S. forces, military planners did not mind the clamor created by Senator Keating and other Republicans about the dangers of a military threat in Cuba precisely because such remarks would "condition" U.S. public opinion in the event Washington decided to use force to eliminate the Castro regime. "Actually, getting ready to invade Cuba is what we were doing," the official remarked off-handedly in 1979 oral history interview, clearly referring to the meaning of preparatory measures undertaken before the detection of Soviet missiles in mid-October.[122] While this statement, made well after the fact, by itself does not prove that a political go-ahead for an invasion had been given, it offers suggestive evidence that such a perception did exist at senior military command levels.

On the other hand, of course, a clear reluctance among senior Kennedy administration figures to make a final commitment to using military force also repeatedly manifested itself, to the frustration of Lansdale and others who advocated a no-holds-barred approach to deposing Castro. And an internal CIA memorandum written on the eve of the crisis tends to corroborate McNamara's contention that prior to the crisis, top officials acted gingerly when confronted with options that might require open military action. "During the past year," an aide wrote CIA Deputy Director Richard Helms on 16 October 1962, "while one of the options of the [Mongoose] project was to create internal dissension and resistance leading to eventual U.S. intervention, a review shows that policymakers not only shied away from the military intervention but were generally apprehensive of sabotage proposals."[123]

The early October exhortations to step up sabotage suggest that the SGA had begun to shed some of its inhibitions. But whether Mongoose's second phase might have led to eventual U.S. military intervention in Cuba is uncertain. So the question stands: Would the United States have attacked Cuba in the fall of 1962 if the Soviets had continued to supply Cuba with military equipment—but refrained from deploying surface-to-surface missiles? A definitive answer remains elusive, and may never be known, as the only man who knew John F. Kennedy's intentions died in Dallas in November 1963. But the evidence belies categorical claims that the notion of a U.S. attack on Cuba never entered policymakers' minds. Clearly, when Washington detected the Soviet missiles in mid-October, the prospect of military intervention assumed a far more immediate and realistic character. But, far from gathering dust in some cabinet, as some former officials would have us believe, Pentagon plans for action against Castro were already being revivified at the express direction of the secretary of defense, who in turn acted at President Kennedy's behest.

Although a firm conclusion that a U.S. invasion of Cuba was in the offing is not possible, it seems reasonable to conclude that in late September and early October, 1962, Kennedy or his top aides seriously considered an air strike, blockade or other overt military pressure against Castro. The administration may also have considered helping a third country to take some military action against Cuba and may well have been moving into position to launch a full-scale invasion should Cuba resist limited military actions or should U.S.-backed covert operations produce widescale revolt inside Cuba.

Despite the documentary evidence to the contrary, some scholars of the missile crisis continue to trust the denials of former Kennedy administration officials (and McNamara in particular) that military action against Cuba received serious attention prior to Washington's discovery of the Soviet nuclear-capable missiles in mid-October. To support their assertion that the process of forming a U.S. military option "began from scratch" after the discovery of missiles, Bruce Allyn, James G. Blight and David A. Welch assign heavy weight to the transcripts of the 16 October 1962 ExComm meetings at which the president and his advisers first discussed the Soviet missile emplacement. Those transcripts, the authors wrote in the journal *International Security,* "nowhere refer to any prior decision to invade Cuba, any established intention to invade Cuba, or even any previous exploration of the desirability of such an invasion. If indeed there had been serious consideration of the possibility, one would expect it to be reflected in those early, formative discussions, because an invasion would have been a comparatively well-formulated option already on the table."[124]

In my view, however, the evidence of the 16 October transcripts remains ambiguous. Aside from the fact that portions of the transcripts are still classified, that the precrisis planning had been a closely-held secret even within the government, and that the discovery of the missiles placed the Cuban affair on an entirely different basis, the full transcripts—as opposed to the edited version cited by Allyn, Blight and Welch[125]—actually *do* contain allusions to prior military planning. At one point in the 16 October meetings, as Robert F. Kennedy is discussing a full-scale invasion as one U.S. option in response to the Soviet missile deployment, the transcript records the following presidential interjection:

JFK: I don't believe it takes us, at least, uh . . . How long did it take to get in a position where we can invade Cuba? Almost a month? Two months?

McNamara: No, sir.

Speaker: Right on the beach . . .

At that juncture government censors blacked out a half-page or so exchange involving the president, McNamara, and Gen. Maxwell D. Taylor, chairman of the Joint Chiefs of Staff. It would be interesting to know what was said. But the three evidently were discussing the extent of precrisis military preparations, for when the transcript resumes, Taylor says, apparently in response to a comment from the president, "Uh, at least it's enough to start the thing going . . . It ought to be enough."[126] The president's query, moreover, wondering how long *it had taken* to get into a position "where we can invade Cuba," certainly suggests an invasion, although of course it hardly establishes whether he had intended to order one. The president's uncertainty as to whether the effort had taken one month or two is also consistent with this chapter's description of a buildup that accelerated in late summer following NSAM 181 on 23 August and then intensified in late September and the first two weeks of October. It seems clear, to sum up the significance of this particular piece of evidence, that an informed assessment of the 16 October 1962 transcripts must await their full declassification.[127]

The possibility that a preelection "October surprise" was being hatched by the Kennedy administration raises some intriguing questions: Did the Cuban missile crisis that did occur actually supplant an imminent non-nuclear crisis stemming from U.S. irritation with Castro, which had been exacerbated by the conventional Soviet buildup on the island? Did Khrushchev's decision to deploy the missiles, taken in the spring of 1962 under the mistaken impression that a U.S. attack was then firmly set, in the end deter a threat to Cuba that only arose in the fall?

If an eventual U.S. intervention was likely, then there would seem to be some truth to Igor Statsenko's claim that "the Soviet strategic rockets stationed in Cuba did not give rise to, but on the contrary prevented the further dangerous development of the Caribbean crisis," deterred a conventional war, and "saved revolutionary Cuba"—at the price, of course, that General Statsenko does not care to mention, of nearly igniting World War III.[128] Recall that in 1962 U.S. policymakers had not yet learned perhaps the principal lesson of Vietnam—that military intervention against popular Third World nationalism risks unanticipated and debilitating expenditures of lives, resources, and political and moral capital, with no assurance of victory. Some historians have argued that the Kennedy administration's "success" in the missile crisis led its principal authors to conclude, with spectacularly disastrous results, that the graduated escalation of military pressure would produce a similarly successful outcome in Vietnam.[129] The new evidence concerning U.S. behavior toward Cuba before the missile crisis, along with the recent claim from Soviet sources that as many as 42,000 Soviet troops were on the island in October 1962, between four and nine times the number estimated by U.S. intelligence,[130] and that Soviet forces in Cuba were equipped with short-range tactical nuclear weapons and the authority to use them,[131] thus raises yet another question: Had the missile crisis not intervened, would we have learned the "lesson of Vietnam"—or worse—in Cuba?

With many documents still classified and serious historical scholarship still sparse, further research is required to clarify the issue of precrisis (and preelection) U.S. intentions. The purpose of this chapter has been to illuminate and invite further consideration of a previously neglected aspect of the crisis. In the meantime, the retrospective accounts of former officials, which have played and are likely to continue to play an unusually important part in determining both the history and political lessons of the Cuban missile crisis, should be welcomed but treated with caution. Most of these recollections may be correct, most of the time. But as one former senior Kennedy administration official interviewed for this chapter remarked about another (not for attribution, naturally), "Sometimes he remembers it the way he wishes it was, rather than the way it was."

NOTES

This chapter was previously published, in different form, as Occasional Paper No. 89-1 of the Nuclear Age History and Humanities Center (NAHHC), Tufts University, and in *Diplomatic History* 14 (Spring 1990), 163-98. The author would like to acknowledge the support of NAHHC and its director, Martin J. Sherwin, as well as assistance from Philip Nash, Brian Balogh, Barton J. Bernstein, Raymond Garthoff, Daniel Ellsberg, Marc Trachtenberg, Scott Sagan, Mark White, and Laurence Chang of the National Security Archive.

1. Principal accounts by former officials include George Ball, *The Past Has Another Pattern: Memoirs* (New York, 1982); McGeorge Bundy, *Danger and Survival: Choices about the Bomb in the First Fifty Years* (New York, 1988); Raymond L. Garthoff, *Reflections on the Cuban Missile Crisis* (Washington, 1987), and rev. ed., 1989 (all citations are to the revised version unless otherwise noted); Roger Hilsman, *To Move a Nation: The Politics of Foreign Policy in the Administration of John F. Kennedy* (New York, 1967); Robert F. Kennedy, *Thirteen Days: A Memoir of the Cuban Missile Crisis* (New York, 1969); Arthur M. Schlesinger, Jr., *A Thousand Days: John F. Kennedy in the White House* (Boston, 1965); idem, *Robert Kennedy and His Times* (Boston, 1978); and Theodore Sorensen, *Kennedy* (New York, 1965). Robert S. McNamara offers some general comments, but no full account or analysis, in his *Blundering into Disaster: Surviving the First Century of the Nuclear Age* (New York, 1987). Important secondary works include Elie Abel, *The Missile Crisis*(Philadelphia, 1966; citations from Bantam paperback ed.); Graham T. Allison, *Essence of Decision: Explaining the Cuban Missile Crisis* (Boston, 1976); and Herbert S. Dinerstein, *The Making of a Missile Crisis: October 1962* (Baltimore, 1976). For a recently issued anthology of articles on the crisis, see Robert A. Divine, ed. with commentary *The Cuban Missile Crisis* (New York, 1988). To date, no comprehensive secondary work incorporating the wealth of materials declassified over the past decade has appeared. For a study based on recent recollections by participants on both sides, however, see James G. Blight and David A. Welch, *On the Brink: Americans and Soviets Reexamine the Cuban Missile Crisis* (New York, 1989, rev. ed. 1990; citations from the 1989 edition); see also Bruce J. Allyn, James G. Blight, and David A. Welch, "Essence of Revision: Moscow, Havana, and the Cuban Missile Crisis," *International Security* 14 (Winter 1989/90): 136-72. Two articles presenting declassified transcripts and minutes of Excomm meetings are "White House Tapes and Minutes of the Cuban Missile Crisis," Marc Trachtenberg, ed., *International Security* 10 (Summer 1985): 164-203; and "October 27, 1962: Transcripts of the Meetings of the Ex-

Comm," McGeorge Bundy, transcriber; James G. Blight, ed., *International Security* 12 (Winter 1987/88): 30-92. For the Soviet perspective see Strobe Talbott, trans. and ed., Edward Crankshaw, intro, *Khrushchev Remembers* (Boston, 1970), 488-505; Strobe Talbott, trans. and ed., Edward Crankshaw, foreword and Jerrold L. Schecter, intro., *Khrushchev Remembers: The Last Testament* (New York, 1976), 509-14; and Ronald R. Pope, ed., *Soviet Views on the Cuban Missile Crisis: Myth and Reality in Foreign Policy Analysis* (Lanham, MD, 1982). For Castro's role see Tad Szulc, *Fidel: A Critical Portrait* (New York, 1986; paperback ed., 1987), 588-657, and Philip Brenner, "Cuba and the Missile Crisis," *Journal of Latin American Studies* 22:1 (February 1990): 115-42. Essential archival materials are at the John F. Kennedy Library in Boston, but the National Security Archive in Washington.DC, has gathered an extensive collection of declassified documents from various sources and has organized a detailed chronology of the crisis.

2. Those few authors who cursorily commented on U.S. military preparations prior to the crisis or on Soviet claims that Washington was readying an attack on Cuba tended to downplay the former and discount the latter. Raymond L. Garthoff, for example, wrote in the 1987 edition of his *Reflections on the Cuban Missile Crisis,* that Soviet analysts "incorrectly conclude from evidence that there was a policy and firm plan for a new invasion of Cuba by the United States' armed forces." He then added, somewhat sarcastically: "No doubt a military contingency 'plan' was on file (the United States in 1941 even had a 'war plan' for conflict with Great Britain), but there was no political decision or intention to invade Cuba before October 1962." Garthoff, *Reflections* (1987 ed.), 5. In the same vein, Graham T. Allison, author of *Decision: Explaining the Cuban Missile Crisis,* declared flatly in late 1987: "The United States had no such plans or intentions." Graham T. Allison, "Lessons of the Cuban Missile Crisis," *Boston Globe,* 26 October 1987. (After seeing an early draft of this chapter and supporting documentation provided by the author, both Allison and Garthoff reversed their earlier views on the subject and gave more serious attention to precrisis U.S. military activity.)

3. A notable exception is Scott Sagan, "Nuclear Alerts and Crisis Management," *International Security* 9 (Spring 1985): 99-139, esp. 106-07. For discussions of the historiography of the defense-of-Cuba motive for emplacing the missiles, see Welch and Blight, *On the Brink,* 294-96, 301-2; Pope, *Soviet View,* ix-x, 153-59, 227-49; and Laurence J. Chang, "Historical Reassessment of the Cuban Missile Crisis," presented to the Society of Historians of American Foreign Relations annual meeting, Williamsburg, VA, 15 June 1989.

4. Soviet recollections of the decision to send the missiles differ. Sergei Khrushchev insists that his father told him in June 1962 that the missiles were being sent for the sole purpose of defending Cuba. Comments at public forum, Kennedy School of Government, Harvard University, 15 February 1989. By contrast, Fyodor Burlatsky, a Khrushchev speech writer, recalled

that Khrushchev's "main" motive was "the first step to strategic parity." Blight and Welch, *On the Brink,* 229. For various recent Soviet assessments of the rationale for the decision see Blight and Welch, *On the Brink,* 229, 234-43, 249-50, 257-58; "Meeting Sheds New Light on Cuban Missile Crisis," *The New York Times,* 14 October 1987; Richard Ned Lebow, "Provocative Deterrence: A New Look at the Cuban Missile Crisis," *Arms Control Today,* July/August 1988, 15-16; Global Classroom Project, "The Cuban Missile Crisis," a televised teleconference sponsored by Tufts University and Lomonosov Moscow State University, 30 April 1988, transcript available at Nuclear Age History and Humanities Center, Tufts University, Medford, Massachusetts.

5. *Khrushchev Remembers,* 494. Khrushchev also gave this explanation at the time of the crisis, writing Kennedy that the "Soviet government decided to render assistance to Cuba with means of defense against aggression—only with means for defensive purposes . . . We have supplied them to prevent an attack on Cuba—to prevent rash acts." Khrushchev to Kennedy, 28 October 1962, in David L. Larson, ed., *The "Cuban Crisis" of 1962: Selected Documents and Chronology* (Boston, 1963), 162. For Khrushchev's postcrisis explanation to the Soviet people and leadership, see Khrushchev, "In Defense of Cuba," *The Worker Supplement,* 23 December 1962, quoted in Henry Pachter, *Collision Course: The Cuban Missile Crisis and Coexistence* (New York, 1963), 243-248; and Divine, ed., *Cuban Missile Crisis,* 102-8. For precrisis Soviet claims of hostile U.S. intent toward Cuba see, for example, the *Tass* statements of 11 and 13 September 1962. And for an important example of the defense-of-Cuba argument in Soviet historical treatments see Anatoly A. Gromyko, "The Caribbean Crisis, Part I: The U.S. Government's Preparation of the Caribbean Crisis," *Voprosy istorii* [Questions of history] 7 (July 1971): 135-44, reprinted in Pope, ed., *Soviet Views,* 161-94.

6. Comments to the Institute of Politics, John F. Kennedy School of Government, Harvard University, 13 October 1987. A tape recording of the discussion is available at the institute's offices. Bundy makes a similar assertion in *Danger and Survival,* 416, in which he states that the possibility that the Soviets feared U.S. action against Cuba "simply did not occur to us in Washington before October 15." Here he acknowledges, as he did not in his Harvard remarks, that from Moscow's perspective the U.S. posture toward Cuba may have appeared provocative and threatening:

> We knew that we were not about to invade Cuba and we saw no reason for the Russians to take a clearly risky step because of a fear that we ourselves understood to be baseless. We did not understand that Khrushchev might take our hostile words about Cuba, and the very attitudes of our own people that we understood so well on October 16, as meaning that all we had learned from the Bay of Pigs was that we should do it right next time. Khrushchev certainly knew of our program of covert action against Cuba, and he could

hardly be expected to understand that to us this program was not a
prelude to stronger action but a substitute for it.

7. Comments to the Institute of Politics, John F. Kennedy School of Government, Harvard University, 13 October 1987, emphasis in spoken remarks.
For a similar comment by McNamara, see Lebow, "Provocative Deterrence," 16.

8. *CINCLANT Historical Account of Cuban Crisis,* 29 April 1963, Admiral
Robert L. Dennison, commander in chief Atlantic, declassified September
1986 per Freedom Of Information Act request filed by WGBH-TV (hereafter CINCLANT report). The author first discussed the report and its
significance in understanding the precrisis U.S. posture toward Cuba in
James G. Hershberg, "Before the Missiles of October," *Boston Phoenix,* 8
April 1988. Dennison, who died in 1980, denied in a 1973 oral history
interview that the United States threatened Cuba militarily prior to 16
October 1962. "Before the crisis invasion was farthest from our minds. In
other words, there were then no plans to invade Cuba. Everybody familiar
with our own history would know that would be farthest from our intentions." Interview No. 10 of Admiral Robert L. Dennison, USN (Ret.) by Dr.
John T. Mason, Jr., 17 July 1973, #10-395, Oral History Department, United
States Naval Institute, Annapolis, Maryland. Dennison's claim that anyone
"familiar with our own history" would dismiss the possibility of U.S.
military intervention in Cuba is, to put it mildly, open to question.

9. One seven-page chapter of the CINCLANT report, entitled "Joint Uncon-
ventional Warfare Task Force Atlantic," remains classified in full. Other
deletions, ranging from a few words to a paragraph, are scattered through
the report. However, at least 95 percent of the document is declassified. The
deletions appear to concern references to commando operations (either by
the military or under the Mongoose rubric) and intelligence sources in Cuba,
to some operational details of invasion plans, and perhaps to the role of
nuclear weapons in contingency plans or to their movement during the
crisis.

10. Department of Defense Operations During the Cuban Crisis, a report by
Adam Yarmolinsky, special assistant to the secretary of defense, 12 February 1963, ed. and intro. Dan Caldwell, in *The Naval War College Review*
32 (July-August 1979): 91, 93 (hereafter Defense Operations Report).

11. Many of the newly released documents were cited or quoted in *Alleged
Assassination Plots Involving Foreign Leaders,* an interim report of the
Senate Select Committee to Study Governmental Operations with Respect
to Intelligence Activities, S. Rept. 94-465, 94th Cong., 1st sess., 134-69
(hereafter *Alleged Assassination Plots*). The newly released documents,
however, also include material omitted from the report.

12. Telephone interviews with McGeorge Bundy, Abram J. Chayes, Ray Cline,
Roswell Gilpatric, U. Alexis Johnson, Robert S. McNamara, Dean G. Rusk,
and Adam Yarmolinksy, October 1987. McNamara said "there sure as hell
wasn't any massing of forces before the 16th" and attributed the actions to
routine contingency planning, "although that may appear contrary to the

documents." He added: "The best evidence that we didn't make any serious preparations prior to the 16th is what we had to do when the President and I learned of the missiles." Only then, McNamara said, did the United States commence gathering forces. Told of the contents of the CINCLANT report, Bundy, in an interview, described the measures as "pure contingency planning." He also advanced the hypothesis that Kennedy ordered readiness measures to demonstrate his toughness to the military. In his book, Bundy maintained that "as far as I can remember" the United States took no special military preparations before the crisis and therefore Kennedy "had to begin on the sixteenth [of October] almost from a standing start." Bundy, *Danger and Survival*, 413-14. It is unclear why Bundy makes this assertion. He may not have been informed of the preliminary actions described in this chapter (the chain of command that is most fully documented runs from Kennedy to McNamara to the Joint Chiefs to Admiral Dennison), or he may have regarded them as insignificant or ineffective, or he may simply not, or not wish to, recall them.

13. Cuban missile crisis scholarship combines an unruly mix of contemporary documents and retrospective accounts and analyses, many of which incorporate explicit or cloaked personal or political agendas, whether on the part of former government officials, political scientists and nuclear strategists, or even (perish the thought!) supposedly detached academics. I, for instance, was annoyed to hear prominent former government officials making statements that seemed to conflict with documents I had seen, and I was interested in ascertaining and setting forth, fairly, the factual basis for my annoyance. This chapter resulted: Caveat lector.

14. *Khrushchev Remembers*, 493. More recent information from Soviet sources indicates that Khrushchev discussed the idea of sending missiles to Cuba with leading Soviet officials, including Deputy Prime Minister Anastas Mikoyan and Defense Minister Marshal Rodion Malinovsky, and perhaps others, in late April or early May 1962—prior to the trip to Bulgaria. See Raymond L. Garthoff, "Cuban Missile Crisis: The Soviet Story," *Foreign Policy* 72 (Fall 1988): 61-80, esp. 63-66.

15. Also, the paucity of internal Soviet documentation has hampered attempts to reconstruct what Kremlin leaders knew or thought about U.S. actions or intentions (secret and public) toward Cuba. This situation appears to be improving, however.

16. The most comprehensive analysis of the relationship between the Cuban missile crisis and domestic politics is Thomas G. Paterson and William J. Brophy, "October Missiles and November Elections: The Cuban Missile Crisis and American Politics, 1962," *Journal of American History* 73 (June 1986): 87-119. See also Montague Kern, Patricia W. Levering, and Ralph B. Levering, *The Kennedy Crises: The Press, the Presidency, and Foreign Policy* (Chapel Hill, 1983), 99-122.

17. Sorensen, *Kennedy*, 755.

18. Schlesinger, *A Thousand Days*, 800-801; Sorensen, *Kennedy*, 754-55, 758. Keating's sources for his allegations, including claims in early October that

the Soviets were deploying offensive missiles, remain cloaked in secrecy. See Thomas G. Paterson, "The Historian as Detective: Senator Kenneth Keating, the Missiles in Cuba, and His Mysterious Sources," *Diplomatic History* 11 (Winter 1987): 67-70.

19. McGeorge Bundy, "Memorandum on Cuba for conference," 13 September 1962, cited in Paterson and Brophy, "October Missiles," 96.

20. For the full text of Kennedy's statement see transcript of news conference with Pierre Salinger, 4 September 1962, 6:10 P.M., National Security Files, box 36, folder: "Cuba, General 9/62," Kennedy Library; or *New York Times,* 5 September 1962.

21. Bundy, "Memorandum on Cuba for the press conference." For Kennedy's 13 September 1962 statement see *Public Papers of the Presidents of the United States. John F. Kennedy, 1962* (Washington, 1963), 674.

22. Kennedy, *Thirteen Days,* 4-5; Schlesinger, *A Thousand Days,* 798-99.

23. Kennedy, *Thirteen Days,* 2-3; Hilsman, *To Move a Nation,* 165, 170.

24. Allison, *Essence of Decision,* 190-92; Hilsman, *To Move a Nation,* 172-73. On McCone's warning see especially Bundy, *Danger and Survival,* 419-20.

25. For the U-2 delay see Hilsman, *To Move a Nation,* 175-6, 180; Allison, *Essence of Decision,* 122, 192; Bundy, *Danger and Survival,* 687.

26. Hilsman, *To Move a Nation,* 180; Allison, *Essence of Decision,* 189.

27. The Defense Operations Report, written several months after the event, offers contradictory evidence on whether military action was intended prior to the crisis. It states (p. 8) that the advance preparations "were taken in contemplation of possible execution of the contingency plans" but then adds that the actions were ordered "as a matter of prudence."

28. Jean R. Moenk, *USCONARC Participation in the Cuban Crisis 1962,* declassified copy available from National Security Archive, Washington, D.C.

29. Trumbull Higgins, *The Perfect Failure: Kennedy, Eisenhower, and the CIA at the Bay of Pigs* (New York, 1989; Norton, paperback ed.), 71.

30. On the links between the Guatemala and Bay of Pigs episodes, see esp. Richard H. Immerman, *The CIA and Guatemala: The Foreign Policy of Intervention* (Austin, TX, 1982), 187-97.

31. Moenk, *USCONARC Participation in the Cuban Crisis 1962,* 1, 3, 6-7.

32. National Security Action Memorandum No. 100, 5 October 1961, quoted in *Alleged Assassination Plots,* 136.

33. Moenk, *USCONARC Participation in the Cuban Crisis 1962,* 6.

34. Kennedy to Rusk et al., 30 November 1961, quoted in *Alleged Assassination Plots,* 139.

35. The SGA comprised National Security Adviser McGeorge Bundy, Under-secretary of State U. Alexis Johnson, Deputy Secretary of Defense Roswell Gilpatric, CIA Director John McCone, General Lyman Lemnitzer, chairman of the Joint Chiefs of Staff, Attorney General Robert F. Kennedy, and General Maxwell D. Taylor, Kennedy's military adviser, who chaired the group. Secretary of State Rusk and Secretary of Defense McNamara,

though not formal members, attended some meetings. See *Alleged Assassination Plots*, 140.

36. Ibid., 142fn.
37. E. G. Lansdale, "The Cuba Project," 18 January 1962, Mongoose Freedom of Information Act documents collection, National Security Archive, Washington, D.C. (hereafter Mongoose FOIA documents).
38. Moenk, *USCONARC Participation in the Cuban Crisis 1962*, 17.
39. Lansdale, "Memorandum for members, Caribbean Survey Group," 20 January 1962, Mongoose FOIA documents.
40. Most of the military support details were censored in the recently released version. Lansdale, "The Cuba Project," 20 February 1962, Mongoose FOIA documents; *Alleged Assassination Plots*, 142-47.
41. "Guidelines for Operation Mongoose," 14 March 1962, Mongoose FOIA documents; *Alleged Assassination Plots*, 144-47.
42. *Alleged Assassination Plots*, 147.
43. The SGA took pains to have the record avoid any explicit reference to presidential approval of the guidelines, but a memorandum of the 16 March 1962 meeting, at which the guidelines were circulated and "used as the basis of the discussion," indicated that Kennedy received a "progress report" on Mongoose and that after "prolonged consideration of the visibility, noise level and risks entailed, General Lansdale and the Special Group (Augmented) were given tacit authorization to proceed in accordance with the Guidelines." A week later, after reading the memorandum, the SGA tried to take full responsibility, disclaiming presidential approval, tacit or otherwise. See *Alleged Assassination Plots*, 145fn.
44. "Guidelines for Operation Mongoose," 5 March (draft) and 14 March, 1962, Mongoose FOIA documents. In the latter version, references to Cuba and Cuban resources were replaced by references to the "target" government and "indigenous" but the wording of these passages is otherwise identical.
45. Arthur M. Schlesinger, Jr., *Robert Kennedy and His Times*, 514.
46. *Alleged Assassination Plots*, 140; Joan Didion, *Miami* (New York, 1987), 90-91, cited in Welch and Blight, *On the Brink*, 364; John Prados, *President's Secret Wars: CIA and Pentagon Covert Operations from World War II through Iranscam* (rev. ed., New York, 1988), 211-13.
47. Lansdale to SGA, "Operation Mongoose, 13-19 April," 19 April 1962; "Operation Mongoose, 20-26 April," 26 April 1962; "Operation Mongoose, 27 April-3 May," 3 May 1962, Mongoose FOIA documents.
48. Lansdale to SGA, "Progress, Operation Mongoose," 5 July 1962, Mongoose FOIA documents; *Alleged Assassination Plots*, 154.
49. Lansdale to SGA, "Review of Operation Mongoose," 25 July 1962, Mongoose FOIA documents.
50. *Moenk, USCONARC Participation in the Cuban Crisis 1962*, 4-5.
51. Benjamin T. Harris to Lansdale, "End of Phase I," 23 July 1962, Mongoose FOIA documents.
52. Lansdale to SGA, "Progress, Operation Mongoose," 5 July 1962, Mongoose FOIA documents.

53. Lansdale to SGA, "Contingency Plan," 31 July 1962, Mongoose FOIA documents; Lansdale to SGA, "Review of Operation Mongoose," 25 July 1962, Mongoose FOIA documents.

54. CIA, "National Intelligence Estimate 85-2-62: The Situation and Prospects in Cuba," 27 July 1962, Mongoose FOIA documents.

55. *Alleged Assassination Plots,* 74, 78-86.

56. *Alleged Assassination Plots,* 7, 263-64.

57. *Alleged Assassination Plots,* 83-84, 131, 134-35, 148-54, 156.

58. Cecil B. Currey, *Edward Lansdale: The Unquiet American* (Boston, 1988), 248.

59. Lansdale to SGA, "Review of Operation Mongoose," 25 July 1962, Mongoose FOI Documents.

60. Lansdale to SGA, "Contingency Plans," 31 July 1962, Mongoose FOIA Documents.

61. Statement by General Benjamin T. Harris, "Military," 7 August 1962, appendix to Lansdale to SGA, "Stepped Up Course B," 8 August 1962, Mongoose FOIA documents.

62. Lansdale to U. Alexis Johnson, 20 July 1962, Mongoose FOIA documents.

63. For public coverage of the maneuvers, see: "Big Maneuver Opens," *New York Times,* 10 April 1962; "President Joins Fleet Maneuvers," *New York Times,* 14 April 1962; "President Sees Atlantic Fleet Hunt and Destroy 'Enemy' Submarine" and "9,000 Marines Land," *New York Times,* 15 April 1962; "10,000 Marines in Sea Games," *New York Times,* 16 April 1962; "Marines Maneuver on Isle," *New York Times,* 25 April 1962.

64. "40,000 to Take Part in Atlantic Exercise," *New York Times,* 29 April 1962.

65. For Whip Lash see Lansdale to Special Group (Augmented), 10 May 1962, Mongoose FOIA documents; for Quick Kick see "Command History-CINCLANTFLT, 1962," OPNAV Report 5750-5, submitted 21 May 1963, cited in Garthoff, *Reflections,* 6.

66. Garthoff ignored the issue of prior military exercises in the first edition of *Reflections on the Cuban Missile Crisis* but inserted references in the revised edition (pp. 6-7) after reading a draft of this chapter.

67. I. D. Statsenko, "On Some Military-Political Aspects of the Caribbean Crisis," *Latinskaya Amerika* (Latin America) 6 (November-December 1977): 108-17. My thanks to Raymond L. Garthoff for alerting me to this source and providing a copy. See also Pope, *Soviet Views,* 247-49.

68. Lansdale to SGA, "Review of Operation Mongoose," 25 July 1962, Mongoose FOIA documents.

69. Bundy, *Danger and Survival,* 415.

70. *Alleged Assassination Plots,* 161-65.

71. Garthoff's conclusion that the intensified contingency planning during this period was attributable solely to the arms buildup in Cuba thus strikes me as overly narrow. See Garthoff, *Reflections,* 52.

72. McGeorge Bundy to secretary of state et al., National Security Action Memorandum No. 181, 23 August 1962. This sentence is blacked out in the

version of NSAM-181 at the JFK Library, but it appears in the same
document in the Cuban missile crisis document collection of the National
Security Archive, Washington, D.C. It is also quoted in *Alleged Assassination Plots*, 147. For the distinction between phase one of Operation Mongoose and the stepped-up course B see Lansdale to Special Group (Augmented), "Stepped Up Course B," 8 August 1962, Mongoose FOIA
documents.

73. McGeorge Bundy to Secretary of State et al. NSAM 181, 23 August, 1962.
    This sentence is blacked out in the version of NSAM at the JFK Library but
    appears in the same document in the National Security Archive's Cuba
    Missile Crisis collection.
74. McGeorge Bundy to secretary of state et al., National Security Action
    Memorandum No. 181, 23 August 1962, National Security Files, box
    335A-338, folder: "NSAM 181 Cuba(A) Aug. 23, 1962," Kennedy Library.
75. The specifics of OPLAN 312 are summarized in CINCLANT report, 17-20.
76. CINCLANT report, 162.
77. John F. Kennedy to McNamara, 21 September 1962, President's Official
    Files, box 77, "Defense, July-Dec., 1962," Kennedy Library.
78. CINCLANT report, 19.
79. CINCLANT report, 162-63. This sequence of preparations is also recounted
    in "The Air Force Response to the Cuban Crisis," USAF Historical Division
    Liaison Office, Headquarters USAF, n.d., 21.
80. Kennedy to McNamara, 21 September 1962, declassified at author's request, 25 Feb. 1991, NLK-89-10, President's Official Files, box 77, "Defense, July-Dec. 1962," Kennedy Library.
81. CINCLANT report, 20-22.
82. Defense Operations Report, 1.
83. Letter from Colonel Wright to Elie Abel, 18 March 1970, cited in NSA
    Chronology, 104.
84. CINCLANT report, 39; Moenk, *USCONARC Participation in the Cuban
    Crisis 1962*, 7. Details of the air strike plan, known as "Rockpile," appear
    to have been redacted, but it apparently called for destroying the SAM sites
    as well as bases for Soviet-supplied Komar rocket-launching torpedo boats
    at the Cuban port of Mariel.
85. CINCLANT report, 58; Moenk, *USCONARC Participation in the Cuban
    Crisis 1962*, 8, citing top secret 2 October messages between CINCSTRIKE
    and CINCLANT. In an October 1987 telephone conversation with the
    author, McNamara said he did not recall the 20 October target date and
    discounted its significance.
86. Defense Operations Report, 1. See also CINCLANT report, 39-40. The
    CINCLANT report notes that the blockade orders, while not executed,
    "were, however, the forerunners to the quarantine operations which were
    ultimately placed into effect."
87. Defense Operations Report, 1. The CINCLANT report is not so categorical
    in relating the exercises, which it describes as "routinely scheduled," to the
    covert contingency preparations. It states, however, that "it is of interest

that as early as 10 October the National Military Command center began inquiring informally of CINCLANT as to the nature and scope of PHIBRIGLEX-62. Without ever relating the exercise to the Cuban situation, there were indications of high-level interest in it." CINCLANT report, 3.

88. Abel, *Missile Crisis,* 86. This pungent detail was leaked to the press at the time, and one must assume that those in charge of the exercise did not worry about Castro's or Moscow's reaction. For coverage of PHIBRIGLEX see "Marines Set Atlantic Tests," *New York Times,* 17 October 1962; "Navy-Marine Force in Caribbean Game," *New York Times,* 21 October 1962; and "Navy and Marine Force Heads for Exercise off Puerto Rico," *New York Times,* 22 October 1962.

89. The National Security Archive's chronology (p. 105-6) gives the date of this directive as 2 October 1962, as do notes of this document taken and provided to me by Daniel Ellsberg, who reviewed classified documents relating to the crisis for a 1964 internal Pentagon study. The CINCLANT report does not provide the date of McNamara's directive but notes that it was passed by the JCS to CINCLANT on 8 October, suggesting that it reached the Joint Chiefs in time to trigger the 6 October directives. CINCLANT report, 41. This sequence is also implicit in the Defense Operations Report, 7-8.

90. CINCLANT report, 42; Defense Operations Report, 7.

91. CINCLANT report, 42.

92. Kennedy, statement of 13 September 1962, *Public Papers of the Presidents, 1962,* 674.

93. Carl Kaysen to secretary of defense and chairman, Joint Chiefs of Staff, 3 October 1962. For two differently sanitized versions of the directive see National Security Files, box 273-274, folder: "Department of Defense, Sept.-Dec. 1962," and President's Official Files, box 77, folder: "Defense, July-Dec. 1962," both at Kennedy Library.

94. McNamara to Kennedy, "Presidential Interest in SA-2 Missile System and Contingency Planning for Cuba," 4 October 1962, National Security Files, box 35A-36, folder: "Cuba, General, Oct. 1-Oct. 14, 1962," Kennedy Library.

95. Ibid.

96. Major General C. V. Clifton to McNamara, 5 October 1962, National Security Files, box 35A-36, folder: "Cuba, General, Oct. 1-14 1962," Kennedy Library.

97. This account of the 4 October 1962 meeting is drawn from two sources: *Alleged Assassination Plots,* 147, and McCone, "Memorandum of Mongoose Meeting Held on Thursday October 4, 1962," cited in NSA Chronology, 107B-107C, and Prados, *President's Secret Wars,* 213, 497.

98. CINCLANT report, 40; USCONARC History, 8, 20.

99. Defense Operations Report, 1, 8; CINCLANT report, 40. The Defense Operations Report states that "Atlantic Fleet forces were already moving toward a high peak of readiness because of a heavy schedule of training

operations which were under way, but further specific orders for highest readiness were issued October 6."

100. U.S. Marine Corps Summary, 8 October 1962; cited in NSA Chronology, 107D.

101. Defense Operations Report, 8.

102. U.S. Marine Corps Summary, 11 October 1962, cited in NSA Chronology, 107I.

103. Defense Operations Report, 1; CINCLANT report, 46.

104. Defense Operations Report, 15; CINCLANT report, 110.

105. "The Air Force Response to the Cuban Crisis," USAF Historical Division Liaison Office, Headquarters USAF, n.d., 21.

106. U.S. Marine Corps Emergency Action Center, "Summary of Items of Significant Interest; Period 090701-100700 October 1962," U.S. Marine Corps Historical Center; copy in National Security Archive Cuban missile crisis collection.

107. CINCLANT Report, 44; USCONARC History, 9.

108. CINCLANT report, 45. The report states that the "conferees were to determine requirements, methods and costs" of prepositioning troops and other preparatory actions. It went on to list actions "taken or being taken to improve readiness" for the air strike plan that would be completed by 20 October; these included prepositioning of forces, equipment, and "war consumables." As for the invasion plan (OPLAN 314), the report then noted, in the context of the 12 October 1962 meeting, that "actions to increase . . . readiness included" prepositioning the 120 units.

109. The early stages of the buildup may have been a secret within the Cabinet as well. Then-Secretary of State Dean Rusk said any redeployments of forces or changes in military readiness toward Cuba should have been discussed in the Cabinet or in his regular meetings with McNamara but were not. "I don't recall any [U.S. military preparations] that preceded the location of the missiles in Cuba," Rusk said. He added that he presumed the readiness steps outlined in the CINCLANT report represented "normal contingency planning" but that it was "theoretically possible" that the State Department was deliberately excluded from military planning that took place "outside of Cabinet channels." Rusk, telephone interview with author, October 1987.

110. CINCLANT report, 39.

111. Samuel V. Wilson, telephone interview with author, November 1987.

112. Paterson and Brophy, "October Missiles," 88, 97, 119.

113. Harris to Kennedy, "The Shape of this Campaign," 4 October 1962; cited in Kern, Levering, and Levering, *Kennedy* 117-18.

114. Paterson and Brophy note that Kennedy succumbed to domestic pressures in mid-September, when he decided to sell Hawk missiles to Israel following intense lobbying by American Jews. Paterson and Brophy, "October Missiles," 87-88. Another example of Kennedy's sensitivity to domestic politics in his conduct of foreign policy during the period under scrutiny in

this chapter was his flip-flop on retaining most-favored-nation trade status for Yugoslavia, a policy which he (in line with the State Department) at first supported but then, under pressure from Congress, abandoned. George F. Kennan, *Memoirs, 1950-1963* (Boston, 1972), 293-305.

115. Bundy, *Danger and Survival,* 410-13.

116. Graham Allison elides this issue in *Essence of Decision* (47-50). He contends that, although the desire to deter a U.S. invasion seems like a "persuasive" explanation for the Soviet missile deployment, this explanation does "not withstand careful examination." There was no need to send MRBMs to deter a major U.S. attack, he writes, since "a sizeable contingent of Soviet troops" would have sufficed. Leaving aside the fact that challenging a superpower conventionally on its doorstep hardly seems like a feasible strategy (it was for that very reason that the United States decided to send nuclear-equipped bombers and missiles rather than massive ground forces to Western Europe in the late 1940s and 1950s), it is not clear why the fact that the Soviets could have taken a different route to reach their goal of defending Cuba constitutes an argument against the possibility that they may have attempted to take a far quicker, if riskier, shortcut. "Cuban defense might have been a subsidiary effect of the Soviet gamble," Allison concludes, "but not its overriding objective." Note the wording: by describing Cuban defense as a subsidiary *effect,* yet denying that it was an overriding *objective,* Allison evades the question of whether defending Cuba may have been a subsidiary Soviet *objective,* or motive, rather than a coincidental *effect.*

117. The two promises Kennedy made to the Soviets on the night of 27 October 1962, viewed in the context of whether they represented concessions on the part of the United States, parallel each other in some respects. A natural corollary of the assertion that the Kennedy administration had not considered attacking Cuba prior to the crisis is that the United States therefore gave up nothing by promising not to attack. In a similar vein, some former Kennedy aides have ardently insisted that the private promise to Khrushchev to withdraw Jupiter missiles from Turkey, as relayed by Robert Kennedy to Soviet Ambassador Anatoly Dobrynin on 27 October, did not constitute a concession or a "deal" because the president had already ordered their removal—a claim strongly challenged by some historians. One wonders whether the vehemence of the assertions that Kennedy had ordered the missiles removed from Turkey and that the administration never considered military action against Cuba prior to the crisis stems in part from a reluctance to acknowledge that the United States conceded anything to end the crisis. See Donald L. Hafner, "Bureaucratic Politics and 'Those Frigging Missiles': JFK, Cuba and U.S. Missiles in Turkey," *Orbis* 21 (Summer 1977): 307-33; Barton J. Bernstein, "The Cuban Missile Crisis: Trading the Jupiters in Turkey," *Political Science Quarterly* 95 (Spring 1980): 97-125, esp. 102-04, 112; Garthoff, *Reflections,* 71n; and Philip Nash, "Essence of Revision: Jupiter Missiles and the Cuban Missile Crisis" (Nuclear Age History and Humanities Center, Occasional Paper #89-2,

Medford, MA, 1989). Bundy, among others, has pointed out the political costs of the no-invasion pledge (*Danger and Survival,* 407)—costs that Kennedy presumably would not have incurred gratuitously—and, siding with the revisionist view of Ball and Bernstein, confirms the absence of a presidential decision to remove the Jupiters from Turkey prior to 27 October (428-36). In discussing the issue in his latest work Bundy seems to have only a mild case of what might be termed the deal-denial syndrome. He writes that administration officials "denied in every forum that there was any deal, and in the narrowest sense what we said was usually true, as far as it went."

118. Garthoff, *Reflections,* 140-48; Henry A. Kissinger, *White House Years* (Boston, 1979), 632-35. When Kennedy issued a statement to the public on 28 October 1962 to welcome Khrushchev's announcement that the Soviet Union would withdraw its missiles, he omitted a line contained in the original draft wherein he gave his "assurance that the United States will not invade Cuba since the necessity for military action would disappear with the removal of offensive weapons." Statement and draft are in National Security Files, box 36A37, folder: "Cuba, General, Oct. 28-31, 1962," Kennedy Library.

119. Anderson, telephone interview with author, October 1987.

120. McNamara, telephone interview with author, 5 November 1987; U. Alexis Johnson and Roswell Gilpatric, telephone interviews with author, October 1987.

121. McNamara, telephone interview with author, November 1987. McNamara made no mention of Mongoose operations in his memorandum to Kennedy on Cuban contingency planning on 4 October, which was the same day the SGA met.

122. Oral history interview, Vice Adm. (ret.) William P. Mack, 23 March 1979, 389-90, U.S. Naval Institute, in National Security Archive Cuban Missile Crisis collection, document #3285. My thanks to Mark White of Rutgers University for calling my attention to this quotation.

123. *Alleged Assassination Plots,* 146.

124. Allyn, Blight, and Welch, "Essence of Revision," 145-46; Blight and Welch, *On the Brink* (2nd. ed.), 330-31.

125. "White House Tapes and Minutes," 171-194.

126. ExComm transcripts, Off the Record Meeting on Cuba, 16 October 1962, 11:50 A.M.-12:57 P.M., audiotape 28.1, p. 21-22, President's Office Files, JFKL; later on October 16, in an ExComm meeting that evening, Taylor also refers to prior movements of military forces to the southeastern United States "under the general guise of, uh, of preparations for that part of the country," and McNamara notes that "the military planning has been carried on for a considerable period of time, is well under way," although the defense secretary does add that the "only thing we *haven't* done, really, is to consider fully these alternatives." ExComm transcripts, Off the Record Meeting on Cuba, 16 October 1962, 6:30 P.M. -7:55 P.M., pp. 28-29. My thanks to Phil Nash, Scott Sagan, and Mark White for altering me to the relevant quotations.

127. For an early attempt, see Mark J. White, "Belligerent Beginnings: John F. Kennedy on the Opening Day of the Cuban Missile Crisis," *Journal of Strategic Studies* 15:1 (March 1992), 30-49, esp. 39.
128. I. D. Statsenko, "On Some Military-Political Aspects of the Caribbean Crisis," 115, quoted in Pope, ed., *Soviet Views*, 248.
129. Garthoff doubted "that the experience of the Cuban missile crisis had much to do with Vietnam policymaking." *Reflections*, 164. McNamara seemed to lend some credence to this argument, however, when he commented in 1987 that the rationale for using limited bombing against North Vietnam "was exactly the same rationale as for preferring the quarantine during the Cuban missile crisis." (In other words, the strategy in both cases was to apply maximum coercive pressure without provoking full-scale war between the superpowers.) McNamara also said his experience with "low-probability, highly adverse consequences" during the missile crisis was "very influential in my decisions relating to Vietnam." Quoted in Welch and Blight, *On the Brink*, 193-94.
130. Ibid., 241, 356.
131. "Cuban Missile Crisis More Volatile Than Thought," *Washington Post*, 14 January 1992.

9

The Kennedy-Khrushchev Letters:
An Overview

Philip Brenner

The recently released communiques between President John F. Kennedy and Chairman Nikita S. Khrushchev,* from the period immediately after the Soviet leader announced the withdrawal of the ballistic missiles from Cuba on October 28, 1962, underscore that the crisis did not end until November 20.[1] They also highlight several new lessons about the crisis.

In their so-called agreement of October 27 and October 28, the U.S. president promised to lift the quarantine around Cuba and "to give assurances against an invasion of Cuba," while the Soviet leader promised to withdraw "the weapons which you describe as 'offensive.' "[2] Kennedy qualified his pledge with two conditions: (a) that the "weapons systems" would be removed "under appropriate United Nations observation and supervision"; and (b) that the Soviets would "undertake, with suitable safeguards, to halt the further introduction of such weapons systems into Cuba." Khrushchev's unwillingness to acknowledge that he had placed missiles in Cuba, even as late as October 28, and his determination to emphasize that the Soviets viewed the weapons in Cuba as defensive, led him to use the phrase "the weapons which you describe as 'offensive'." This phrasing created an opportunity that Kennedy quickly seized.

U.S. officials had been concerned about IL-28 fighter-bombers that the Soviet Union had sent to Cuba along with the ballistic missiles because the

---

* Khrushchev was chairman of the Soviet Council of Ministers as well as General Secretary of the Communist party.

bombers had the capability of carrying nuclear bombs. During the height of the crisis, Kennedy focused on the missiles, but early in November he authorized the U.S. ambassador to the United Nations, Adlai Stevenson, to give the Soviet U.N. ambassador a list of "offensive" weapons, including the IL-28 bombers, to be removed from Cuba in addition to the missiles.[3] The confrontation over the removal of the IL-28s created a second crisis that lasted until November 20, when Kennedy announced publicly that the Soviets had agreed to remove the bombers and he ordered the military alert reduced from Defense Condition 2. Much of the November correspondence focuses on the IL-28s.

On November 12, Khrushchev acknowledged Kennedy's concern about the bombers and offered his "gentleman's word" to remove the IL-28s, "although not now but later." The Soviet leader's formulation here echoes the secret promise Attorney General Robert F. Kennedy made to Soviet Ambassador Anatoly Dobrynin during the height of the crisis to remove ballistic missiles from Turkey at a later date. But the president's brother had demanded that the promise be kept secret. The United States, it was believed, could not publicly trade missiles in Turkey for those in Cuba, because it neither wanted to offend its NATO ally nor undermine its own credibility. Despite the seemingly parallel circumstances that now faced Khrushchev, President Kennedy was unyielding. In a message received by Moscow on November 13, he insisted on an announcement about the bombers' removal, though he indicated a willingness to keep secret "the time period for withdrawing the IL-28 aircraft." The next day, Khrushchev relented and agreed to "the withdrawal of the IL-28s within mentioned 30 days. . . ."

Meanwhile, Cuba was insisting—as Khrushchev alluded in his letter of November 12—that it would not permit withdrawal of the IL-28s, because they had been given to Cuba. Moreover, President Fidel Castro was demanding that U.N. inspection of Cuban territory could be undertaken only if there were a reciprocal inspection of U.S. territory—where there were alleged base camps used by the Central Intelligence Agency for training anti-Castro guerrillas. Just as the United States did not trust Cuba, and sought verified safeguards against the return of offensive weapons, so Cuba wanted to make certain that the United States upheld its pledge not to support terrorists who were attacking Cuba. The Il-28s were Cuba's bargaining chip to secure a firm agreement with the United States not to invade Cuba. Yet, unknown to Castro, Khrushchev gave up the bombers on November 14, the day before the Cuban president wrote a strong letter to U.N. Acting Secretary General U Thant expressing Cuba's position.

The IL-28 crisis thus made clear that the Soviet Union would not provide a security umbrella for Cuba. Khrushchev could not and did not claim in November, as he did earlier, that he acceded to the U.S. demands on the IL-28s in return for Cuban security. Indeed, Kennedy toughened the conditions on the U.S. pledge not to invade Cuba, and in effect, provided no pledge at all.

On November 6, he emphasized that his "assurances against an invasion of Cuba" were predicated on the "verified removal of the missile and bomber systems, together with real safeguards against their reintroduction." Then the president added a new element: "that Cuba can never have normal relations with the other nations of this hemisphere unless it ceases to appear to be a foreign military base and adopts a peaceful course of non-interference in the affairs of its sister nations." Six weeks later, on December 14, Kennedy reiterated this formula for guaranteeing no invasion: "We do need to have adequate assurances that all offensive weapons are removed from Cuba and are not reintroduced, and that Cuba itself commits no aggressive acts against any of the nations of the Western Hemisphere." As "adequate assurances" included on-sight inspection, which Cuba rejected, this formulation established conditions that could not be met. Moreover, the Kennedy administration's addition of a demand for no "aggressive acts" was so broad that it could have interpreted much Cuban behavior as "aggressive."

Despite the qualified nature of the pledge, there is no evidence that the United States activated any plans to invade Cuba after the missile crisis, and thus in effect honored the pledge. In 1970, the Nixon administration offered a new U.S. promise to the Soviets not to invade Cuba by restating the 1962 agreement with fewer conditions. Henry Kissinger, President Richard Nixon's national security adviser at the time, gave a communique to the Soviets that

> noted with satisfaction the assurance of the Soviet government that the understandings of 1962 were still in force. We defined these as prohibiting the emplacement of any offensive weapon of any kind or any offensive delivery system on Cuban territory. We affirmed that in return we would not use military force to bring about a change in the governmental structure of Cuba.[4]

Cuba has abided by the 1970 conditions, and in effect, the Nixon pledge replaced the Kennedy pledge, and has been the basis of U.S. policy since then.

Khrushchev's failure to obtain concessions from Kennedy was not for want of trying. On November 14 and again on December 10 he sought to have Kennedy's no-invasion pledge codified in "an appropriate document" at the United Nations. Noting that he wanted the U.S. pledge to last beyond the anticipated remaining six years during which Kennedy would be in office, Khrushchev asserted that "it is necessary to fix the assumed commitments in the documents of both sides and register them with the United Nations."

Kennedy refused. Indeed, Kennedy's tone in the postcrisis letters was tough and businesslike. Where Khrushchev injected touches of warmth—about the defeat of Kennedy's adversary, Nixon, in the 1962 California gubernatorial race, or about Kennedy's family—Kennedy focused exclusively on U.S. objectives and was almost condescending to the Soviet leader. Notably, at a conference in Havana in January 1992, Castro suggested that Kremlin officials judged that Kennedy had humiliated Khrushchev in the crisis and its aftermath, although the president had admonished his advisers not to describe the outcome as a victory.[5] The Cuban leader conjectured that this contributed to Khrushchev's ouster two years later as Communist party general secretary, which Castro argued ultimately confronted the United States with a more virulent and debilitating arms race than it would have encountered with the more pacifically-oriented Khrushchev.

Finally, the letters demonstrate that both Kennedy and Khrushchev had little understanding of Cuba or regard for it. Kennedy casually suggested on November 3, for example, that the quarantine might "be of assistance to [Soviet Deputy Premier] Mr. [Anastas] Mikoyan in his negotiations with Premier Castro," as if Castro might be intimidated by such a show of force. Yet the Cuban leader refused even to meet with Mikoyan for a week, because of his anger about the missile withdrawal, and was prepared even for a nuclear war. Similarly, Khrushchev knew of Castro's anger, but continued to deal secretly with Kennedy about the IL-28s, even to the point of agreeing to their withdrawal without first consulting the Cuban leader.

From Cuba's perspective, the U.S. and Soviet attitudes reinforced the belief that Cuba was vulnerable to a future U.S. attack, which was likely, and was betrayed by the Soviet Union. It is notable, then, that Cuba increased its support for revolutionary movements in Latin America after the crisis, in part to "overextend" the United States and undermine its ability to strike at Cuba.[6] In turn, the U.S. stepped up military aid to the region, and in the 1970s this aid became a basis for the rise of despotic military regimes in Latin America.

In a curious way, then, the letters help us to understand the limitations of the two leaders who brought us to the brink of nuclear destruction and then with extraordinary wisdom avoided war. They did not appreciate the extent to which Cuba was a part of the Cuban missile crisis, and so they did not recognize that it had to be a party to the full resolution of the crisis. That Kennedy and Khrushchev—two enormously skillful leaders—had such limitations points to a profound new lesson which is coming to replace the old notion, that the missile crisis demonstrated how crises ought to be managed. The new lesson of the missile crisis is that in the nuclear age crises cannot be managed, but must be avoided; and crisis avoidance is best achieved through diplomacy, not through the use or threat of force.

NOTES

1. Ten letters—from October 22 to October 28, 1962—had been declassified and published in 1973. In 1987, the National Security Archive (a private research library in Washington, D.C.) requested the declassification of thousands of documents related to the Cuban missile crisis, including the post-October 28 correspondence between Kennedy and Khrushchev. More than two thousand of these Freedom of Information Act requests were filed on my behalf. The petition for the letters and for more than 700 other documents was denied. The Archive then retained the pro bono services of a team of lawyers at Crowell & Moring, led by Stuart Newberger, to seek release of the documents. As the lawsuit proceeded, I asked the Soviet government if it would be willing to release the letters. In April 1991 [*Washington Post,* April 11, 1991] it announced that it had no objection to the release of the correspondence, and it provided a list of 15 letters in its possession to the U.S. State Department. The U.S. government responded on January 6, 1992 by releasing all fifteen. Of these, two had been published in full and one in part in 1991 [Edward Claflin, *JFK Wants to Know* (New York: Morrow, 1991)] and had been quoted in Michael Beschloss, *The Crisis Years: Kennedy and Khrushchev, 1960-1963* (New York: Edward Burlingame Books, 1991). One letter—from December 19, 1962—actually had been declassified in 1962.
2. Letter from President Kennedy to Chairman Khrushchev, October 27, 1962, *Department of State Bulletin,* November 19, 1973, p. 649; text of Chairman Khrushchev's message, as recorded and translated by the U.S. Foreign Broadcast Information Service, October 28, 1962, *Department of State Bulletin,* November 19, 1973, p. 650.
3. It is this list to which Khrushchev makes reference in his November 5 letter. See: Department of State, Incoming Telegram No. 1606, November 2, 1962, from Adlai Stevenson to Secretary of State (available at the National Security Archive, Washington, D.C.). Also: Raymond L. Garthoff, *Reflections on the Cuban Missile Crisis,* rev. ed. (Washington, D.C.: Brookings Institution, 1989), pp. 107-109.

4. Henry Kissinger, *The White House Years* (Boston: Little, Brown, and Co., 1979), p. 634. Notably, six weeks later, the White House learned that Soviets appeared to be in the process of building a submarine base at the Cuban port of Cienfuegos. The Nixon administration relied, in part, on the 1962 understanding to demand the Soviets cease construction of the base. What we know now is that the administration was not merely interpreting the language in the 1962 understanding about "offensive" weapons. In his November 6, 1962 letter, Kennedy explicitly referred to the exclusion of submarine bases as part of the understanding: "I hope you will understand that we must attach the greatest importance to the personal assurances you have given that submarine bases will not be established in Cuba."

5. Robert F. Kennedy, *Thirteen Days: A Memoir of the Cuban Missile Crisis* (New York: New American Library, 1969), pp. 127-128. The tripartite Havana conference—held from January 8-12, 1992—was hosted by the Cuban government and sponsored by the Center for Foreign Policy Development at Brown University's Thomas J. Watson Jr. Institute for International Studies.

6. "Playboy Interview: Fidel Castro," *Playboy,* January 1967, p. 70.

TEXT OF THE LETTERS

November 3, 1962

Dear Mr. Chairman:

. . . You are, of course, aware that Premier Castro has announced his opposition to measures of verification on the territory of Cuba. If he maintains this position this would raise very serious problems. So far as incoming shipments are concerned, I understand that efforts are being made to have the International Red Cross carry out the necessary measures at sea and I hope that these will be successful. In the meantime, perhaps the existence of the quarantine can be of assistance to Mr. Mikoyan in his negotiations with Premier Castro. . . .

Sincerely, /s/JFK

November 5, 1962

Dear Mr. President,

　　I have just received information from Mr. V. Kusnetsov, our representative at the negotiations in New York for liquidation of the tense situation around Cuba, that Mr. Stevenson handed him a list of weapons which your side calls offensive. I have studied the list and, I must confess, the approach of the American side to this matter has seriously worried me. In such a move, I will say frankly, I see a wish to complicate the situation, because it is impossible indeed to place into the category of "offensive" weapons such types of weapons which have always been reffered [*sic*] to as defensive weapons even by a man uneducated militarily—by a common soldier, not to say of an officer....

　　That is why I would ask you, Mr. President, to meet our anxiety with understanding, to take measures on your side in order not to complicate the situation and to give your representatives a directive to eliminate the existing tension on the basis upon which both of us have agreed by having exchanged public messages. You spoke to the effect that missiles which you called offensive should be removed from Cuba. We agreed to that. You in your turn gave assurances that the so-called "quarantine" would be promptly removed and that no invasion of Cuba would be made, not only by the U.S. but by other countries of the Western hemisphere either.

　　Let us then bring the achieved understanding to a completion, so that we could consider that each side has fulfilled its pledges and the question has been settled. If, however additional demands are made, then that means only one thing—the danger that the difficulties on the way to eliminating tension created around Cuba will not be removed. But that may raise then new consequences....

　　Sincerely, N. Khrushchev

November 6, 1962

Dear Mr. Chairman,

I am surprised that in your letter, which I received yesterday, you suggest that in giving your representative in New York a list of the weapons we consider offensive there was any desire on our part to complicate the situation. Our intention was just the opposite: to stick to a well-known list, and not to introduce any new factors. But there is really only one major item on the list, beyond the missiles and their equipment, and that is the light bombers with their equipment. This item is indeed of great importance to us....

Your letter says—and I agree—that we should not complicate the situation by minor things. But I assure you that this matter of IL-28s is not a minor matter for us at all. It is true, of course, that these bombers are not the most modern of weapons, but they are distinctly capable of offensive use against the United States and other Western Hemispheric countries, and I am sure your own military men would inform you that the continued existence of such bombers in Cuba would require substantial measures of military defense in response by the United States. Thus, in simple logic these are weapons capable of offensive use. But there is more in it than that, Mr. Chairman. These bombers could carry nuclear weapons for long distances, and they are clearly not needed, any more than missiles, for purely defensive purposes on the island of Cuba. Thus in the present context their continued presence would sustain the grave tension that has been created, and their removal, in my view, is necessary to a good start on ending the recent crisis. . . .

I therefore hope that you will promptly recognize that when we speak of the need to remove missiles and bombers, with their immediate supporting equipment, we are not trying to complicate the situation but simply stating what was clearly included in our understanding of October twenty-seventh and twenty-eighth. I shall continue to abide fully by the undertakings in my letter of October twenty-seventh, and specifically, under the conditions stated in that letter I will hold to my undertaking "to give assurances against an invasion of Cuba." This undertaking has already come under attack here and is likely to become increasingly an object of criticism by a great many of my countrymen. And the very minimum that is necessary in regard to these assurances is, as we agreed, the verified removal of the missile and bomber systems, together with real safeguards against their reintroduction.

I should emphasize to you directly, Mr. Chairman, that in this respect there is another problem immediately ahead of us which could become very serious indeed, and that is the problem of continuing verification in Cuba. Your representatives have spoken as if this were entirely a problem for the Castro regime to settle, but the continuing verification of the absence of offensive weapons in Cuba is an essential safeguard for the United States and the other countries of this hemisphere, and is an explicit condition for the undertakings which we in our turn have agreed to. The need for this verification is, I regret to say, convincingly demonstrated by what happened in Cuba in the months of September and October. . . .

Finally, I would like to say a word about longer range matters. I think we must both recognize that it will very difficult for any of us in this hemisphere to look forward to an real improvement in our relations with Cuba if it continues to be a military outpost of the Soviet Union. We have limited our action at present to the problem of offensive weapons, but I do think it may be important for you to consider whether a real normalization of the Cuba problem can be envisaged while there remains in Cuba large numbers of Soviet military technicians, and major weapons systems and communications complexes under Soviet control, all with the recurrent possibility that offensive weapons might be secretly and rapidly reintroduced. That is why I think there is much wisdom in the conclusion expressed in your letter of October 26th, that when our undertakings against invasion are effective the need for your military specialist in Cuba will disappear. That is the real path to progress in the Cuban problem. And in this connection in particular, I hope you will understand that we must attach the greatest importance to the personal assurances you have given that submarine bases will not be established in Cuba.

I believe that Cuba can never have normal relations with the other nations of this hemisphere unless it ceases to appear to be a foreign military base and adopts a peaceful course of non-interference in the affairs of its sister nations. These wider considerations may belong to a later phase of the problem, but I hope that you will give them careful thought. . . .

Sincerely, JFK

November 12, 1962

Dear Mr. President,

I would like to express my satisfaction that the mutual obligations taken in accordance with the exchange of messages between us are being carried out both by your side and our side. One can say that certain favourable [*sic*] results are already seen at this time. We appreciate your understanding of the situation and your cooperation in carrying out the obligations taken by our side. We, on our part, will as always honor our obligations. And I would like to inform you that our obligations with regard to dismantling and removal of both missiles and warheads have already been fulfilled. . . .

Thus, if we proceed from our understanding which was expressed in your message of October 27 and in our reply of October 28, then we, the Soviet side, have carried out our obligations and thereby have created possibility for complete elimination of tension in the Caribbean. Consequently, now it is your turn, it is for your side to carry out precisely your obligations. We have in mind that apart from the long term obligations that the United States itself will not attack Cuba and will restrain other countries of the Western Hemisphere from doing that, the most important thing which is required to-day [*sic*] is to give moral satisfaction to world public opinion and tranquillity [*sic*] to peoples. And what is required from you side to that end is to lift the so-called quarantine and of course to stop violating the territorial waters and air space of Cuba. . . .

Now the elections in your country, Mr. President, are over. You made a statement that you were very pleased with the results of these elections. They, the elections, indeed, were in your favor. This success does not upset us either—though that is of course you internal affair. You managed to pin your political rival, Mr. Nixon, to the mat. This did not draw tears from our eyes either. . . .

Now about the matter that, as you state, worries you today about the IL-28 planes which you call an offensive weapon. We have already given you our clarification on this point and I think you can not but agree with us. However, if you do not agree—and this is your right—ask intelligence after all and let it give you an answer based not on guesswork but on facts. If it really knows anything it must tell you the truth and namely that it is long since the IL-28s have been taken out of production and out of use in our armed forces. And if some planes still remain now—and a certain number of them have been brought by us to Cuba—that was done as a result of your action last year when you increased the budget and called up reservists. We on our part had to take measures in response at that time, having postponed taking those planes out of use as well.

Had there been no such action on your part we would not have IL-28s in existence because they would have been used for scrap. Such is this "formidable offensive" weapon. If your intelligence is objective it must give a correct appraisal of these 12-year old planes and report to you that they are incapable of offensive actions. We brought them to Cuba only because they can be used as a mobile means of coastal defense under the cover of anti-aircraft fire from their own territory. They can not [sic] however fly beyond the limits of that cover since they will be immediately destroyed either by modern anti-aircraft means or by simple conventional artillery; not to speak of interceptors before which they are entirely defenseless. But all this must be known not only to the intelligence but to all engaged in military matters.

Nevertheless we regard your concern with understanding though on our part we share the desire of the Government of Cuba to possess defensive weapons which would permit to defend the territorial integrity of its country.

Therefore if you met this with understanding and if we agreed with you on solving other questions in implementing the mutually assumed obligations then the question of IL-28 bombers would be solved without difficulties.

In what way should this cooperation, in our understanding find its expression and what would facilitate the solution of this question?

We state to you that these bombers are piloted solely by our fliers. Consequently you should not have any fears that they can be used to do harm to the United States or other neighbouring [sic] countries in Western Hemisphere. And since you and your allies in Western Hemisphere have taken an obligation not to invade Cuba then it would seem this weapon should not pose any threat for you. Moreover we are aware of what military means are in your possession. If the enemy were threatening us with such weapon we would ignore that threat completely for it would cause us no anxiety whatsoever. . . .

As you ascertained yourself we have removed the missiles, we also removed everything else related to missiles, all the equipment necessary for their use and recalled the personnel manning those missiles. Now that the missiles are removed the question of IL-28s is an incomprehensible argument because the weapon as I have already said is of no value as a combat weapon at present, to say nothing of the future. Let us come to an agreement on this question as well, let us do away with tension, let us fulfil [sic] the mutual pledges made in our messages. Your brother Robert Kennedy mentioned as one variant of solving the question of IL-28 aircraft that those planes should be piloted by Soviet fliers only. We agree to this. But we are also ready to go further—We will not insist on permanently keeping those planes on Cuba. We have our difficulties in this question. Therefore we give a gentleman's word that we will remove the IL-28 planes with all the personnel and equipment related to those planes, although not now but later. We would like to do that some time later when we determine that the conditions are ripe to remove them. We will advise you of that.

I think that an agreement on such basis will enable us to complete the elimination of all the tension that existed and will create conditions for life to resume its normal course, that is the blockade would be immediately removed; the pledges of the sides would be registered in the appropriate documents in the United Nations Organization; non-invasion of Cuba and strict observance of her sovereignty guaranteed; the UN posts established in the countries of the Caribbean so that neither one nor the other side would indeed undertake any unexpected actions to the detriment of another state....

We displayed an understanding with regard to the positions of each other and came out of a critical situation through mutual consessions [sic] to the satisfaction of all peoples of the world. Let us now give joy to all peoples of the world and show that this conflict really became a matter of yesterday, let us normalize the situation.

Sincerely, [unsigned]

Unofficial Translation

During the second meeting with A.F. Dobrynin on the evening of November 12, R. Kennedy, under instruction from the President, formulated the U.S. proposal in this way: "N.S. Khrushev [sic] and the President agree in principle that the IL-28 aircraft shall be withdrawn within a certain period of time. Following this agreement the US will immediately, even tomorrow, lift all quarantine, without waiting for the completion of the aircraft pullout. The US side would, of course, prefer that the agreed time period for withdrawing the IL-28 aircraft were made public. However, if the Soviet side has any objections to making it public, the President will not insist. N.S. Khrushev's word would be quite suffice. As for the period of time, it would be good if the aircraft were withdrawn within, say, 30 days." (This proposal was received in Moscow on November 13).

[The Department of State has been unable to locate an original version of President Kennedy's November 12, 1962 message. The above version was furnished to the department by the Soviet Embassy in late 1991.]

November 14, 1962

Dear Mr. President,

I have read with great satisfaction the reply of the President of the United States and I agree with the considerations expressed by the President. . . .

The question of the withdrawal of the IL-28s within mentioned 30 days does not constitute any complicated question. Yet this period will probably not be sufficient. As I already said in my oral message I can assure the President that those planes will be removed from Cuba with all the equipment and flying personnel. It can be done in 2-3 months. But for me, for our country it would be a great relief if the state of tension that evolved in the Caribbean were liquidated as soon as possible. I have in mind what I have already said, namely: to lift immediately the quarantine that is blockade; to stop the flights of the US planes over Cuba; to write down the mutual committments [*sic*] ensuing from the messages of the President and mine of October 27 and 28 to which end your representatives and ours have to prepare with the participation of the UN acting Secretary General U Thant an appropriate document. This is the main thing now.

You understand that when we say that it is necessary to announce now the withdrawal of the IL-28s at the time when your planes are flying over Cuba it creates for us no small difficulties. I have no doubt that you will understand— and the Cuban Government understands this—that such actions constitute violation of sovereignty of the Cuban state. Therefore it would be a reasonable step to create in this respect also conditions for the normalization of the situation and this in a great degree would make it easier to meet your wish of expediting the withdrawal of the IL-28 planes from Cuba. . . .

It is hard to say for me what specific agreement is possible on the question of UN observation posts. But we as well as the Government of Cuba have already expressed a desire to come to terms on this question. If the question of the observation posts is of interest to the US—and I think it must be of interest—then I consider it wise to come to an agreement on this. I think that the Government of Cuba will not object to the UN posts, of course on the condition of respect for the sovereignty of Cuba, on the condition of treating her as equal which must mean that on the territory of other countries of the Caribbean and in a corresponding region of the US there will be also set up similar UN posts, that is on the condition that reciprocity will be observed in this question. . . .

Sincerely [unsigned]

December 10, 1962

Dear Mr. President,

. . . I think you will agree that if our arrangement for settling the Cuban crisis fails it will undermine a possibility for manoeuvre which you and we would resort to for elimination of danger, a possibility for compromise in the future if similar difficulties arise in other areas of the world, and they really can arise. We attach great significance to all this, and subsequent development will depend on you as President and on the U.S. Government.

We believe that the guarantees for non-invasion of Cuba given by you will be maintained and not only in the period of your stay in the White House, that, to use an expression, goes without saying. We believe that you will be able to receive a mandate at the next election too, that is that you will be the U.S. President for six years, which would appeal to us. At our times, six years in world politics is a long period of time and during that period we could create good conditions for peaceful coexistence on earth and this would be highly appreciated by the peoples of our countries as well as by all other peoples.

Therefore, Mr. President, I would like to express a wish that you follow the right way, as we do, in appraising the situation. Now it is of special importance to provide for the possibility of an exchange of opinion through confidential channels which you and I have set up and which we use. But the confidential nature of our personal relations will depend on whether you fulfill—as we did—the commitments taken by you and give instructions to your representatives in New York to formalize these commitments in appropriate documents. This is needed in order that all the peoples be sure that tension in the Carribean [*sic*] is a matter of yesterday and that now normal conditions have been really created in the world. And for this it is necessary to fix the assumed commitments in the documents of both sides and register them with the United Nations. . . .

Please convey to your wife and your whole family wishes of good health from myself, my wife and my entire family.

[Unsigned]

December 14, 1962

Dear Mr. Chairman:

. . . You refer to the importance of my statements on an invasion of Cuba and of our intention to fulfill them, so that no doubts are sown from the very start. I have already stated my position publicly in my press conference on November 20th, and I am glad that this statement appears to have your understanding; we have never wanted to be driven by the acts of others into war in Cuba. The other side of the coin, however, is that we do need to have adequate assurances that all offensive weapons are removed from Cuba and are not reintroduced, and that Cuba itself commits no aggressive acts against any of the nations of the Western Hemisphere. As I understand you, you feel confident that Cuba will not in fact engage in such aggressive acts, and of course I already have your own assurance about the offensive weapons. So I myself should suppose that you could accept our position—but it is probably better to leave final discussion of these matters to our representatives in New York. . . .

Thank you for your expressions of good wishes to me and my family, and let me in turn send you and your wife and family our personal good wishes for the coming year.

[Unsigned]

INDEX

Abel, Elie 133, 161
   The Missile Crisis 133
Acheson, Dean 5, 14, 16, 21, 61,
   223, 227, 228
"actor-observer" fallacy 143
Adenauer, Konrad 80, 93
Adzhubei, Aleksei I. 188
Alekseev, Aleksandr 44, 49, 50, 51,
   141, 199, 202
Allison, Graham 103, 146, 149, 223
   Essence of Decision 103, 134, 146
Allyn, Bruce 228, 264, 265
Alpha 66 142
Anderson, George W., Jr. 19, 147,
   262
Anderson, Paul 227
Aragones Navarro, Emilio 195, 196
Argentina 82
Armstrong, Scott vii
Aron, Raymond 3

Ball, George 22, 24, 63, 75, 90, 95
Bartlett, Charles
   Facing the Brink 134
Batista, Fulgencio 242
Bay of Pigs 9, 42, 61, 67, 106, 142,
   165, 169, 170, 173, 187-191, 197,
   206, 220, 229, 230, 238, 239,
   240, 242, 253
Berlin Wall 11, 169, 170, 240
Bernstein, Barton 134, 161, 164, 194
Biryuzov, Sergei 44, 139, 195
"Black Saturday" (October 27) 19,
   22, 47
Blight, James 135, 228, 264, 265
Bobrow, David 207
Bohemia 191

Bohlen, Charles 174, 228, 230
Bolivia 82
Bolshakov, Georgy 12
Bowles, Chester 61, 62
Brazil 82
Brophy, William J. 260
Brzezinski, Zbigniew 177
Bundy, McGeorge 12, 14, 17, 22,
   23, 25, 62, 67, 68, 69, 78, 83, 86,
   88, 95, 102, 138, 163, 166, 167,
   178, 223, 238-241, 260
Bundy, William 5
Burlatsky, Fyodor 49, 50, 175

Canada 82
Cardona, Miro 188
Castro, Fidel 42, 44, 51, 67, 79, 96,
   97, 142, 153, 169, 176, 187, 189,
   191-200, 203, 204, 205, 206, 207,
   220, 237-239, 241-243, 245, 246,
   248, 251, 256, 262, 282, 284, 286
   removal of 243-3
Castro, Raúl 44, 195, 249
Central Intelligence Agency (CIA)
   77, 106, 142, 147, 165, 173, 189,
   205, 206, 223, 241-243, 246, 248,
   282
Chayes, Abram 23, 73
CINCLANT 43, 221
Clausewitz, Carl von 2, 4
Cleveland, Harlan 75, 76
Clifford, Clark 6
Clines, Thomas 246
Cold War 27, 132, 169, 180
conferences on crisis
   Antigua (1991) 49, 200
   Harvard University (1987) 136

Havana (1992) 49, 136, 193-194, 199
Moscow (1989) 48-49, 51, 136, 150
Cordier, Andrew 100, 150, 228
covert action 9, 18-19, 42-43, 67, 135, 142, 147, 220, 237-239, 241-247, 251, 252, 255, 257, 258, 260, 262, 263, 264
Cuba 171
    discovery of missiles in 12-13, 41-44, 46, 67, 172, 192, 220
    Soviet defense of 138-139, 141
Cuban Communist party 42, 195
Cuban missile crisis
    and use of force 1-2
    and opinion of voters 260
    as historical paradigm 131-132
    as precedent for Vietnam War 180, 266
    end of 20
Cuban Revolutionary Council 188
Cuban Student Directorate 191
Currey, Cecil B. 248

de Calliers, François 6
de Gaulle, Charles 80, 93
del Valle Jímenez, Sergio 197, 198
Denmark 81
Dennison, Robert Lee 221, 226, 239, 242, 253, 254, 257, 258
de Staercke, Andrew 82
Detzer, David 224
Diefenbaker, John 82
Dillon, C. Douglas 86, 88, 99, 131, 199
Dinerstein, Herbert 197
diplomacy 5-7
Dobrynin, Anatoly 21-23, 46, 47, 49, 52, 56, 57, 66, 70, 94, 95, 97, 99, 102, 103, 134, 150, 151, 168, 199, 228, 282, 294

Dorticós, Osvaldo 67, 190, 192, 195, 202
Dulles, John Foster 5, 6, 7, 11

Eisenhower, Dwight D. 4, 7, 11, 57, 58, 60, 89, 101, 140, 166, 242
    and installment of Jupiters 60, 101
"Elite" see ExComm
Ellsberg, Daniel 27
Escalante, Fabian 190
escalation 10, 12-14, 18-19, 21-22, 48, 68-69, 83, 89, 90, 97, 98, 100, 103, 132, 145, 149-150, 174, 175, 180, 190, 193, 195, 198, 201, 251, 266
Executive Committee of the President (ExComm) 13-15, 19, 20, 52, 57, 67, 68, 70, 71, 79, 83, 87-90, 95, 102, 134, 135, 143, 144, 146, 147, 149-151, 162, 163, 166, 167, 172, 174, 199, 205, 219, 220, 222, 225, 226
    first meeting of 68

Fanfani, Amintore 81
Finletter, Thomas 76, 93, 98
Fomin, Aleksandr 47, 144
Franqui, Carlos 194
Freedom of Information Act (FOIA) 153, 239
Fulbright, J. William 165, 168

Galbraith, John Kenneth 165
Garthoff, Raymond 16, 17, 143, 179
Gates, Thomas 60
Germany 170
    and defense 10-11
Gilly, Adolfo 197
Gilpatric, Roswell 22, 95, 141
Great Britain 81
Greece 82
Gribkov, Anatoly 46, 49, 52, 193

Gromyko, Andrei A. 44, 46, 49, 50-52, 70, 139, 141, 174
Guantanamo Bay 201, 242, 255, 258
Guevara, Che 189, 195, 196

Halper, Thomas 20
Hare, Raymond 75, 98
Harriman, W. Averell 10, 74, 75, 76, 77
Harris, Benjamin T. 246
Harris, Louis 249, 260
Harvey, William King 248
Hawk's Cay Conference 171
Helms, Richard 248, 263
Hershberg, James 221
Hickenlooper, Bourke 23
Hilsman, Roger 20, 23, 25, 26, 63, 133, 165, 167
    To Move a Nation 133
Hitler, Adolf 4, 162, 169
Horelick, Arnold 139
House Appropriations Committee 23, 98
Hoy 198

Independence 258
Institute of Military History 49
Integrated Revolutionary Organizations (ORI) 195
intercontinental ballistic missiles (ICBMs) 18, 41, 42, 65, 69, 105, 106, 140, 141, 147
intermediate-range ballistic missiles (IRBMs) 13, 42, 58, 59, 62, 66, 87, 98, 104, 134, 137, 139-141, 150
International Security 264
Italian Socialist party 81
Italy 81, 99
Izvestia 188

Jenner, William 5

John Fitzgerald Kennedy Library 134
Johnson, Lyndon B. 90, 106, 145, 180
Johnson, U. Alexis 145, 249
Joint Chiefs of Staff 220, 221
Joint Congressional Committee on Atomic Energy 60
Journal of American History 260
Julien, Claude 193, 202
Jupiters 21, 57, 59, 63, 65, 66, 69, 72, 84-86, 97-99, 101, 104, 107, 134, 140, 145, 150, 151, 168, 169, 177, 194, 228
    and exchange with missiles in Cuba 21-23, 48, 57, 71-74, 91, 150-152, 282

Keating, Kenneth B. 166, 229, 240, 263
Kennan, George 5, 12
Kennedy, John F. 8, 9, 11-13, 15, 17, 21, 22, 45, 52, 56, 57, 63, 68, 71, 72, 74, 75, 77, 78, 83, 84, 88, 100, 101, 103, 106, 132, 134, 140, 142, 143, 146, 150-152, 161-166, 168, 169-174, 178, 179, 181, 187, 188, 191, 197, 203, 205, 206, 219, 221, 222, 224, 225, 226, 229, 238-241, 243, 245, 246, 250, 252, 253, 256, 257, 260, 263, 281, 283
    and presidential election 165, 173
    as viewed by administration 8
    Why England Slept 170
Kennedy, Robert 9, 12, 14, 16-18, 21-24, 47, 52, 57, 66, 69, 73, 74, 83, 89, 93-97, 99, 100, 102, 103, 104, 106, 133, 134, 146, 150, 151, 166, 177, 199, 205, 220, 222-225, 227-231, 243, 244, 257, 282, 292, 294
    Thirteen Days 60, 69, 94-96, 133

Khrushchev, Nikita 10-12, 16, 17, 22, 41, 42-44, 46-48, 50, 51, 58, 59, 65-70, 72, 85, 86, 96, 97, 101, 106, 133, 136-138, 140, 141, 145, 153, 161, 162, 164, 165, 167, 169, 171, 172, 173-175, 178, 179, 181, 187, 193, 194, 196, 199, 200, 202, 203, 238, 240, 281, 283, 294
Khrushchev, Sergei 141
Kissinger, Henry 4, 6, 7, 13, 26, 283
Kohler, Foy 67
Komer, Robert 99
Kozlov, Frol 139
Kreisky, Bruno 86, 91
Kusnetsov, V. 286

Lansdale, Edward 189, 243, 244-249, 251, 263
"Lantphibex 1-62" 188, 250
Laos 9
LeMay, Curtis 24, 230
Lemnitzer, Lyman 24
limited war 3, 15, 21, 24, 25, 27, 46-47, 56, 64, 148, 221, 223, 226, 264, 289
Lippmann, Walter 91, 175
Literaturnaya Gazeta 175
Lovett, Robert 228
Luce, Henry R. 26

MacArthur, Douglas 168
Macmillan, Harold 81
Malinovsky, Rodion 41, 44, 50, 65, 66, 139, 140, 141, 176
Marshall, George C. 5, 8
Matthews, Herbert 197
McCarthy, Joseph 7
McCloy, John 228, 230
McCone, John 60, 64, 68, 78, 79, 90, 223, 241, 257
McGhee, George C. 62

McNamara, Robert 1, 9, 13-17, 19-22, 25, 26, 56, 62, 68-72, 75, 83, 89, 90, 93-95, 98, 99, 102, 133, 142, 144, 147, 167, 193, 207, 221-223, 226, 230, 239, 242, 243, 249, 251, 253, 254, 257, 259, 260, 262, 263, 265
McNaughton, John 98
medium-range ballistic missiles (MRBMs) 13, 42, 68-70, 77, 87, 98, 103, 104, 137, 139, 141, 149, 219, 222, 238, 241
Mexico 82
Mikoyan, Anastas 44, 51, 59, 66, 139, 201-204, 206, 284, 286
Mikoyan, Sergo 49-51, 141, 180, 188, 189, 197, 202
multilateral forces (MLF) 76, 78

Nathan, James 180
National Security Archive vii, 239
Netherlands, the 82
Nitze, Paul 26, 62, 73, 84, 104, 223
Nixon, Richard 58, 59, 165, 166, 283
Norstad, Lauris 62
North American Treaty Organization (NATO) 58, 76, 78, 82, 86-88, 90-92, 98
and response to potential trade of Jupiters 79-82
Norway 81

O'Donnell, Kenneth 224, 225, 231
Operation Mongoose 18, 42, 67, 142, 147, 149, 189, 190, 203, 206, 207, 220, 237, 239, 242, 243, 244-252, 257, 262-264
and suspension of activities 18-19
OPLAN 312 190, 219, 221, 242, 253, 254, 258
OPLAN 314 219, 221, 242, 253, 258
OPLAN 316 219, 221, 242, 253, 254, 258

Organization of American States
(OAS) 43, 82, 142, 188

Paterson, Thomas G. 138, 260
Penkovsky, Oleg 17-18
"Phibriglex-62" 190, 221, 254, 255
Pliyev, Issa A. 46, 145, 199
Polaris 99, 100
Policy Planning Council 75, 178
Poltava 20
Powers, Thomas 147, 225
Pravda 189

quarantine 72, 78, 81, 82, 100, 104,
132, 133, 161, 163, 166, 173,
197, 224, 281
"Quick Kick" 188, 250

Radio Americas 189
Radio Swan 189
Revolucion 197, 198, 202
Risquet Valdes, Jorge 195, 198
Roca, Blas 195
Rosen, Peter 25
Rostow, Walt Whitman 75, 77, 78,
178
Rusk, Dean 8, 11, 16, 22, 23, 46, 57,
62, 63, 68, 77, 79, 83, 94, 95, 98-
100, 102, 150, 151, 163, 167,
222, 223, 226, 228
Russell, Richard 165, 168

Sagan, Scott 17, 148
Sarper, Raul 62
Scali, John 47, 144
Schell, Jonathan 14
Schelling, Thomas 7, 178
Schlesinger, Arthur 8, 9, 11, 20, 22,
24, 26, 72, 133, 137, 152, 161,
162, 206
A Thousand Days 133
Second Declaration of Havana 191,
194

Senate Foreign Relations Committee
23, 165
Shackley, Theodore 246
Sidey, Hugh 8
Sorensen, Theodore 8, 22, 56, 57,
66, 72, 73, 88, 95, 96, 102, 133,
161-163, 165, 167, 171, 172, 179,
196, 220, 223-225, 228, 230, 231,
239
Special Group (Augmented) (SGA)
243-245, 247, 249, 251, 252, 257,
264
Sputnik 58
Statsenko, Igor D. 250, 266
Steel, Ronald 161, 164, 167, 174
Stevenson, Adlai 23, 71, 72, 73, 75,
102, 203, 230, 282, 286
Stone, I. F. 161, 163, 164
Strategic Air Command (SAC) 12,
18, 82, 201
Strategic Missile Forces 44, 45
Sulzberger, Cyrus 82
surface-to-air missiles (SAMs) 15,
79, 145, 196, 198, 199, 220, 221,
241, 256
Sverdlovsk
dowing of American U-2 in 11
Szulc, Tad 192

Taft, Robert A. 168
Tass 66, 67, 138
Taylor, Maxwell 15, 89, 222, 225,
252, 262, 265
Thant, U 100, 150, 177, 201, 203,
228, 282
Thomas, Hugh 191
Thompson, Llewellyn 22, 70, 83,
86, 88, 90, 95, 145, 174
Trachtenberg, Mark 152
"Trollope ploy" 88-89, 91, 94
Truman, Harry S 6, 168
Tuchman, Barbara 10

Turkey 57, 59, 65, 75, 78, 85, 86,
    91, 98-100, 150, 151, 169, 205,
    282
26th of July Movement 42

U-2 16, 79, 83, 89, 92, 97, 145, 146,
    148, 198, 199, 241
Uruguay 82

Vienna 62, 169, 170, 173, 240
Vieques 43, 188, 190, 250, 255
Volkogonov, Dimitri 49, 52

war, theory of 2-3
weapons, atomic 4
    and American defense planning 9
Weintel, Edward
    Facing the Brink 134
Welch, David 135, 228, 264, 265
"Whip Lash" 250
Wilson, Samuel V. 260

Yalta 5
Yarmolinsky, Adam 239, 254